Organizational Resilience and Artificial Intelligence

Organizational Resilience and Artificial Intelligence is your essential companion for steering any enterprise through today's turbulent landscape. Drawing from real-world crises—including global supply chain shocks, natural disasters, and cyber threats—this book demystifies *organizational resilience* and arms you with proven frameworks, tools, and strategies needed to thrive when adversity strikes.

Discover why resilience goes far beyond risk management, introducing a holistic approach that integrates proactive planning, adaptive leadership, robust communication, and a culture of learning and innovation. Through vivid case studies—such as manufacturers recovering after floods and companies maintaining operations in a pandemic—you'll see the pivotal role business resilience plays not only in sustaining critical services, but also in supporting communities and sustaining long-term stakeholder trust.

Inside, you'll learn to:

- *Identify and assess* vulnerabilities across operations, supply chains, and technologies
- *Strengthen situational awareness* to anticipate and manage emerging risks
- Develop *business continuity plans and adaptive processes* that ensure readiness for both foreseeable and "black swan" events
- Foster *cross-functional collaboration* and stakeholder engagement
- *Build* a culture of agility, innovation, and continuous improvement
- *Measure, test, and enhance* resilience with actionable checklists and guidelines

Whether you're a top executive, Risk or BC professional, or an emerging leader, this guide offers a practical, *research-backed roadmap* to embedding resilience into every layer of your organization. The future belongs to those who are prepared—start building your organization's resilience today, and ensure you can not only weather disruption, but emerge stronger than ever before.

Security, Audit and Leadership Series

Series Editor: Dan Swanson, Dan Swanson and Associates, Ltd., Winnipeg, Manitoba, Canada.

About the Book Series

The scope and mandate for cybersecurity and internal audit continues to evolve each year, as does the complexity of the business environment and speed of the changing risk landscape in which it must operate. The fundamental goal of this exciting series is to produce leading-edge books on critical subjects facing security and audit executives and practitioners. Key topics addressed include Leadership, Cybersecurity, Security Leadership, Privacy, Strategic Risk Management, Auditing IT and Technology, and Audit Management and Leadership.

If you're interested in submitting a proposal for a book to be included in the series, please email the series editor, Dan Swanson: dswanson_2008@yahoo.ca

Bridging the Gap: *Strengthening the Bond between Audit Committee and Internal Audit*
By Denise Cicchella

CISO: Evolution of a Vocation
Confessions of a Recovering CISO
By Ron Baklarz

Dark Faces in Cyber Places: *Shattering Stereotypes and Leading with Legacy in Cybersecurity*
By Devon Bryan

Logic Before Language: *Rethinking AI in the Age of Illusion, Bertrand Russell and the Future of Real AI*
By Martin Milani

Relevant Impact: *A Field Guide to Integrated Assurance*
By Patrick M. Hayes

Cybersecurity and the Art of Cyberwar
By Dan Shoemaker, Tamara Shoemaker, and Amir Jabri

Trust Hacked: *What Firewalls, Failures, and the Frontlines Taught Me About Trust*
By Nia Luckey

Organizational Resilience and Artificial Intelligence: *A Practical Framework for Crisis Leadership, Adaptability and Sustainable Performance*
By Arnab Mukherjee and Sachin Kumar

Organizational Resilience and Artificial Intelligence

A Practical Framework for Crisis Leadership, Adaptability and Sustainable Performance

Arnab Mukherjee and Sachin Kumar

CRC Press
Taylor & Francis Group
Boca Raton London New York

CRC Press is an imprint of the
Taylor & Francis Group, an **informa** business

Designed cover image: Shutterstock ID: 2490792321

First edition published 2026
by CRC Press
2385 NW Executive Center Drive, Suite 320, Boca Raton FL 33431

and by CRC Press
4 Park Square, Milton Park, Abingdon, Oxon, OX14 4RN

CRC Press is an imprint of Taylor & Francis Group, LLC

ISBN: 9781032981864 (hbk)
ISBN: 9781032981888 (pbk)
ISBN: 9781003597520 (ebk)

DOI: 10.1201/9781003597520

Typeset in Sabon
by KnowledgeWorks Global Ltd.

To the leaders, innovators, and resilience practitioners who embrace both human intelligence and artificial intelligence to build stronger, safer, and future-ready organizations.

Contents

About this book

As disruptions grow more frequent and unpredictable, resilience has become a strategic foundation—not just a defensive capability.

But in today's world, *resilience without Artificial Intelligence is incomplete.*

This book brings together two powerful pillars:

1. **Organizational Resilience**
   Rooted in global best practices, crisis leadership, supply chain strength, communication excellence, adaptability, and learning culture.
2. **Artificial Intelligence for Resilience**
   A modern extension that transforms how organizations anticipate threats, manage crises, optimize decisions, and accelerate recovery.

Through real-world case studies, AI-driven models, and practical frameworks, this book provides leaders with:

- Intelligent risk forecasting
- AI-enabled crisis management
- Smart decision support
- Automated resilience workflows
- Adaptive learning systems
- AI-driven supply chain resilience
- Tools to future-proof organizations

This is a hands-on guide for leaders preparing not only for today's disruptions but for *the intelligent, interconnected challenges of tomorrow.*

About the authors

Arnab Mukherjee is a recognized subject matter expert in Business Continuity and Organisational Resilience with over two decades of experience designing, implementing, and auditing resilience frameworks across complex organizations. Drawing on specialist knowledge of continuity, crisis management, and enterprise risk, he currently serves as Business Continuity Crisis Manager at Vodafone Qatar, where he leads major resilience initiatives and supports critical national telecom operations during disruptive events. He holds a Master of Science in Business Continuity from Norwich University, Vermont, USA, and has extensive hands-on experience in enterprise risk management, end-to-end continuity strategy, testing and exercising, and independent audits of continuity capabilities.

Throughout his career, he has provided real-time support in crisis situations including strikes, road blocks, floods, network outages, and other significant business disruptions, ensuring that essential services remain available and recover rapidly. He played a key role in managing the COVID-19 response, coordinating safe telecom operations and enabling vaccination for all employees, and successfully established and ran a dedicated WAR Room during the FIFA World Cup 2023 to monitor telecom infrastructure and supply chain resilience. He has led or audited more than 100 organizations against ISO 22301 and ISO 27001, giving him a unique perspective on how standards can be translated into practical, value-creating resilience.

He is a multiple award winner from the Business Continuity Institute (BCI) in Asia and the Middle East, reflecting his contribution to advancing resilience practice in the region. A regular speaker at global business continuity and risk conferences, he is known for turning complex resilience concepts into actionable strategies that boards, executives, and practitioners can apply. This book on Organisational Resilience brings together his field experience, standards expertise, and crisis leadership to offer a practical roadmap for organizations seeking to thrive in an age of disruption.

Sachin Kumar is an experienced Risk Management professional with over 15 years of expertise in Business Continuity, Enterprise Risk, and Information Security. He holds several certifications, including CISA,

CIRM, PMP, and ISO 22301 Business Continuity Trainer. He has demonstrated expertise across various sectors, such as motorsports, tourism, financial services, and manufacturing. His leadership roles have involved developing and implementing comprehensive Business Continuity and Disaster Recovery programs, conducting risk assessments, and managing enterprise security and compliance initiatives.

He has held senior positions at notable organizations, including the Dubai Economy and Tourism Authority, Yas Marina Circuit, PricewaterhouseCoopers, and Ventures Middle East. His accomplishments include leading cybersecurity maturity assessments, enhancing IT disaster recovery programs, and receiving an appreciation award from NCEMA for his contribution to UAE Business Continuity Management Standards.

His core competencies include conducting risk assessments, business impact analyses, strategy design, contingency planning, recovery planning, exercise management, and continuous improvement. He leads the process and staff to identify and mitigate risks, vulnerabilities, and potential business interruptions for the organization and its stakeholders. He is also an active member of ARISE, a UN-affiliated initiative for disaster-resilient societies. His mission is to ensure the safety of people, the protection of corporate intellectual property, and the continuity of essential resources, functions, and business services in the face of unforeseen challenges.

In addition to his technical skills, he has managed numerous successful projects, published key organizational policies, and implemented advanced tools for crisis communication and business continuity automation. He holds an MBA in Marketing and a B.Tech in Electronics & Communication, further solidifying his strong foundation in both technical and management domains. His recent certification is from MIT in Business Resilience and Crisis Management.

Preface

The world has entered an era where shocks are faster, crises are deeper, and uncertainty is constant. Traditional resilience is no longer enough.

We have witnessed organizations collapse despite strong structures—and others thrive through massive disruptions. The differentiator is no longer just planning.

It is *the fusion of human leadership and Artificial Intelligence.*

AI gives organizations the ability to sense earlier, respond faster, and recover smarter. Combined with strong leadership, culture, and governance, AI becomes a strategic force multiplier for resilience.

This book brings together our combined experience in crisis consulting, AI adoption, emergency response, and global resilience initiatives.

Our goal is to provide a *practical, clear, and modern framework* that leaders can implement immediately.

—Arnab Mukherjee and Sachin Kumar

Acknowledgments

This book reflects the collective wisdom of resilience professionals, crisis responders, AI innovators, and global industry experts.

We thank all mentors, collaborators, and organizations whose experiences, research, and challenges shaped every framework presented here.

> Supply chain resilience is often overlooked—until a disruption makes its importance impossible to ignore. Arnaud's analysis highlights the critical need to strengthen resilience across the entire end-to-end global supply chain, beginning with sourcing and supplier stability, through logistics and manufacturing, and ultimately to final delivery. In today's interconnected world, a single disruption—whether geopolitical conflict, natural disaster, transportation bottleneck, or material shortage—can create cascading impacts across multiple regions and industries. Building an adaptive, forward-looking supply chain enables organizations to anticipate volatility, safeguard business continuity, and ensure consistent value delivery to customers. This includes integrating sustainability, regulatory compliance, and ethical sourcing practices, which are increasingly essential in global markets. Developing strong capabilities in risk assessment and mitigation helps teams better understand how global events influence supply chains and what proactive strategies can minimize exposure. Achieving true resilience is a collaborative effort, requiring coordinated support across all supply chain functions.
>
> Michael W Janko MBCP, MBCI, ARM, CBCLA | Director Global Business Continuity | The Goodyear Tire & Rubber Company

> In an uncertain world, resilience stems from three disciplined practices. First, decentralize decision-making to where learning occurs fastest, but centralize control over irreversible consequences. Build guardrails—like "blast radius" containment and ethical thresholds—directly into your operating system to enable safe experimentation. Second, measure exploration by reduced uncertainty, not shipped features. Use an "Evidence Ladder" to fund progress and track learning velocity. Celebrate teams that efficiently eliminate dead ends. Third, protect critical investments

during downturns: strategic platforms (your innovation infrastructure), exploratory research (your future compass), and talent development (your adaptable core). These generate the option value needed for recovery. Sustainable innovation requires distributing learning while systematically managing risk. Protect your organization's capacity to learn, adapt, and grow—especially when times are tough.

Dr. Karan Kumar, Governance, Risk & Compliance @Microland I Doctor of Business Administration @SSBM Geneva I Advisory Board Member @CyberEd I AI Governance Strategist I Author I ROI Architect I CSA TAISE ContributorI

In today's dynamic and unpredictable business environment, adaptability and flexibility are paramount for achieving organizational resilience and sustainable success. The ability to pivot quickly is essential for navigating market volatility, technological shifts, and global crises. Organizations must proactively anticipate change through strategic foresight. This involves rigorous environmental scanning to detect emerging trends, comprehensive scenario planning to prepare for diverse futures, and fostering a culture of organizational learning for continuous improvement and swift knowledge integration. The key takeaways emphasizing the importance of adaptability and flexibility:

1. Mandatory for Success: Adaptability and flexibility are not optional, but vital requirements for organizational resilience and achieving long-term, sustainable success in a constantly changing business landscape..
2. Proactive Preparation: Resilience is built by anticipating change, not just reacting to it. This requires structured activities like:
   - Environmental Scanning: Monitoring external forces.
   - Scenario Planning: Preparing for multiple futures.
   - Organizational Learning: Integrating new knowledge swiftly.

Anandarup Sen, CBCI, Director, Firm Resilience I Business Continuity I Mogan & Stanley

"Artificial Intelligence (AI) is not merely optimizing organizational resilience; it is redefining it by excelling at processing vast, heterogeneous datasets at speeds impossible for humans, allowing organizations to shift from identifying what happened to predicting what might happen. By shifting the focus from recovery metrics to predictive anticipation, AI enables organizations to absorb shocks through proactive mitigation and agile adaptation. But the real value of AI is realized when it can predict a disruptive future outcome of a digital initiative and the steps needed to balance its benefits against the associated risks. The future of organizational resilience, however, requires AI governance, coupled with a decisive human role in oversight, without cognitive bias, to balance technological innovation with ethical, effective, and equitable responsibility. This chapter illustrates how artificial intelligence can empower organizations to anticipate, contain, withstand, and recover from disruptions, safeguarding business interests and reputation in an increasingly complex risk environment."

Agnidipta Sarkar | Chief Evangelist | ColorTokens Inc.

As a resilience professional with extensive international experience, I have observed distinct paradigms in organizational resilience. The public sector is characterized by its procedural rigor and well-defined hierarchies and leverages established responsibilities to ensure cohesive execution.The private sector's agility and commercial flexibility drive innovation but often lead to fragmented approaches to organisational resilience, with siloed efforts caused by unclear definitions and accountability. This can result in strategic misalignment and inefficient resource allocation, especially where corporate policy overlaps functional responsibility. For effective BCM and crisis management, organisations must define goals, delineate roles, and provide robust structures. Top-down leadership at Board or Executive Committee level, is essential for holistic coordination and the cultivation of resilience as an organizational imperative rather than a collection of isolated initiatives. Given the growing threat landscape of geopolitical volatility and hybrid warfare, appointing a Chief Resilience Officer is crucial, particularly in sectors vital to national infrastructure.

Norman Heit | Global Director Vodafone Group | Critical Infrastructure, Resilience & Geopolitical Risk | Supervisory Board Member Vodafone Germany

Drawing on 20 years of corporate security leadership, I have contributed to advancing organisational resilience in Qatar through a preparedness-led operating model. As a subject-matter expert and Head of Corporate Security, I have supported the safe delivery of high-profile events including FIFA World Cup Qatar 2022 and AFC tournaments, translating complex risk environments into actionable readiness measures for business operations. During periods of disruption—including the Gulf blockade and heightened geopolitical volatility linked to US-Iran tensions I have strengthened decision-making under uncertainty and enhanced multi-stakeholder crisis coordination. I have elevated awareness and enabled cross-functional engagement through scenario-based exercises, including the national Watan Exercise, aligning people, processes, and partners for a cohesive response. My experience underscores that resilience is built through disciplined planning, training, and exercising, where preparedness remains the critical determinant of sustained performance and recovery.

Meshaal Al-Ibrahim | Head of Corporate Security | LLB in Law

"The importance of supply chain resilience highlighted in this chapter strongly aligns with my professional experience in business continuity and crisis management across global consulting and financial institutions. While working with KPMG in India, I supported business continuity coordination during the 2010 Chennai Floods, where severe disruptions to transportation, workforce mobility, and vendor operations required rapid activation of contingency plans and close collaboration with stakeholders to sustain critical services. Later, during my tenure at Goldman Sachs, I was involved in operational resilience activities during the major blackout that affected large parts of Manhattan following Hurricane Sandy, which disrupted power, transportation, and technology infrastructure across the city. While the Goldman Sachs Hudson Street facility remained operational due to resilient infrastructure and contingency planning, the incident highlighted the importance of robust continuity strategies, supplier coordination, and crisis communication to sustain critical financial operations during large-scale disruptions."

Debjyoti Mukherjee | CISSP, CRISC, CCSK, CBCP. |
Associate Director - Data and AI Governance |
Royal bank of Canada

Across three decades spanning oil and gas, petrochemicals, utilities, mining, and defence, I have worked across operations, strategy, emergency response, crisis management, and risk and resilience functions, experiencing disruptions firsthand at every level. One observation has remained constant: *an ounce of prevention is worth a pound of cure.* The organizations that weathered disruptions most effectively were those that had embedded continuity thinking into business strategy, not bolted it on as an afterthought. This meant aligning leadership commitment, integrating risk considerations into capital decisions, and rigorously exercising response capabilities before a crisis demanded them. Resilience is not built in a boardroom during a crisis; it is built quietly, deliberately, and continuously, long before the disruption arrives. True organizational resilience is a leadership commitment, not a compliance exercise.

Atiq Bajwa, FBCI, CBCP | Chief Risk
Officer | Sulaiman AlRajhi Holding

Chapter 1

Understanding resilience

Learning Objective

- Define organizational resilience and explain its importance in today's business environment.
- Distinguish between traditional risk management and resilience-based approaches.
- Identify and describe the core elements of a resilience management framework.
- Analyze the interconnectedness of organizations and communities in resilience planning.
- Develop strategies for building high reliability and adaptive capacity within organizations.

1.1 INTRODUCTION

Imagine that you are a Business Continuity Manager. And you've drafted a Business Resilience Plan or a new Resilience Strategy, to be embedded in the Organization Resilience Plan. You're pitching this plan to a skeptical, conservative Quality Head, who has no understanding of your domain. Let's call him Arun. I think we all know at least one Arun, right?

How would that go?

Arun, I've got this incredible idea for a completely new Resilience Strategy Approach. It's called the Remote Working System. I can see from your face that you're having some problems with this. Don't worry. I know it's very complicated. I don't want to take you through the gory details, I just want to tell you about some of the benefits of this strategy. First of all, it cleverly uses redundancy by having the critical resources supporting from remote workplace—before they're actually needed, to create a buffer against the unexpected. And it cleverly leverages the technology so that we have no dependency to come to office for work. The point is that we can use different approaches where we can use resources to support even if they are traveling outside the country. And the design is completely

DOI: 10.1201/9781003597520-1

modular. You have a system and can be implemented at any given time. The point is, that if team fails, another can take over, creating a virtually foolproof system.

I can see I'm losing you, Arun, but stay with me, because here is the really killer feature. The Resilience Strategy is completely adaptive. It's able to address not only our internal team but also external vendors can be a part of the strategy. It actually also does this with incredible prudence, detecting and reacting to every single incident, and furthermore, remembering every previous incident, in case they are ever encountered again. What I'm pitching you today is actually not a stand-alone strategy. The solution is embedded in the larger system of the organization, and it works in complete harmony with that system, to create this unprecedented level of continuity and protection of business. So Arun, just tell me honestly, what do you think of my new Resilience Strategy?

And Arun may say something like, I sincerely appreciate the effort and passion that have gone into your plan, blah blah blah. But honestly, it's total nonsense. You seem to be saying that the key selling points of your strategy are that it is inefficient and complex. Didn't they teach you 80–20? And furthermore, you're saying that this strategy is siloed. It overreacts, makes things up as it goes along, and is actually designed for someone else's benefit. I'm sorry to break it to you, but I don't think this one is a winner.

If we went with Arun's philosophy, I think we'd actually end up with a more efficient approach. And efficiency is always important in the short term. Less complex, more efficient, more bang for the buck. Who could say no to that? Unfortunately, there's one very tiny problem, and that is that the user of this solution, you or I, would probably die within one week of the disaster, when we encountered such situation where the office site is unavailable.

I first became interested in business continuity and resilience, when I was asked a very unusual question by the CEO of a global telecom company. And the question was: What do we have to do to make sure that if the Core Data Center fails? A seemingly innocent question, but actually, it's a little trickier than you might think, considering that the average cost of making another data center will cost more than millions of dollars. That is less than half of the organization total value of the assets.

After doing my research over the years and handling more than 20 real-time crisis over past two decades, what I found was that the same six principles that I saw underpinning the proposal of remote working system actually cropped up again and again, from redundancy through to embeddedness. In fact, I saw these principles not only during COVID-19 but also found them being very characteristic of long-lived outages, like War scenarios, etc. We also went on to look at other business interruptions and found that these very same properties also characterized businesses that were resilient and long-lived, and we noted their absence from ones which were short-lived.

1.2 RESILIENCE: A FRAMEWORK FOR ORGANIZATIONAL SUCCESS

Consider a major automotive assembler, a company we'll call "AutoCorp," operating a network of sophisticated manufacturing plants across North America. For decades, AutoCorp has relied on a "just-in-time" supply chain, receiving components from around the globe shortly before they are needed on the assembly line. This efficiency allowed for lean inventories and maximized profits until disruptions occurred.

In early 2020, reports of a novel virus began to emerge. Initially considered a distant threat, the virus, later known as COVID-19, quickly spread worldwide, causing factory closures and disrupting international shipping routes. A significant bottleneck developed in the supply of semiconductors, essential chips used in various automotive systems.

AutoCorp, like many of its competitors, faced a shortage. Assembly lines halted, production targets dropped, and thousands of workers were furloughed. Dealerships struggled to meet customer demand, affecting the stock price and raising concerns about long-term viability.

Other automakers, including a hypothetical 'Resilient Motors,' had invested in resilience measures. Resilient Motors diversified its supplier base, maintained strategic stocks of critical components, and developed adaptable manufacturing processes.

The different outcomes of AutoCorp and Resilient Motors highlight the importance of organizational resilience. AutoCorp faced challenges due to disruptions, while Resilient Motors adapted and continued operations, maintaining market share and reliability. The semiconductor shortage revealed vulnerabilities in AutoCorp's supply chain and emphasized the need for resilience in an interconnected world.

Imagine a manufacturing plant, 'Heartland Manufacturing,' located in America's rust belt. Its assembly lines produce components for the agricultural machinery industry, supporting a national network of distributors.

Inside, skilled workers assemble mechanisms, supported by a logistics network that transports products and receives raw materials. Heartland Manufacturing is a key part of a complex supply chain.

Unexpectedly, a severe flood occurs. The local river overflows, flooding Heartland Manufacturing, damaging the factory floor, electrical systems, and machinery.

Transportation links are disrupted, isolating the plant from suppliers and customers. Production halts, orders remain unfulfilled, and revenue declines. The community faces economic uncertainty, and farmers struggle without replacement parts.

The flood tests Heartland Manufacturing's resilience. Their recovery depends on their ability to restore operations and supply chains. The event impacts employees and the community, causing immediate financial hardship and uncertainty.

Maria, a single mother who worked at Heartland Manufacturing for fifteen years, faces eviction due to lost wages. John, a veteran machinist nearing retirement, fears the permanent closure of the plant. Local businesses dependent on plant employees experience decreased sales, affecting the community's economy.

As the floodwaters recede, the town faces economic challenges. The community, once supported by Heartland Manufacturing, now confronts a bleak outlook. For many, the flood represents both a natural disaster and a personal crisis.

The flood tests Heartland Manufacturing's resilience. With outdated insurance and inadequate cross-training, they face a difficult recovery. Six months later, the plant operates at 60% capacity, losing market share to more responsive competitors.

In contrast, 'AgriParts,' a competitor affected by the flood, had implemented resilience programs. They diversified their supplier base, invested in protective measures, and empowered employees to adapt.

AgriParts activated its emergency response plan, sourcing components from alternative vendors, minimizing flood damage, and assisting employees with temporary housing and financial support. They resumed operations quickly and communicated with customers transparently.

Long-term, Heartland Manufacturing faced layoffs and reputational damage, while AgriParts strengthened its position, gaining customer trust and employee loyalty. AgriParts demonstrated resilience, emerging as a leader in the agricultural machinery industry.

1.2.1 The interconnectedness of organizations

The story of Heartland Manufacturing reveals a crucial imperative for modern organizations: In an increasingly complex and interconnected world, resilience is not just about surviving crises, but about exhibiting the high reliability that communities and stakeholders expect in the face of adversity.

'There is an intrinsic relationship between organisational resilience and improving the resilience of communities.' This means that the strength and well-being of a community are fundamentally linked to the ability of its organizations to withstand and recover from crises.

The Resilient Organisation definition emphasizes that 'enabling the continued operation of organisations, in and following crises, significantly impacts on the medium to long term recovery and health of the wider community.' This highlights that organizations are not isolated entities; their ability to function during and after a disruption directly affects the community's access to essential goods, services, and employment.

Consider Heartland Manufacturing in our earlier example. Had the company been more resilient, the community would have suffered less economic hardship, as wages and tax revenue would have continued to flow. Resilient organizations provide a stabilizing force, minimizing the ripple effects of disasters on local economies and social structures.

Furthermore, the document acknowledges the 'interconnectedness of modern organizations, where disruptions can have significant and widespread impacts globally.' This implies that a failure in one organization can trigger a cascade of failures throughout its network, potentially affecting multiple communities across geographical boundaries.

In essence, a community's resilience is directly proportional to the resilience of its constituent organizations. When organizations are prepared to face disruptions, they contribute to a more robust and sustainable community. The resilience of essential industries such as grocery stores and gas stations allows communities to function after a disaster. Enabling the continued operation of organisations, in and following crises, significantly impacts on the medium to long term recovery and health of the wider community.' This is because organizations are the economic engines that drive community recovery. When a major employer like Heartland Manufacturing falters, the effects can linger for years, impacting employment rates, property values, and overall quality of life.

Moreover, the resilient framework acknowledges the 'interconnectedness of modern organisations, where disruptions can have significant and widespread impacts globally.' It's no longer a matter of isolated events; a failure in one organization can trigger a cascade of failures throughout its network, potentially affecting multiple communities and even destabilizing global systems. Consider, for example, a single data breach at a major financial institution. The resulting loss of consumer confidence, regulatory scrutiny, and legal liabilities can trigger a ripple effect of distrust and financial instability across global markets, impacting investors, businesses, and individuals worldwide.

In essence, organizational resilience is not just about protecting an individual company; it's about safeguarding the stability and well-being of the communities and global systems on which we all depend. A resilient organization is a responsible organization, one that recognizes its role as a vital component of a larger, interconnected whole.

1.2.2 The demand for high reliability

The story of Heartland Manufacturing highlights an important requirement for modern organizations: resilience is not just about surviving crises but also demonstrating high reliability that communities and stakeholders expect in challenging situations. As Resilient Organizations mentions, "There is increasing demand for organisations to exhibit high reliability in the face of adversity; decision makers must address not only the crises that they know will happen, but also those that they cannot foresee."

This demand for high reliability arises from several factors:

Increased Interdependence: Modern supply chains and business networks are tightly coupled, meaning that a disruption in one area can quickly affect the entire system. Stakeholders expect organizations to maintain consistent service levels even when facing unexpected challenges.

Growing Customer Expectations: In today's competitive marketplace, customers have more choices than ever before. They are less tolerant of disruptions and may switch to competitors if an organization fails to meet its promises.

Regulatory Scrutiny: Governments and regulatory agencies are increasingly focused on ensuring the resilience of critical infrastructure and essential services. Organizations that do not meet these standards may face fines, penalties, or legal actions.

Reputational Risk: In the age of social media, a single crisis can quickly damage an organization's reputation and reduce customer trust. Demonstrating resilience helps maintain a positive image and preserve brand value.

High reliability requires organizations to adopt a proactive and comprehensive approach to resilience management, addressing all aspects of the organization, from its culture and leadership to its processes and technologies (Figure 1.1).

Decision-makers must now address both predictable disruptions and emergencies, as well as unforeseen events known as "black swan" events that defy prediction. Traditional risk management approaches, which focus on mitigating known threats, are no longer sufficient. Organizations must develop the capacity to adapt and improvise in the face of unforeseen challenges, preparing for unknown risks that can emerge from a complex and interconnected world. This requires a shift in mindset from a reactive, defensive posture to a proactive, adaptive one.

For example, the COVID-19 pandemic caught many organizations unprepared. Those with resilience strategies, such as flexible supply chains, remote

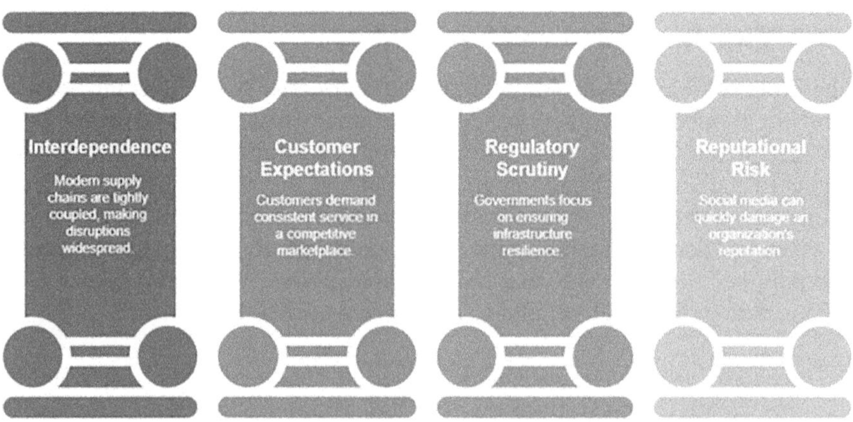

Figure 1.1 Building Resilience Amidst Modern Business Challenges

work capabilities, and strong communication channels, adapted more quickly and minimized disruptions. Others struggled to survive.

The expanding threat landscape, characterized by both known and unknown risks, underscores the need for organizations to embrace resilience as a core strategic imperative. It is not a matter of if a crisis will occur, but when and how. Organizations that fail to prepare for the unexpected are increasingly vulnerable to disruptions that can threaten their survival.

Additionally, the increasing reliance on technology amplifies both opportunities and vulnerabilities. Technology enables greater efficiency, innovation, and connectivity, but also creates new avenues for disruption. Our reliance on technology providers forces organizations to become resilient to a wider range of threats, including cyberattacks, data breaches, and system failures.

Recent events, such as ransomware attacks on hospital networks and cloud outages affecting thousands of websites, highlight the risks of relying on complex and interconnected technologies. These incidents underscore the need for robust cybersecurity measures and contingency plans.

Overall, the expanding threat landscape and growing reliance on technology emphasize the urgent need for organizations to prioritize resilience as a core strategic goal. Failure to prepare for unexpected challenges makes organizations increasingly vulnerable to disruptions that can jeopardize their existence.

1.2.3 Defining resilience and setting the stage

1.2.3.1 The challenge of defining resilience

This emphasis on high reliability necessitates that organizations adopt a proactive and comprehensive approach to resilience management. Such an approach must go beyond traditional risk management and encompass all aspects of the organization, including its culture, leadership, processes, and technologies. However, before delving into the specifics of resilience management, it is essential to address a fundamental challenge: defining what resilience truly *is*.

As experts have noted, "The term resilience has been used freely across a wide range of academic disciplines and in many different contexts. There is little consensus regarding what resilience is ..." This lack of a universally accepted definition can create confusion and impede efforts to build organizational resilience in a meaningful manner.

Resilience has been studied in various fields ranging from ecology and psychology to materials science, each bringing its own perspective and terminology. What constitutes resilience in a child facing adversity may differ significantly from what constitutes resilience in a financial institution facing a market crash.

Therefore, it is imperative to establish a clear and actionable definition of organizational resilience, one that is tailored to the specific challenges and opportunities faced by organizations in today's complex environment. This book aims to provide such a definition, grounded in research and practical experience, and applicable across diverse industries and organizational contexts. The goal of this book is to offer a practical, research-backed definition of resilience that organizations can utilize to assess their current state, identify areas for improvement, and develop strategies for thriving amid uncertainty.

1.3 RESILIENCE DEFINED

Some consolidated list of organizational resilience definitions is as follows:

1. "Organizational Resilience [is] the ability of an organization to anticipate, prepare for, respond and adapt to today's volatile business climate to survive and prosper."
2. "Organizational resilience is the ability of an organization to absorb and adapt in a changing environment to enable it to deliver its objectives and to survive and prosper. More resilient organizations can anticipate and respond to threats and opportunities, arising from sudden or gradual changes in their internal and external context."
3. "Organizational resilience is a function of the overall vulnerability, situation awareness, and adaptive capability of an organization in a complex, dynamic, and interdependent system."
4. "Resilience is the ability of an organization to rebound following a crisis or a disaster event. It is the ability to absorb strain. Building resilience into organizations entails a shift from a reactive to a proactive approach for crisis management and disaster recovery."

It's important to note these key themes that run through the different definitions:

- *Situation Awareness*: Understanding the context in which the organization operates.
- *Proactivity*: The ability to anticipate and prepare for future challenges.
- *Adaptability*: The capacity to adjust to changing circumstances.
- *Survival & Prosperity*: The goal of not only surviving but thriving in the long term.

When discussing organizational resilience, it is important to recognize the variety of definitions available and then specify which definition your work will be using, as outlined in the introduction.

"We present a framework built around three core components: *situation awareness*, *management of core vulnerabilities*, and *adaptive capacity*. This framework serves as a practical roadmap for building more resilient organizations, tested and refined through real-world case studies."

"By providing a clear and actionable definition of resilience, this aims to help organizations transform themselves from reactive entities into proactive agents of change."

"Therefore, it is essential to establish a clear and actionable definition of organizational resilience, tailored to the specific challenges and opportunities faced by organizations today. The goal of this book is to provide a practical, research-backed definition of resilience that organizations can use to assess their current state, identify areas for improvement, and develop strategies for thriving amid uncertainty."

"This book offers a pragmatic framework for assessing and improving organizational resilience, applicable across various industries and organizational structures. Our definition is based on concrete elements that organizations can directly influence and measure."

"Specifically, we define organizational resilience as a function of an organization's:

Situation awareness: The ability to understand and perceive its environment.

Management of core vulnerabilities: The capability to mitigate critical points of failure.

Adaptive capacity: The ability to adjust to changing conditions and learn from experience.

Effectively managing these elements enables organizations to withstand disruptions, adapt to change, and ultimately succeed in a complex and dynamic environment" (Figure 1.2).

Figure 1.2 Organizational Resilience Framework

1.4 INTRODUCING THE RESILIENCE MANAGEMENT FRAMEWORK

This book presents a pragmatic framework for assessing and improving organizational resilience, applicable across various industries and organizational structures. Organizational resilience is defined as a function of three key elements, which will be explored in detail in subsequent chapters:

Situation Awareness: The ability to understand and accurately perceive the organization's environment, both internal and external. This involves identifying potential threats and opportunities, monitoring key trends, and maintaining an understanding of the organization's strengths and weaknesses.

Management of Core Vulnerabilities: The proactive identification, assessment, and mitigation of the most critical points of failure within the organization. These "core vulnerabilities" are those that, if compromised, could affect the organization's operations and overall resilience significantly.

Adaptive Capacity: The organization's ability to learn, adapt, and innovate in response to changing conditions. This includes developing a culture of agility, empowering employees to make decisions, and creating flexible processes and systems.

Mastering these three core elements helps organizations build a foundation for resilience, enabling them to handle crises and operate effectively in a complex and dynamic environment. The following chapters will provide a detailed roadmap for implementing this framework, offering practical tools, examples, and strategies for building a more resilient organization.

1.5 CHAPTER ROADMAP

In the following pages, we will delve into the critical importance of *Situation Awareness*, exploring practical strategies for enhancing an organization's ability to perceive and understand its environment. We will then turn our attention to *Managing Core Vulnerabilities*, providing a step-by-step guide to identifying and mitigating the most critical points of failure within the organization. Finally, we will examine *Adaptive Capacity*, offering insights into how organizations can foster a culture of agility, innovation, and continuous learning to thrive in the face of constant change. By the end of this chapter, you will have a clear understanding of the three core elements of organizational resilience and the tools to begin measuring the resilience of your organization (Table 1.1).

Table 1.1 Organisation Resilience Measurement

Situation awareness	*Management of core vulnerabilities*	*Adaptive capacity*
Situational awareness and horizon scanning • Interviews, surveys, and reports • Collecting information from key stakeholders and verifying that data • Consequence scenarios understanding causes and consequences of crises	*Risk management—risk-based approach* • Assessing critical infrastructure: • Energy, information and communications, banking and finance, transportation • Vital human services • Mitigating risks with resilience strategies	*Leadership in crisis* • Visibility and availability of leadership • Decision-making, effective communication • Adapt to change and innovate
Select critical organizational components • Identify essential internal and external components for continued services and operations	*Business continuity planning* • Graceful degradation, agile restoration, critical thinking • Response and Recovery	*Crisis management and emergency response* • Readiness Exercises and Disaster Simulations (REDS) • Identification and continuous testing of vulnerabilities in simulated crisis situations
The interconnectedness of organizations • Assurance to interested parties, • Community focus • Interconnectedness	*Supply chain resilience* • Supply chain governance • Visibility • Supply chain risks • Supplier engagement • Supply chain velocity • Communication within supply chain • Product stewardship • Inventory management • Diversification and redundancy	*Adaptability and flexibility* • Room for autonomous change • Learning capacity • Leadership role • Resources • Workforce resilience • Culture of promoting adaptive capacity
		Learning and Innovation • Information and knowledge to handle unexpected problems • Expertise required handle unusual situation occurs • Training required to acquire roles of key personnel • Access to expert assistance during issues or crisis

1.5.1 Situational awareness

How situational awareness impacts organizational resilience? Here are five key resilience indicators related to situational awareness and we discuss the challenges organizations face in understanding their roles, risks, and recovery priorities.

Key Points

1. *Roles and Responsibilities*:
   - Organizations struggle with clarity regarding roles and responsibilities, leading to issues such as undervalued staff, lack of consultation, mistrust in decision-makers, and disengagement from the organizational vision.
   - A silo mentality often hampers communication and collaboration, especially in geographically distributed teams.
   - Organizations with clearly defined roles may experience rigidity that limits flexibility and adaptive capacity during crises.
2. *Understanding of Hazards and Consequences*:
   - While some organizations are aware of specific high-profile hazards (e.g., earthquakes, pandemics), overall awareness of potential risks is limited.
   - Many organizations tend to be reactionary rather than proactive in crisis management, often failing to consider the broader implications of various hazards.
   - Despite having some pandemic planning in place, organizations often overlook the long-term effects of such events on human resources and fail to adopt an all-hazards planning approach.
3. *Connectivity Awareness*:
   - Organizations generally understand their immediate operating environment but lack a comprehensive awareness of their connectivity with all stakeholders.
   - Awareness of internal stakeholders is often minimal; few organizations actively engage staff or consider them as key stakeholders in crisis planning.
   - Smaller organizations tend to have a better understanding of their internal dynamics compared to larger ones.
4. *Insurance Awareness*:
   - Knowledge regarding business interruption insurance and other aid options is inconsistent across organizations.
   - Many participants assume coverage exists without understanding the specifics or limitations, leading to unrealistic expectations about financial assistance during crises.
   - There is a general lack of awareness about the potential scarcity of professionals needed for processing insurance claims after large-scale events.

5. *Recovery Priorities*:
   - Organizations exhibit a limited understanding of their minimum business requirements and recovery priorities during crises.
   - Many organizations focus inwardly and fail to recognize the importance of collaboration with other entities in the community during recovery efforts.
   - Only a few organizations have clearly identified their key response and recovery priorities, which can hinder effective crisis management.

1.6 CONCLUSION

This book emphasizes that enhancing situational awareness is crucial for improving organizational resilience. By addressing the gaps in understanding roles, hazards, connectivity, insurance, and recovery priorities, organizations can better prepare for and respond to crises, ultimately leading to more robust resilience strategies.

1.6.1 Management of core vulnerabilities

The identification and management of core vulnerabilities within organizations and their impact on overall resilience. It outlines five key indicators that highlight common issues faced by organizations in planning and executing effective risk management strategies.

Key Points

1. *Planning Strategies*:
   - Larger organizations often have ongoing risk identification processes and emergency planning, typically driven by parent companies or industry demands.
   - Many organizations focus narrowly on specific risks rather than adopting an all-hazards approach.
   - Drivers for planning include insurance requirements, pandemic awareness, and directives from parent companies.
   - Discrepancies in vision among decision-makers regarding emergency plans can lead to ineffective planning.
2. *Participation in Exercises*:
   - Most organizations primarily conduct fire evacuation drills, with limited participation in broader emergency management exercises.
   - Barriers to exercising plans include staff availability and concerns about disrupting daily operations.
   - Some organizations express reluctance to exercise due to a lack of confidence in their plans.

3. *Capability and Capacity of Internal Resources*:
   - Internal resources are divided into physical, human, and process resources.
   - Many organizations lack contingency planning for alternative office spaces and underestimate the importance of co-dependencies between services.
   - Human resources are crucial, yet many organizations do not fully appreciate the challenges in retaining or recruiting staff post-crisis.
   - Organizations often overlook the impacts of crises on staff engagement and succession planning.
4. *Capability and Capacity of External Resources*:
   - Organizations often fail to recognize the importance of external resources in response and recovery efforts.
   - Critical services such as electricity, telecommunications, and transportation are acknowledged as vulnerabilities, but many organizations do not adequately plan for service outages or their implications.
   - There is limited planning for maintaining supply chains during crises, with few organizations establishing preferential agreements with suppliers.
5. *Organizational Connectivity*:
   - While some organizations maintain good relationships with critical partners, there is insufficient planning to sustain these connections during crises.
   - A lack of formal engagement in crisis planning can hinder effective collaboration during emergencies.

1.7 CONCLUSION

The book emphasizes that addressing core vulnerabilities is essential for enhancing organizational resilience. By improving planning strategies, participation in exercises, internal and external resource capabilities, and connectivity with stakeholders, organizations can better prepare for and respond to crises. The findings highlight the need for a comprehensive approach to resilience that encompasses both internal processes and external relationships.

1.7.1 Adaptive capacity

Adaptive capacity is a key component of organizational resilience, emphasizing the cultural and structural elements that enable timely and appropriate decision-making during crises, while also identifying and maximizing opportunities. It outlines five critical indicators of adaptive capacity, supported by examples from case studies.

Key Indicators of Adaptive Capacity

1. *Silo Mentality*:
    - Silo mentality refers to decentralized structures within organizations that foster individualistic approaches, poor communication pathways, and limited understanding of overall organizational vision.
    - Negative impacts include unclear roles, lack of trust, destructive relationships, and non-transparent governance.
    - Case studies reveal that attempts to address silo mentality at executive levels often fail to filter down effectively, exacerbating its negative effects during crises.
2. *Communications and Relationships*:
    - Effective communication pathways are vital but often hindered by silo mentality and geographic or departmental barriers.
    - Internal communication issues arise between general staff and senior executives, while external communications with stakeholders are often overlooked in crisis planning.
    - Organizations struggle with transferring critical information during emergencies due to reliance on traditional systems like email or telecommunications.
3. *Strategic Vision and Outcome Expectancy*:
    - A clear organizational vision improves resilience by guiding decision-making during crises.
    - Many organizations fail to align day-to-day operations with their vision or use it effectively in emergency management.
    - Organizations with a strong sense of purpose tend to have higher expectations for recovery, while those with unclear visions exhibit lower resilience.
4. *Information and Knowledge*:
    - Specialized knowledge held by individuals is often inaccessible during emergencies due to insufficient systems for information sharing.
    - Organizations rarely plan for alternative methods of communication when traditional networks fail, limiting their ability to transfer critical information during crises.
    - Mentoring programs or cross-training staff could mitigate these issues but are underutilized.
5. *Leadership, Management, and Governance Structures*:
    - Leadership plays a crucial role in adaptive capacity, yet many organizations rely on decentralized decision-making without planning for the centralized coordination required during large-scale emergencies.
    - Poor emergency communication systems and unclear response priorities hinder effective crisis management.
    - Organizations often lack awareness of the consequences of geographically widespread events or large-scale disruptions.

1.8 CONCLUSION

The book highlights the importance of addressing these indicators to enhance adaptive capacity and overall organizational resilience. It underscores the need for proactive measures such as improving communication pathways, aligning operations with strategic vision, facilitating knowledge sharing, and developing robust leadership structures. These steps are essential for organizations to effectively respond to crises and thrive in dynamic environments.

Creating an Organizational Resilience Framework involves integrating several key characteristics that help organizations withstand disruptions and adapt to changing environments. Here are some practical steps and characteristics to consider when building your framework:

Characteristics of Organizational Resilience

1. *Adaptability*: The ability to adjust to changing circumstances.
2. *Agility*: The capacity to respond quickly to disruptions.
3. *Cohesion*: Strong internal relationships and communication.
4. *Innovation*: Encouraging creative solutions to challenges.
5. *Risk Awareness*: Identifying and mitigating potential risks.
6. *Learning Culture*: Continuous learning and improvement (Figure 1.3).

Figure 1.3

Practical Steps for Achieving Resilience

1. Conduct Risk Assessments
    - *Identify Risks*: Use tools like SWOT analysis or risk matrices to identify potential threats.
    - *Assess Impact*: Evaluate the potential impact of each risk on operations.
    - *Develop Mitigation Strategies*: Create plans to reduce or manage identified risks.

2. Implement Business Continuity Planning (BCP)
    - *Develop Continuity Plans*: Outline procedures for maintaining operations during disruptions.
    - *Test Plans Regularly*: Conduct regular drills or tabletop exercises to ensure readiness.
    - *Review and Update Plans*: Regularly review and update plans based on lessons learned.

3. Foster a Learning Culture
    - *Encourage Feedback*: Create an environment where employees feel comfortable sharing insights and feedback.
    - *Provide Training*: Offer training programs that focus on resilience, adaptability, and innovation.
    - *Celebrate Successes and Failures*: Use both successes and failures as learning opportunities.

4. Enhance Communication and Collaboration
    - *Cross-Functional Teams*: Encourage collaboration across departments to foster a cohesive response to challenges.
    - *Clear Communication Channels*: Establish open and transparent communication channels.
    - *Regular Updates*: Keep stakeholders informed about organizational changes or challenges.

5. Embed Innovation
    - *Encourage Experimentation*: Provide resources and support for innovative projects.
    - *Foster a Culture of Innovation*: Recognize and reward innovative thinking.
    - *Stay Updated on Emerging Trends*: Monitor industry trends and technologies that could impact resilience.

6. Ensure Adaptability and Agility
    - *Flexible Processes*: Implement processes that can adapt quickly to changing conditions.

- *Agile Methodologies*: Adopt agile methodologies in project management to enhance responsiveness.
- *Stay Alert to Market Changes*: Continuously monitor market conditions and adjust strategies accordingly.

7. Build Strong External Relationships
   - *Stakeholder Engagement*: Engage with suppliers, partners, and customers to build strong relationships.
   - *Community Involvement*: Participate in community activities to enhance reputation and build support networks.
   - *Collaborate with Peers*: Share best practices with industry peers to stay informed about resilience strategies (Table 1.2).

Table 1.2 Organizational resilience checklist

Category	*Actions*
1. Risk Management	• Conduct *regular risk assessments* using tools like SWOT analysis or risk matrices. • *Identify and prioritize risks* (e.g., operational, financial, reputational, cybersecurity). • Develop *mitigation strategies* for high-priority risks (e.g., diversifying suppliers). • Assign *clear responsibilities* for risk management tasks. • *Review and update risk assessments* quarterly or after major disruptions.
2. Business Continuity Planning (BCP)	• Develop *comprehensive business continuity plans* for critical operations. • *Identify key roles and responsibilities* for continuity efforts. • *Regularly test continuity plans* through drills, tabletop exercises, or simulations. • Ensure *all employees are trained* on their roles in continuity efforts. • *Update continuity plans* based on lessons learned from tests or real incidents.
3. Learning Culture	• Provide *ongoing training and development opportunities* (e.g., resilience training). • Encourage *feedback and continuous improvement* through surveys or debriefs after incidents. • *Celebrate successes and learn from failures* to foster a culture of growth. • Promote *knowledge sharing* across teams and departments.
4. Communication and Collaboration	• Establish *clear communication channels* for internal and external stakeholders. • Develop a *crisis communication plan* for timely and accurate information sharing.

(Continued)

Table 1.2 Organizational resilience checklist *(Continued)*

Category	*Actions*
	• Foster *cross-functional collaboration* to break down silos and improve coordination. • Conduct *regular team meetings* to discuss resilience efforts and address challenges.
5. Innovation	• Encourage *experimentation and innovation* by providing resources for new ideas. • Foster a *culture of innovation* by recognizing and rewarding creative solutions. • Stay updated on *emerging trends and technologies* (e.g., AI for risk prediction). • Implement *pilot programs* to test innovative approaches before scaling.
6. Adaptability and Agility	• Implement *flexible processes* that can quickly adapt to changing conditions. • Adopt *agile methodologies* in project management to improve responsiveness. • Continuously *monitor market conditions* and adjust strategies as needed. • Empower employees to *make decisions and take action* during disruptions.
7. External Relationships	• Build *strong relationships with key stakeholders* (e.g., suppliers, customers, regulators). • Engage with the *local community* to enhance reputation and build support networks. • Collaborate with *industry peers* to share best practices and stay informed. • Develop *partnerships with emergency response organizations* for faster recovery.
8. Employee Well-Being	• Implement *employee well-being programs* to support mental and physical health. • Provide *resources for stress management* (e.g., counseling, mindfulness training). • Ensure *work-life balance* to prevent burnout and maintain productivity. • Recognize and reward employees for their contributions to resilience efforts.
9. Technology Resilience	• Implement *robust cybersecurity measures* to protect against data breaches and cyberattacks. • Ensure *data backups and disaster recovery plans* are in place and regularly tested. • Invest in *redundant systems* to minimize downtime during disruptions. • Train employees on *cybersecurity best practices* to reduce vulnerabilities.

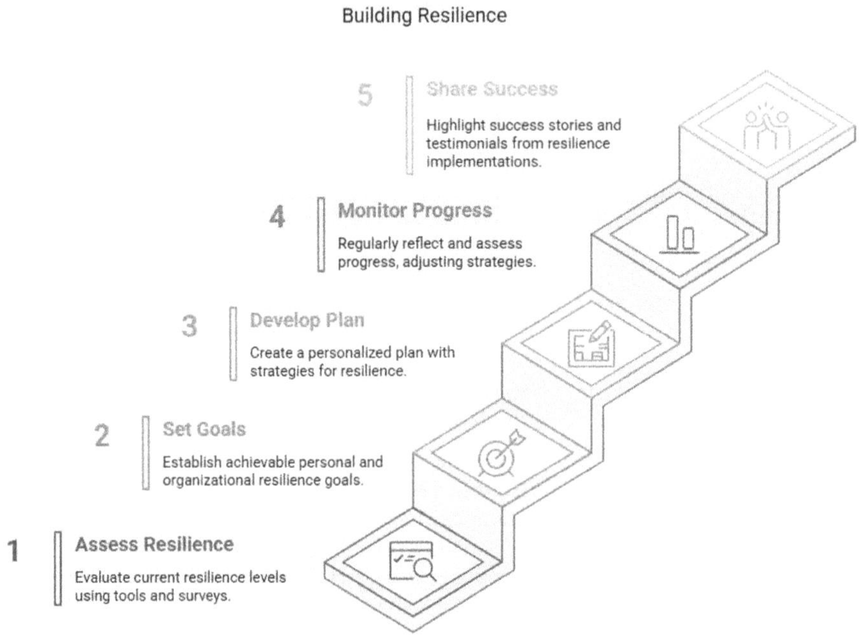

Figure 1.4

Implementation Steps

1. *Assess Current Resilience*: Evaluate their current level of resilience using self-assessment tools or surveys.
2. *Set Resilience Goals*: Set achievable goals for improving resilience, both personally and organizationally.
3. *Develop a Resilience Plan*: Create a personalized resilience plan that includes strategies for managing stress, building support networks, and enhancing emotional intelligence.
4. *Monitor Progress*: Regular reflection and self-assessment to monitor progress and adjust strategies as needed.
5. *Share Success Stories*: Case studies or testimonials from individuals or organizations that have successfully implemented resilience strategies are included in this book (Figure 1.4).

1.8.1 Call to action/engagement

The following chapters will provide a detailed roadmap for implementing this framework, offering practical tools, real-world examples, and actionable strategies for building a more resilient organization.

But building resilience is not a passive exercise; it requires active engagement, critical thinking, and a willingness to challenge conventional wisdom.

We invite you, the reader, to embark on this journey with us. As you delve into the following chapters, consider how these concepts apply to your own organization. Identify your own Core vulnerabilities. Assess your organization's adaptive capacity. And ask yourself: Are we truly prepared to face the inevitable challenges that lie ahead?

The future belongs to those who are prepared. Let's work together to build a more resilient world, one organization at a time.

"Whether you are a seasoned executive seeking to safeguard your organization's long-term viability, a risk management professional tasked with mitigating emerging threats, or an emerging leader eager to champion a culture of adaptability, this book offers a roadmap for building a truly resilient organization – one that can not only withstand the inevitable storms but emerge stronger and more adaptable than before."

"As you delve into the following chapters, consider how these concepts apply to your own role and responsibilities. Identify your organization's unique vulnerabilities. Assess your team's adaptive capacity. And ask yourself: Are we truly prepared to face the inevitable challenges that lie ahead, and are we positioned to seize the opportunities that arise from adversity? In a world of increasing uncertainty, how prepared is your organization to face the challenges ahead?"

"The future belongs to those who are prepared. Let's work together to build a more resilient world, one organization at a time."

Chapter 2

Risk management

Risk-based approach

Learning Objective

- Identify and assess risks and vulnerabilities in critical infrastructure.
- Integrate risk management with business continuity and resilience planning.
- Analyze the unique risk profiles of different critical infrastructure sectors.
- Develop and apply comprehensive strategies for risk mitigation and adaptation.
- Evaluate lessons from real-world case studies to improve risk management practices.

2.1 INTRODUCTION

Risk management has evolved from a peripheral business function to a central strategic imperative, particularly when addressing the complex challenges of protecting critical infrastructure. In today's interconnected world, where disruptions can cascade across sectors with unprecedented speed and magnitude, adopting a risk-based approach has become essential for organizational resilience and national security. This chapter explores the multifaceted nature of risk management as it applies to critical infrastructure protection, emphasizing the importance of systematic assessment, strategic mitigation, and adaptive resilience.

The concept of risk itself encompasses a degree of inherent uncertainty. As noted in our research, risk management activities are often described as "vague and uncertain," requiring a comprehensive "understanding of uncertainty" to be effective. This uncertainty is particularly pronounced in critical infrastructure contexts, where threats range from natural disasters and technological failures to deliberate attacks and systemic vulnerabilities. The complexity is further amplified by the interdependencies between different infrastructure sectors, where a failure in one system can trigger cascading effects across multiple domains.

DOI: 10.1201/9781003597520-2

Enterprise Risk Management (ERM), defined as "the process of planning, organizing, leading, and controlling the activities of an organization in order to minimize the effects of risk," provides a framework for addressing these challenges. This approach extends beyond traditional risk management by considering not only financial and accidental losses but also strategic, operational, and previously unrecognized risks. The goal is not merely to prevent negative outcomes but to create a foundation for organizational stability and growth even in uncertain environments.

The evolving risk landscape presents organizations with increasingly complex challenges. Rapid technological change, geopolitical tensions, and ongoing climate-related issues create a dynamic environment where risk factors are constantly shifting.

This reality demands a more sophisticated approach to risk management—one that is proactive rather than reactive, comprehensive rather than siloed, and strategic rather than merely tactical.

This chapter will examine risk management through the lens of critical infrastructure protection, focusing on five key sectors: Energy, Information and Communications, Banking and Finance, Transportation, and Vital Human Services. Each of these sectors presents unique vulnerabilities and risk profiles, yet they share common challenges and interdependencies that necessitate coordinated approaches to risk assessment and mitigation.

We will also explore a significant case study—the BP Deepwater Horizon oil spill of 2010—to illustrate the catastrophic consequences that can result from inadequate risk management practices. This disaster, which claimed eleven lives and caused unprecedented environmental damage, offers valuable lessons about the importance of comprehensive risk assessment, effective crisis management, and organizational preparedness.

Finally, we will discuss resilience strategies that can help organizations not only mitigate risks but also adapt and thrive in the face of disruption. These strategies represent the evolution of risk management from a defensive posture focused on protection to a more dynamic stance that embraces adaptation and continuous improvement.

By the conclusion of this chapter, readers will have gained insights into the techniques for assessing risks and vulnerabilities in critical infrastructure, approaches for integrating risk management with business continuity and resilience planning, and an understanding of the role that technology plays in both risk assessment and mitigation efforts. These insights will provide a foundation for developing more robust and adaptive risk management practices in an increasingly complex and uncertain world. Critical infrastructure forms the backbone of modern society, providing essential services that underpin economic prosperity, public health, and national security. The assessment of these vital systems requires a sophisticated understanding of their unique vulnerabilities, interdependencies, and the evolving threat landscape they face. This section examines the risk assessment approaches for five key infrastructure sectors, highlighting their distinctive characteristics while identifying common challenges and mitigation strategies.

2.2 ASSESSMENT OF CRITICAL INFRASTRUCTURE

2.2.1 Introduction

Risk management has transformed from a secondary business function into a strategic imperative, particularly in the context of safeguarding *Critical Infrastructure* (*CI*). These systems, including *Energy*, *Information and Communications*, *Banking and Finance*, *Transportation*, and *Vital Human Services*, form the foundation of economic prosperity, national security, and public health.

This section outlines a detailed assessment of these critical sectors, focusing on their unique vulnerabilities, interdependencies, and strategies for mitigating risk.

2.2.2 Critical infrastructure sectors overview

2.2.2.1 Energy sector

The energy infrastructure represents one of the most fundamental components of national critical infrastructure, providing the power that enables virtually all other sectors to function. As noted by the Cybersecurity and Infrastructure Security Agency (CISA), the U.S. energy infrastructure is divided into three interrelated segments: electricity, oil, and natural gas. With more than 6,413 power plants nationwide and approximately 1,075 gigawatts of installed generation capacity, this vast network faces numerous vulnerabilities that demand rigorous risk assessment.

The complexity of the energy sector is evident in its diverse generation sources. Approximately 48% of electricity is produced by combusting coal, 20% in nuclear power plants, and 22% by combusting natural gas, with the remainder coming from hydroelectric plants, oil, and renewable sources. This diversity, while providing resilience through redundancy, also creates multiple potential points of failure that must be assessed and managed.

Risk assessment in the energy sector must account for both physical and cyber vulnerabilities. Physical threats include natural disasters, aging infrastructure, and potential terrorist attacks on generation facilities, transmission lines, or fuel supply chains. The heavy reliance on pipelines to distribute products across the nation highlights the interdependencies between the Energy and Transportation Systems Sectors, creating additional risk vectors that cross sectoral boundaries.

Cybersecurity threats present an increasingly significant risk to energy infrastructure. As control systems become more automated and interconnected, the potential for cyberattacks to disrupt energy supplies grows correspondingly.

The energy sector has been proactive in addressing these risks, with substantial information sharing of best practices across the sector through industry groups. Many sector owners and operators have extensive experience with infrastructure protection abroad and have recently focused their attention on cybersecurity challenges. The Department of Energy, as the designated Sector Risk Management Agency, has developed the Energy Sector-Specific Plan that details how the National Infrastructure Protection Plan risk management framework is implemented within the context of the energy sector's unique characteristics and risk landscape. This plan emphasizes the importance of public-private partnerships, given that more than 80% of the country's energy infrastructure is owned by the private sector.

Risk assessment methodologies in the energy sector often employ a multilayered approach that considers threats, vulnerabilities, and consequences. These assessments must account for the "enabling function" that energy provides across all critical infrastructure sectors, making the cascading impacts of energy disruptions particularly severe. The interdependencies between electricity, oil, and natural gas systems further complicate risk assessments, requiring analysts to consider how failures in one energy subsector might affect others.

Climate-related risks have gained increasing prominence in energy sector risk assessments. Extreme weather events, changing temperature patterns, and water availability concerns all pose threats to energy infrastructure. For instance, power plants that rely on water for cooling may face operational constraints during droughts, while transmission lines are vulnerable to damage from storms and wildfires. These climate considerations must be integrated into comprehensive risk assessment frameworks

- *Risks*:
  - Physical: Natural disasters, aging infrastructure, terrorism.
  - Cyber: SCADA systems, remote access vulnerabilities.
- *Mitigation*:
  - Redundancy in energy sources.
  - Cybersecurity frameworks (NIST, ISO 27001).
  - Public-private coordination.

2.2.3 Information and communications sector

The Communications Sector has evolved dramatically over the last 25 years, transforming from predominantly a provider of voice services into a competitive and interconnected industry using terrestrial, satellite, and wireless transmission systems.

This evolution has created new capabilities but also introduced new vulnerabilities that require sophisticated risk assessment approaches.

The interconnected nature of modern communications infrastructure presents unique challenges for risk assessment. As CISA notes, satellite, wireless, and wireline providers depend on each other to carry and terminate their traffic, and companies routinely share facilities and technology to ensure interoperability. This interdependence means that vulnerabilities in one part of the network can potentially affect the entire communications ecosystem.

Risk assessment in the communications sector must address both physical and cyber threats. Physical vulnerabilities include damage to transmission infrastructure from natural disasters, deliberate attacks on critical nodes, and disruptions to power supplies. Cyber vulnerabilities encompass a range of threats, from denial-of-service attacks and malware to sophisticated intrusions that could compromise the confidentiality, integrity, or availability of communications services.

The Communications Sector is closely linked to numerous other critical infrastructure sectors, creating complex interdependencies that must be factored into risk assessments. For example, the Energy Sector provides power to run cellular towers, central offices, and other critical communications facilities. Conversely, the Energy Sector relies on communications to aid in monitoring and controlling the delivery of electricity. Similar interdependencies exist with the Information Technology, Financial Services, Emergency Services, and Transportation Systems Sectors.

The Department of Homeland Security, as the designated Sector Risk Management Agency for the Communications Sector, has developed a sector-specific plan that implements the National Infrastructure Protection Plan risk management framework. This plan emphasizes the importance of collaboration between the private sector, which owns and operates the majority of communications infrastructure, and the federal government. Together, they work to predict, anticipate, and respond to sector outages and understand how they might affect the ability of national leadership to communicate during times of crisis.

Risk assessment methodologies in the communications sector often employ a system-based approach that considers the resilience of networks rather than just individual components. This approach recognizes that modern communications systems are designed with redundancy and alternative routing capabilities that can mitigate the impact of localized failures. However, it also acknowledges that certain high-impact, low-probability events could potentially cause widespread disruptions that overwhelm these built-in resilience mechanisms.

Emerging technologies present both opportunities and challenges for risk assessment in the communications sector. The deployment of 5G networks, the Internet of Things (IoT), and increasing automation all offer potential improvements in efficiency and capability, but also introduce new attack surfaces and potential vulnerabilities. Risk assessment frameworks must evolve to address these emerging technologies and the novel threats they may face.

- *Risks:*
  - Physical: Damage to transmission towers and data centers.
  - Cyber: Malware, ransomware, denial-of-service attacks.

- *Mitigation*:
  - System-level redundancy.
  - 5G network security and IoT monitoring.

2.2.4 Banking and finance sector

The Financial Services Sector represents a vital component of national critical infrastructure, facilitating the transactions and investments that drive economic activity. This sector includes thousands of depository institutions, providers of investment products, insurance companies, other credit and financing organizations, and the providers of critical financial utilities and services that support these functions.

The diversity of financial institutions presents challenges for risk assessment. As CISA notes, financial institutions vary widely in size and presence, ranging from some of the world's largest global companies with thousands of employees and many billions of dollars in assets, to community banks and credit unions with a small number of employees serving individual communities. This diversity necessitates risk assessment approaches that can be scaled and adapted to different organizational contexts.

Risk assessment in the financial sector must address a wide range of threats, including cybersecurity attacks, fraud, physical security breaches, and systemic risks that could affect market stability. The sector faces a complex risk environment characterized by rapid technological change, evolving regulatory requirements, and the potential for contagion effects where problems in one institution can quickly spread to others. Large-scale power outages, natural disasters, and an increase in the number and sophistication of cyberattacks demonstrate the wide range of potential risks facing the sector. These risks can affect the sector's ability to perform its core functions: depositing funds and making payments to other parties, providing credit and liquidity to customers, investing funds for both long and short periods, and transferring financial risks between customers.

The Department of the Treasury, designated as the Sector Risk Management Agency for the Financial Services Sector, has developed a sector-specific plan that details how the National Infrastructure Protection Plan risk management framework is implemented. This plan recognizes the unique regulatory environment of the financial sector, which includes oversight from multiple federal and state agencies.

Risk assessment methodologies in the financial sector often employ a multilayered approach that considers operational, credit, market, and liquidity risks. These assessments must account for both institution-specific vulnerabilities and broader systemic risks that could affect market stability. The interconnected nature of financial markets means that risk assessments must consider potential contagion effects and cascading failures.

Technology plays an increasingly important role in financial sector risk assessment. Advanced analytics, artificial intelligence, and machine learning are being employed to identify patterns and anomalies that might indicate emerging risks. However, the growing reliance on technology also creates new vulnerabilities, particularly in the areas of cybersecurity and operational resilience.

Regulatory frameworks significantly influence risk assessment practices in the financial sector. Requirements such as stress testing, capital adequacy assessments, and business continuity planning create standardized approaches to identifying and managing risks. These regulatory requirements have evolved in response to past financial crises and continue to adapt to address emerging threats.

- *Risks*:
  - Systemic risk from global interconnected markets.
  - Cyberattacks (SWIFT system vulnerabilities).
- *Mitigation*:
  - Real-time fraud detection (AI/ML).
  - Compliance with Basel III, DORA.

2.2.5 Transportation sector

The Transportation Systems Sector encompasses a vast network of infrastructure that enables the movement of people and goods across the nation and internationally. As CISA notes, this sector consists of seven key subsectors: Aviation, Highway and Motor Carrier, Maritime Transportation System, Mass Transit and Passenger Rail, Pipeline Systems, Freight Rail, and Postal and Shipping.

The scale and diversity of transportation infrastructure present significant challenges for risk assessment. The aviation subsector includes approximately 19,700 airports, heliports, and landing strips, along with aircraft, air traffic control systems, and various support services. The highway and motor carrier subsector encompasses more than 4 million miles of roadway, more than 600,000 bridges, and more than 350 tunnels. Similar complexity exists across the other transportation subsectors, creating a multifaceted risk landscape.

Risk assessment in the transportation sector must address both physical and cyber vulnerabilities. Physical threats include natural disasters, accidents, and potential terrorist attacks on transportation infrastructure or vehicles. Cyber threats encompass risks to the increasingly automated and interconnected control systems that manage transportation operations, from air traffic control to pipeline monitoring. The Department of Homeland Security and the Department of Transportation, designated as the Co-Sector Risk Management Agencies for the Transportation Systems Sector, have developed a sector-specific plan that implements the National Infrastructure Protection Plan risk management framework. This collaborative approach reflects the shared responsibilities for transportation security and resilience.

Risk assessment methodologies in the transportation sector often employ a system-based approach that considers the interconnections between different modes of transportation and their dependencies on other infrastructure sectors. For example, the heavy reliance on pipelines to distribute products across the nation highlights the interdependencies between the Energy and Transportation Systems Sectors.

The transportation sector faces unique challenges related to the movement of hazardous materials. Approximately 65% of hazardous liquids and nearly all of the nation's natural gas are transported through pipeline systems spanning more than 2.5 million miles. Risk assessments must consider the potential consequences of accidents or attacks involving these materials, including environmental damage and threats to public safety.

Technology is transforming transportation systems and creating new considerations for risk assessment. Autonomous vehicles, smart infrastructure, and integrated traffic management systems offer potential improvements in efficiency and safety but also introduce new vulnerabilities. Risk assessment frameworks must evolve to address these emerging technologies and the novel threats they may face.

The international dimensions of transportation add complexity to risk assessment efforts. Global supply chains, international shipping lanes, and cross-border transportation networks create dependencies on infrastructure and security measures outside of national control. Risk assessments must consider these international factors and the potential for disruptions originating in other countries.

- *Risks*:
  - Physical: Accidents, terrorism, natural disasters.
  - Cyber: Autonomous transport system vulnerabilities.
- *Mitigation*:
  - Scenario-based drills and simulations.
  - Smart traffic management systems.

2.2.6 Vital human services (Healthcare and Public Health)

The Healthcare and Public Health Sector protects all sectors of the economy from hazards such as terrorism, infectious disease outbreaks, and natural disasters. This sector's critical infrastructure includes hospitals, clinics, public health agencies, pharmaceutical manufacturers, and the supply chains that support healthcare delivery. Risk assessment in the healthcare sector must address a diverse range of threats, from pandemic diseases and bioterrorism to cyberattacks on medical devices and patient records. The COVID-19 pandemic has highlighted the importance of robust risk assessment and preparedness planning in this sector, revealing both strengths and vulnerabilities in healthcare infrastructure.

The Healthcare and Public Health Sector is highly dependent on other critical infrastructure sectors for continuity of operations and service delivery. As CISA notes, these dependencies include Communications, Emergency Services, Energy, Food and Agriculture, Information Technology, Transportation Systems, and Water and Wastewater Systems. Risk assessments must consider these interdependencies and the potential for cascading failures across sectors.

The Department of Health and Human Services, designated as the Sector Risk Management Agency for the Healthcare and Public Health Sector, has developed a sector-specific plan that implements the National Infrastructure Protection Plan risk management framework. This plan emphasizes the importance of collaboration between public and private stakeholders, given that the vast majority of the sector's assets are privately owned and operated.

Risk assessment methodologies in the healthcare sector often employ an all-hazards approach that considers both intentional threats and natural disasters. These assessments must account for the unique characteristics of healthcare delivery, including the need for continuous operations during emergencies and the potential for surge demands that exceed normal capacity.

Supply chain vulnerabilities represent a significant concern for healthcare sector risk assessments. The global nature of pharmaceutical and medical supply manufacturing creates dependencies on international production and distribution networks.

Disruptions to these supply chains, whether from natural disasters, geopolitical tensions, or other factors, can have serious implications for healthcare delivery.

Cybersecurity risks have gained increasing prominence in healthcare sector risk assessments. The digitization of patient records, the proliferation of networked medical devices, and the growing use of telemedicine create new attack surfaces for malicious actors. Ransomware attacks on healthcare facilities have demonstrated the potential for cyber threats to disrupt critical care and put patient safety at risk.

Workforce considerations play an important role in healthcare sector risk assessments. As noted in the research, the healthcare sector faces challenges related to an aging workforce, with significant percentages of workers approaching retirement age in various healthcare fields. These demographic trends create potential vulnerabilities related to knowledge transfer, succession planning, and maintaining adequate staffing levels during crises.

- *Risks*:
  - Pandemic response, biosecurity, ransomware on medical devices.
- *Mitigation*:
  - Telemedicine resilience planning.
  - National stockpiles and supply chain diversification.

2.3 STEPS FOR CONDUCTING AN ENTERPRISE RISK MANAGEMENT WORKSHOP

How to conduct an effective ERM workshop, emphasizing key aspects for organizational resilience:

1. *Preparation and Planning*
    - *Define Objectives*: Clearly state the goals of the workshop. For example:
        - Identify key enterprise risks.
        - Assess the potential impact of these risks.
        - Develop mitigation strategies.
        - Enhance risk awareness and accountability.
    - *Identify Participants*: Select a diverse group of stakeholders from different departments and levels within the organization. This ensures a comprehensive view of potential risks.
    - *Gather Information*: Collect relevant data, reports, and information about the organization's strategic objectives, operations, and past incidents.
    - *Create an Agenda*: Structure the workshop with specific activities, time allocations, and breaks.
    - *Prepare Materials*: Develop presentation slides, risk assessment templates, and any other necessary handouts.
    - *Select a Facilitator*: Choose someone with expertise in ERM and workshop facilitation skills.
2. *Workshop Execution*
    a. *Introduction and Context Setting*
        - *Welcome and Introductions*: Start by welcoming participants and having them introduce themselves.
        - *Explain Objectives*: Clearly state the workshop's objectives and expected outcomes.
        - *Define ERM*: Provide a brief overview of Enterprise Risk Management and its importance for organizational resilience. Refer to the document's definition of risk management activities as inherently "vague and uncertain" and requiring an "understanding of uncertainty."
        - *Set the Stage*: Explain the current risk landscape and any recent events or trends that highlight the need for ERM.

    b. *Risk Identification*
        - *Brainstorming Session*: Facilitate a brainstorming session to identify potential risks across different categories. Use the lists provided in the document as a starting point:
            - Natural Disasters
            - Economic Disasters
            - Personnel Disasters
            - Physical Disasters

You may have developed a list of your enterprise's risks that looks similar to this:

Physical Disasters
•Industrial Accidents
•Supply Chain
•Value Chain
•Product Failure
•Fires
•Environmental
•Health & Safety

Personnel Disasters
•Strikes
•Workplace Violence
•Vandalism
•Employee Fraud

Natural Disasters
•Hurricanes
•Earthquakes
•Floods
•Tornadoes
•Drought

Criminal Disasters
•Product Tampering
•Terrorism
•Kidnapping & Hostages

Information Disasters
•Theft of Proprietary Information
•Hacking, Data Tampering
•Cyber Attacks

Economic Disasters
•Recessions
•Stock Market Downturns
•Rating Agency Downgrade

Reputation Disasters
•Rumors
•Regulatory Issues
•Litigation
•Product Liability
•Media Investigations
•Internet Reputation

Figure 2.1

    - Criminal Disasters
    - Information Disasters
    - Reputation Disasters
    - *Don't Forget*: Risks related to Partners, Government, Human Capital, Infrastructure, Competitors, Customers, Substitutes, New Entrants, Suppliers, and Stakeholders (Figure 2.1).
  - *Categorize Risks*: Group the identified risks into relevant categories for easier analysis.
  - *Document Risks*: Record each identified risk with a clear description.

c. *Risk Assessment*
  - *Probability and Impact*: For each identified risk, assess the probability of occurrence and the potential impact on the organization. Use a matrix similar to the one in the document (Consequences vs. Probability of Disruption).
  - *Qualitative vs. Quantitative*: Determine whether to use qualitative (High, Medium, Low) or quantitative (numerical values) assessments.
  - *Risk Prioritization*: Prioritize risks based on their assessed probability and impact. Focus on the high-priority risks that require immediate attention (Figure 2.2).

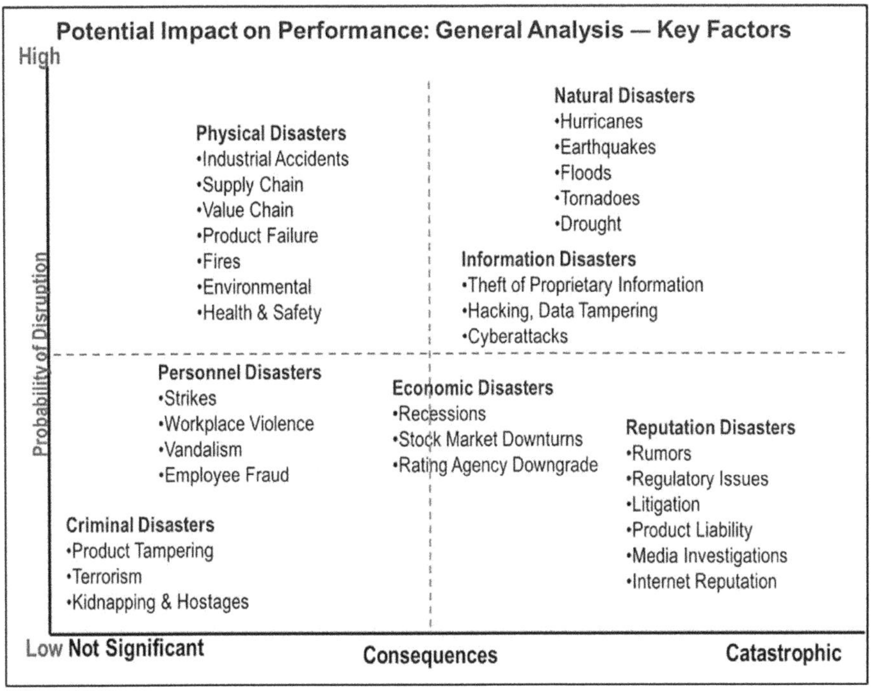

Figure 2.2

d. *Risk Mitigation Strategies*
   - *Develop Mitigation Plans*: For each high-priority risk, develop specific mitigation strategies. These may include:
     - Risk Avoidance
     - Risk Reduction
     - Risk Transfer (e.g., insurance)
     - Risk Acceptance
   - *Assign Responsibilities*: Clearly assign responsibility for implementing each mitigation strategy to specific individuals or teams.
   - *Set Timelines*: Establish realistic timelines for implementing the mitigation strategies.

e. *Action Planning and Follow-Up*
   - *Create Action Plans*: Develop detailed action plans for each mitigation strategy, outlining the specific steps, resources required, and responsible parties.
   - *Establish Monitoring Mechanisms*: Set up mechanisms for monitoring the progress of the action plans and the effectiveness of the mitigation strategies.
   - *Schedule Follow-Up Meetings*: Plan regular follow-up meetings to review progress, address any issues, and update the risk assessment as needed.

3. *Wrap-Up and Documentation*
    - *Summarize Key Findings*: Review the key findings of the workshop, including the identified risks, their assessed impact, and the proposed mitigation strategies.
    - *Document Results*: Compile a comprehensive report documenting the workshop's activities, results, and action plans.
    - *Communicate Results*: Share the report with relevant stakeholders and ensure that the findings are integrated into the organization's ERM framework.

Key Considerations

- *Critical Thinking*: Encourage participants to use critical thinking skills to challenge assumptions and consider different perspectives (as highlighted below).

  Critical thinking is the ability to see problems from multiple perspectives, expose critical underlying assumptions, challenge and reverse one's assumptions, and reformulate basic arguments (Figure 2.3).
- *Understanding Uncertainty*: Acknowledge the inherent uncertainty in risk management and the need for flexibility and adaptability.
- *Active Analysis*: Promote "active analysis" through continuous scanning, monitoring, and issue management.
- *Business Implications*: Ensure that the risk management team understands the business implications of their decisions and recommendations.

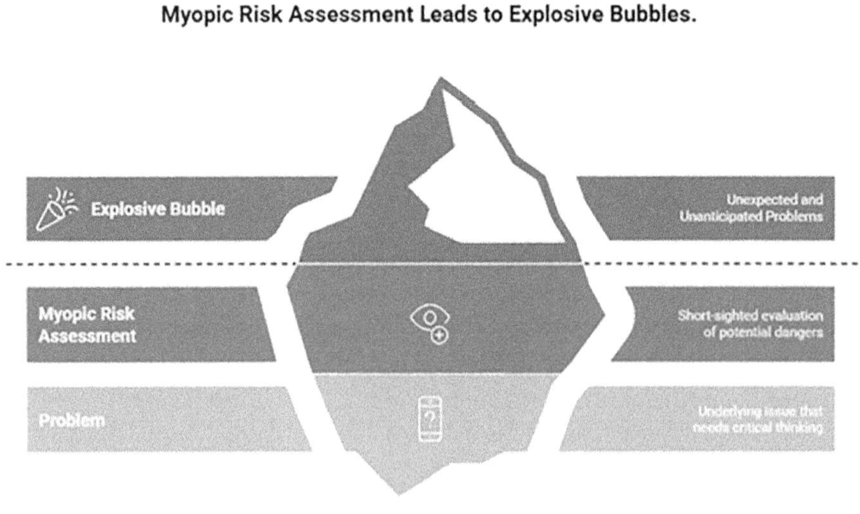

Figure 2.3

2.4 CASE STUDY: BP DEEPWATER HORIZON OIL SPILL (2010)

2.4.1 Background and context

The Deepwater Horizon was an ultra-deepwater, semi-submersible offshore drilling rig owned by Transocean and leased to BP for drilling operations in the Macondo Prospect, located approximately 41 miles off the southeast coast of Louisiana. At the time of the incident, the rig was drilling an exploratory well at a water depth of approximately 5,000 feet. The operation involved multiple companies, creating a complex web of responsibilities and potential accountability gaps.

BP leased the rig from Transocean, while critical processes such as cementing the well were performed by Halliburton's subsidiary, Sperry-Sun. Other companies involved included Dril-Wuip, Oceaneering, M-I-SWACO, Cameron, and Weatherford. This distributed responsibility structure would later be identified as a contributing factor to the disaster, as it complicated oversight and created potential communication breakdowns.

The Deepwater Horizon operation was taking place in a challenging regulatory environment. The Minerals Management Service (MMS), the regulatory body responsible for offshore oil drilling at the time, had been criticized for lax enforcement and insufficient technical expertise. A report by the General Accountability Office (GAO) later described MMS as showing "a series of inconsistencies and omissions in their National Environmental Policy Act analyses" and lacking "organization, guidance, technical expertise, and qualified personnel."

2.4.2 Chronology of the incident

The disaster unfolded in a series of catastrophic events. On April 20, 2010, a surge of natural gas blasted through a concrete core that had recently been installed to seal the well for later use. The gas traveled up the drilling riser and ignited, causing an explosion that killed 11 workers and injured 17 others. The rig burned for approximately 36 hours before sinking on April 22.

When the rig capsized, the riser pipe that connected the wellhead to the rig was damaged, allowing oil to begin spewing into the Gulf of Mexico. Initial response efforts by BP included releasing a small fleet of response vessels, planning relief wells, skimming oily surface water, implementing protective boom to prevent oil from reaching the shoreline, and placing chemical dispersants in the spill site to break up the oil.

Efforts to seal the leaking well were initially unsuccessful. BP attempted various solutions, including a containment dome, a "top kill" procedure, and a "junk shot" approach, all of which failed to stop the leak. As a backup measure, BP began drilling relief wells in May. To reduce the leak, a tube tool was inserted into the ruptured riser pipe, and a containment cap was used to collect the oil and pump it to the gulf surface.

After nearly three months of continuous leakage, BP was finally able to stop the flow of oil on July 15, 2010. The well was permanently sealed on September 19, 2010, after releasing an estimated 4.9 million barrels (210 million gallons) of crude oil into the Gulf of Mexico. The spill contaminated approximately 400 square miles of the sea floor and 1,300 miles of shoreline along the Gulf of Mexico.

2.4.3 Risk management failures

The Deepwater Horizon disaster resulted from a series of risk management failures across multiple dimensions. Investigations, including the BP report of 2010, the Commission Report of 2011, and the Joint Report of 2011, identified several critical shortcomings.

2.4.4 Inadequate risk assessment and planning

BP's Gulf Oil Spill Response Plan, though approved by MMS, was later described as a "cookie-cutter" document that shared similar errors with plans prepared by the same contractor for other oil companies. The plan detailed clean-up equipment and techniques, surface containment methods, and the use of chemical dispersants, but critically omitted adequate measures for preventing or stopping a blowout. Furthermore, BP received a categorical exclusion for its exploration plan for the Macondo Prospect, allowing the company to drill without preparing a detailed site-specific environmental assessment. This exclusion was based on the outdated assumption that "the impacts from the common operations are expected to be negligible to non-existent."

2.4.5 Failure to learn from previous incidents

The Deepwater Horizon disaster did not occur in isolation but followed a series of safety incidents involving BP operations. In 2005, BP's refinery in Texas City exploded, and their Thunder Horse rig in the Gulf of Mexico experienced an accident. In 2006, a BP pipeline leaked in Prudhoe Bay. Reports indicated that BP was still addressing violations from these previous incidents when the Deepwater Horizon explosion occurred, suggesting a pattern of inadequate risk management and a failure to implement lessons learned.

2.4.6 Organizational and cultural factors

Investigations revealed significant organizational and cultural factors that contributed to the disaster. These included:

- Cost-cutting measures that potentially compromised safety
- Pressure to complete the project quickly, leading to rushed decisions

- Inadequate communication and coordination among the multiple companies involved
- A culture that did not sufficiently prioritize safety and risk management

A U.S. congressional investigation concluded that "the companies involved in the Gulf of Mexico oil spill made decisions to cut costs and save time that contributed to the disaster." These findings highlight how organizational priorities and cultural factors can significantly influence risk management effectiveness.

The Deepwater Horizon disaster offers several critical lessons for risk management practices:

2.4.7 Comprehensive risk assessment

1. The disaster highlights the importance of comprehensive risk assessment that considers worst-case scenarios, not just likely outcomes. BP's risk assessment processes failed to adequately account for the possibility of a catastrophic blowout, despite previous incidents in the industry that should have raised awareness of this risk.

   Organizations must develop risk assessment methodologies that identify and evaluate all potential failure modes, including low-probability, high-impact events. These assessments should consider not only technical factors but also organizational, human, and external variables that could contribute to risk.

   Integration of Safety Culture
2. The investigation findings emphasize the critical role of organizational culture in risk management. A strong safety culture must be integrated into all aspects of operations, with clear accountability and incentives aligned with safety objectives rather than just production targets or cost reduction.

   Leadership commitment to safety and risk management is essential, as demonstrated by the negative consequences of BP's apparent prioritization of cost-cutting and production speed over safety considerations. Organizations should regularly assess their safety culture and address any gaps or misalignments.
3. Effective Crisis Management Planning

   The BP response illustrates the importance of having robust crisis management plans in place before a disaster occurs. Organizations should invest in developing comprehensive crisis management capabilities, including:
   - Designated crisis management teams with clear roles and responsibilities
   - Pre-established communication protocols and messaging strategies
   - Regular crisis simulation exercises to test and improve response capabilities

- Relationships with external crisis management experts who can provide immediate support
- These preparations should be viewed not as optional expenses but as essential investments in organizational resilience.

4. Regulatory Oversight and Compliance

   The disaster revealed significant weaknesses in the regulatory framework for offshore drilling, leading to substantial reforms. Organizations should not rely solely on meeting minimum regulatory requirements but should instead adopt a proactive approach to compliance that exceeds baseline standards.

   This approach includes engaging constructively with regulatory bodies, participating in industry standard-setting initiatives, and implementing internal oversight mechanisms that provide effective checks and balances on operational decisions affecting safety and environmental protection.

2.5 CONCLUSION

The BP Deepwater Horizon oil spill stands as a stark reminder of the catastrophic consequences that can result from inadequate risk management. The disaster's root causes spanned technical failures, organizational shortcomings, regulatory weaknesses, and crisis management deficiencies—illustrating the multifaceted nature of risk in complex operations.

The lessons learned from this tragedy have driven significant improvements in risk management practices, both within the oil and gas industry and more broadly across high-risk sectors. These improvements include more comprehensive risk assessment methodologies, stronger safety cultures, better crisis management preparedness, enhanced regulatory frameworks, and more effective contractor management approaches.

However, maintaining these improvements requires ongoing commitment and vigilance. The passage of time can lead to complacency, with the hard-won lessons of past disasters gradually fading from organizational memory. Sustaining effective risk management practices demands continuous reinforcement of safety culture, regular testing of crisis response capabilities, and persistent investment in risk assessment and mitigation.

By studying the Deepwater Horizon disaster and implementing its lessons, organizations can develop more robust approaches to managing the complex risks inherent in critical infrastructure operations. This case study thus serves not only as a cautionary tale but also as a catalyst for positive change in how we understand and address risk in our increasingly interconnected and complex world.

In an increasingly complex and interconnected world, traditional approaches to risk management that focus solely on prevention are no longer sufficient. Organizations responsible for critical infrastructure must develop comprehensive resilience strategies that enable them not only to mitigate risks but also to adapt and recover when disruptions inevitably occur. This section explores the concept of resilience in the context of critical infrastructure protection and examines strategies for integrating resilience into risk management frameworks.

2.6 RISK MITIGATION WITH RESILIENCE STRATEGIES

Risk assessment and resilience planning are complementary processes that together form a comprehensive approach to managing critical infrastructure. Risk assessment identifies potential threats, vulnerabilities, and consequences, providing the foundation for understanding what might go wrong. Resilience planning builds on this understanding to develop strategies for maintaining functionality when disruptions occur.

The relationship between these processes can be conceptualized as a continuum. Risk assessment looks at the probability and impact of specific events, while resilience planning considers the broader capacity of systems to withstand and recover from a range of potential disruptions, including those that cannot be precisely predicted. Both perspectives are essential for effective critical infrastructure protection.

Integrating risk assessment with resilience planning requires a shift in mindset from a purely preventive approach to one that balances prevention with preparation for recovery. This integration involves several key steps:

- Using risk assessment findings to identify critical functions and services that must be maintained during disruptions
- Developing performance metrics that define acceptable levels of service during various disruption scenarios
- Designing systems with redundancy, diversity, and modularity to enhance their ability to withstand and recover from shocks
- Creating adaptive management structures that can respond flexibly to emerging threats and changing conditions
- This integrated approach recognizes that while risk assessment helps identify specific vulnerabilities that can be addressed through targeted interventions, resilience planning provides the broader framework for ensuring system functionality even when unexpected disruptions occur.

Key Resilience Strategies

1. Effective resilience planning encompasses a range of strategies that address different aspects of risk management. These strategies can be categorized based on their primary approach to managing risk:
2. Risk Transfer Mechanisms

   Risk transfer involves shifting the financial burden of risk to another entity, typically through insurance or contractual arrangements. While this approach does not eliminate the risk itself, it provides financial resources that can support recovery efforts when disruptions occur.

3. For critical infrastructure operators, risk transfer mechanisms might include:
   - Specialized insurance policies covering physical damage, business interruption, and cyber incidents
   - Contractual arrangements with suppliers that include service level agreements and penalty clauses
   - Public-private partnerships that distribute risk across multiple stakeholders
   - Catastrophe bonds and other alternative risk transfer instruments that provide access to capital markets

These mechanisms are particularly important for low-probability, high-impact events where prevention may not be economically feasible. By ensuring that financial resources are available for recovery, risk transfer supports resilience even when disruptions cannot be prevented.

2.6.1 Risk reduction approaches

Risk reduction focuses on decreasing either the probability or the impact of adverse events. These approaches typically involve physical hardening, operational improvements, or technological enhancements that make systems less vulnerable to disruption.

Effective risk reduction strategies for critical infrastructure include the following:

- Physical hardening of facilities against natural disasters and deliberate attacks
- Implementation of redundant systems and backup capabilities
- Regular maintenance and upgrading of aging infrastructure components
- Adoption of industry best practices and standards for safety and security
- Training and certification programs that enhance workforce capabilities

The effectiveness of risk reduction approaches depends on their alignment with the specific vulnerabilities identified through risk assessment. By targeting the most significant vulnerabilities, these strategies can substantially improve resilience while making efficient use of limited resources.

2.6.2 Risk anticipation methods

Risk anticipation involves developing the capability to identify emerging threats before they materialize into actual disruptions. This forward-looking approach enables proactive responses that can prevent or mitigate potential impacts.

Key risk anticipation methods include the following:

- Horizon scanning to identify emerging trends and potential threats
- Early warning systems that provide timely alerts about developing situations
- Predictive analytics that use data patterns to forecast potential disruptions
- Scenario planning exercises that explore possible future conditions
- Intelligence sharing networks that facilitate the exchange of threat information

As noted in the research, horizon scanning involves the "systematic examination of potential threats, opportunities and likely future developments resulting from the disruptive event, including (but not restricted to) those at the margins of current thinking and planning." This approach helps organizations prepare for novel and unexpected risks that might otherwise be overlooked.

2.6.3 Risk avoidance strategies

Risk avoidance involves eliminating exposure to specific threats by changing operations, locations, or activities. While complete avoidance is rarely possible for critical infrastructure, targeted avoidance strategies can significantly reduce vulnerability to particular risks.

Examples of risk avoidance in critical infrastructure contexts include the following:

- Relocating facilities away from high-risk areas such as flood plains or earthquake zones
- Redesigning systems to eliminate dangerous processes or materials
- Outsourcing high-risk functions to specialized providers with greater expertise
- Implementing "security-by-design" principles that eliminate vulnerabilities in new systems
- Establishing clear operational boundaries that prohibit activities with unacceptable risk profiles
- Risk avoidance strategies must be carefully evaluated to ensure that they do not simply transfer risk to other parts of the system or create new vulnerabilities. When properly implemented, however, these strategies can eliminate entire categories of risk from consideration.

2.6.4 Altering risk characteristics

Sometimes risks cannot be avoided entirely, but their characteristics can be altered to make them more manageable. This approach involves changing the nature of the risk to reduce its potential impact or increase the system's ability to respond effectively.

Strategies for altering risk characteristics include the following:

- Disaggregating large, concentrated risks into smaller, more manageable components
- Implementing circuit breakers or other automatic controls that limit cascading failures
- Creating modular designs that allow for isolation of affected components
- Developing staged response protocols that escalate based on threat severity
- Establishing clear thresholds for intervention before risks reach critical levels

By altering the characteristics of risks, organizations can transform potentially catastrophic threats into more manageable challenges that can be addressed through standard response procedures.

2.7 INTEGRATION OF RESILIENCE INTO BUSINESS CONTINUITY PLANNING

Resilience strategies must be integrated into broader business continuity planning to ensure a coordinated approach to managing disruptions. Business continuity planning focuses on maintaining essential functions during adverse events, making it a natural complement to resilience-focused risk management.

Effective integration of resilience into business continuity planning involves several key elements:

1. Identifying Critical Functions and Dependencies

   The first step in integrating resilience into business continuity planning is identifying the functions that are truly essential for organizational mission fulfilment. This analysis should consider not only internal operations but also external dependencies on suppliers, utilities, and other infrastructure sectors.

   For critical infrastructure operators, this identification process should include the following:

   - Mapping of essential services and the systems that support them
   - Analysis of interdependencies with other infrastructure sectors
   - Identification of single points of failure and critical nodes
   - Assessment of minimum service levels required during disruptions
   - Prioritization of recovery sequences based on criticality

   This comprehensive understanding of critical functions and dependencies provides the foundation for developing targeted resilience strategies that protect the most essential capabilities.

2. Developing Adaptive Response Capabilities

   Resilience requires the ability to adapt quickly to changing conditions during disruptions. This adaptability depends on having flexible response capabilities that can be adjusted based on the specific nature and severity of the event.

   Key elements of adaptive response capability include the following:

   - Scalable emergency response structures that can expand or contract as needed
   - Cross-trained personnel who can perform multiple functions during staffing shortages
   - Decentralized decision-making authority that enables rapid local responses
   - Real-time monitoring systems that provide situational awareness
   - Alternative operating procedures for various degraded conditions

   These capabilities enable organizations to maintain essential functions even when facing unexpected or unprecedented disruptions, a core aspect of resilience.

3. Establishing Robust Communication Protocols

   Effective communication is essential for coordinating responses during disruptions and maintaining stakeholder confidence. Resilient organizations develop communication protocols that can function even when normal channels are compromised.

   Critical elements of resilient communication include the following:

   - Redundant communication systems using different technologies and pathways
   - Pre-approved message templates for common disruption scenarios
   - Clear roles and responsibilities for communication during emergencies
   - Regular stakeholder engagement to build relationships before crises occur
   - Transparent information sharing that maintains trust during disruptions

   As demonstrated in the BP Deepwater Horizon case study, communication failures can significantly exacerbate the impact of disruptions. Robust communication protocols help prevent these secondary failures and support more effective response and recovery efforts.

4. Implementing Regular Testing and Exercises

   Resilience strategies must be regularly tested to ensure their effectiveness and to build organizational capacity for response. Testing and exercises provide opportunities to identify gaps, train personnel, and refine procedures before actual disruptions occur.

   Effective testing approaches include the following:

   - Tabletop exercises that simulate decision-making during various scenarios
   - Functional drills that test specific capabilities such as emergency communications

- Full-scale exercises that involve multiple organizations and stakeholders
- Surprise tests that evaluate readiness without advance preparation
- After-action reviews that capture lessons learned and drive improvements

These activities build both technical capabilities and the human dimensions of resilience, including familiarity with emergency procedures and confidence in response capabilities.

5. Ensuring Continuous Improvement

Resilience is not a static condition but a dynamic capability that must evolve as threats, technologies, and organizational contexts change. Continuous improvement processes ensure that resilience strategies remain relevant and effective over time.

Key elements of continuous improvement include the following:

- Regular review and updating of risk assessments and resilience plans
- Incorporation of lessons learned from exercises and actual incidents
- Monitoring of emerging threats and technological developments
- Benchmarking against industry best practices and standards
- Investment in research and innovation to enhance resilience capabilities

As noted in the research, risk management systems should "become smarter with use, leading to adaptability." This adaptive capacity is essential for maintaining resilience in a rapidly changing risk environment.

2.7.1 Measuring resilience effectiveness

To ensure that resilience strategies are achieving their intended outcomes, organizations must develop meaningful metrics and evaluation approaches. Measuring resilience effectiveness presents unique challenges because it involves assessing both the prevention of negative outcomes and the capacity to respond when disruptions occur.

Effective approaches to measuring resilience include the following:

- Performance-Based Metrics

  Performance-based metrics focus on the system's ability to maintain essential functions during and after disruptions. These metrics might include:

  - Recovery time objectives (RTOs) that specify how quickly functions must be restored
  - Minimum service levels that must be maintained during disruptions
  - Degradation rates that measure how quickly performance declines under stress
  - Restoration curves that track the pattern of recovery after disruptions

- Adaptation metrics that assess how effectively systems evolve based on experience

  These metrics provide concrete measures of resilience outcomes, enabling organizations to assess whether their strategies are delivering the desired level of protection for critical functions.
- Capability-Based Assessments

  Capability-based assessments evaluate the organization's readiness to respond to disruptions rather than actual performance during events. These assessments might examine:
  - Resource availability, including personnel, equipment, and supplies
  - Redundancy levels for critical systems and components
  - Training and exercise completion rates
  - Documentation quality and accessibility
  - Coordination mechanisms with external partners

  These assessments provide insights into resilience potential, helping organizations identify gaps before they are exposed during actual disruptions.
- Scenario-Based Evaluations

  Scenario-based evaluations use hypothetical disruption scenarios to assess resilience capabilities. These evaluations might involve:
  - Modeling and simulation of system performance under various conditions
  - Tabletop exercises that test decision-making processes
  - Stress tests that evaluate breaking points under extreme conditions
  - Red team exercises that simulate adversarial actions
  - Multi-stakeholder simulations that test coordination capabilities
  - These evaluations provide insights into how systems might perform during specific, types of disruptions, helping to identify vulnerabilities that might not be apparent during normal operations.
- Learning-Focused Metrics

  Learning-focused metrics assess the organization's ability to adapt and improve based on experience. These metrics might include:
  - Implementation rates for lessons learned from incidents and exercises
  - Time required to identify and address emerging vulnerabilities
  - Innovation investments related to resilience enhancement
  - Knowledge sharing activities within and across organizations
  - Continuous improvement project completion rates

These metrics recognize that resilience depends not just on current capabilities but also on the ability to evolve and adapt over time.

By combining these different measurement approaches, organizations can develop a comprehensive understanding of their resilience effectiveness. This understanding supports targeted improvements and helps demonstrate the value of resilience investments to stakeholders.

Key elements of continuous improvement in resilience planning include:

2.7.1.1 Continuous improvement in resilience planning

Resilience planning must evolve continuously to address changing threats, technologies, and organizational contexts. This evolution requires a structured approach to capturing lessons learned, identifying emerging risks, and implementing improvements.

2.7.1.2 Systematic after-action reviews

After-action reviews following both exercises and actual incidents provide valuable insights into resilience strengths and weaknesses. These reviews should:

- Involve all relevant stakeholders and participants
- Focus on systemic issues rather than individual performance
- Document both successes and areas for improvement
- Identify specific, actionable recommendations
- Establish clear responsibility for implementation

By systematically capturing and addressing lessons learned, organizations can steadily enhance their resilience capabilities over time.

2.7.1.3 Horizon scanning for emerging risks

As noted in the research, horizon scanning involves the systematic examination of potential threats, opportunities, and likely future developments. This forward-looking process helps organizations identify emerging risks before they materialize into actual disruptions.

Effective horizon scanning includes:

- Monitoring technological developments that could create new vulnerabilities
- Tracking social, political, and economic trends that might affect risk profiles
- Analyzing near-miss incidents within the organization and across the sector
- Engaging with external experts and stakeholders to identify emerging concerns
- Reviewing academic research and industry publications for early warning signals

By maintaining awareness of emerging risks, organizations can adapt their resilience strategies proactively rather than reactively.

2.7.1.4 Technology integration for enhanced resilience

Technological advances offer new opportunities to enhance resilience through improved monitoring, analysis, and response capabilities. Organizations should continuously evaluate and integrate appropriate technologies into their resilience strategies.

Promising technological approaches include:

- Internet-of-Things (IoT) sensors for real-time monitoring of infrastructure conditions
- Artificial intelligence and machine learning for anomaly detection and predictive analytics
- Digital twins that enable simulation and testing of response strategies
- Blockchain and distributed ledger technologies for secure information sharing
- Advanced visualization tools that enhance situational awareness during disruptions

While technology alone cannot ensure resilience, thoughtful integration of appropriate technologies can significantly enhance both prevention and response capabilities.

2.7.1.5 Cross-sector collaboration and information sharing

The interconnected nature of critical infrastructure means that resilience cannot be achieved in isolation. Organizations must collaborate across sectors to share information, coordinate planning, and develop integrated response capabilities.

Effective cross-sector collaboration includes:

- Information sharing about threats, vulnerabilities, and incidents
- Joint planning and exercises that test cross-sector coordination
- Development of compatible standards and protocols
- Mutual aid agreements that enable resource sharing during disruptions
- Collaborative research and development on common resilience challenges

These collaborative efforts help address the interdependencies that characterize modern critical infrastructure, enhancing resilience across the entire system rather than just within individual organizations or sectors.

2.7.1.6 Building a culture of resilience

Ultimately, resilience depends not just on plans and technologies but on organizational culture. A culture of resilience values preparedness, adaptability, and continuous learning, embedding these principles into everyday operations rather than treating them as separate activities.

Key elements of a resilience culture include:

- Leadership commitment to resilience principles and investments
- Employee awareness and engagement in resilience activities
- Recognition and rewards for contributions to resilience enhancement
- Transparent communication about risks and response capabilities
- Integration of resilience considerations into routine decision-making

By fostering this culture, organizations can ensure that resilience becomes a core organizational capability rather than just a collection of plans and procedures.

2.8 DECISION POINTS—COMMUNICATING RISK: KEY CONSIDERATIONS

This diagram emphasizes the critical role of communication in effective risk management. It highlights that the ability to make and execute decisions is crucial for the survival of an enterprise, especially in a crisis (Figure 2.4).

1. *The Importance of Communication*
    - *Crisis Management*: Management is most strongly tested in a crisis. The ability to make and execute decisions is critical for the survival of the enterprise.
    - *Problem Characterization*: Real problems must be characterized in terms recognizable to all stakeholders before they can be solved.
    - *Intelligence Collection*: Correct and effective assessments allow decision-makers to prioritize activities, allocate resources, and adjust to events quickly.
2. *The Challenge of Information*
    - *Information Overload*: The availability of data far exceeds our capacity to digest it and develop it into meaningful intelligence.
    - *Data Fusion*: Bringing together seemingly unrelated pieces of information to form a comprehensive package for analysis requires seamless communication and constant scrutiny of data.
3. *Decision-Making Issues Related to Risk*
    - *Actions*: Decision-makers need to be able to identify, alter, neutralize, share, diversify, mitigate, transfer, contain, offset effects, reduce exposure, alleviate impact, change negative outcomes to positive, insure against loss, monitor, hedge, use derivatives, control, and discount risks.
    - *Leadership*: Decision-making requires observation, orientation, decision-making, and action.

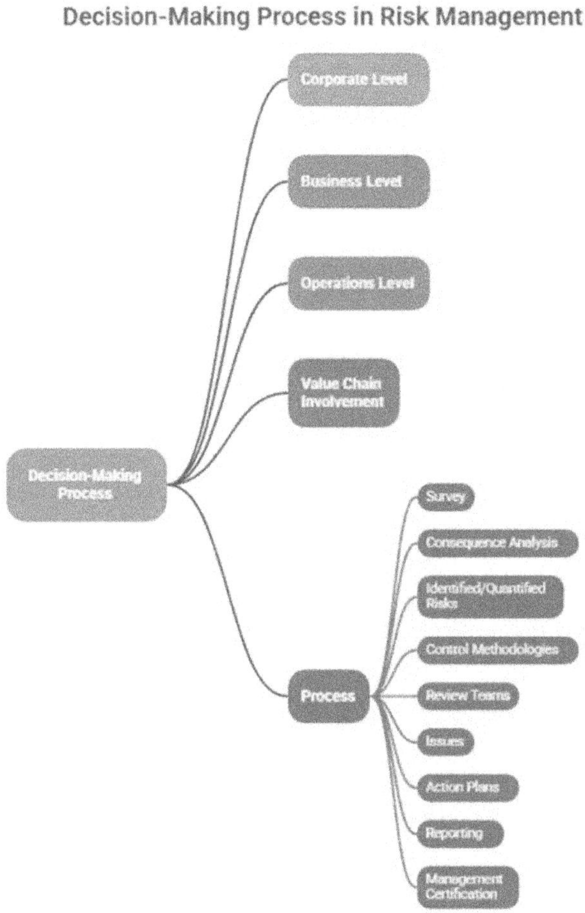

Figure 2.4

4. *Decision-Making Influences*
   - *Complexity*: Greater complexity increases the degree of impact.
   - *Speed*: Acceleration of change influences decision-making.
   - *Resource Base*: More complexity requires greater energy to maintain.
   - *Shocks*: Supply, demand, and raw material shocks impact decisions.
   - *Technology*: Limitations of technology solutions can constrain decisions.
   - *Information*: Near-unlimited access to information can lead to overload and decision paralysis.
5. *Decision Cascades*
   - *Decision Cascades*: When a person makes a decision, others observing the decision may copy it, avoiding further analysis. If the initial decision was incorrect, the error is compounded throughout the organization.

6. *Why Communicate Risk?*
   - *Brand Disasters*: Poor or nonexistent communication can turn risk realization into brand disasters (e.g., Firestone Tire Recall, Exxon Valdez Oil Spill, Coke Belgium Contamination).
7. *Key Components of a Risk Communication Program*
   - *Panic*: Prevent panic.
   - *Surprise*: Avoid surprise.
   - *Forgotten*: Ensure risks are not forgotten.
   - *Employees*: Keep employees informed.
   - *Lack of Information*: Address information gaps.
   - *Government Involvement*: Manage government involvement.
   - *Social Ramifications*: Consider social ramifications.
   - *Conflict*: Manage conflicts.
   - *Confusion*: Reduce confusion.
   - *Intense Media Scrutiny*: Prepare for media scrutiny.
   - *Internet Ramifications*: Address internet-related issues.
8. *Elements of a Risk Communication Strategy*
   - *Strategy*: Develop an overarching communication strategy.
   - *Audiences*: Identify target audiences.
   - *Messages*: Craft clear and concise messages.
   - *Methodology*: Determine the communication methods.
9. *Risk Perception*
   - *Risk = Hazard + Outrage*: Public perception of risk may not resemble risk assessment. The document introduces the formula Risk = Hazard + Outrage, implying that people's perception of risk is not solely based on the hazard itself but also on the outrage it generates.
   - *Voluntary vs. Imposed Risks*: Risks perceived as voluntary, under individual control, having clear benefits, fairly distributed, natural, statistical, generated by a trusted source, familiar, and affecting adults are more acceptable. Risks perceived as imposed, controlled by others, having little benefit, unfairly distributed, manmade, catastrophic, generated by an untrusted source, exotic, and affecting children are less acceptable.
10. *Risk Communication Strategies*
    - *High Risk—High Outrage*: Crisis Communications
    - *High Risk—Low Outrage*: Precaution Advocacy
    - *Low Risk—High Outrage*: Outrage Management
11. *Effective Risk Communication: The 5 Ws and H*
    - *WHO*: Identify internal/external audiences.
    - *WHAT*: Determine the degree of complexity.
    - *WHY*: Work on solutions, not finger-pointing.
    - *WHEN*: Timing is critical.
    - *WHERE*: Choose your ground, know your turf.
    - *HOW*: Consider the manner, method, and effectiveness of communication.

12. *The Communication Process*
    - *Sender-Receiver Model*: Effective risk communication involves a sender transmitting a message to a receiver, who then interprets, thinks about, and understands the message.
13. *Building Trust and Credibility*
    - *Key Principles*:
        - Accept and involve stakeholders as partners.
        - Accept each stakeholder's specific concerns.
        - Be honest and open, never misleading stakeholders.
        - Work with recognized and accepted credible sources.
        - Meet the needs of the media.

In summary, "Decision Points – Communicating Risk" emphasizes that effective risk communication is essential for managing risks, building trust with stakeholders, and making informed decisions, especially during crises. The presentation provides a framework for developing a risk communication strategy that considers the audience, message, method, and context.

2.9 CONCLUSION

In today's interconnected and rapidly evolving risk landscape, effective decision-making hinges on the ability to reduce uncertainty across all organizational levels—strategic, operational, tactical, and throughout the value chain. The illustrated process emphasizes that robust risk management is not a linear exercise but an integrated cycle involving risk surveys, consequence analysis, and the identification and quantification of risks, threats, hazards, and vulnerabilities. These steps must be complemented by the implementation of appropriate control methodologies and thorough review by cross-functional teams. Addressing issues, developing actionable plans, and transparent reporting are critical to ensure management certification and organizational accountability. As highlighted by Geary W. Sikich's insight, asking precise but misguided questions can lead to false positives and ineffective outcomes. Therefore, organizations must foster a culture of critical thinking, continuous feedback, and adaptive learning to ensure that risk assessments are meaningful and drive resilient, informed decision-making in the face of uncertainty.

Chapter 3

Leadership in crisis

Learning Objectives

- Guide organizations through adversity with agility, decisiveness, and empathy.
- Develop crisis communication skills tailored for different stakeholders.
- Balance short-term response with long-term recovery and growth strategies.

3.1 OVERVIEW

I wanted to share some thoughts and experiences on management and leadership that have had a profound impact on my career.

In 1980, I had the privilege of meeting Bob Townsend, the former CEO of Avis Rent a Car and the author of "Up the Organization." This book, which remains a must-read at the Wharton Business School even after 50 years, is a treasure trove of wisdom on leadership and culture-building without ego.

When Bob Townsend walked into my office, he asked for just 15 minutes of my time. Five hours later, I was left in awe of his energy and insights. He introduced me to his book, which I immediately read cover to cover that night. It resonated deeply with my own ideologies about leading people and provided me with a structured framework that I have followed ever since.

Interestingly, that same year, I was overlooked for a promotion to CEO. Bob Townsend advised me to further my education, but to avoid an MBA, as he believed the world needed more leaders, not managers. This distinction between management and leadership has shaped my understanding and approach ever since.

Management, as I see it, is about control—balancing quality, time, and money. Yet, true leadership is about people. A story that encapsulates this difference involves Dwight Eisenhower during World War II. He would demonstrate to his generals that pushing a chain leads to unpredictable results, but pulling it ensures it follows. This principle applies to leadership—if you push people, you don't know where they'll go, but if you lead them, they will follow.

 DOI: 10.1201/9781003597520-3

During my time in China, where I built a company from a handful to 8,000 employees, I experienced the power of leading by example. One rainy afternoon, I jumped into a trench with workers to correct a technical issue. This act of solidarity and hands-on leadership became a powerful symbol within the company, reinforcing the lesson that true leaders are willing to get into the trenches with their teams.

Great leaders like Mahatma Gandhi and Ronald Reagan exemplify this principle. Gandhi united diverse groups and achieved monumental change through peaceful means, while Reagan demonstrated empathy by prioritizing his staff's well-being. Leadership is about channeling power back to the people, creating a cycle of empowerment and trust.

Leadership, much like creativity, is a gift that cannot be bought or sold—it can only be honed and polished. It is the rarest and most valuable commodity on our planet, more so than food, water, or minerals. The world needs leaders who can guide without ego and inspire others to follow.

3.2 ADAPTIVE AND INNOVATIVE LEADERSHIP

3.2.1 Leadership values and characteristics: The Fukushima Daiichi example

The Fukushima Daiichi nuclear disaster in March 2011 is a powerful case study in adaptive and innovative leadership. When a massive earthquake and tsunami struck the plant, leaders faced unprecedented technical and human challenges.

Initial Impact

- The earthquake prompted an automatic shutdown of reactors 1–3.
- External power sources were lost due to earthquake damage.
- Emergency diesel generators activated to maintain cooling systems.

Tsunami Aftermath

- 41 minutes after the earthquake, tsunami waves over 14 meters high hit the plant.
- Seawater pumps, diesel generators, and electrical systems were submerged and damaged.
- A station blackout occurred, isolating the reactors from their ultimate heat sink.

3.2.2 Leadership challenges

The Fukushima disaster presented unprecedented challenges for TEPCO's leadership and the Japanese government. Key issues included:

- *Information Management*: Initial confusion and delays in information sharing hampered early response efforts.

Figure 3.1 Picture of Naohiro Masuda.

- *Decision-Making Under Pressure*: Leaders faced critical decisions with incomplete information and under extreme time constraints.
- *Communication*: Effective communication with the public, employees, and international partners proved challenging amidst the evolving crisis.
- *Resource Allocation*: Managing limited resources and personnel in a high-risk environment required careful prioritization (Figure 3.1).

Naohiro Masuda, the plant manager, exemplified crisis leadership by:

- Acting decisively under extreme pressure, immediately evacuating workers and initiating emergency protocols.
- Continuously adapting strategies as the situation evolved, reassessing risks, and adjusting plans in real time.
- Demonstrating technical competence and leveraging deep institutional knowledge to inform decisions.
- Maintaining calm and composure, providing stability and reassurance to his team.
- Practicing transparent communication, openly sharing information and uncertainties to build trust and facilitate sense-making.
- Empowering his team by delegating responsibilities and trusting their expertise, while ensuring clarity through feedback loops.
- Taking personal accountability for outcomes, reinforcing a culture of responsibility and openness.

- Prioritizing critical tasks and resource allocation, focusing on restoring cooling systems and preventing further escalation.
- Showing resilience and empathy, supporting his team's psychological well-being and maintaining morale through adversity.

These leadership characteristics enabled Masuda to guide his team through the crisis at Fukushima Daini, ultimately preventing a meltdown and safely shutting down all four reactors. His approach to crisis management has since become a prominent case study in effective leadership during extreme circumstances.

Naohiro Masuda demonstrated exceptional crisis leadership during the Fukushima Daiichi nuclear disaster, taking several crucial steps to restore cooling and power while motivating his team:

- Immediate assessment: Masuda quickly organized reconnaissance teams to assess the damage to the plant, allowing him to prioritize actions.
- Strategic power restoration: He directed the team to run cables from a waste-processing building 800 meters away to restore power, rather than overloading the functioning unit.
- Efficient resource allocation: Masuda ordered motors, cables, and generators from various sources across the country to address equipment shortages.
- Hands-on approach: He led a team of 200 workers to manually lay 9 kilometers of heavy cables in just 30 hours, a task that would normally take a month.
- Calm under pressure: Masuda remained at his desk throughout the crisis, providing a sense of stability and ensuring he was always accessible to his team.
- Clear communication: He made staff repeat instructions back to him to ensure clarity and shared understanding in the high-stress environment.
- Empowerment and trust: Masuda delegated tasks and trusted his team to execute them, fostering a sense of shared responsibility.
- Transparency and accountability: He reinforced a culture of openness by taking personal responsibility for any mistakes made.
- Sense-making process: Masuda engaged in ongoing discussions with his team to create clarity and adapt to the evolving situation.
- Personalized leadership: He tailored instructions to each team member's strengths and limitations, leveraging his familiarity with the staff.
- Stress management: Masuda assigned roles to team members, recognizing that having clear tasks could help alleviate stress in a crisis situation.
- Focus on safety: He prioritized the well-being of his staff and the nearby community, working tirelessly to prevent the need for reactor venting.

Through these actions, Masuda successfully led his team to restore cooling to all reactors, averting a potential meltdown and demonstrating exemplary crisis leadership skills.

3.2.3 Case study: New Zealand's response to the Christchurch Earthquake (2011)

3.2.3.1 Background and context

On *February 22, 2011*, a *6.3 magnitude earthquake* struck *Christchurch, New Zealand*, causing significant loss of life and widespread destruction. *185 people were killed*, thousands injured, and much of the central city was left in ruins. The earthquake's shallow depth and proximity to the city center made it particularly devastating.

The New Zealand government's *adaptive and innovative leadership* played a critical role in *emergency response, recovery, and long-term resilience-building.*

- Establishing a unified command structure for rapid resource mobilization and agency coordination.
- Demonstrating flexibility in decision-making, adjusting strategies in response to ongoing aftershocks and emerging data.
- Empowering community groups like the Student Volunteer Army, illustrating distributed leadership.
- Practicing transparent, empathetic communication tailored to different stakeholder groups.
- Embedding resilience into long-term recovery by creating the Canterbury Earthquake Recovery Authority (CERA) to oversee sustainable rebuilding (Table 3.1).

The Christchurch case illustrates the principles of adaptive leadership: diagnosing the system, mobilizing stakeholders, regulating distress, empowering communities, and listening to diverse voices.

Table 3.1 Leadership lessons from Christchurch

Leadership quality	*Example*
Visibility and accessibility	Frequent press briefings, direct community engagement
Collaboration	Leveraging volunteer networks alongside emergency services
Adaptive decision-making	Adjusting strategies based on evolving risks and feedback
Empathy and reassurance	Acknowledging trauma, offering optimism
Long-term vision	Aligning recovery with economic and community resilience

3.3 DECISION-MAKING AND EFFECTIVE COMMUNICATION

3.3.1 Tailored crisis communication strategies

Effective crisis communication requires leaders to adapt their messaging to the needs of different stakeholders (Table 3.2).

Core Principles

- Transparency: Share facts, acknowledge unknowns.
- Frequency: Communicate early and often.
- Consistency: Align messages across spokespeople.
- Empathy: Address fears and impacts.
- Adaptability: Update messaging as facts change (Table 3.3).

Table 3.2 Christchurch Principles

Stakeholder group	*Communication approach*	*Example*
Internal teams	Clear, task-oriented, confirm understanding	Fukushima: staff repeated instructions
General public	Empathetic, frequent, factual, reassuring	Giuliani's 9/11 briefings
Media	Proactive, factual, counter misinformation	Christchurch daily press briefings
Regulators and governments	Technical, compliance-focused, transparent	TEPCO updates to nuclear regulators
Community volunteers/ NGOs	Inspirational, collaborative, action-oriented	Christchurch Student Volunteer Army
Business sector	Economic impacts, continuity, recovery incentives	CERA's business recovery plans

Table 3.3 Decision-making framework: Cynefin model

Domain	*Leadership approach*	*Example*
Chaotic	Act, stabilize, then understand	Giuliani's rapid 9/11 decisions
Complex	Sense, analyze, respond	Christchurch's evolving earthquake response
Complicated	Use expert advice, established processes	TEPCO's technical reactor strategies
Clear	Follow standard procedures	NZ's pre-earthquake drills

3.3.2 Case study: Rudolph Giuliani—Mayor of New York City during 9/11

Giuliani's leadership during 9/11 is a masterclass in crisis leadership:

- Immediate, visible presence at Ground Zero, demonstrating commitment and control.

- Clear, consistent, and empathetic communication to inform and reassure the public.
- Decisive action under pressure, establishing command centers and coordinating agencies.
- Empowerment of teams, streamlining collaboration across departments.
- Projecting calm and resolve, instilling public confidence.

Despite some later criticisms (e.g., resource allocation, long-term health concerns), Giuliani's approach highlights the importance of presence, communication, decisiveness, and collaboration in crisis leadership (Table 3.4).

3.4 RESILIENT LEADERSHIP QUALITIES

Table 3.4 Key characteristics of effective crisis leaders

Resilient quality	*Case example*
Seeing reality clearly	Masuda confronting reactor damage (Fukushima)
Balancing strategy and detail	Giuliani balancing operations and recovery (9/11)
Encouraging diverse views	Christchurch leaders integrating broad input
Decisiveness with incomplete data	Giuliani's rapid evacuation decisions
Collaborative problem solving	Christchurch's alliances across sectors
Listening to unpopular advice	Masuda's engineers advocating seawater cooling
Calm, courage, and positivity	Mandela during apartheid imprisonment
Risk taking in uncertainty	Steve Jobs' bold product launches at Apple's low point
Action over perfection	Christchurch's fast infrastructure reopening
Owning mistakes	TEPCO's eventual admission of failures

3.5 LEADERSHIP IN ORGANIZATIONAL RESILIENCE

Inspirational organizational leadership including commitment to resilience which successfully balances the needs of all internal and external stakeholders and business priorities and which would be able to provide good management and decision-making during times of crisis and change as well as continuous evaluation of strategies and work programs against organizational goals. Their awareness and understanding of their operating environment, their ability to manage vulnerabilities, and their ability to adapt in response to rapid change.

Leadership plays a crucial role in organizational resilience by setting the tone for how the organization responds to crises, manages uncertainty, and continuously adapts to changing conditions. Here's an in-depth look at what leadership entails in the context of organizational resilience:

1. *Crisis Leadership*
   - Effective crisis leadership requires leaders to be *decisive and act quickly* during times of uncertainty or disruption. This includes the ability to make difficult decisions under pressure, often with incomplete information.
   - Crisis leaders must be *visible and accessible to staff*, providing a calming influence while demonstrating confidence in the organization's ability to overcome challenges.
   - They should take a *proactive approach by anticipating potential crises* and preparing for them in advance through risk assessments and scenario planning.
2. *Decision-Making*
   - Strong leadership ensures that decision-making processes are well-defined and communicated. During a crisis, this means having established protocols for quickly gathering relevant information and making informed choices.
   - Leaders should be capable of balancing short-term needs with long-term objectives, avoiding "knee-jerk" reactions that may compromise the organization's future.
   - Inclusive decision-making that involves relevant stakeholders can enhance the quality of decisions and ensure that multiple perspectives are considered.
3. *Strategic Vision*
   - Resilient organizations have leaders who provide a clear vision of what the organization aims to achieve, even in times of crisis. This vision should align with the organization's mission and core values, providing a sense of purpose to guide actions.
   - Leaders must be able to translate this vision into specific, actionable strategies that address the challenges posed by the crisis while positioning the organization for future success.
   - A strategic vision also includes setting priorities for the organization during and after a crisis, such as identifying critical operations that must continue to maintain minimum functionality.
4. *Continuous Evaluation of Strategies*
   - Resilient leadership involves regularly assessing the effectiveness of existing strategies and making adjustments based on new information, changing circumstances, or lessons learned from past crises.
   - Continuous evaluation helps ensure that the organization's plans remain relevant and capable of addressing evolving risks and opportunities.
   - This process should include monitoring key performance indicators and other metrics to track progress and identify areas for improvement.

5. *Communication and Transparency*
   - Strong leadership is characterized by open, transparent communication, especially during times of uncertainty. Leaders should keep employees, stakeholders, and partners informed about the organization's situation, actions being taken, and what is expected of them.
   - Communication should be two-way, with leaders also listening to feedback and concerns from employees and stakeholders. This helps to build trust and foster a culture of engagement.
   - Honest and empathetic communication during a crisis can help reduce anxiety and maintain morale, as people feel more secure when they know what is happening and what they need to do.
6. *Empowering and Motivating Staff*
   - Leaders in resilient organizations empower their teams by delegating responsibility and encouraging employees to take initiative. This helps to distribute the workload during a crisis and allows leaders to focus on strategic decision-making.
   - Motivating staff involves recognizing and rewarding efforts, especially when employees go above and beyond during challenging times. It also means providing the support and resources they need to perform their roles effectively.
   - Leadership should foster a culture where employees feel valued and are committed to the organization's goals, as high levels of engagement can enhance the overall resilience of the organization.
7. *Adaptive Leadership*
   - Adaptive leaders are flexible and open to change, quickly shifting their strategies and approaches as circumstances evolve. This involves being willing to reconsider previous decisions and trying new methods when the current ones are not effective.
   - Adaptive leadership also includes learning from experiences, whether successes or failures, and integrating these insights into future plans and practices.
   - Encouraging a culture of learning and development among staff can also help organizations stay adaptive, as employees will be better equipped to manage changes in their work environment.
8. *Ethical and Value-Based Leadership*
   - During times of crisis, leaders must maintain ethical standards and adhere to the organization's values, even when it is difficult. This helps to uphold the organization's reputation and stakeholder trust.
   - Value-based leadership involves making decisions that are not only financially sound but also socially responsible, ensuring that the organization contributes positively to the well-being of its community and stakeholders.
   - Maintaining ethical leadership during a crisis can inspire employees to act with integrity and strengthen their commitment to the organization.

9. *Developing Future Leaders*
   - A resilient organization does not rely on a single person for leadership; it cultivates leadership skills across all levels. By identifying and developing future leaders, organizations ensure that there are capable individuals ready to step up during a crisis.
   - Leadership development programs and mentoring can help build a strong leadership pipeline, ensuring continuity in times of transition or disruption.

3.5.1 Integrating leadership with other resilience indicators

Leadership is intertwined with other resilience indicators such as:

- *Staff Engagement and Culture*: Leaders set the tone for a culture of resilience, where employees feel empowered to take action.
- *Situation Awareness*: Leaders encourage awareness by promoting open communication and vigilance regarding internal and external changes.
- *Proactive Posture*: Strategic leadership includes anticipating potential crises and preparing the organization to act swiftly and effectively.
- *Planning Strategies*: Leaders are responsible for driving the planning process, setting priorities, and ensuring that plans are adaptable to changing circumstances.

In essence, leadership in resilient organizations is about more than managing the status quo; it is about inspiring others to navigate through uncertainty, adapt to changing conditions, and emerge stronger from adversity.

3.6 CRISIS LEADERSHIP COMPETENCY MODEL

The *Crisis Leadership Competency Model* is designed to equip leaders with the skills and behaviors necessary to guide organizations through high-pressure, high-uncertainty situations (Figure 3.2). Drawing on established frameworks and research, the model includes nine core competencies, each critical for effective crisis management and organizational resilience (Table 3.5).

3.6.1 Application and importance

- *Situational Awareness* enables leaders to anticipate and respond proactively, minimizing damage and leveraging opportunities.
- *Team Leadership* and *Communication* ensure coordinated, motivated efforts and reduce confusion or misinformation.
- *Connectivity* and *Credibility* build trust and facilitate collaboration with stakeholders, which is essential for resource mobilization and unified action.

Figure 3.2 Crisis Leadership Competencies

Table 3.5 Crisis leadership competency model: Core components

Competency	*Description and key behaviors*
1. Situational awareness	The ability to perceive, understand, and anticipate the dynamics of a crisis. Leaders gather real-time information, assess risks, and recognize changing conditions to inform timely and effective decisions.
2. Team Leadership	Inspiring, coordinating, and empowering teams to work cohesively under stress. This includes delegating tasks, building trust, and maintaining morale during uncertainty.
3. Communication	Conveying clear, accurate, and timely information to internal and external stakeholders. Effective crisis leaders are transparent, empathetic, and consistent in their messaging.
4. Connectivity	Building and sustaining relationships and networks inside and outside the organization. This enables rapid information sharing, resource mobilization, and collective action during a crisis.
5. Courage and perseverance	Demonstrating resolve, composure, and moral fortitude in the face of adversity. Leaders must persist through setbacks, make tough calls, and inspire confidence in others.
6. Credibility	Earning and maintaining trust through integrity, consistency, and competence. Credible leaders are relied upon to act ethically and deliver on promises, especially under pressure.
7. Decisiveness	Making timely, well-informed decisions despite ambiguity or incomplete data. This includes the willingness to take calculated risks and adapt as new information emerges.
8. Emotional effectiveness	Managing one's own emotions and responding empathetically to the emotions of others. This supports psychological safety, reduces panic, and fosters resilience.
9. Integrative thinking	Synthesizing diverse perspectives and complex information to develop creative, holistic solutions. Leaders must see the big picture, connect short-term actions to long-term goals, and avoid siloed thinking.

- *Courage, Decisiveness, and Emotional Effectiveness* help leaders remain steady, make tough choices, and support their teams' well-being under duress.
- *Integrative Thinking* allows leaders to navigate complexity and uncertainty, ensuring that responses are both innovative and aligned with organizational values and long-term objectives.

In the realm of crisis management, the principles outlined in this passage can be reframed to align with key crisis leadership concepts. Let's examine these ideas through the lens of a crisis management expert:

3.6.2 The new crisis leadership paradigm

In today's interconnected world, crises can emerge swiftly and unexpectedly, challenging traditional leadership models. The modern crisis leader must adapt to a new playbook that emphasizes *flexibility, transparency, and shared responsibility.*

3.6.3 Transparent communication

During a crisis, leaders must prioritize open and frequent communication. This approach builds trust and creates psychological safety, even in uncertain times. For instance:

- Acknowledge what is known and unknown about the situation
- Provide regular updates, even when full information is not available
- Use multiple communication channels to reach all stakeholders
- Decisive action with incomplete Information

Crisis leaders must balance the need for swift action with the reality of incomplete data. This requires:

- Developing a framework for *rapid decision-making*
- Implementing a flexible crisis management plan that can *adapt to new information*
- Continuously *reassessing and adjusting strategies* as the situation evolves

3.6.4 Values-Driven leadership

In times of upheaval, an organization's core values and purpose become critical anchors. Effective crisis leaders:

- Clearly articulate and *reinforce organizational values*
- Use these values as guiding principles for *decision-making*

- Ensure all actions align with the organization's fundamental purpose
- *Empowerment and Shared Responsibility*

Contrary to the instinct to centralize control, effective crisis management often involves distributing power and responsibility. Leaders should:

- *Delegate authority* to those closest to the situation
- Encourage *innovation and problem-solving* at all level
- Foster a culture of collective responsibility for crisis resolution

3.6.5 The adaptive crisis leader

The modern crisis leader is not defined by unwavering certainty, but by the ability to navigate uncertainty with agility and transparency. By embracing these principles, leaders can guide their organizations through crises while building trust, fostering innovation, and maintaining alignment with core values.

For more suitable for a crisis leadership workshop, here's how I'll approach it:

- *Focus on Actionable Insights:* I'll emphasize practical takeaways and advice that participants can implement immediately.
- *Clarity and Conciseness:* I'll simplify complex ideas and remove jargon to ensure the content is easily digestible.
- *Emphasis on Leadership Competencies:* I'll highlight the specific skills and traits that crisis leaders need to succeed.

Engagement and Interactivity: I'll pose questions and prompts to encourage participants to reflect on their own experiences and challenges

3.7 CRISIS LEADERSHIP: BEYOND MANAGEMENT

We're not just talking about crisis management; we're focusing on *crisis leadership*—a critical skill that's often missing when organizations face major challenges. We'll explore how to avoid the "reputation train wreck" that can follow even a well-managed crisis.

3.7.1 What's the difference?

Many organizations are prepared for crises, but why do things still go wrong? It often comes down to a failure in leadership. Crisis management focuses on *processes* and *procedures*. Crisis leadership focuses on *people* and *decisions*.

- *Crisis Management:* Deals with the *what* and *how* of responding to an event.
- *Crisis Leadership:* Deals with the *who* and *why*—guiding people through uncertainty and making tough choices.

3.7.2 Setting the stage: Understanding the crisis landscape

Before we dive into leadership competencies, let's ensure we are all on the same page when talking about a crisis.

A true crisis has three key elements:

1. *Surprise:* It's unexpected. It catches you off guard.
2. *Immediacy:* It demands immediate action. You can't wait until next week.
3. *Threat:* It poses a risk to people, the environment, assets, business operations, or reputation—often all of the above.

Think about a time when you faced a crisis. Which of these elements was most challenging for you?

Today's Crisis: A Shifting Landscape

- *Globalization:* Crises spread faster and farther than ever before.
- *Politicization:* Every crisis is under a microscope.
- *Climate Change:* Impacts supply chains and emergency response.
- *24/7 News and Social Media:* News cycles are constant, and stakeholders are always watching.
- *Fake News:* Misinformation can spread rapidly and damage your reputation.

These factors compound crises, making them more complex and harder to manage. Failures often occur at the interfaces between different teams.

- *What are some ways you think we can reduce the chance of "fake news" spreading so rapidly?*

3.7.3 The rise of "Smoldering crises"

Here's a crucial point: Many crises today aren't sudden explosions; they *smolder* beneath the surface. These are the incidents that go undetected, unreported, ignored, or downplayed until a trigger event turns them into a full-blown crisis. Most often they're caused by management complacency, negligence, or even cover-ups.

The good news? *70% of crises could be prevented.*

How? By addressing risks and threats *before* they escalate.

Common Themes and Factors

- Globalization and the systematic risk
- Ever crisis gets politicized
- Climate is having a huge impact
- Breaking news and 24-hour cable news
- Internet that blurs the news cycles
- Social networks bring all stakeholders close

This results in compounded crises, leading to the phase of "uber crises." It becomes difficult to manage as failures occur in the interfaces between teams.

3.7.4 Actionable steps

Here are things you can do now.

1. Increase quality readership.
2. Be informed of the impact of globalization and systemic risks.
3. Be aware of the common themes and factors that occur during a crisis.
4. Communicate more effectively.

3.8 MATURITY LEVEL

Here are some Leadership Questions which can address the requirements of the Leadership skills in a Resilient Organization.

Leadership Qualities and Development

1. *Role Models and Integrity:* What specific actions can leadership take to demonstrably become *role models* of integrity? How do you currently assess this quality in your leaders?
2. *Strategic Thinking and Goal Orientation:* How does your organization cultivate strategic thinking at all levels? How are individual and team goals aligned with overall organizational priorities, *especially* during times of uncertainty?
3. *Leadership Development:* What are the most effective methods your organization uses to develop leaders at *all* levels, not just at the top? How can leadership development programs be adapted for crisis readiness?

Decision-Making in Crisis

4. *Consultation vs. Speed:* In a crisis, is it ever justifiable for top management to make decisions with minimal consultation? What safeguards

need to be in place to ensure those decisions are still ethical and well-informed?

5. *Timely Decisions:* Can you share examples of when quick, decisive action made a significant positive impact during a past crisis? What factors enabled those rapid decisions?
6. *Staying Ahead of the Curve:* How can top management proactively anticipate potential crises and ensure the organization remains "ahead of the curve"? What early warning systems or horizon-scanning techniques are used and how leadership team is involved?
7. *Meritocracy in Decision-Making:* Does seniority triumph expertise when making decisions? How does your organization ensure that the most qualified individuals, regardless of their position, have a voice during a crisis?

Communication and Employee Empowerment

8. *Leading by Example:* What concrete steps does top management take to "lead by example" and foster a culture of resilience? What specific behaviors demonstrate commitment to organizational values during a crisis?
9. *Understanding Organizational Goals:* How effectively do employees understand what the organization is trying to achieve, and how is that understanding reinforced during times of crisis?
10. *Raising Concerns:* Do employees feel comfortable raising problems with senior management, *especially* during a crisis? What mechanisms are in place to encourage open communication and feedback?
11. *Access to Authority:* During a crisis, do staff have direct access to individuals with the authority to make decisions? How is this ensured, and what are the potential roadblocks?

Organizational Resilience

12. *Internal Leadership Depth:* If your organization were struck by a crisis today, do you have sufficient leadership depth to respond effectively? What are the key gaps, and how can they be addressed?
13. *Acceptance of Limited Consultation:* How can management gain staff acceptance for making decisions with limited consultation during a crisis, without damaging morale or trust?
14. *Workload Management:* How does your organization monitor and manage staff workloads to prevent excessive stress and burnout, *especially* during prolonged crises?
15. *Regular Re-evaluation:* How often does your organization re-evaluate its goals and objectives? How are these re-evaluations used to improve crisis preparedness?

These rephrased questions are designed to be more engaging and thought-provoking, suitable for a dynamic workshop environment. They encourage participants to reflect on their own experiences, share insights, and identify areas for improvement within their organizations. They also emphasize the importance of proactive leadership, open communication, and organizational resilience in navigating crises effectively.

3.9 PROFILES IN RESILIENT LEADERSHIP

- *Steve Jobs:* Ruthless focus, visionary decisions, transformational leadership, attention to detail, innovation-driven culture, high standards.
- *Nelson Mandela:* Revolutionary and charismatic leadership, principled stance, reconciliatory approach, democratic and servant leadership, Ubuntu philosophy.
- *Stephen Hawking:* Adaptability, perseverance, clear communication, focus on strengths despite adversity.
- *Walt Disney:* Visionary thinking, risk-taking, communication, adaptability, collaboration, customer focus, perseverance.
- *Christina Noble:* Vision, perseverance, compassion, innovation, inspiration, overcoming personal adversity to lead global humanitarian efforts.

Winston Churchill: Decisive action, morale-boosting communication, coalition-building, strategic focus, hands-on leadership, alliance management, adaptability.

3.10 REFERENCE: WORKSHOP FOR BUILDING CRISIS LEADERS

Several organizations offer workshops and courses designed to build crisis leadership skills:

Crisis Leadership Programs

1. The Business Continuity Institute (BCI) offers an Organizational Crisis Leadership E-Learning Course. This advanced-level course covers key elements of crisis leadership, developing leadership styles and skills, and managing multiple stakeholders.
2. The Centre for Humanitarian Leadership provides a Crisis Leadership Program (CLP) with three levels:
    - CLP Seed: For those with 0–2 years of experience
    - CLP Grow: For those with 2–8 years of experience
    - CLP Extend: For those with over 8 years of experience
3. Aventis Learning offers a one-day workshop titled “Crisis Leadership: More About People Than Protocol” on April 15, 2025. This course focuses on transforming crisis management into effective leadership.

4. Oxford Management Centre provides a "Leading Through Crisis" training course. This program covers crisis stages, decision-making processes, and leadership interventions.
5. PwC's Crisis Leadership Centre offers a holistic approach to crisis leadership training, focusing on personal resilience, emotional intelligence, and adaptability.
6. Deakin University, through Future Learn, offers a three-week online course on Crisis Leadership. This introductory-level course explores crisis management from an organizational perspective.
7. The Disruptive Leadership Institute provides a Crisis Leadership Masterclass, emphasizing communication and collaboration during crisis events.
8. NorQuest College in Edmonton, Alberta, is hosting a 45-minute workshop on Managing Through Crisis.

These programs vary in duration, format, and focus, allowing individuals to choose the most suitable option for their specific needs and experience level.

3.11 CONCLUSION

Leadership in crisis is about more than managing processes—it is about guiding people through uncertainty, making tough decisions, and inspiring collective resilience. The case studies and leadership profiles in this chapter demonstrate that effective crisis leaders are adaptive, communicative, decisive, and resilient. By cultivating these qualities, leaders can better prepare their organizations to withstand and grow from future crises.

Chapter 4

Situational awareness and horizon scanning

Learning Objective

- *Improve organizational responsiveness and adaptability* by fostering a change-ready culture, empowering teams, and using structured feedback and decision frameworks.
- *Apply effective data collection and analysis techniques* for horizon scanning using tools like STEEP, SEIPS, and dashboard technologies.
- *Utilize predictive analytics* to shift from reactive to proactive situational awareness through real-time monitoring, pattern recognition, and scenario planning.
- *Strengthen decision-making* by integrating risk assessments and predictive models to anticipate and respond to emerging challenges.
- *Leverage strategic foresight* to continuously scan the external environment and align organizational strategies with future trends.

Today, organizations operate in an increasingly dynamic environment where the average lifespan of companies has decreased from 55 years in the 1970s to merely 15 years today. This VUCA (vulnerability, uncertainty, complexity, and ambiguity) environment demands proactive approaches to identifying both immediate threats and long-term opportunities.

4.1 HORIZON SCANNING IN ORGANISATIONAL RESILIENCE

Horizon scanning is a systematic, forward-looking process that enables organizations to anticipate, prepare for, and respond to emerging risks, opportunities, and disruptions in their business environment. It is a core business intelligence activity that supports organizational resilience by enhancing an organization's understanding of its business landscape, increasing awareness of what is happening around it, and interpreting what that information means for both the present and the future136.

 DOI: 10.1201/9781003597520-4

Key Elements of Horizon Scanning

- *Understanding the Business Landscape:* Horizon scanning involves gathering information from a wide range of sources—such as news, academic research, expert opinions, and social media—to build a comprehensive picture of the current and emerging business environment.
- *Awareness of External Changes:* It systematically examines external trends, signals, and developments across domains like technology, regulation, economics, society, and the environment. This enables organizations to detect early warning signs of change that may otherwise go unnoticed.
- *Interpretation for Strategic Action:* The process is not just about collecting data, but also about analyzing and interpreting what these changes mean for the organization now and in the future. This includes scenario development, risk assessment, and strategic planning to ensure the organization can adapt and thrive in changing conditions.

4.1.1 Scope: novel, unexpected, and persistent issues

Horizon scanning explores:

- *Novel and Unexpected Issues:* By looking beyond conventional industry boundaries, horizon scanning identifies outlier events, disruptive innovations, and weak signals that could become significant.
- *Persistent Problems and Trends:* It also tracks ongoing trends and recurring challenges, ensuring organizations are not blindsided by slow-moving but impactful shifts.

4.1.2 Process overview

The horizon scanning process typically includes:

- *Scoping:* Defining the focus area or strategic question to guide the scanning effort.
- *Environmental Scanning:* Systematically collecting information on trends, signals, and potential disruptors from diverse sources.
- *Analysis and Synthesis:* Identifying patterns, connections, and potential impacts; developing scenarios to visualize alternative futures.
- *Strategic Response:* Using insights to inform decision-making, risk management, resource allocation, and resilience planning.

4.1.3 Contribution to organizational resilience

Horizon scanning strengthens organizational resilience by:

- *Anticipating Risks and Opportunities:* Providing early warnings about emerging threats and opportunities, allowing proactive adaptation rather than reactive crisis management.
- *Enhancing Agility and Adaptability:* Enabling organizations to adjust strategies and operations in response to changing conditions, thus maintaining business continuity and competitive advantage.
- *Supporting Crisis Management:* Offering foresight that helps in preparing contingency plans for potential disruptions, such as regulatory changes, supply chain shocks, or technological shifts.
- *Facilitating Innovation:* Guiding research and development efforts toward areas with the greatest future impact, and helping organizations seize new market opportunities.

4.1.4 Business intelligence foundation

Horizon scanning is fundamentally a business intelligence activity, relying on the systematic collection, analysis, and interpretation of information and knowledge. It transforms raw data into actionable insights that inform strategic decision-making and resilience planning (Table 4.1).

"Horizon scanning is a strategic foresight technique for identifying potential opportunities and threats. It systematically examines emerging trends and developments that could impact an organization or sector. The scope of horizon scanning extends beyond immediate concerns, focusing on long-term implications."

Horizon scanning is essential for any organization aiming to build resilience in an increasingly complex and unpredictable world. It enables leaders to look beyond the immediate horizon, challenge assumptions, and prepare for a range of possible futures.

Table 4.1 Horizon scanning and organizational resilience

Aspect	*Description*
Purpose	Anticipate risks, opportunities, and disruptions; inform strategic and resilience planning
Scope	Novel/unexpected issues, persistent trends, weak signals, cross-sectoral developments
Process	Scoping, data collection, analysis, scenario development, strategic response
Benefits	Early warning, agility, innovation, risk mitigation, competitive advantage, preparedness
Foundation	Business intelligence-systematic use of information and knowledge

4.2 EARLY DETECTION OF THREATS AND OPPORTUNITIES

Horizon scanning is a proactive, systematic process that enables organizations to identify and assess potential threats, risks, and vulnerabilities before they escalate into critical issues. This early detection is fundamental to building and maintaining organizational resilience.

Early Detection of Threats and Vulnerabilities

- *Systematic Monitoring:* Horizon scanning involves continuously examining a wide range of information sources—such as news, regulatory updates, technological developments, and geopolitical events—to spot early warning signs of emerging threats and vulnerabilities.
- *Identifying Weak Signals:* By capturing weak signals and trends, organizations can detect issues that may not yet be mainstream but could significantly impact operations if left unaddressed.
- *Complex Threat Analysis:* The process allows organizations to consider the complexity of threats, challenge assumptions, and review how risk events could unfold, providing a deeper understanding of potential vulnerabilities.

Contribution to Organizational Resilience

- *Proactive Risk Management:* Early identification of risks enables organizations to develop mitigation strategies before threats materialize, reducing potential negative impacts and enhancing business continuity.
- *Operational Readiness:* By integrating horizon scanning with threat intelligence, organizations can anticipate change, allocate resources efficiently, and make informed decisions to protect assets and operations.
- *Strategic Adaptation:* Horizon scanning supports scenario planning and resilience strategies, allowing organizations to adapt to evolving risks and seize emerging opportunities.

Practical Implementation

- *Data Collection and Analysis:* Use advanced tools and interdepartmental coordination to collect, analyze, and synthesize data from diverse sources, ensuring comprehensive coverage and timely detection of threats.
- *Risk Prioritization:* Assess and prioritize identified threats based on their likelihood and potential impact, aligning them with organizational objectives and resilience planning.
- *Continuous Improvement:* Regularly update and refine horizon scanning processes to stay ahead of new and evolving risks, leveraging technologies like AI and data analytics for enhanced capability.

Methods and Tools

- *PESTLE and SWOT Analyses:* Employ frameworks such as PESTLE (Political, Economic, Social, Technological, Legal, Environmental) and SWOT (Strengths, Weaknesses, Opportunities, Threats) to systematically evaluate external and internal risk factors.
- *Expert Input and Collaboration:* Engage with experts and relevant stakeholders to validate findings and ensure a robust understanding of the threat landscape.

Horizon scanning equips organizations with the foresight needed to detect threats and vulnerabilities early, enabling timely action and strengthening overall resilience in a volatile and uncertain environment.

4.2.1 Case study: Nokia's collapse vs. Fuji's adaptation

What happened to Nokia is no secret. The company, once a dominant player in the mobile phone industry, faced a dramatic downfall. Historically, Nokia had been an adaptive company, moving in and out of various industries such as paper, electricity, and rubber. This flexibility allowed it to reinvent itself successfully over the years. In the early 1990s, anticipating the rise of cell phones, Nokia strategically pivoted from being a conglomerate to focusing solely on the telecom business. This decision initially paid off, solidifying Nokia's position as a leader in the mobile phone market.

However, the reasons behind Nokia's failure were rooted in several strategic missteps. Despite its history of adaptability, Nokia struggled to recognize the increasing importance of software in the mobile phone industry. The company's strong focus on hardware innovation, such as improvements in camera quality, overshadowed the crucial developments in software and user experience that were being pioneered by its competitors. This oversight was evident when Nokia dismissed the iPhone's 2007 launch as a niche product, despite its user-centric design that soon redefined the industry standards.

Nokia's underestimation of the smartphone transition was a classic case of a company being enthralled by its past success. The company had built its legacy on reliable hardware, and this success blinded it to the rapidly changing technological landscape. Additionally, Nokia overestimated the strength of its brand, believing that its market dominance and brand loyalty would allow it to catch up quickly even if it was late to the smartphone game. This assumption proved fatal as consumer preferences shifted rapidly toward smartphones equipped with sophisticated software ecosystems like iOS and Android.

Furthermore, Nokia failed to recognize that brands in the high-tech era are not as resilient as they once were. Consumers have grown to expect constant innovation and when companies fall behind, they are quick to punish them. This was particularly true in the tech industry where the pace of innovation is relentless. Nokia's late entry into the smartphone market, coupled with its inadequate response to the emerging trends, turned out to be a deadly combination. The company's market share plummeted from 50% in 2007 to a mere 3% in 2013, culminating in its eventual sale to Microsoft. This highlighted the critical importance of situational awareness and horizon scanning in maintaining organizational resilience in the face of disruptive changes.

Nokia's Critical Failures

1. *Internal Blind Spots:* Middle managers withheld critical feedback about software deficiencies in Nokia's Symbian OS, fearing retaliation from temperamental leaders.
2. *External Threat Dismissal:* Nokia famously dismissed the iPhone's 2007 launch as a niche product, despite its user-centric design that would soon redefine industry standards.
3. *Cultural Inertia:* The company prioritized incremental hardware improvements (e.g., camera quality) over ecosystem innovation (apps, touchscreens), becoming entrapped by past successes.

Lack of Horizon Scanning

1. Focused on optimizing existing supply chains and feature phones instead of exploring smartphone platform dynamics.
2. Overlooked the rise of Android and iOS ecosystems, which redefined mobile computing (Figure 4.1).

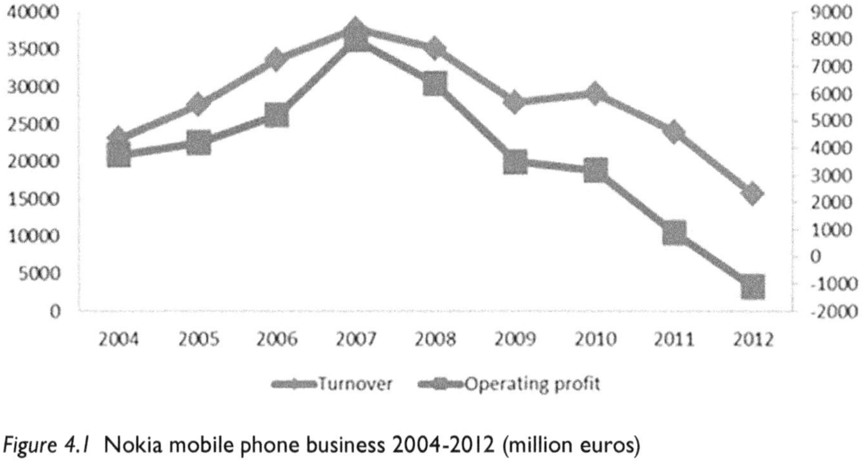

Figure 4.1 Nokia mobile phone business 2004-2012 (million euros)

Source: Disruptive innovation.

4.2.2 Contrast with Fuji's adaptation

When digital photography threatened traditional film, both Kodak and Fuji faced similar challenges, but with drastically different outcomes. Take the example of Fuji and Kodak, two companies with strong intellectual property and over a century of existence. Both had to cease their production of film-based cameras following the advent of digital technology and cameras. However, these companies experienced different outcomes based on their responses to these technological changes.

Fujifilm redefined its business strategy by diversifying into healthcare, medical imaging equipment, and other sectors. This proactive approach allowed Fuji to maintain stability, with a market capitalization of over 21 billion. On the contrary, Kodak, a firm resistant to change, diversified into printing solutions but failed to capitalize on new opportunities effectively. This reluctance to adapt led to a significant decline in stock prices, culminating in bankruptcy.

In today's fast-paced world, the ability to anticipate and respond to disruptive trends is vital for organizational resilience. The contrasting trajectories of Fuji and Kodak underscore the importance of situational awareness and horizon scanning. By continuously monitoring and interpreting the evolving business environment, companies can make informed decisions, mitigate risks, and seize opportunities, ensuring their long-term success.

Kodak's Failure

- *Situational Awareness Gap:* Ignored the 1983 Sony Mavica (first digital camera) and internal R&D warnings about film's decline.
- *Strategic Myopia:* Clung to film's profitability, dismissing digital photography as a threat. Later attempted to monetize digital through restrictive platforms (e.g., KodakOne blockchain), which misunderstood market fluidity.

Fuji's Success

- *Horizon Scanning:* Anticipated film's demise and diversified into healthcare (e.g., MRI contrast agents), cosmetics (Astalift), and digital imaging.
- *Adaptive Leadership:* CEO Minoura encouraged exploring adjacencies, leveraging existing capabilities in chemicals and materials.

Result: Kodak filed for bankruptcy in 2012, while Fuji thrived with a $21B market cap by 2025 (Figure 4.2).

4.2.3 Lessons for organizational resilience

1. *Kodak's Failure:* Despite inventing the first digital camera in 1975, Kodak ignored internal R&D warnings about film's decline. They clung to film's profitability and later attempted misguided strategies like the

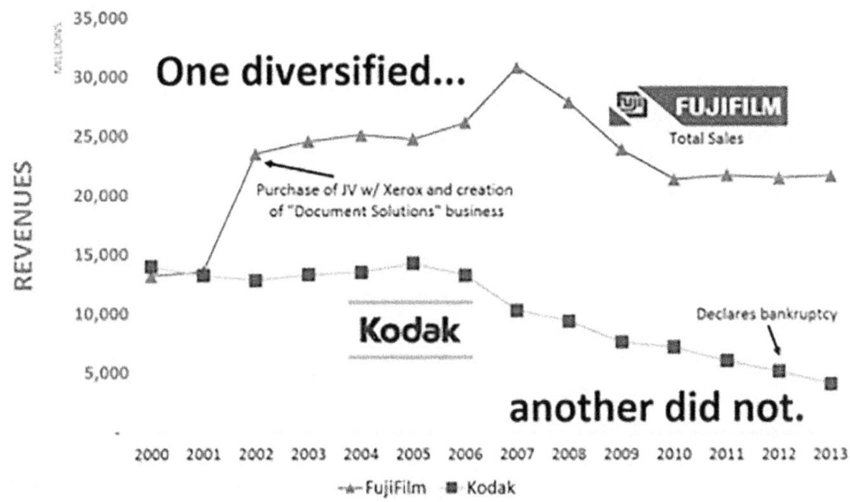

Figure 4.2 A Tale of Two Film Manufacturers

Source: Fujifilm and Kodak Annual reports.

KodakOne blockchain platform, which fundamentally misunderstood market dynamics.[1] Kodak filed for bankruptcy in 2012.

2. *Fuji's Success:* Anticipating film's inevitable decline, Fuji proactively diversified into healthcare (MRI contrast agents), cosmetics (Astalift), and digital imaging. CEO Minoura encouraged exploration of adjacent markets, leveraging existing capabilities in chemicals and materials science. Today, Fuji maintains a market capitalization of over $21 billion.

Key Lessons

- Complacency and insularity can blind established market leaders to disruptive threats
- Effective situational awareness requires psychological safety for employees to report warning signs
- Diversification based on core competencies provides resilience against industry disruptions

4.3 CONTEXT OF THE ORGANIZATION

4.3.1 Horizon scanning and organizational understanding

Horizon scanning is a proactive, systematic process that enhances an organization's understanding of its business landscape by continuously monitoring, identifying, and analyzing emerging trends, risks, opportunities, and disruptions across a broad range of domains—including technology, regulation, economics, society, and the environment. This process is fundamental to organizational resilience and is deeply embedded in business intelligence activities, relying on the collection and interpretation of information and knowledge.

Enhancing Awareness of the Business Landscape

- *Comprehensive Environmental Awareness:* Horizon scanning involves the systematic examination of both the immediate and extended environment to detect early signals of change. This includes monitoring news, regulatory updates, scientific developments, social trends, and even weak signals that may not yet be mainstream but could become highly significant.
- *Identification of Key Drivers:* By mapping out drivers of change—such as technological innovation, shifting consumer preferences, or geopolitical events—organizations gain a richer, more nuanced understanding of the forces shaping their current and future operating environment.

Interpreting What Information Means—Now and for the Future

- *Scenario Analysis:* Horizon scanning supports the development of alternative future scenarios, allowing organizations to visualize how emerging trends and uncertainties might impact their business. This enhances strategic planning and helps decision-makers prepare for a range of possible futures.
- *Risk and Opportunity Assessment:* Through continuous scanning, organizations can identify both novel and persistent issues. This includes outlier events (e.g., pandemics, regulatory shocks) as well as long-term trends (e.g., climate change, digital transformation), enabling them to assess potential impacts and adjust strategies accordingly.
- *Agility and Preparedness:* By interpreting early signals and trends, organizations can move from reactive to proactive postures-seizing opportunities, mitigating risks, and building resilience before disruptions occur.

Exploring Novel, Unexpected Issues, and Persistent Trends

- *Novel and Unexpected Issues:* Horizon scanning is particularly valuable for uncovering weak signals and "unknown unknowns"—issues that may not be on the organization's radar but could have significant future impact. For example, early awareness of a new technology or regulatory change can provide a critical head start.
- *Persistent Problems or Trends:* It also ensures ongoing vigilance against slow-moving but impactful issues, such as demographic shifts or evolving compliance requirements, which may not be urgent but are strategically important.

Business Intelligence Foundation

- *Information and Knowledge-Based:* Horizon scanning is fundamentally a business intelligence activity, leveraging diverse information sources and analytical methods to transform raw data into actionable insights. This supports not only risk management but also innovation, resource allocation, and stakeholder engagement.

Practical Benefits

- *Competitive Advantage:* Early identification of trends and disruptions allows organizations to innovate ahead of competitors and adapt more rapidly to change.
- *Strategic Foresight:* Integrating horizon scanning into strategy cycles ensures that plans are robust, future-proof, and responsive to a dynamic environment.
- *Resilience:* Ultimately, horizon scanning strengthens organizational resilience by ensuring that leaders are not blindsided by change, but are instead equipped to navigate uncertainty with confidence.

4.3.2 Case study: toys "R" Us

Toys "R" Us, once the dominant toy retailer, filed for bankruptcy in 2017 after years of declining sales and mounting debt. Its downfall illustrates the consequences of inadequate horizon scanning.

Key Failures in Horizon Scanning

1. *Missed E-Commerce Revolution:* Rather than building its own robust online platform, Toys "R" Us outsourced its digital presence to Amazon through a 2000 partnership agreement. This shortsighted decision gave Amazon the opportunity to dominate the online toy market, while Toys "R" Us lagged behind.
2. *Delayed Digital Investment:* By the time Toys "R" Us attempted to catch up with e-commerce, competitors had already captured the market with better prices, wider selections, and superior customer experiences.
3. *Stagnant Business Model:* The company continued investing in large physical stores while failing to innovate the in-store experience. Meanwhile, competitors like Apple and Disney reimagined retail by creating interactive, experiential stores.
4. *Poor Customer Experience:* As online shopping became more convenient, Toys "R" Us stores became known for being disorganized, with poor inventory management and long checkout lines, further driving customers away.
5. *Financial Inflexibility:* High debt from a leveraged buyout limited the company's ability to invest in necessary digital transformation initiatives.

Organizational Resilience Lessons from Toys "R" Us

- Systematic horizon scanning is essential for identifying emerging risks and opportunities early
- Companies must develop flexible strategies adaptable to changing market conditions
- Financial structures should support, not hinder, necessary innovation investments
- Customer experience should evolve with changing consumer expectations

4.4 INFORMED DECISION MAKING

4.4.1 Horizon scanning and informed decision making

Horizon scanning is a structured, forward-looking process that enables organizations to systematically monitor both their internal and external environments for information relevant to their activities. This process is fundamental for making informed decisions at all organizational levels, especially when aiming to prevent or respond more effectively to crises and emergencies.

How Horizon Scanning Supports Informed Decision Making

- *Comprehensive Data Collection:* Organizations gather information from diverse sources, including news articles, reports, expert opinions, academic papers, and social media, to form a holistic understanding of the current and emerging landscape.
- *Pattern and Trend Analysis:* By evaluating collected data, organizations can identify patterns, trends, and weak signals that may indicate future opportunities, risks, or disruptions.
- *Scenario Development:* Insights from horizon scanning are used to develop various future scenarios, helping decision-makers visualize alternative outcomes and prepare accordingly.
- *Risk Assessment:* Each scenario is assessed for potential impacts, allowing organizations to weigh both positive and negative outcomes and prioritize risks.
- *Strategic Decision Making:* The insights gained directly inform decisions and planning, enabling organizations to allocate resources efficiently, adapt strategies, and take pre-emptive action to mitigate risks or seize opportunities.

Organizational Benefits

- *Early Warning and Crisis Prevention:* Horizon scanning acts as an early warning system, allowing organizations to detect and address potential threats before they escalate into crises.

- *Enhanced Preparedness and Resilience:* By anticipating changes in the environment, organizations can develop contingency plans and build resilience against uncertainty and disruption.
- *Organization-Wide Communication:* Findings from horizon scanning can be communicated throughout the organization, ensuring that all levels are informed and can contribute to a coordinated response.
- *Continuous Improvement:* Regular reassessment and stakeholder engagement ensure that the process remains relevant and adaptive to new information and changing circumstances.

4.4.2 Practical example

"Horizon scanning enhances the decision-making processes by offering a structured framework to assess various possibilities and encourages an organization-wide culture of risk awareness and preparedness."

Key Steps in Horizon Scanning for Decision Making

- Scoping and framing relevant issues
- Gathering and analyzing information from internal and external environments
- Interpreting signals and trends to identify implications
- Developing and prioritizing scenario
- Communicating insights and integrating them into decision-making at all organizational levels

Horizon scanning empowers organizations to make informed, proactive decisions by continuously monitoring and interpreting relevant information from their environments. This approach not only helps prevent crises but also ensures a more agile and resilient organizational response to emerging challenges.

Horizon scanning extends beyond situational awareness by systematically identifying emerging trends, potential disruptions, and future scenarios. It's not about predicting the future with certainty, but about understanding potential developments and their implications to inform strategic decisions.[1]

Situational awareness refers to an organization's ability to perceive, comprehend, and project critical factors affecting its current operations. It focuses on:

- Understanding the present moment and near-term future
- Monitoring immediate operational contexts
- Enabling real-time decision-making and response

Unlike horizon scanning, which looks years ahead, situational awareness deals with the immediate environment, helping organizations respond to current challenges and opportunities (Table 4.2).

Table 4.2 Key differences between situational awareness and horizon scanning

Aspect	*Situational awareness*	*Horizon scanning*
Timeframe	Present and immediate future	Medium- to long-term futures
Scope	Specific operational contexts	Broader, systemic perspective
Purpose	Informs immediate actions	Supports strategic planning
Methodology	Often reactive and tactical	Structured and systematic

4.4.3 Effective organizations integrate both situational awareness and horizon scanning to balance short-term operations with long-term strategic resilience

4.4.3.1 Case study: shell oil company

Shell has pioneered the integration of situational awareness and horizon scanning since the 1960s, enabling it to navigate industry disruptions and prepare for future uncertainties.[6,7]

4.4.3.2 Shell's approach to situational awareness

Shell's situational awareness involves real-time monitoring of operational environments, geopolitical developments, and market dynamics, allowing it to:

- Respond quickly to supply disruptions, regulatory changes, and safety incidents
- Maintain operational efficiency in volatile regions
- Adjust production and logistics in response to immediate threats

During the 1973 oil crisis, Shell's ability to rapidly assess and respond to embargoes and supply constraints allowed it to maintain supply chains and minimize disruptions, outperforming competitors who were slower to react.[6]

4.4.3.3 Shell's horizon scanning and scenario planning

Shell's scenario planning process, initiated in 1967, became a model for multinational corporations. Key elements include:

1. *Research:* Ongoing, structured research into global trends such as energy transitions, technological innovation, climate change, and societal shifts.
2. *Scenario Building:* Shell regularly constructs multiple plausible future scenarios (e.g., "Mountains" and "Oceans" in the 2013 "New Lens Scenarios") to stress-test strategies and challenge conventional thinking.
3. *Application:* Scenarios are used in strategic planning, investment decisions, and risk management across Shell's business units.

Shell's scenarios in the 1970s anticipated both the rise of OPEC and the potential for oil to become a limited resource. As Pierre Wack, one of Shell's scenario planners, noted: "The aim of a scenario is therefore to question, challenge or influence the decision-makers' 'microcosm.' Scenarios should then help decision-makers to question their own mental models and modify them if necessary."

4.4.3.4 *Structured approaches to horizon scanning*

Organizations can adopt frameworks such as:

1. *SEIPS Framework:* Analyzes work systems and their impact through six components: Person, Tasks, Tools/Technology, Environment, Organization, and External Influences.
2. *STEEP Analysis:* Categorizes external factors into Social, Technological, Economic, Environmental, and Political domains to anticipate disruptions. For example, JP Morgan uses STEEP analysis to guide investment strategies amid geopolitical and economic volatility.
   - *Benefits of Shell's Integrated Approach:*
     - Short-term: Maintains operational continuity and risk management
     - Long-term: Anticipates and adapts to industry shifts, such as the energy transition toward renewables
     - Competitive advantage: By seeing both immediate challenges and future trends, Shell positions itself strategically in a volatile industry

4.5 STRUCTURED APPROACHES

Horizon scanning employs systematic frameworks like *SEIPS* (Systems Engineering Initiative for Patient Safety) and *STEEP* (Social, Technological, Economic, Environmental, Political) to identify emerging risks and opportunities. These frameworks provide structured methodologies for analyzing complex systems and external environments. Below are detailed examples of their application:

4.5.1 SEIPS framework

SEIPS is a human factors framework used to analyze work systems and their impact on safety. It structures horizon scanning around six components: *Person*, *Tasks*, *Tools/Technology*, *Environment*, *Organization*, and *External Influences.*

Example: NHS Mental Health Trust Horizon Scanning

Context: A UK mental health trust faced rising referrals of young people (15–17 years) during the COVID-19 pandemic, straining capacity, and staff well-being.

Steps Using SEIPS

1. *Work System Mapping*
   - *Person:* High staff turnover and burnout in mental health teams.
   - *Tasks:* Referral processing delays due to outdated electronic forms.
   - *Tools/Technology:* Poorly designed risk-assessment software.
   - *Environment:* Noisy office spaces disrupting administrative workflows.
   - *Organization:* Limited bed capacity forcing out-of-area referrals.
   - *External Influences:* Pandemic-driven surge in mental health cases.
2. *Forward-Looking Analysis*
   - *Exacerbated Risks:* Increased referrals would amplify delays if software issues persisted.
   - *Emerging Risks:* Potential reversion to placing young patients in adult wards due to bed shortages.
   - *Mitigations:* Relocating administrative staff to quieter offices and redesigning referral forms.

Outcome: The trust prioritized IT upgrades and staff retention strategies to address systemic risks.

4.5.2 STEEP analysis

STEEP categorizes external factors into *Social, Technological, Economic, Environmental, and Political* domains to anticipate disruptions.

Example 1: JP Morgan's Economic Horizon Scanning

Context: JP Morgan uses STEEP to guide investment strategies amid geopolitical and economic volatility4.

STEEP Breakdown

- *Social:* Aging populations increasing demand for retirement products.
- *Technological:* AI-driven trading algorithms reshaping market dynamics.
- *Economic:* Inflation trends and central bank policy shifts.
- *Environmental:* Climate-related financial disclosures affecting asset valuations.
- *Political:* Trade wars impacting global supply chains.

Outcome: By monitoring these factors, JP Morgan advised clients to diversify into renewable energy ETFs and hedge against inflation.

JP Morgan's Economic Horizon Scanning dashboard plays a critical role in the bank's WAR Room, especially during periods of rapid political and economic change. The dashboard aggregates and visualizes real-time data, policy developments, and market reactions, enabling leaders to make informed, timely decisions under pressure.

Key Enhancements to Decision-Making

1. *Real-Time Policy and Market Monitoring*
   - The dashboard consolidates executive orders, regulatory changes, and macroeconomic indicators as they happen. For example, during the first days of the Trump administration, JP Morgan's WAR Room tracked dozens of new policies and their immediate effects on global markets, such as currency fluctuations and trade tariffs.
   - This live feed allows decision-makers to quickly assess the scope, scale, and likely impact of each development, minimizing lag between event and response.
2. *Scenario Analysis and Risk Assessment*
   - The dashboard enables the WAR Room team to model various scenarios based on incoming data—such as the potential inflationary effects of new tariffs or the impact of regulatory rollbacks on the banking sector.
   - By visualizing possible outcomes and stress-testing assumptions, leadership can prioritize actions and allocate resources to mitigate risks or seize emerging opportunities.
3. *Cross-Functional Collaboration*
   - The dashboard acts as a single source of truth, accessible to asset managers, economists, compliance officers, and executive leadership. This ensures alignment and rapid information sharing, which is crucial when evaluating complex, multi-dimensional risks.
   - For instance, when President Trump announced a 25% tariff on Canadian goods, the WAR Room was able to immediately assess currency impacts and advise trading desks in real time.
4. *Informed, Agile Decision-Making*
   - With the dashboard's synthesized insights, JP Morgan's WAR Room can issue guidance, adjust trading strategies, and communicate with clients faster and with greater confidence.
   - The ability to digest and act on a high volume of information overnight—as highlighted by JP Morgan's all-night WAR Room operations—demonstrates the dashboard's role in enabling agile, evidence-based decisions during volatile periods (Table 4.3).

Table 4.3 Dashboard value in the WAR room

Dashboard feature	*Decision-making benefit*	*Example from recent use*
Real-time policy/news aggregation	Immediate situational awareness	Tracking Trump's executive orders
Scenario modeling tools	Rapid risk assessment and contingency planning	Analyzing tariff/inflation impacts
Shared, cross-team access	Faster, aligned collaboration and response	Coordinated asset management
Visual analytics and alerts	Quick identification of critical issues and market movements	Monitoring currency fluctuations

4.6 CONCLUSION

JP Morgan's Economic Horizon Scanning dashboard transforms the WAR Room from a reactive crisis center into a proactive decision-making hub. By providing real-time, actionable intelligence and facilitating collaboration, the dashboard ensures JP Morgan can anticipate, assess, and respond to economic and policy shocks with speed and precision.

Example 2: United Nations Environment Programme's (UNEP)'s Environmental Foresight

Context: The UNEP scans for emerging ecological threats.

STEEP Application

- *Social*: Public demand for sustainable packaging.
- *Technological*: Advances in carbon capture and biodegradable materials.
- *Economic*: Subsidy shifts toward green energy.
- *Environmental*: Melting permafrost releasing methane.
- *Political*: Global agreements on plastic waste reduction.

Outcome: UNEP advocated for bans on single-use plastics and promoted circular economy policies.

The UNEP leverages advanced dashboard technologies to support its Environmental Foresight and decision-making processes, particularly in "WAR Room" or crisis-response settings. These dashboards aggregate, visualize, and analyze environmental data and public sentiment, enabling rapid, evidence-based action on emerging environmental threats.

Key Dashboard Tools and Features

1. *World Environment Situation Room (WESR) Dashboard*
   - *Federated Data System:* WESR integrates global, regional, and national environmental data, providing policymakers with real-time access to essential climate variables and environmental indicators.
   - *DPSIR Framework:* The dashboard organizes data using the Drivers, Pressures, States, Impacts, and Responses model, allowing users to trace environmental issues from root causes to policy responses.
   - *Visualization:* Offers interactive maps, trend graphs, and scenario modeling to assess the current state and projected changes in climate, biodiversity, pollution, and more.
   - *Decision Support:* Empowers users to guide mitigation and adaptation measures, assess climate risks, and attribute events to underlying causes, supporting both immediate and long-term policy decisions.
2. *UNEP Live and webLyzard Dashboard*
   - *Web Intelligence Portal:* Aggregates global environmental indicators, news, and social media sentiment.

Table 4.4 Enhancing WAR room decision-making

Dashboard feature	*WAR room benefit*	*Example use case*
Real-time environmental data	Immediate situational awareness	Tracking pollution spikes or extreme weather
Scenario modeling and trend analysis	Proactive risk assessment and contingency planning	Assessing impacts of policy changes or disasters
Public sentiment analytics	Understanding stakeholder and public response to environmental events	Shaping crisis communication strategies
Integrated policy response tracking	Coordinated, multi-level action and monitoring	Aligning national and international responses
Visualization of geographic patterns	Rapid identification of hotspots and emerging issues	Mobilizing resources to affected regions

- *Real-Time Analytics:* Tracks public opinion, stakeholder influence, and the evolution of environmental dialogue across regions and languages.
- *Visual Tools:* Includes word trees, geographic maps, and entity maps to identify trending topics, contested issues, and key actors in environmental debates.
- *Crisis Communication:* Facilitates rapid understanding of how environmental events are perceived and discussed, enabling targeted communication and stakeholder engagement.

3. *Sustainability Risk Tool Dashboard*
    - *Risk Tool Database:* Provides a comprehensive overview of environmental and social risk assessment tools, including their methodologies and use cases.
    - *Scenario Planning:* Supports financial institutions and policymakers in forward-looking risk assessment and scenario analysis, integrating findings from climate risk reports and market trends (Table 4.4).

4.6.1 Case example

During the release of a major UNEP foresight report, the WAR Room used dashboards to:

- Track online coverage and public sentiment on topics like solar radiation modification and climate interventions.
- Visualize geographic spread and intensity of environmental crises.
- Aggregate data from scientific sources, policy updates, and stakeholder communications for real-time situational awareness.
- Inform rapid policy briefings and targeted outreach to governments and media156.

Table 4.5 Comparison of SEIPS vs. STEEP

Framework	*Focus*	*Use case example*	*Key outputs*
SEIPS	Work system safety	Healthcare capacity planning	Process maps, risk mitigation strategies
STEEP	Macro-environment	Financial/ecological trend analysis	Scenario planning, investment/policy guidance

4.7 CONCLUSION

UNEP's dashboard-driven approach empowers its WAR Room to move from reactive crisis management to proactive, data-driven environmental foresight. By integrating real-time data, scenario modeling, and public sentiment analytics, UNEP ensures that decision-makers can anticipate, assess, and respond to complex environmental challenges with speed and precision (Table 4.5).

Benefits of Structured Approaches

- *SEIPS:* Identifies latent risks in operational workflows (e.g., administrative bottlenecks).
- *STEEP:* Reveals cross-domain interdependencies (e.g., how political regulations affect technological adoption).
- Both frameworks convert raw data into *actionable foresight*, enabling proactive decision-making.

For organizations, adopting these methods transforms horizon scanning from a reactive exercise into a strategic asset.

4.7.1 Outcomes

Situational awareness typically leads to tactical responses, while horizon scanning informs strategic decisions and organizational adaptations.

4.8 CONCLUSION

In practice, both processes are valuable and complementary. Organizations need situational awareness for day-to-day operations and immediate risk management, while horizon scanning helps them prepare for longer-term changes and build resilience against future uncertainties. By effectively combining both approaches, organizations can navigate the complexities of the present while strategically positioning themselves for future success.

Chapter 5

Crisis management and emergency response

Learning Objectives Alignment

- Protect Lives, Safeguard Assets, Maintain Continuity, Uphold Reputation: Each case demonstrates how decisive action, transparency, and stakeholder engagement are critical to minimizing harm and preserving trust.
- Effective emergency response depends on rapid, coordinated action to minimize harm, save lives, and protect property, with clear roles, responsibilities, and communication channels established in advance.
- Foster Adaptability, Learning, and Continuous Improvement: All three organizations institutionalized lessons learned, updated protocols, and invested in resilience, turning crises into catalysts for improvement.
- Develop Protocols for Coordinated Multi-Agency Response: Effective crisis management requires clear frameworks for collaboration with regulators, law enforcement, suppliers, and other stakeholders.
- Establish and Operate a Crisis Command Center: Centralized command centers, empowered with clear authority and robust communication tools, are essential for orchestrating effective, timely responses.

5.1 INTRODUCTION

In today's rapidly evolving business landscape, organizations face an unprecedented array of threats that can disrupt operations, damage reputations, and even threaten lives. The digital landscape, while offering tremendous opportunities, has transformed the nature of crisis management. As highlighted in the original document, "We live in an era where there is an overwhelming urge to share every experience in real time on social media." I would like to begin by sharing an image of a sign I recently encountered online. This sign is intended for display in the emergency stairwell of a public building and reads: *"In case of fire, exit building before tweeting about it"* (Figure 5.1).

This sign, while humorous, accurately reflects our society today. We live in an era where there is an overwhelming urge to share every experience in real time on social media. This tendency poses significant challenges for organizations in terms of crisis management.

DOI: 10.1201/9781003597520-5

Figure 5.1 Signage

This reality creates a situation where organizations must respond and communicate at unprecedented speeds, contend with the public nature of all events, and struggle to get ahead of stories that quickly gain momentum.

Effective crisis management in the 21st century requires a proactive mindset rather than a merely reactionary approach. As Captain Chris Hsiung from the Mountain View Police Department articulated, organizations must engage in both online and offline proactive initiatives daily to build trust and establish credibility with their stakeholders, creating a "bank of community trust" that can be drawn upon during times of crisis.

This chapter explores three pivotal case studies that illustrate different dimensions of crisis management and emergency response: Toyota's accelerator pedal recall, Johnson & Johnson's Tylenol crisis, and Maersk's response to the NotPetya cyberattack. Each case offers valuable insights into strategies for protecting lives, safeguarding assets, maintaining operational continuity, and upholding organizational reputation while fostering adaptability, learning, and continuous improvement.

5.2 DEFINITION OF CRISIS MANAGEMENT

5.2.1 Crisis

A crisis is a sudden, significant negative event that threatens to harm an organization, its stakeholders, or the general public. Crises are often unpredictable or escalate faster than anticipated, requiring rapid decision-making and extraordinary measures to limit damage and maintain continuity. Examples include natural disasters, major product failures, cyberattacks, and reputational scandals.

Crises are unique, rare, unforeseen or poorly managed events, or combinations of such events, that can create exceptional challenges for an organization and are not well served by prescriptive, pre-planned responses.

Crisis management is the developed capability of an organization to prepare for, anticipate, respond to, and recover from crises. This capability is not normally part of routine organizational management, and should be consciously and deliberately built and sustained through capital, resource, and time investment throughout the organization.

Crisis management is a subset of business continuity. A crisis management plan provides a framework for management to respond to a crisis. Developing the crisis management program and having it ready to be implemented before a crisis occurs is likely more effective. The crisis management plan would include role/responsibilities of staff and crisis management team, processes, templates to follow, and escalation rules (Table 5.1).

Table 5.1 Crisis management vs incident management

Crisis management	*Incident management*
Crises are unique, rare, *unforeseen* or poorly managed events, or combinations of such events, that can create *exceptional* challenges for an organization and are not well served by prescriptive, pre-planned responses.	Incidents are generally *foreseeable* and amenable to *pre-planned* response measures, although their specific timing, nature, and spread of implications are variable and therefore unpredictable in detail.
Crises have a higher sense of *urgency* and might require the response to run over *longer periods of time* to ensure that impacts are minimized.	Incident response usually spans a *short time* frame of activity and is resolved before exposure to longer-term or permanent significant impacts on the organization
Operations are intact, and media and social networks are involved.	Operations are impacted, but no media response is required.
Examples Crisis	Examples of Major Incidents
• Natural Disaster: Example: 2004 Indian Ocean earthquake (Tsunami) • Technological crisis: Examples: Chernobyl disaster, Exxon Valdez oil spill, Heartbleed security bug • Confrontation crisis: Example: Rainbow/PUSH's (People United to Serve Humanity) boycott of Nike • Crisis of malevolence: Example: 1982 Chicago Tylenol murders • Crises of skewed management values: Example: Sears sacrifices customer trust • Workplace violence: Example: DuPont's Lycra	• In 1985, in Colombia, a volcano erupted that destroyed the village of Armero. • Uganda in 1980 during the famine and period of starvation • Bhopal gas tragedy killed up to 15,000 people • 9/11, the second attack

5.3 KEY POINTS OF BS 11200:2014—CRISIS MANAGEMENT

1. *Understanding Crisis Management*
    - *Definition of Crisis vs. Incident:*
        - *Incident*: A disruptive event that can be managed with pre-planned procedures.
        - *Crisis*: An abnormal, unstable situation threatening an organization's strategic objectives, reputation, or viability, often requiring flexible, creative, and strategic responses beyond routine plans.
        - *Example:*
            - A minor IT outage (incident) can be managed by IT support, but a major data breach exposing customer data (crisis) threatens reputation and may require executive intervention, legal response, and public communication.
    - *Origins of Crises:*
        - Crises can arise from:
            - Extreme disruptive incidents (e.g., natural disasters, major accidents, criminal acts).
            - Poorly managed incidents that escalate.
            - Latent problems (e.g., governance failures, "workarounds," blame culture) that incubate and erupt unexpectedly.
    - *Case Study:*
        - The Deepwater Horizon oil spill (BP, 2010) began as a technical failure but escalated into a crisis due to poor initial management, lack of transparency, and systemic safety culture issues.
2. *Core Principles for Crisis Management Capability*
    - *Proactive and Systematic Approach:*
        - Crisis management should be a forward-looking, systematic process involving regular planning, training, and improvement.
        - *Example:*
            - Organizations like airlines conduct regular crisis simulations to prepare for rare but catastrophic events such as plane crashes or hijackings.
    - *Integration with Other Disciplines:*
        - Crisis management is interconnected with risk management, business continuity, and security management.
        - *Example:*
            - During the COVID-19 pandemic, organizations integrated crisis management with business continuity to maintain operations and protect staff.
    - *Leadership and Decision-Making:*
        - Top management must provide clear direction, make timely decisions, and uphold organizational values during a crisis.

- *Case Study:*
    - Johnson & Johnson's Tylenol crisis (1982): Leadership's swift product recall and transparent communication preserved public trust.

3. *Crisis Management Process*
    - *Preparation and Planning:*
        - Develop crisis management structures, roles, and responsibilities.
        - Establish clear criteria for escalating incidents to crises.
        - *Example:*
            - A manufacturing company defines clear thresholds for when a product defect becomes a recall-level crisis.
    - *Situational Awareness and Communication:*
        - Maintain up-to-date knowledge of events and their potential impacts.
        - Communicate proactively with stakeholders, media, and the public.
        - *Case Study:*
            - The Fukushima nuclear disaster (2011): Delayed and unclear communication worsened public anxiety and eroded trust.
    - *Strategic Response and Adaptability:*
        - Crises often require flexible, creative problem-solving and may demand deviation from standard procedures.
        - *Example:*
            - During the 2010 Icelandic volcano eruption, airlines and governments had to coordinate rapidly and adapt travel policies as the situation evolved.
4. *Crisis Leadership*
    - *Role of Top Management:*
        - Leaders must set the tone, make high-stakes decisions, and communicate values.
        - *Case Study:*
            - In the aftermath of 9/11, New York City's leadership coordinated emergency services, public information, and recovery efforts under extreme pressure.
    - *Decision-Making Under Pressure:*
        - Use structured frameworks to support rapid, informed decisions despite uncertainty.
        - *Example:*
            - Hospitals use triage protocols during mass casualty incidents to prioritize care.
5. *Crisis Communication*
    - *Principles of Crisis Communications*: Crisis communication processes, steps for dealing with the media, and the need for a trained media spokesperson are discussed. Developing a crisis communications segment for the emergency operations plan and how emergency

communications differ from daily communication are covered. Special communication needs of the audience, appropriate technologies, and the value of empathic listening and effective feedback are highlighted.
- *Crisis Communications Overview*: Crisis communications support personal and public safety by providing guidance information to answer risks. Differences between day-to-day and emergency communications, including the importance of timeliness, consistency, and clear language, are outlined. Standards such as NFPA 1600, NIMS ICS, and BS25999 are mentioned. Guidelines for defining communication structures and protocols are provided.
- *Using Technology in Crisis Communications*: Technology can increase message speed and delivery, broaden recipients, and manage communication processes. Limitations and the need for manual processes when technology fails are noted. Tools like cell phones, satellite phones, and computer network resources are listed. Considerations for message content, purpose, and recipient are discussed.
- *Effective Crisis Communication Strategies*: The "10 Cs of Good Crisis Communications" include being cooperative, clear, concise, and consistent. Establishing relationships with media representatives and the role of an organizational spokesperson are emphasized. The importance of image, active listening, and understanding cultural differences is highlighted. Information sharing needs and privacy concerns are addressed.
- *Components of a Crisis Communications Plan*: A crisis communications plan should include external and internal procedures, escalation and notification messages, technology guidelines, joint information centers, potential issues and resolutions, and supporting documents/templates.
- *Media Engagement:*
  - Proactively engage with media to provide facts and correct rumors.
  - *Example:*
    - Organizations designate trained spokespeople and prepare holding statements for likely scenarios.

6. *Training, Exercising, and Learning*
   - *Regular Training and Drills:*
   - Conduct exercises to test plans, build skills, and identify gaps.
     - *Case Study:*
       - Airports conduct annual full-scale emergency exercises involving multiple agencies to rehearse crisis response.
   - *Learning from Crises:*
     - Review and update crisis management plans based on lessons learned from real events and exercises.
     - *Example:*
       - After-action reviews following Hurricane Katrina led to major reforms in U.S. emergency management (Table 5.2).

Table 5.2 Distinguishing incidents from crises (from BS 11200:2014)

Characteristic	*Incident*	*Crisis*
Predictability	Generally foreseeable	Unique, rare, unforeseen
Onset	Sudden or gradual	Sudden or escalation from incident
Urgency	Short-term, resolvable	High urgency, longer duration
Impact	Limited, predefined response possible	Strategic, organization-wide, uncertain
Media Scrutiny	Little, unless escalates	High, reputation at risk
Manageability	By plans/procedures	Requires flexible, creative response

5.3.1 Conclusion

BS 11200:2014 emphasizes that crisis management is a distinct, strategic discipline requiring proactive preparation, strong leadership, effective communication, and continual learning. Real-world crises—from product recalls to natural disasters—demonstrate the need for adaptable, values-driven responses that go beyond routine incident management. Integrating crisis management with business continuity, risk, and security management builds true organizational resilience.

5.4 EMERGENCY RESPONSE

Emergency response is the immediate and coordinated reaction to an unforeseen event or crisis. It involves actions taken to minimize harm, save lives, and protect property. A rapid and effective response can significantly reduce the impact of a crisis. Emergency response is focused on the immediate and short-term needs of those affected, often involving emergency services, public assistance, and community participation.

Introduction to Emergency Management: Emergencies are unpredictable and always changing. Organizations are never fully protected from risk, even with comprehensive mitigation programs. Plans help in managing emergencies. Current changes in emergency management include efforts to address the special needs of children and pets. EM practitioners need to develop critical thinking and assessment skills to address diverse disaster issues.

Emergency Management Must Be...

1. *Comprehensive* emergency managers consider and take into account all hazards, all phases, all stakeholders, and all impacts relevant to disasters.
2. *Progressive* emergency managers anticipate future disasters and take preventive and preparatory measures to build disaster-resistant and disaster-resilient communities.

3. *Risk-Driven* emergency managers use sound risk management principles (hazard identification, risk analysis, and impact analysis) in assigning priorities and resources.
4. *Integrated* emergency managers ensure unity of effort among all levels of government and all elements of a community.
5. *Collaborative* emergency managers create and sustain broad and sincere relationships among individuals and organizations to encourage trust, advocate a team atmosphere, build consensus, and facilitate communication.
6. *Coordinated* emergency managers synchronize the activities of all relevant stakeholders to achieve a common purpose.
7. *Flexible* emergency managers use creative and innovative approaches in solving disaster challenges.
8. *Professional* emergency managers value a science and knowledge-based approach based on education, training, experience, ethical practice, public stewardship, and continuous improvement.

Why Emergency Management is important to Continuity of Operations

- Emergency management and business continuity are risk-driven
- An emergency event can directly damage resources
- Events also indirectly threaten supporting infrastructure (i.e., Essential personnel availability)
- Goal is to lessen negative impacts and protect life and human safety while ensuring a secure environment to support continued operations

5.4.1 Writing emergency response plan

- The emergency operations plan describes actions to be taken in response to natural, manmade, or technological hazards
- Specifies tasks to be performed by specific organizational elements at projected times
- Emergency planning is not a one-time event—emergency planning process is cyclical
- Business continuity and emergency management planning is becoming part of organization management
- Tend to follow the Plan, Do, Check Act (PDCA) cycle
- Ensures that continuity and EM activities support organizational resilience
- PDCA cycle is being used in the ISO 22320, National Fire Protection Association (NFPA) 1600, and ASIS International management system standards

5.4.1.1 Plan components

- *Some typical sections that may be used in emergency plans*
- *Introduction*
  - Plan purpose, Authority and responsibility assignment, Distribution record, Change log
- *Table of contents*
- *Situation and Assumptions*
  - Hazards addressed by the plan
  - Relative probability and impact
  - Areas likely to be affected
  - Vulnerable critical facilities
  - Limits of the plan
  - Identified hazards will occur
  - Individuals and organizations will execute their assigned responsibilities
  - Assistance may be needed and, if so, will be available
- Concept of Operations
  - The division of governmental and organizational responsibilities
  - When the plan will be activated—and when it will be inactivated
  - Alert levels and the basic actions that accompany each level
  - Forms and processes necessary to request assistance of various types
- Organization and Assignment of Responsibilities
  - Lists the general areas of responsibility assigned by organization and position
  - Identifies shared responsibilities, reporting relationships, and lines of authority
- Administration and Logistics
  - Police, Hospital, Ambulance, Fire Station Details
  - NGO
  - Transportation
  - Assumed resource needs for high-risk hazards
  - Potential resource availability
  - Mutual aid agreements
  - Policies on augmenting response staff with public employees and volunteers
  - A statement that addresses liability issues
  - Resource management policies (acquisition, tracking, and financial record-keeping
  - The general sequence of actions before, during, and after an event
- Authorities and References
  - Laws, statutes, ordinances, executive orders, regulations, formal agreements
  - Pre-delegation of emergency authorities
  - Pertinent reference materials, including related plans

- Functional Annexes
    - The Direction and Control Annex,
    - The Communications Annex,
    - The Warning Annex
    - The Emergency Public Information (EPI) Annex,
    - The Evacuation Annex,
    - The Mass Care Annex
    - The Health and Medical Annex,
    - The Resource Management Annex (Figure 5.2)

5.4.1.2 Response vs recovery

Response Activities Include

- Applying intelligence and other information to lessen the effects or consequences of an incident
- Increased security operations
- Continuing investigations into the nature and source of the threat
- Ongoing public health and agricultural surveillance and testing processes
- Immunization, isolation, or quarantine
- Specific law enforcement operations aimed at preempting, interdicting, or disrupting illegal activity

Much of the emphasis in emergency management is on response to disaster. The majority of government resources are oriented toward response. Organizations must prepare to initiate response activities on their own because first responders may be delayed in arrival.

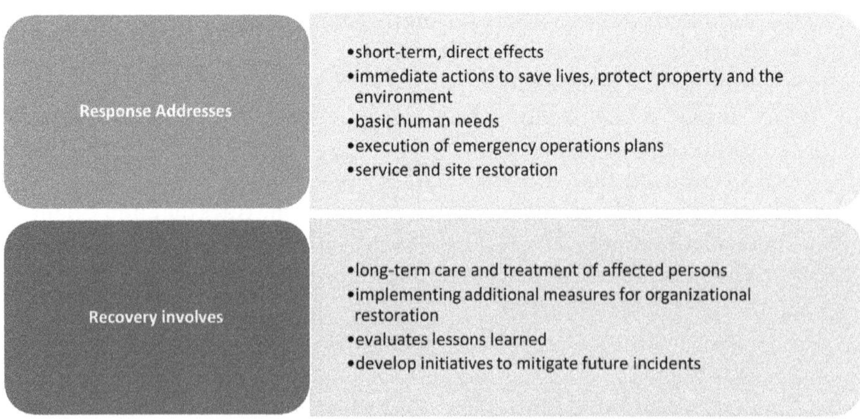

Figure 5.2 Response Vs Recovery

Recovery Activities Include

- The development, coordination, and execution of service- and site-restoration plans
- The reconstitution of government operations and services
- Individual, private-sector, nongovernmental, and public assistance programs to provide housing and to promote restoration
- Long-term care and treatment of affected persons
- Additional measures for social, political, environmental, and economic restoration
- Evaluation of the incident to identify lessons learned
- Post-incident reporting
- Development of initiatives to mitigate the effects of future incidents

There is never any definable point that marks the transition from response to recovery. Recovery is the move to reestablish normalcy and order. From an organizational perspective, recovery can mean a return to emergency management normalcy. Mitigation practices should be considered when recovering and reconstructing.

5.5 INCIDENT COMMAND CENTER

5.5.1 ICS organizational structure and elements

This section provides a detailed overview of the Incident Command System (ICS) organizational structure, its elements, and the roles and responsibilities essential for effective incident management, particularly as incidents grow in complexity and scale (Figures 5.3 and 5.4).

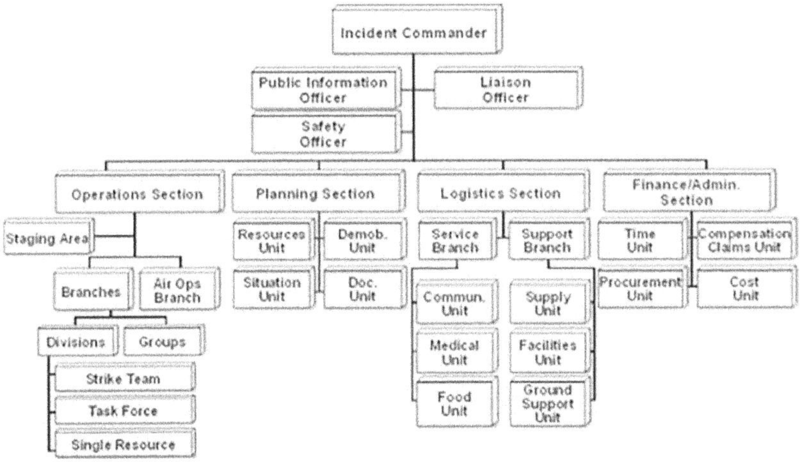

Figure 5.3 Incident Command System

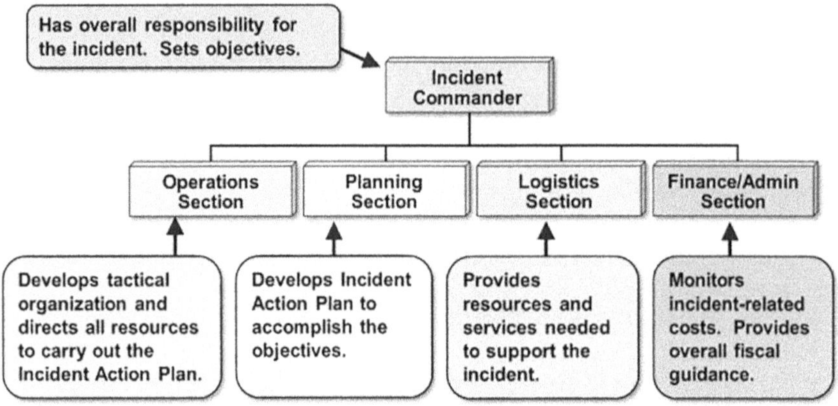

Figure 5.4 Incident Command Organisation Structure roles and responsibilities

5.5.2 ICS—who does what?

Key Components of ICS Structure

- *Command Staff:* Reports directly to the Incident Commander and includes critical roles such as:
  - Public Information Officer (PIO): Manages information dissemination and media relations.
  - Safety Officer (SO): Ensures responder and public safety.
  - Liaison Officer (LNO): Coordinates with assisting and cooperating agencies.
  - Additional roles (e.g., Legal Counsel, Medical Advisor) may be assigned as needed.
- *General Staff:* Responsible for the main functional areas of incident management, typically including:
  - Operations Section: Manages tactical operations and resources.
  - Planning Section: Collects and evaluates information to develop action plans.
  - Logistics Section: Provides facilities, services, and materials.
  - Finance/Administration Section: Manages financial, cost analysis, and administrative aspects.
  - Intelligence/Investigations Section (if established): Handles information and intelligence gathering, especially in criminal or complex incidents.
- *Other Organizational Elements:*
  - Section: Major functional area (e.g., Operations, Planning).
  - Branch: Manages a functional or geographical aspect of operations, situated between the Section Chief and Divisions/Groups.
  - Division: Responsible for operations within a defined geographic area.
  - Group: Handles specific functional areas within the Operations Section.

- Unit: Handles specific tasks within Planning, Logistics, or Finance/Admin.
- Task Force: Mixed resources assembled for a specific mission with a leader and common communications.
- Strike Team/Resource Team: Same kind/type of resources with a designated leader.
- Single Resource: An individual or team with a supervisor.

Key Points Relevant to Emergency Response

1. *Unified Command (UC) Definition and Role*
   - UC is activated when incidents cross jurisdictions or require multi-agency response (e.g., spills affecting multiple states, agencies, or tribal lands).
   - UC brings together Incident Commanders from all major organizations involved, allowing for shared decision-making, resource allocation, and a single set of objectives and strategies.
   - Each UC member retains their own legal and functional responsibilities while collaborating on response management.
2. *When and How UC is Used*
   - UC is appropriate whenever multiple jurisdictions, agencies, or statutory authorities are involved.
   - Membership is determined by jurisdictional authority, functional responsibility, and the ability to commit resources.
   - The structure is flexible, adapting as the incident evolves.
3. *UC Responsibilities in Emergency Response*
   - Develop common incident objectives, strategies, and priorities.
   - Approve a single Incident Action Plan (IAP) for all responders, ensuring unity of effort.
   - Assign roles and responsibilities within the command and general staff.
   - Coordinate logistics, resources, and communications.
   - Engage the media and public with a unified voice (often through a Joint Information Center).
   - Ensure worker and public health and safety.
   - Establish joint decision-making and documentation procedures.
4. *Decision-Making and Conflict Resolution*
   - Consensus-based: UC strives for consensus but allows for deferral to the agency with primary jurisdiction if needed.
   - Efficient and timely: UC is not a committee; it is an empowered leadership team focused on rapid, effective response.
5. *Integration with ICS*
   - UC replaces the single Incident Commander within ICS for multi-agency events.
   - ICS/UC is scalable and adaptable, expanding or contracting as the situation requires.

- Support agencies (without direct jurisdiction) participate through liaison roles or by supporting ICS sections.

6. *Training and Preparedness*
   - The document encourages joint training and exercises using UC to build familiarity and interoperability among agencies.
   - Promotes a common response culture and language across all responders.

Emergency Response Benefits

- Enhanced Coordination: UC ensures all agencies work from a shared plan, reducing duplication and confusion.
- Resource Optimization: Pooled resources and unified logistics maximize efficiency.
- Clear Communication: Unified messaging to responders, the public, and the media.
- Flexibility: Structure adapts to the size and complexity of the incident.
- Consistent, Effective Response: UC is the nationally recognized standard for managing complex emergencies in the U.S.

5.5.3 In summary

The document establishes Unified Command as the cornerstone of effective multi-agency emergency response, providing clear structures, roles, and processes to ensure coordinated action, rapid decision-making, and optimal use of resources during complex incidents (Figure 5.5).

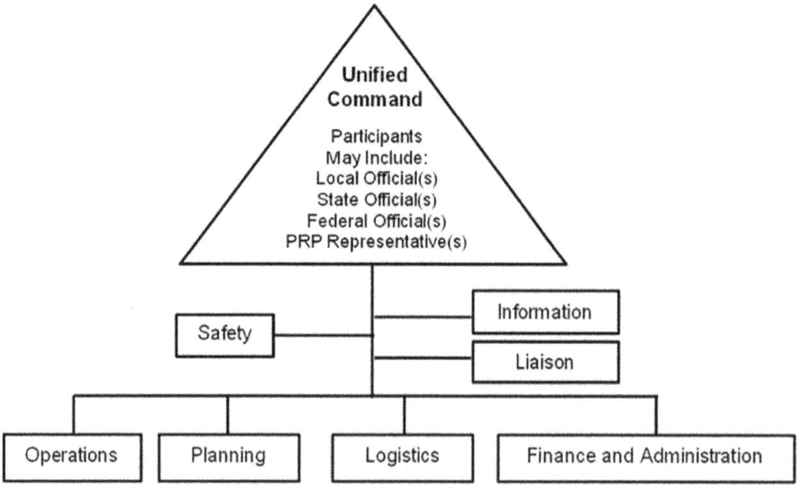

Figure 5.5 Relationship between ICS and UC.

5.6 WAR ROOM

5.6.1 How to establish a crisis command center (WAR room) and its operations

Establishing a robust crisis command center—commonly called a WAR Room—is critical for effective incident response and business continuity, especially in sectors like telecommunications. Referring to some of the best practices and external expert sources, here's a comprehensive guide:

1. *Purpose and Benefits of a Crisis Command Center*

   A crisis command center (WAR Room) serves as a dedicated space—physical or virtual—where key stakeholders and subject matter experts (SMEs) gather to manage and resolve major incidents. Its main benefits include:
   - Centralized decision-making and coordination
   - Rapid, clear communication among cross-functional teams
   - Enhanced adaptability and real-time problem-solving
   - Reduced distractions and miscommunication
   - Efficient stakeholder updates without interrupting response efforts.
2. *Planning and Preparation*
   a. *Governance Structure*
      - *Define roles and responsibilities:* Assign clear roles such as Incident Commander, Crisis Management Team (CMT), Business Continuity Coordinators, and functional SPOCs (Single Points of Contact).
      - *Establish decision-making processes:* Ensure everyone understands escalation paths and authority levels.

   b. *Location and Access*
      - *Identify multiple locations:* Prepare both on-site and off-site options to ensure accessibility regardless of the crisis.
      - *Access control:* Limit entry to authorized personnel to maintain focus and security.

   c. *Physical and Technical Setup*
      - *Dedicated space:* Use a room solely for crisis management, equipped with large tables, whiteboards, screens, and collaboration tools.
      - *Technology:* Ensure high-speed internet, video conferencing, secure communications (landline, satellite, radio phones), and backup power (generators, batteries).
      - *Supplies:* Stock essentials—computers, printers, stationery, markers, post-its, emergency kits, and catering if long shifts are expected.
3. *Operational Procedures*
   a. *Activation*
      - *Trigger criteria:* Activate the command center based on predefined scenarios (e.g., network outage, cyberattack, natural disaster).

    - *Notification:* Use a call tree or automated alerts to assemble the crisis team rapidly.
  b. *Incident Command System*
    - *Single point of command:* An Incident Commander leads the response, sets objectives, and ensures coordinated action.
    - *Team structure:* Organize into specialized units-incident response, communications, IT support, facilities, and business monitoring.
  c. *Communication and Information Management*
    - *Real-time dashboards:* Use interactive dashboards for monitoring incidents, network status, and key metrics.
    - *Collaboration tools:* Employ chat rooms, document sharing, and conference calls for seamless teamwork.
    - *Stakeholder updates:* Designate regular briefings for executives and external stakeholders without disrupting operations.
  d. *Documentation and Reporting*
    - *Incident logs:* Maintain detailed records of actions, decisions, and communications.
    - *Templates:* Use standardized incident reporting templates for consistency.

4. *Specialized Features for Telecom WAR Rooms*
  - *Network Operations Monitoring:* Integrate alarm systems, sensor data, and network analytics for rapid detection and response to outages or cyber incidents.
  - *Fraud and Cybersecurity Monitoring:* Set up dedicated teams and dashboards for fraud detection and cyber threat response.
  - *Business Activity Monitoring:* Display real-time dashboards for critical business functions (call centers, supply chain, retail operations).
5. *Training and Testing*
  - *Regular drills:* Conduct mock incidents to test readiness and refine procedures.
  - *Ongoing training:* Keep all team members updated on tools, protocols, and evolving threats.
6. *Continuous Improvement*
  - *Post-incident reviews:* Analyze each crisis response to identify lessons learned and update playbooks.
  - *Inventory management:* Periodically review and replenish supplies and ensure all equipment is functional (Table 5.3).

Table 5.3 Sample layout and team structure

Area/team	*Function*
Command center	Executive decision-making
Incident commander room	Incident assessment and communication
Business activity monitoring	Real-time dashboards for critical functions
Printer/facilities room	Support, IT, and logistics

Key *Takeaways*

- *Preparation is everything*: Dedicate and equip your WAR Room in advance.
- *Clear roles and communication*: Avoid confusion with well-defined responsibilities and communication channels.
- *Technology and supplies*: Ensure robust infrastructure and resources.
- *Regular review*: Test, train, and update your command center operations continuously.

Example of a Typical WAR Room (Figure 5.6)

By following these best practices, your organization can ensure rapid, coordinated, and effective crisis response, minimizing disruption and safeguarding critical operations

5.7 CONCLUSION: ESTABLISHING A CRISIS COMMAND CENTER AND MULTI-AGENCY RESPONSE

The three case studies examined in this chapter—Toyota's accelerator pedal recall, Johnson & Johnson's Tylenol crisis, and Maersk's NotPetya cyberattack—offer valuable insights into different aspects of crisis management and emergency response. While each crisis presented unique challenges; several common themes emerge that can guide organizations in developing robust crisis management capabilities.

5.7.1 The critical role of a crisis command center

A central lesson from these case studies is the importance of establishing a crisis command center as a focal point for coordinating response efforts. In each case, the affected organization needed a centralized mechanism for gathering information, making decisions, and implementing actions across multiple functions and locations.

An effective crisis command center should include the following elements:

1. *Clear Leadership Structure*: The crisis command center should have a clearly defined leadership structure with designated roles and responsibilities. This structure should include representatives from key functions such as operations, communications, legal, human resources, and technical specialists relevant to the specific crisis.
2. *Comprehensive Information Management*: The command center should serve as a central hub for gathering, analyzing, and disseminating information related to the crisis. This includes monitoring the situation, tracking response efforts, and maintaining a common operating picture for all stakeholders.

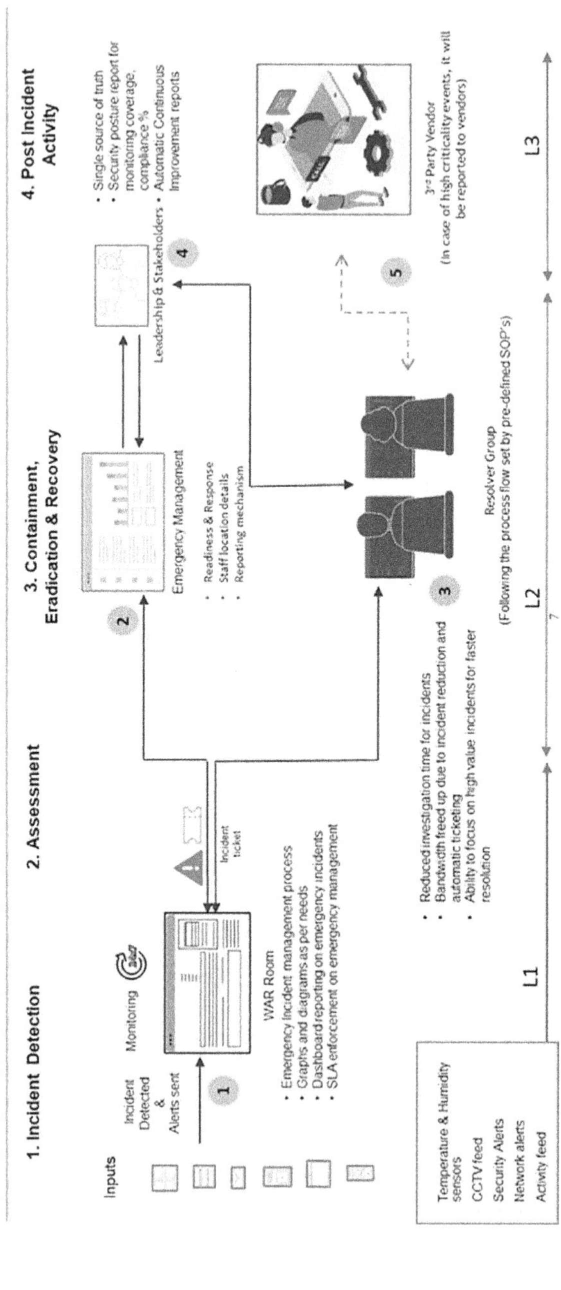
1. Incident Detection
2. Assessment
3. Containment, Eradication & Recovery
4. Post Incident Activity
Inputs
Incident Detected & Alerts sent
Monitoring
WAR Room
Emergency Incident management process
Graphs and diagrams as per needs
Dashboard reporting on emergency incidents
SLA enforcement on emergency management
Incident ticket
Emergency Management
Readiness & Response
Staff location details
Reporting mechanism
Leadership & Stakeholders
Single source of truth
Security posture report for monitoring coverage, compliance %
Automatic Continuous Improvement reports
Temperature & Humidity sensors
CCTV feed
Security Alerts
Network alerts
Activity feed
Reduced investigation time for incidents
Bandwidth freed up due to incident reduction and automatic ticketing
Ability to focus on high value incidents for faster resolution
Resolver Group
(Following the process flow set by pre-defined SOP's)
3rd Party Vendor
(In case of high criticality events, it will be reported to vendors)
L1
L2
L3
Figure 5.6

3. *Decision-Making Authority*: The crisis command center must have the authority to make critical decisions quickly without excessive bureaucracy. This requires pre-established delegation of authority and clear escalation paths for issues that require higher-level approval.
4. *Communication Capabilities*: The command center should be equipped with robust communication tools to facilitate internal coordination and external engagement. This includes systems for communicating with employees, customers, partners, regulators, and the media.
5. *Resource Coordination*: The crisis command center should have the ability to mobilize and coordinate resources across the organization, including personnel, equipment, facilities, and financial resources.
6. *Documentation and Record-Keeping*: Thorough documentation of the crisis and response efforts is essential for post-incident analysis, legal compliance, and organizational learning. The command center should maintain detailed records of all decisions, actions, and communications.
7. *Developing Protocols for Coordinated Multi-Agency Response:* Modern crises often require coordination with external agencies and stakeholders, as demonstrated in all three case studies. Toyota worked closely with regulatory agencies like NHTSA; Johnson & Johnson coordinated with law enforcement, the FDA, a retailer; and Maersk collaborated with cybersecurity experts, government agencies, and global partners. Effective protocols for coordinated multi-agency response should include:
   - *Pre-established Relationships*: Organizations should develop relationships with relevant external agencies before a crisis occurs. This includes identifying key contacts, understanding agency roles and capabilities, and establishing communication channels.
   - *Clear Communication Protocols*: Protocols should define how information will be shared between the organization and external agencies, including what information will be shared, with whom, and through what channels.
   - *Joint Training and Exercises*: Regular joint training and exercises with external agencies can help identify gaps in coordination and build familiarity with each other's procedures and capabilities.
   - *Defined Roles and Responsibilities*: Protocols should clearly define the roles and responsibilities of each participating agency or stakeholder, including who has authority for different aspects of the response.
   - *Integrated Planning*: Crisis response plans should be developed with input from relevant external agencies to ensure alignment and compatibility.
   - *Unified Command Structure*: In complex crises involving multiple agencies, a unified command structure can help ensure coordinated decision-making and resource allocation.
   - *Fostering Adaptability, Learning, and Continuous Improvement*: Perhaps the most important lesson from these case studies is the need for organizations to foster adaptability, learning, and continuous

improvement in their approach to crisis management. Each of the organizations examined—Toyota, Johnson & Johnson, and Maersk—emerged from their respective crises with valuable lessons that informed improvements to their crisis management capabilities.

Organizations can foster adaptability, learning, and continuous improvement by:

a. *Conducting Thorough Post-Incident Reviews*: After a crisis, organizations should conduct comprehensive reviews to identify what worked well, what didn't, and why. These reviews should involve all relevant stakeholders and focus on identifying actionable improvements.
b. *Updating Plans and Procedures*: Crisis management plans and procedures should be regularly updated based on lessons learned from actual incidents, exercises, and changes in the organization's risk profile.
c. *Investing in Training and Development*: Organizations should invest in ongoing training and development for crisis management teams, ensuring they have the knowledge, skills, and capabilities needed to respond effectively to evolving threats.
d. *Embracing a Culture of Preparedness*: Crisis management should be integrated into the organization's culture, with leadership emphasizing the importance of preparedness, resilience, and continuous improvement.
e. *Leveraging Technology and Innovation*: Organizations should leverage emerging technologies and innovative approaches to enhance their crisis management capabilities, from advanced monitoring and early warning systems to sophisticated simulation and modelling tools.

5.8 CASE STUDY 1

5.8.1 Strategies: Toyota—accelerator pedal recall

In the realm of crisis management, few cases illustrate the complexities and challenges of navigating a major corporate crisis as vividly as Toyota's accelerator pedal recall of 2009–2010. This crisis, which threatened the very foundation of one of the world's most respected automotive manufacturers, provides invaluable insights into crisis management strategies, their implementation, and their effectiveness in protecting lives, safeguarding assets, maintaining operational continuity, and upholding organizational reputation.

5.8.2 The crisis unfolds

The crisis began in August 2009 when a tragic accident occurred in California. A Lexus ES 350, a Toyota brand vehicle, experienced uncontrolled acceleration, resulting in a high-speed crash that claimed the lives of four people. This incident received significant media attention and brought to light potential dangers associated with unintended acceleration in Toyota vehicles. What initially appeared to be an isolated incident would soon escalate into one of the most challenging crises in Toyota's history, testing the company's crisis management capabilities and threatening its long-standing reputation for quality and reliability.

The timeline of events reveals how rapidly the crisis escalated. Following the fatal accident, the National Highway Traffic Safety Administration (NHTSA) launched an investigation into sudden acceleration issues in Toyota vehicles in September 2009. By November 2009, Toyota announced a voluntary recall of approximately 4.2 million vehicles due to the risk of floor mat entrapment causing unintended acceleration. This recall affected several popular models, including the Camry and Prius. However, the crisis deepened in January 2010 when Toyota expanded the recall to include an additional 2.3 million vehicles, citing concerns over sticking accelerator pedals. This brought the total number of recalled vehicles to nearly 6 million. In a highly publicized move that underscored the severity of the situation, Toyota halted sales of eight of its models affected by the accelerator pedal recall in February 2010, causing significant disruption to its production and sales operations.

The U.S. government's formal investigation into the safety issues related to unintended acceleration in Toyota vehicles further intensified the crisis. Congressional hearings were held, during which Toyota executives were questioned about the company's handling of the situation. By April 2010, Toyota faced a $16.4 million fine from the NHTSA for failing to promptly notify the agency about the accelerator pedal defect, violating federal safety regulations.

5.8.3 Initial response and strategic missteps

Toyota's initial response to the crisis revealed significant strategic missteps that would later necessitate a more comprehensive approach to crisis management. When reports of unintended acceleration first emerged, Toyota's response was characterized by denial and dismissal of the problem. The company initially attributed the incidents to driver error or improper installation of floor mats, rather than acknowledging potential mechanical or design flaws in their vehicles. This defensive stance proved problematic for several reasons. First, it created the perception that Toyota was prioritizing its reputation over customer safety, damaging trust among consumers and regulatory bodies. Second, it delayed the implementation of effective solutions to address the actual causes of the problem. Third, it allowed the crisis to escalate as more incidents were reported and media coverage intensified.

Toyota's reluctance to acknowledge the full extent of the problem was particularly evident in its communication strategy. The company's messaging was often technical and lacked empathy for affected customers, further alienating stakeholders during a critical period. This approach stood in stark contrast to best practices in crisis communication, which emphasize transparency, empathy, and a clear commitment to resolving the issue.

The company's organizational structure also contributed to its ineffective initial response. Toyota's decision-making was highly centralized in Japan, creating delays in responding to a crisis that was primarily unfolding in the U.S. This geographical and cultural disconnect hampered Toyota's ability to understand the severity of the situation from an American perspective and to respond with appropriate urgency.

5.8.4 Strategic pivot and comprehensive crisis management

Recognizing the inadequacy of its initial response, Toyota implemented a comprehensive crisis management strategy that addressed multiple dimensions of the problem. This strategic pivot included several key components:

Leadership Engagement: Toyota's top leadership, including President Akio Toyoda, became directly involved in managing the crisis. Toyoda personally appeared before the U.S. Congress to apologize for the company's safety issues and to outline steps being taken to address them. This high-level engagement signaled the company's commitment to resolving the crisis and taking responsibility for its failures.

Transparent Communication: Toyota shifted from a defensive communication stance to one characterized by greater transparency and accountability. The company acknowledged the seriousness of the issues, provided regular updates on its investigation and recall efforts, and established dedicated channels for customer inquiries and concerns.

Comprehensive Recall Program: Toyota implemented one of the largest recall programs in automotive history, affecting millions of vehicles worldwide. The company not only recalled affected vehicles but also suspended production and sales of certain models until safety issues could be resolved. This decisive action, while costly in the short term, demonstrated Toyota's commitment to customer safety.

Technical Solutions: Toyota developed and implemented technical solutions to address the identified problems. For vehicles affected by the floor mat issue, Toyota redesigned the accelerator pedal and floor area. For those with sticky accelerator pedals, the company engineered a reinforcement bar to prevent the pedal from sticking. Additionally, Toyota installed brake override systems in its vehicles, which would cut engine power when both the accelerator and brake pedals were pressed simultaneously.

Organizational Restructuring: Toyota restructured its quality control and decision-making processes to enable faster responses to safety concerns. This included establishing regional quality committees with the authority to initiate recalls without waiting for approval from Japan, thereby addressing the centralization issues that had hampered its initial response.

Stakeholder Engagement: Toyota actively engaged with various stakeholders, including customers, dealers, regulators, and the media. The company established a quality advisory panel composed of independent experts to review its quality assurance processes and make recommendations for improvement.

Long-term Quality Initiatives: Beyond addressing the immediate crisis, Toyota launched long-term initiatives to enhance quality control throughout its global operations. This included extending vehicle development timelines to allow for more thorough testing, increasing the number of quality engineers, and implementing more rigorous safety evaluation procedures.

5.8.5 Outcomes and lessons learned

The effectiveness of Toyota's crisis management strategy can be evaluated through various outcomes. In the short term, the company experienced significant financial losses, with recall costs estimated at over $2 billion and additional losses from decreased sales and market share. Toyota's stock price also declined substantially during the crisis.

However, the long-term outcomes reflect the effectiveness of Toyota's comprehensive approach to crisis management. By 2011, independent investigations by NASA and NHTSA concluded that there were no electronic defects in Toyota vehicles that would have caused unintended acceleration. The investigations identified driver error, floor mat entrapment, and sticky accelerator pedals as the primary causes of the reported incidents.

Toyota's sales and market share gradually recovered in the years following the crisis, suggesting that the company's efforts to rebuild trust were largely successful. Moreover, Toyota implemented lasting changes to its organizational structure and quality control processes, creating a more responsive and safety-focused corporate culture.

Several key lessons emerge from Toyota's experience:

Proactive Risk Identification: Organizations must proactively identify potential risks and address them before they escalate into crises. Toyota's failure to recognize and address early warning signs of acceleration problems contributed to the severity of the crisis.

Transparent and Empathetic Communication: Effective crisis communication requires transparency, empathy, and a clear commitment to resolving the issue. Toyota's initial defensive stance damaged trust, while its later, more transparent approach helped rebuild relationships with stakeholders.

Decisive Action: In a crisis involving safety concerns, decisive action is essential. Toyota's comprehensive recall program, while costly, demonstrated the company's commitment to customer safety and helped restore confidence in the brand.

Organizational Flexibility: Crisis management requires organizational structures that enable rapid decision-making and response. Toyota's centralized decision-making initially hampered its response, highlighting the importance of regional autonomy in global organizations.

Continuous Learning: Effective crisis management involves learning from the experience and implementing changes to prevent similar crises in the future. Toyota's organizational restructuring and enhanced quality control processes reflect this commitment to continuous improvement.

The Toyota accelerator pedal recall crisis underscores the complex interplay of technical, communication, and organizational factors in crisis management. It demonstrates how a company's initial response can exacerbate a crisis, while a comprehensive, multi-faceted approach can effectively address the immediate issues and create a foundation for long-term recovery and improvement. For organizations seeking to develop robust crisis management capabilities, Toyota's experience offers valuable insights into both pitfalls to avoid and strategies to emulate.

5.9 CASE STUDY 2

5.9.1 Crisis communication: Johnson & Johnson—Tylenol crisis (1982)

The 1982 Tylenol crisis stands as one of the most influential case studies in the history of crisis communication and management. When seven people in the Chicago area died after consuming cyanide-laced Tylenol capsules, Johnson & Johnson faced a crisis that threatened not only its most profitable product but also public trust in the entire company. The company's response to this crisis has since become the gold standard for effective crisis communication, demonstrating how transparency, decisive action, and ethical decision-making can preserve and even strengthen an organization's reputation during a catastrophic event.

5.9.2 The crisis unfolds

Before the crisis, Tylenol was the most successful over-the-counter product in the United States with over one hundred million users. The product was responsible for 19% of Johnson & Johnson's corporate profits during the first three quarters of 1982, accounting for 13% of the company's year-to-year sales growth and 33% of its year-to-year profit growth. Tylenol dominated the painkiller market with a 37% market share, outselling the next four leading painkillers combined. Had Tylenol been a standalone company, its profits would have placed it in the top half of the Fortune 500 (Berge, 1998).

The crisis began in the fall of 1982 when an unknown perpetrator replaced Tylenol Extra-Strength capsules with cyanide-laced capsules, resealed the packages, and placed them on the shelves of pharmacies and food stores in the Chicago area. Seven unsuspecting people purchased and consumed these poisoned capsules, resulting in their deaths.

Johnson & Johnson, the parent company of McNeil Consumer Products Company which manufactured Tylenol, suddenly found itself at the center of a crisis that would test its values, leadership, and communication capabilities.

The initial media coverage was devastating. All three major television networks led with the Tylenol story on the first day of the crisis, with CBS putting a human face on the tragedy by reporting: "When 12-year-old Mary Kellerman of Elk Grove Village, Ill., awoke at dawn with cold symptoms; her parents gave her one Extra-Strength Tylenol and sent her back to bed. Little did they know, they would wake up at 7:00 a.m. to find their daughter dying on the bathroom floor" (Kaplin, 1998). Print media followed with equally alarming headlines: Time Magazine's "Poison Madness in the Midwest," Newsweek's "The Tylenol Scare," and The Washington Post's "Tylenol, Killer or Cure."

The media coverage was not only negative but also pervasive. Throughout the crisis, over 100,000 separate news stories ran in U.S. newspapers, and hundreds of hours of national and local television coverage were dedicated to the story. A post-crisis study by Johnson & Johnson revealed that over 90% of the American population had heard of the Chicago deaths due to cyanide-laced Tylenol within the first week of the crisis (Kaplin, 1998).

5.9.3 Johnson & Johnson's crisis communication strategy

What distinguishes the Tylenol case as exemplary is Johnson & Johnson's immediate and comprehensive response to the crisis. The company's approach was guided by its Credo, a one-page document written by Robert Wood Johnson in 1943 that outlined the company's responsibilities to its customers, employees, communities, and shareholders—in that order. This ethical framework would prove invaluable in guiding the company's decision-making during the crisis.

Robert Andrews, assistant director for public relations at Johnson & Johnson, recalled the company's initial encounter with the crisis: "We got a call from a Chicago news reporter. He told us that the medical examiner there had just given a press conference—people were dying from poisoned Tylenol. He wanted our comment. As it was the first knowledge we had here in this department, we told him we knew nothing about it. In that first call we learned more from the reporter than he did from us" (Berge, 1990). This scenario highlights a common challenge in crisis management: organizations often learn about crises affecting them from external sources, particularly in the age of 24-hour media coverage.

Johnson & Johnson chairman, James Burke, responded to the crisis by forming a seven-member strategy team. The team's guidance from Burke was clear and prioritized: first, "How do we protect the people?" and second, "How do we save this product?" This prioritization of public safety over corporate interests would define Johnson & Johnson's approach throughout the crisis.

The company's communication strategy was characterized by several key elements:

Immediate Public Warning: Johnson & Johnson's first action was to alert consumers across the nation, via the media, not to consume any type of Tylenol product until the extent of the tampering could be determined. This immediate warning demonstrated the company's commitment to public safety above all else.

Transparent and Proactive Media Engagement: Before the crisis, Johnson & Johnson had not actively sought press coverage. However, recognizing the benefits of open communications in disseminating warnings and explaining the company's position, Johnson & Johnson established several channels for media engagement.

The company held major press conferences at corporate headquarters, set up a live television feed via satellite to the New York metro area to ensure national coverage, and CEO James Burke appeared on high-profile programs like 60 Minutes and the Donahue show to communicate directly with the public.

Accessible Customer Support: In the first week of the crisis, Johnson & Johnson established a toll-free hotline for consumers to call with inquiries about the safety of Tylenol. The company also created a separate toll-free line for news organizations to receive pre-taped daily messages with updated statements about the crisis (Berge, 1990).

Decisive Product Recall: Johnson & Johnson took the unprecedented step of recalling all Tylenol capsules from store shelves nationwide—31 million bottles with a retail value of over $100 million. This recall went far beyond what was legally required and demonstrated the company's unwavering commitment to consumer safety, even at a significant financial cost.

Transparent Communication of Solutions: When Johnson & Johnson developed its new triple safety seal packaging—a glued box, a plastic seal over the neck of the bottle, and a foil seal over the mouth of the bottle—the company held a press conference at the manufacturer's headquarters to explain the new safety measures. Tylenol became the first product in the industry to use tamper-resistant packaging, just six months after the crisis occurred (Berge, 1990).

5.9.4 The impact of effective crisis communication

Johnson & Johnson's approach to crisis communication had profound effects on both the immediate crisis resolution and the long-term reputation of the company and its product. In the short term, the company's transparent and decisive actions helped contain the crisis and prevent further harm.

By withdrawing all Tylenol products from the market, Johnson & Johnson eliminated the risk of additional poisonings. The company's clear communication about the nature of the crisis and the steps being taken to address it helped manage public fear and uncertainty. The financial impact of the crisis was significant but temporary. The recall and related actions cost Johnson & Johnson an estimated $100 million, and Tylenol's market share plummeted from 37% to just 7% in the immediate aftermath of the crisis. However, the company's effective crisis communication strategy laid the groundwork for a remarkable recovery.

When Tylenol was reintroduced to the market with new tamper-resistant packaging, Johnson & Johnson supported the relaunch with a comprehensive communication campaign that included direct mail, new advertising, and over 2,250 sales representatives making presentations to the medical community. The company also offered coupons for a free product to encourage consumers to return to the brand. The results were extraordinary. Within a year of the crisis, Tylenol had regained 70% of its pre-crisis market share. The product's recovery was so successful that it is often cited as an example of how effective crisis management can not only salvage a brand but also potentially strengthen it. Johnson & Johnson's handling of the Tylenol crisis enhanced its reputation as a company that prioritizes consumer safety and ethical business practices above short-term profits.

5.9.5 Lessons in crisis communication

The Tylenol case has become the foundation for many crisis communication strategies developed by researchers over the last four decades. Several key lessons emerge from Johnson & Johnson's handling of the crisis:

Values-Based Decision-Making: Johnson & Johnson's response was guided by its Credo, which clearly established the company's priorities. This ethical framework enabled quick, consistent decision-making that prioritized public safety over financial considerations.

Transparency and Honesty: The company was forthright about what it knew and didn't know, never attempting to downplay the severity of the situation or deflect responsibility for addressing it, even though the tampering was not the company's fault.

Decisive Action: Johnson & Johnson's nationwide recall demonstrated its commitment to consumer safety and helped establish the company as a responsible corporate citizen.

Proactive Media Engagement: By actively engaging with the media, Johnson & Johnson was able to shape the narrative around the crisis and communicate directly with the public.

Long-Term Perspective: The company was willing to absorb significant short-term costs to protect its long-term reputation and rebuild consumer trust.

Industry Leadership: By developing and implementing new tamper-resistant packaging, Johnson & Johnson not only addressed the immediate crisis but also led the industry in preventing similar incidents in the future.

The Tylenol crisis demonstrates how effective crisis communication can transform a potentially devastating situation into an opportunity to demonstrate organizational values and strengthen stakeholder relationships. Johnson & Johnson's response has become the benchmark against which other corporate crisis responses are measured, illustrating the enduring power of transparent, ethical, and decisive communication in times of crisis.

As noted by crisis communication scholar David Berge, "The Tylenol crisis is without a doubt the most exemplary case ever known in the history of crisis communications. Any business executive, who has ever stumbled into a public relations ambush, ought to appreciate the way Johnson & Johnson responded to the Tylenol poisonings. They have effectively demonstrated how major business has to handle a disaster" (Berge, 1990, p. 19).

The Johnson & Johnson Tylenol case remains relevant today, offering timeless principles for organizations facing crises in an increasingly complex and interconnected world. By prioritizing public safety, communicating transparently, and taking decisive action guided by clear values, organizations can navigate even the most challenging crises while preserving and potentially strengthening their reputations.

5.10 CASE STUDY 3

5.10.1 Incident preparedness and response: Maersk—NotPetya cyberattack

In the digital age, organizations face an evolving landscape of threats that extend beyond traditional physical risks. The 2017 NotPetya cyberattack on A.P. Møller-Maersk, one of the world's largest shipping conglomerates, stands as a watershed moment in corporate crisis management. This case study illustrates the critical importance of incident preparedness and response in the face of sophisticated cyber threats, highlighting how even organizations with substantial resources can be vulnerable to devastating attacks that test their resilience, adaptability, and recovery capabilities.

5.10.2 The NotPetya attack unfolds

On June 27, 2017, a seemingly ordinary summer afternoon in Copenhagen was disrupted when Maersk employees began noticing unusual behavior on their computer screens. Some displays showed messages about repairing file systems, while others more ominously announced that important files had been encrypted and demanded a $300 bitcoin payment for their release.

Within minutes, the scale of the problem became apparent as screens throughout Maersk's headquarters began turning black in rapid succession.

As described by an IT administrator at Maersk (whose name was changed for privacy): "I saw a wave of screens turning black. Black, black, black. Black black black black black" (Greenberg, 2018). The realization that the company was under a massive cyberattack prompted immediate action. Employees ran through hallways, warning colleagues to disconnect their computers from the network. Some even hurdled over locked key-card gates, which had been paralyzed by the malware, to spread the warning to other sections of the building.

Despite these efforts, disconnecting Maersk's entire global network took more than two panicky hours. By the end of this process, every employee had been ordered to turn off their computer and leave it at their desk. The digital phones at every cubicle had also been rendered useless in the emergency network shutdown. Many employees, rendered entirely idle without computers, servers, routers, or desk phones, simply left the building, uncertain when they might return to work.

The maritime giant, responsible for 76 ports on all sides of the earth and nearly 800 seafaring vessels—representing close to a fifth of the entire world's shipping capacity—was effectively dead in the water. The attack had infected approximately 45,000 PCs and 4,000 servers across Maersk's global operations, with an estimated financial impact of $300 million (LRQA, 2023).

5.10.3 Understanding the NotPetya malware

The NotPetya attack was not a conventional ransomware incident, despite its initial appearance. While traditional ransomware encrypts files and offers decryption in exchange for payment, NotPetya was designed primarily as a destructive weapon. It was a sophisticated piece of malware that combined multiple attack vectors to spread rapidly through networks.

NotPetya was propelled by two powerful hacker exploits working in tandem:

Eternal Blue, a penetration tool created by the U.S. National Security Agency but leaked earlier in 2017, and a credential-harvesting tool that allowed the malware to spread laterally through networks. Once inside a system, NotPetya would encrypt the master boot record, making it impossible to start the computer without external intervention.

The malware's origin has been traced back to a Ukrainian accounting software package called M.E.Doc, which was widely used by businesses operating in Ukraine. Russian military hackers had hijacked the software's update servers to create a back door into thousands of computers. While the primary target appeared to be Ukrainian infrastructure as part of the ongoing conflict between Russia and Ukraine, the malware spread globally, affecting multinational corporations like Maersk that had operations in Ukraine.

What made NotPetya particularly devastating was its ability to spread automatically and indiscriminately. As Craig Williams, director of outreach at Cisco's Talos division, noted:

"To date, it was simply the fastest-propagating piece of malware we've ever seen. By the second you saw it, your data center was already gone" (Greenberg, 2018).

5.10.4 Maersk's incident response

Maersk's response to the NotPetya attack demonstrates both the challenges of responding to a catastrophic cyber incident and the resilience that can emerge from effective crisis management. The company's approach included several key elements:

Immediate Containment: The first priority was containing the spread of the malware by disconnecting systems from the network. While this process took longer than ideal, it helped prevent further infection.

Rapid Assessment: Maersk quickly assembled an incident response team to assess the extent of the damage and develop a recovery strategy. An emergency recovery center was established in Great Britain to coordinate the global response.

Shift to Manual Operations: In a remarkable display of adaptability, Maersk rapidly switched from IT-enabled processes to manual, paper-driven models to bypass disabled systems. This approach enabled the organization to restore an estimated 80% of critical functionality and throughput while systems were being cleared and restored (LRQA, 2023).

Prioritized Recovery: Rather than attempting to restore all systems simultaneously, Maersk prioritized the recovery of critical business functions. Two days after the attack, Maersk Line was able to accept bookings from customers with existing accounts. Between 6 and 12 days after the attack, Maersk Line, Damco (Maersk's logistics division), and APM Terminals (Maersk's port operation division) gradually progressed to more normalized operations.

Transparent Communication: Throughout the crisis, Maersk maintained transparent communication with customers, partners, and the public. The company provided regular updates on the situation and the progress of recovery efforts, helping to maintain trust during a period of significant disruption.

Complete Rebuild: Maersk ultimately had to rebuild its entire IT infrastructure, including the installation of 4,000 new servers, 45,000 new PCs, and 2,500 applications. This massive undertaking was completed in just 10 days—a process that would normally take months or even years.

5.10.5 The impact and aftermath

The NotPetya attack had profound impacts on Maersk's operations and the global shipping industry:

Operational Disruption: All 76 of Maersk's global port terminals were affected, with 17 terminals rendered completely inoperable. Ships were unable to unload their cargo, and new shipments could not be processed through Maersk's booking systems.

Financial Losses: The attack cost Maersk an estimated $300 million in lost revenue and recovery expenses. This figure does not include the broader economic impact on Maersk's customers and partners who were unable to ship or receive goods during the disruption.

Reputational Considerations: Despite the significant disruption, Maersk's transparent communication and effective response helped maintain customer trust. The company's ability to continue operations manually demonstrated resilience that actually enhanced its reputation in some respects.

Industry-Wide Awakening: The attack served as a wake-up call for the entire shipping industry, which had traditionally viewed cybersecurity as a secondary concern. As Jim Hagemann, Chairman of Maersk, commented: "We were basically average when it came to cybersecurity, like many companies. This was a wake-up call not just to become good, but to have cybersecurity as a competitive advantage" (LRQA, 2023).

Strategic Shift: Following the attack, Maersk significantly increased its investment in cybersecurity, implementing more robust security measures and developing more comprehensive incident response plans. The company transformed its approach from viewing cybersecurity as a technical issue to recognizing it as a strategic business imperative.

5.10.6 Lessons in incident preparedness and response

The Maersk NotPetya case offers several valuable lessons for organizations seeking to enhance their incident preparedness and response capabilities:

Proactive Risk Assessment: Organizations must regularly assess their vulnerability to cyber threats, particularly as they relate to critical business functions. This includes evaluating dependencies on third-party software and services, which can serve as entry points for attacks.

Comprehensive Incident Response Planning: Effective incident response requires detailed planning that addresses not only technical recovery but also business continuity. Organizations should develop and regularly test incident response plans that include clear roles and responsibilities, communication protocols, and recovery procedures.

Operational Resilience: The ability to maintain critical business functions during a crisis is essential. Organizations should identify alternative methods for conducting essential operations when primary systems are unavailable, as Maersk did by reverting to manual processes.

Supply Chain Security: The NotPetya attack highlighted the importance of securing the entire supply chain, including software updates and third-party applications. Organizations must implement robust controls for managing supply chain risks, such as vendor security assessments and secure update processes.

Backup and Recovery Capabilities: The ability to restore systems and data quickly is crucial for minimizing the impact of a cyber incident. Organizations should maintain secure, offline backups of critical systems and data, and regularly test their recovery procedures.

Cross-Functional Collaboration: Effective incident response requires collaboration across multiple functions, including IT, security, operations, legal, communications, and executive leadership. Organizations should establish cross-functional incident response teams and ensure clear lines of communication.

Transparent Communication: Open and honest communication with stakeholders during a crisis can help maintain trust and manage expectations. Organizations should develop communication plans that address both internal and external stakeholders.

Continuous Improvement: Following an incident, organizations should conduct thorough post-incident reviews to identify lessons learned and opportunities for improvement. These insights should be incorporated into updated incident response plans and security measures.

5.10.7 The evolution of cyber threats and response

The Maersk NotPetya attack represents a pivotal moment in the evolution of cyber threats and organizational responses. It demonstrated that cyber incidents are no longer merely technical issues but can have profound impacts on business operations, financial performance, and even global supply chains.

As cyber threats continue to evolve in sophistication and scale, organizations must adopt a more strategic approach to incident preparedness and response. This includes not only implementing robust technical controls but also developing the organizational capabilities needed to respond effectively to incidents when they occur.

The shipping sector, like many traditional industries, had historically stood apart from developments in cybersecurity, with the majority of critical functions and assets physically isolated by miles of ocean. However, as the Maersk case illustrates, this hands-off approach to cybersecurity has become increasingly risky and costly in the modern threat landscape.

Today, organizations face threats not only from less capable adversaries such as hacktivists and virus writers but also from organized criminals and nation-state sponsored threat actors. The cyber-crime economy is now mature, well-established, and well-developed, requiring a correspondingly sophisticated approach to security.

The Maersk NotPetya attack serves as a powerful reminder that in our interconnected world, no organization is immune to cyber threats. However, it also demonstrates that with effective incident preparedness and response capabilities, organizations can weather even the most severe crises and emerge stronger and more resilient.

5.10.8 In summary

The case studies examined in this chapter demonstrate that effective crisis management is not merely about responding to incidents when they occur but about building organizational capabilities that enable resilience in the face of adversity. By investing in crisis management strategies, communication capabilities, and incident preparedness and response mechanisms, organizations can protect lives, safeguard assets, maintain operational continuity, and uphold their reputations even in the most challenging circumstances.

As the business environment continues to evolve and new threats emerge, the principles illustrated by these case studies—proactive risk management, transparent communication, decisive action, organizational flexibility, and continuous learning—will remain essential for organizations seeking to navigate the complex landscape of crisis management and emergency response in the 21st century (Table 5.4).

Table 5.4 Crisis readiness assessment checklist

Category	*Assessment item*	*Yes*	*No*	*Partial*
Leadership & governance	Crisis management roles and responsibilities are clearly defined			
	Executive leadership is trained in crisis decision-making			
	Authority for crisis decisions is pre-delegated			
Planning & preparation	Crisis management plan is documented and accessible			
	Plan addresses multiple crisis scenarios			
	Plan is reviewed and updated at least annually			
Risk assessment	Potential crisis scenarios are identified and prioritized			
	Early warning indicators are established			
	Supply chain vulnerabilities are assessed			
Communication	Crisis communication protocols are established			
	Spokesperson(s) are identified and trained			
	Multiple communication channels are available			

(Continued)

Table 5.4 Crisis readiness assessment checklist *(Continued)*

Category	*Assessment item*	*Yes*	*No*	*Partial*
Resources & capabilities	Crisis management team is identified and trained			
	Alternate operational procedures exist for critical functions			
	Emergency resources are allocated and accessible			
Testing & training	Crisis simulations are conducted regularly			
	Lessons from exercises are documented and implemented			
	Cross-functional teams participate in training			
Stakeholder management	Key stakeholders are identified for each crisis type			
	Stakeholder communication templates are prepared			
	Regulatory reporting requirements are documented			
Recovery & continuity	Business continuity plans integrate with crisis management			
	Recovery priorities are established			
	Post-crisis review process is defined			

BIBLIOGRAPHY

Berge, D. T. (1990). The first 24 hours: A comprehensive guide to successful crisis communications. Basil Blackwell, Inc.

Berge, D. T. (1998). Recovering from catastrophic loss: A study of the Tylenol poisoning crisis. In D. L. Wilcox, P. H. Ault, & W. K. Agee (Eds.), Public relations: Strategies and tactics (5th ed., pp. 304–305). Longman.

Greenberg, A. (2018, August 22). The untold story of NotPetya, the most devastating cyberattack in history. Wired.

Kaplin, A. (1998). Crisis management and the Tylenol poisonings. In T. L. Beauchamp, & N. E. Bowie (Eds.), Ethical theory and business (5th ed., pp. 124–129). Prentice Hall.

LRQA. (2023). Notpetya ransomware attack on Maersk - key learnings. https://www.lrqa.com/en/insights/articles/notpetya-ransomware-attack-on-maersk-keylearnings/

Chapter 6

Business continuity planning

Learning Objective

- Explain the concept and importance of Business Continuity Management (BCM), including its key components and benefits at organizational, legal, operational, customer, financial, and human levels.
- Describe the BCM lifecycle and its six stages, including policy/program management, organizational understanding, strategy development, response planning, exercising/maintenance, and awareness/training.
- Identify and differentiate between the main types of business continuity plans (Crisis Management, Crisis Communication, IT Disaster Recovery, and Business Recovery) and their roles in organizational resilience.
- Analyze real-world case studies (e.g., Netflix, Toyota, Ochsner Health System, Qatar Diplomatic Crisis) to illustrate resilience, restoration, and critical thinking in business continuity.
- Apply the principles of risk management, crisis management, business recovery, and IT disaster recovery in developing and maintaining an effective business continuity strategy.
- Recognize the importance of continual improvement, training, and stakeholder engagement in sustaining a robust business continuity program.

6.1 SO, WHAT IS BUSINESS CONTINUITY?

Business Continuity is defined as the organization's ability to maintain the delivery of products or services at acceptable, predefined levels following a disruptive incident. Business Continuity Management (BCM) is characterized as a comprehensive management process that identifies potential threats to an organization and evaluates the impacts those threats might have on business operations if they materialize. This process provides a framework for building organizational resilience, enabling an effective response that safeguards key stakeholders' interests, reputation, brand, and value-creating activities.

In BCM, we proactively address threats and their potential impacts, establishing a framework to help the organization recover from disruptive incidents while enhancing its response capabilities. This approach not only protects the

DOI: 10.1201/9781003597520-6

interests of key stakeholders but also preserves the business's value-creating activities, brand, and reputation.

The use of the term "Business Continuity Management" instead of "business continuity planning" is intentional. The term "planning" implies a finite process with a start and end, which can lead to unnecessary bureaucratic procedures. However, business continuity planning remains an essential part of the BCM process. Unlike earlier, narrower, and reactive approaches to BCM, it is now recognized as a dynamic, proactive, and ongoing business-as-usual management process. For BCM to be effective, it must align with or conform to a standard that is practical, realistic, up-to-date, effective, and proven to provide a plausible capability.

The benefits of implementing a successful BCMS are at all levels.

- At the organizational level—Its implementation enhances the organization's reputation and helps it gain a competitive advantage.
- At the legal level—It assists with Legal and Regulatory Compliance.
- At the operating level—It establishes an effective response, which minimizes the impacts of an operational disruption.
- At the customer level—It raises credibility and customer confidence.
- At the financial level—It results in reduced costs and lower insurance premiums.
- At the human level—It encourages cross-team collaboration and improves employee awareness.

Why should an organization adopt Business Continuity Management?

First and foremost, BCM helps an organization provide uninterrupted services. Networks and data centers are critical to its customers, particularly those in media, banking, stock exchanges, and other service sectors. BCM ensures that the capability to provide uninterrupted service for critical infrastructure is in place.

Second, it helps build resiliency and response mechanisms with the aim of safeguarding not only the employees but also all key stakeholders and all the key aspects of the business.

Third, it helps to maintain profitability.

Fourth, it ensures a timely response.

Fifth, it helps meet statutory and legal requirements.

And last but not least, it helps maintain brand, image, and reputation in the market.

BCM helps organizations by:

- Reducing disruption likelihood with preventative measures.
- Ensuring swift response and recovery for employee safety and continuous operations.
- Incorporating legal requirements in the continuity policy.
- Minimizing revenue loss by quickly recovering services and reducing customer impact.

- Limiting critical decisions during crises and reducing dependency on specific personnel.
- Maintaining supplier relationships for quick emergency responses.
- Preserving public image through effective crisis communication.

During a disruptive incident, business continuity answers these three questions for everyone involved:

- Where do I go?
- What should I do?
- When should I do it?

6.2 RESILIENCE APPROACH TOWARDS BUSINESS CONTINUITY

In BCM, we proactively address threats and their potential impacts, establishing a framework to help the organization recover from disruptive incidents while enhancing its response capabilities. This approach not only protects the interests of key stakeholders but also preserves the business's value-creating activities, brand, and reputation.

The use of the term "Business Continuity Management" instead of "business continuity planning" is intentional. The term "planning" implies a finite process with a start and end, which can lead to unnecessary bureaucratic procedures. However, business continuity planning remains an essential part of the BCM process. Unlike earlier, narrower, and reactive approaches to BCM, it is now recognized as a dynamic, proactive, and ongoing business-as-usual management process. For BCM to be effective, it must align with or conform to a standard that is practical, realistic, up-to-date, effective, and proven to provide a plausible capability.

Core Principles of Resilience Approach

- *Integration of Key Components*: This model brings together disaster recovery, business resumption, crisis management, and event management into a unified framework, ensuring that all aspects of continuity and resilience are addressed holistically.
- *Focus on Uncertainty and Complexity*: It highlights that the business environment is characterized by rapid change and fundamental uncertainties, including unknown risks ("unknown unknowns") that cannot be fully anticipated or modeled. He argues that organizations should not rely solely on risk modeling, as overconfidence in models can lead to flawed preparedness.
- *Capacity and Capability Over Prediction*: Rather than attempting to predict every possible disruption, it advocates for building the organization's capacity and capability to respond to consequences as they arise. This means developing targeted flexibility—the ability to adapt

and respond to unforeseen events, rather than preparing for specific, predicted scenarios.

- *Iterative, Top-Down Planning*: It recommends an iterative, top-down approach to risk assessment and business impact analysis (BIA), which helps identify "unknown knowns" (overlooked vulnerabilities or gaps in planning). This approach ensures that planning is dynamic and continuously updated as new information emerges.
- *Graceful Degradation and Agile Restoration*: It introduces the concepts of "graceful degradation" (the ability to maintain essential functions at reduced capacity during disruption) and "agile restoration" (the ability to quickly recover and adapt post-disruption), both of which are central to organizational resilience.
- *Assessment Tools and Exercises*: His methodology includes practical tools, assessment frameworks, and exercises to help organizations evaluate their resilience, test their plans, and identify areas for improvement.

Key Takeaways

- Resilience is about preparation and adaptability, not just prediction.
- Integrated planning ensures all aspects of continuity are addressed.
- Organizations should build flexible, responsive capabilities rather than relying solely on risk models.
- Continuous assessment and improvement are essential for maintaining resilience in an uncertain world.

6.3 GRACEFUL DEGRADATION—NETFLIX'S CHAOS ENGINEERING

Netflix, the global streaming giant serving over 200 million subscribers worldwide, pioneered an innovative approach to resilience called Chaos Engineering. This approach fundamentally changed how organizations think about system reliability and failure management. Rather than waiting for failures to occur naturally, Netflix deliberately introduces controlled failures into their systems to identify weaknesses before they affect customers.

The concept originated in 2010 when Netflix was transitioning from physical data centers to Amazon Web Services (AWS) cloud infrastructure. The engineering team recognized that in large distributed systems, failures are inevitable. Instead of trying to prevent all failures—an impossible task—they developed a strategy to ensure their services would degrade gracefully when components failed, maintaining acceptable service levels even during significant disruptions.

At the heart of Netflix's Chaos Engineering practice is a suite of tools collectively known as the Simian Army. The most famous of these tools, Chaos Monkey, randomly terminates instances in production to ensure that engineers build services that are resilient to instance failures. Other tools in the suite include Latency Monkey (introduces artificial delays), Conformity Monkey (shuts down instances that don't adhere to best practices), and Chaos Kong (simulates the failure of an entire AWS region).

The implementation of Chaos Engineering at Netflix follows a structured methodology:

1. Define the "steady state" that represents normal operation
2. Hypothesize that this steady state will continue during experiments
3. Introduce variables that reflect real-world events (server failures, network issues)
4. Look for differences between the control group and experimental group

This approach has yielded significant benefits for Netflix. By continuously testing their systems against potential failures, they've built an infrastructure that can withstand major disruptions with minimal customer impact. During the 2017 AWS S3 outage that affected numerous internet services, Netflix maintained operations with minimal disruption because their systems were designed to handle such failures.

The Netflix case demonstrates that graceful degradation—the ability of a system to maintain limited functionality even when a large portion of it is inoperable—is achievable through deliberate, controlled testing and design principles that anticipate failure. Organizations across industries have adopted similar approaches, recognizing that in complex systems, resilience comes not from preventing all failures but from designing systems that can continue functioning despite them (Table 6.1).

6.3.1 Conclusion

Netflix's chaos engineering is a practical, systems-thinking approach to ensuring graceful degradation. By intentionally exposing systems to failure and validating their ability to degrade service gracefully—rather than fail outright—Netflix delivers high availability and a seamless user experience, even during unexpected disruption.

Table 6.1 Graceful degradation in Netflix's chaos engineering

Principle	*Netflix practice*
Failure injection	Chaos Monkey randomly terminates instances in production
Observability	Extensive monitoring and feedback loops
Fallback mechanisms	Serve degraded but functional service (e.g., generic recommendations)
Automated recovery	Automated fixes and failover to healthy regions
Controlled experiments	Minimize blast radius, use feature flags, rollback if needed
Continuous improvement	Refine systems based on experiment insights

6.4 AGILE RESTORATION—TOYOTA'S RESPONSE DURING 2011 JAPAN EARTHQUAKE AND TSUNAMI

On March 11, 2011, a magnitude 9.0 earthquake struck off Japan's northeastern coast, triggering a devastating tsunami and nuclear crisis. This triple disaster presented unprecedented challenges to Japanese businesses, with Toyota Motor Corporation facing one of its most significant operational disruptions in history. Toyota's response to this catastrophe has become a textbook example of agile restoration in business continuity management.

Toyota's global supply chain, renowned for its just-in-time inventory system, was severely impacted. The disaster affected 659 of Toyota's suppliers, completely halting production at all Japanese plants for several weeks and reducing global production by 40%. The company faced an estimated production loss of 140,000 vehicles in the immediate aftermath, with financial losses projected at $72 million per day.

What distinguished Toyota's response was its agile restoration approach—a methodology focused on rapidly adapting to changing circumstances and restoring critical functions through flexible, iterative processes. Unlike traditional recovery approaches that follow predetermined plans, agile restoration emphasizes real-time problem-solving and collaborative innovation.

Within hours of the disaster, Toyota activated its emergency response center and deployed disaster assessment teams. Rather than relying solely on formal reporting structures, the company leveraged its keiretsu network—a system of interconnected suppliers with whom Toyota maintained close relationships. This network enabled rapid information sharing about supplier status, damage assessments, and resource availability.

Toyota's restoration strategy included several innovative elements. First, they implemented a comprehensive supply chain visualization initiative, mapping over 30,000 parts to identify critical components and alternative sourcing options. This visualization allowed them to prioritize restoration efforts based on production impact rather than following standard procedures.

Second, Toyota temporarily modified its production processes to accommodate parts shortages. In some cases, they reverted to more manual processes that required fewer electronic components, which were in short supply due to damage to semiconductor manufacturing facilities. This flexibility allowed partial production to resume while suppliers recovered.

Third, Toyota deployed engineering teams to assist suppliers with restoration efforts, sharing technical expertise and resources across organizational boundaries. In one notable case, engineers from multiple companies collaborated to rebuild specialized manufacturing equipment in weeks rather than the months it would typically require.

Perhaps most remarkably, Toyota adjusted its famed production system principles to meet the crisis. While the company normally emphasized efficiency through minimal inventory, they temporarily increased strategic parts inventories for critical components and established redundant supply sources—a significant departure from their standard practices but necessary for resilience.

By May 2011, just two months after the disaster, Toyota had restored 70% of its production capacity. Full production capability returned by September 2011, significantly faster than initial projections. This rapid recovery demonstrated the effectiveness of agile restoration principles in extreme circumstances.

The Toyota case illustrates several key lessons for business continuity. First, relationships and networks often prove more valuable than formal plans during major disruptions. Second, visualization of complex systems enables better decision-making under pressure. Third, the willingness to temporarily modify core business principles may be necessary for effective restoration. Finally, collaborative problem-solving across organizational boundaries can dramatically accelerate recovery timeframes.

Toyota's experience led to lasting changes in their approach to business continuity. The company increased geographic diversification of critical suppliers, implemented more robust risk assessment processes, and institutionalized the agile restoration methodologies developed during the crisis. These changes have strengthened Toyota's resilience against subsequent disruptions, including the COVID-19 pandemic.

6.5 CRITICAL THINKING—HURRICANE KATRINA RESPONSE BY OCHSNER HEALTH SYSTEM

When Hurricane Katrina made landfall near New Orleans on August 29, 2005, it precipitated one of the most catastrophic natural disasters in U.S. history. The hurricane and subsequent flooding devastated the region's healthcare infrastructure, with 11 of 16 hospitals in Orleans Parish forced to evacuate and close. Amid this unprecedented crisis, Ochsner Health System emerged as a remarkable exception—the only full-service hospital to remain operational throughout the disaster and its aftermath.

Ochsner's success in maintaining critical healthcare services during Hurricane Katrina exemplifies the vital role of critical thinking in business continuity—the ability to analyze complex situations, challenge assumptions, evaluate evidence, and make sound decisions under extreme pressure and uncertainty. This approach enabled Ochsner to protect patients and staff while continuing to provide essential medical care when it was most needed.

Ochsner's critical thinking approach to business continuity began well before Katrina struck. The organization had developed a comprehensive hurricane plan based on a critical analysis of previous storms, particularly Hurricane Ivan in 2004, which had prompted a costly but ultimately unnecessary evacuation. Learning from this experience, Ochsner's leadership questioned the conventional wisdom that evacuation was always the safest option during hurricanes. They conducted a rigorous risk assessment that considered multiple factors: the hospital's structural integrity, elevation (27 feet above sea level), backup power systems, water supply, and the medical risks of moving critically ill patients.

This analysis led to a controversial decision: rather than evacuating, Ochsner would shelter in place during major hurricanes, maintaining operations with a core team of staff. This decision reflected critical thinking at its best—evaluating evidence, considering alternatives, and making a reasoned judgment despite external pressure to follow conventional approaches.

When Katrina struck, Ochsner activated its "Code Gray" hurricane protocol, implementing a carefully designed incident command structure. The hospital's leadership team established a command center that became the hub for information gathering, analysis, and decision-making. As conditions deteriorated across the city, Ochsner's leaders faced a cascade of unprecedented challenges requiring rapid critical assessment and action.

One critical decision point came when city water pressure failed. Ochsner's facilities team quickly analyzed the situation and implemented an innovative solution—using available construction equipment to drill a well into the aquifer beneath the hospital, providing a sustainable water source for essential functions. This exemplified critical thinking under pressure—identifying the core problem, generating creative alternatives, and implementing a solution with available resources.

Communication systems presented another major challenge. When conventional telecommunications failed, Ochsner's IT team critically evaluated available options and established a satellite communication system that maintained essential connections with the outside world. They also repurposed internal systems to create information-sharing mechanisms that kept staff informed about rapidly changing conditions.

Perhaps most impressively, Ochsner's medical teams engaged in continuous critical thinking about patient care under disaster conditions. With limited resources and no possibility of transfer for critical patients, physicians and nurses had to evaluate standard protocols, adapt treatments, and make difficult triage decisions. This included converting non-clinical spaces into treatment areas, modifying medication regimens based on available supplies, and developing alternative care protocols when standard equipment wasn't available.

Throughout the crisis, Ochsner's leadership maintained a commitment to evidence-based decision-making despite the emotional intensity of the situation. They established regular briefing cycles where information was gathered, assumptions were challenged, options were evaluated, and decisions were made transparently. This disciplined approach to critical thinking prevented panic reactions and enabled more effective resource allocation.

Ochsner's experience during Hurricane Katrina demonstrates that critical thinking is not just an individual skill but can be institutionalized as an organizational approach to business continuity. By fostering a culture that values analysis over assumption, evidence over emotion, and reasoned judgment over

Table 6.2 Outcomes and lessons

Metric	*Pre-Katrina (2005)*	*Post-reforms (2023)*
Evacuation compliance rate	67%	92%
Levee failure risk	1-in-100 years	1-in-500 years
Economic recovery timeline	14 years	5 years (2028 Ida)

reactive decision-making, organizations can navigate even the most extreme disruptions.

In the years following Katrina, Ochsner Health System has further developed its critical thinking approach to resilience. The organization has implemented structured after-action reviews that critically examine responses to disruptions, identifying both successes and opportunities for improvement. They've also established simulation programs that present complex scenarios requiring critical analysis, helping staff develop these skills before they're needed in real crises (Table 6.2).

6.5.1 Conclusion

Hurricane Katrina exemplifies how unknown unknowns arise from *systemic complexity*, not isolated events. Organizations prioritizing *adaptive resilience* (AWS), *scenario planning* (Bain), and *agile governance* now recover 3× faster than those relying solely on risk modeling. As climate and cyber threats escalate, the lesson is clear: Prepare for the unimaginable by designing systems that thrive amid uncertainty.

6.6 RESPONSE AND RECOVERY—QATAR DIPLOMATIC CRISIS AND BLOCKADE (2017)

On June 5, 2017, Saudi Arabia, the United Arab Emirates, Bahrain, and Egypt severed diplomatic ties with Qatar and imposed a comprehensive blockade, closing land, sea, and air routes to the country. This unprecedented diplomatic crisis created an extraordinary business continuity challenge for Qatar, a nation that imported approximately 90% of its food and a significant portion of construction materials and other essential goods through now-closed borders.

The Qatar diplomatic crisis and subsequent blockade represents one of the most instructive modern case studies in national-scale response and recovery—the systematic process of addressing immediate crisis needs while simultaneously rebuilding systems and capabilities for long-term sustainability. Qatar's approach to this geopolitical and economic disruption offers valuable lessons for organizations facing complex, prolonged business continuity challenges.

Qatar's initial response focused on immediate stabilization. Within 24 hours of the blockade announcement, the government established a crisis management committee with representatives from key ministries, Qatar Airways, the ports authority, and major businesses. This cross-functional team conducted rapid impact assessments across critical sectors—food security, transportation, banking, construction, and energy—to identify immediate vulnerabilities and prioritize response actions.

Food security emerged as the most urgent concern. With dairy products, fresh produce, and poultry previously imported primarily through Saudi Arabia, Qatar faced potential shortages of essential items. The response was swift and multifaceted. Qatar Airways repurposed passenger aircraft for food transportation, establishing new air freight routes from Turkey, Iran, and Oman within days. Simultaneously, the government worked with retailers to prevent panic buying by maintaining price controls and ensuring equitable distribution.

In the transportation sector, Qatar rapidly reconfigured its logistics networks. Hamad Port, which had fortunately opened just months before the crisis, was quickly expanded to handle increased shipping volume. New maritime routes were established with Oman, Turkey, Pakistan, and other nations, replacing the previous hub-and-spoke system that had relied on UAE ports for transshipment.

The financial sector faced different challenges. With Qatari banks cut off from counterparts in blockading countries, there was potential for liquidity issues and disruption to international transactions. Qatar's central bank injected liquidity into the banking system and established new correspondent banking relationships, particularly with Asian financial institutions, to maintain international payment capabilities.

What distinguished Qatar's approach was the rapid transition from emergency response to strategic recovery. Rather than viewing the blockade as a temporary disruption to be endured, Qatari leadership recognized it as a catalyst for fundamental economic transformation. This perspective shift—from crisis management to opportunity identification—characterizes the most effective recovery strategies.

Qatar's recovery strategy emphasized three interconnected priorities: supply chain reconfiguration, domestic capacity building, and economic diversification. Each of these represented a deliberate effort to emerge from the crisis with greater resilience than before.

Supply chain reconfiguration went beyond emergency rerouting to establish entirely new trade relationships and logistics networks. Qatar invested in dedicated shipping lines, purchased its own cargo fleet, and developed new port facilities specifically designed to bypass former regional hubs. These investments created permanent alternatives rather than temporary workarounds.

Domestic capacity building focused on reducing import dependence in critical sectors. The most visible example was dairy production. Before the blockade, Qatar imported 80% of its dairy products from Saudi Arabia. Within months, Qatar established domestic dairy farms with airlifted Holstein cows, achieving self-sufficiency in milk production by April 2018. Similar initiatives in greenhouse agriculture, poultry production, and manufacturing reduced vulnerability to external disruptions.

Economic diversification accelerated existing plans to reduce Qatar's dependence on hydrocarbon exports. The government increased investment in knowledge economy sectors, expanded the Qatar Financial Centre to attract international firms, and leveraged the crisis to reform regulations that had previously limited foreign investment. These structural changes strengthened Qatar's economic foundation beyond the immediate crisis response.

Throughout the blockade period, Qatar maintained a sophisticated communication strategy that balanced transparency about challenges with confidence in recovery efforts. Regular updates from government officials kept citizens informed while carefully managing expectations. This approach maintained public trust and prevented the social disruption that often accompanies economic crises.

By the time the blockade ended in January 2021, Qatar had not only recovered from its initial impacts but had transformed its economy in ways that created greater resilience. Food self-sufficiency had increased from 10% to nearly 30%, new trade relationships had diversified import sources, and domestic industries had developed in previously underdeveloped sectors.

The Qatar case demonstrates that effective response and recovery in business continuity isn't simply about returning to pre-disruption conditions—it's about strategic adaptation that transforms vulnerabilities into strengths. Organizations facing major disruptions can apply similar principles: stabilize immediate operations, reconfigure supply networks, build internal capabilities, and use the disruption as a catalyst for beneficial transformation.

6.7 LEARNING OBJECTIVES

6.7.1 Enabling organizations to anticipate, prepare for, respond to, and recover from disruptions effectively

The foundation of effective business continuity management lies in developing systematic approaches to anticipation, preparation, response, and recovery. Organizations must build capabilities across all four dimensions to achieve true resilience.

Anticipation begins with comprehensive risk identification and assessment. Organizations should implement horizon scanning processes that look beyond immediate threats to identify emerging risks and changing risk landscapes. This includes analyzing geopolitical trends, technological disruptions, climate patterns, and other factors that could create future business interruptions. Netflix's Chaos Engineering approach exemplifies anticipation at its most proactive—deliberately seeking out potential failure points before they manifest in real-world disruptions.

Preparation transforms risk awareness into practical readiness. This includes developing business continuity plans, establishing governance structures, allocating resources, and building organizational capabilities. Effective preparation requires regular exercising of plans and capabilities under realistic conditions. Ochsner Health System's preparation for Hurricane Katrina demonstrated the importance of learning from previous experiences and challenging conventional approaches when developing preparedness strategies.

Response capabilities enable organizations to act decisively when disruptions occur. This requires clear decision-making frameworks, established communication channels, and predefined roles and responsibilities. Toyota's response to the Japan earthquake and tsunami highlights the importance of flexible, adaptive response mechanisms that can function even when formal systems are compromised. Their use of existing relationship networks to gather information and coordinate actions demonstrates that effective response often depends more on organizational culture than on documented procedures.

Recovery focuses on restoring operations and adapting to new realities. Qatar's experience during the diplomatic blockade illustrates how recovery can be transformative rather than merely restorative. By using the crisis as an opportunity to build new capabilities and reduce vulnerabilities, Qatar emerged stronger than before the disruption. Organizations should approach recovery with a similar strategic vision, seeking opportunities to build greater resilience through the recovery process.

To enable these capabilities, organizations should:

Establish integrated risk management frameworks that connect business continuity with enterprise risk management, ensuring that continuity planning addresses the most significant organizational risks.

Develop scenario-based planning approaches that prepare the organization for a range of potential disruptions rather than specific predicted events. This builds adaptive capacity that can respond to unexpected situations.

Implement regular testing and exercising programs that validate plans, build team capabilities, and identify improvement opportunities. These should include both technical tests (e.g., IT recovery) and scenario exercises that test decision-making under pressure.

Create knowledge management systems that capture lessons from disruptions, exercises, and near-misses, ensuring that organizational learning continuously strengthens resilience capabilities.

Foster a resilience-oriented culture where continuity considerations are integrated into everyday decision-making rather than treated as a separate compliance activity.

6.7.2 Understanding the role of continuous improvement in business continuity

Business continuity management is not a static capability but an evolving discipline that requires ongoing refinement and enhancement. Continuous improvement in business continuity involves systematically evaluating and enhancing an organization's ability to maintain operations during disruptions.

The BCM lifecycle, as described earlier, represents a continuous improvement cycle aimed at bolstering organizational resilience through systematic planning and preparedness. This cycle includes six key elements: BCM Policy and Program Management, Understanding the Organization, Developing BCM Strategy, BCM Response, Exercises and Maintenance, and Awareness and Training.

Effective continuous improvement in business continuity requires several key components:

Performance Measurement: Organizations need meaningful metrics to assess their business continuity capabilities. These might include recovery time achievements during exercises, plan coverage across critical functions, training completion rates, or maturity assessments against industry standards. Without measurement, improvement becomes subjective and difficult to validate.

Regular Review Cycles: Business continuity capabilities should be reviewed on scheduled intervals and after significant organizational changes or disruptions. These reviews should examine the continued relevance of recovery strategies, the accuracy of business impact analyses, and the effectiveness of response structures.

Structured Learning Processes: Organizations should implement formal processes to capture and apply lessons from disruptions, exercises, and external events. This includes detailed after-action reviews, root cause analyses, and systematic implementation of identified improvements.

Integration with Management Systems: Business continuity improvement should be integrated with other organizational improvement processes, such as quality management, risk management, and strategic planning. This ensures that continuity considerations are embedded in broader organizational development.

Netflix's Chaos Engineering program exemplifies continuous improvement in action. By constantly testing their systems against potential failures, they create a feedback loop that drives ongoing enhancements to their resilience capabilities. Each test generates insights that inform system design improvements, creating an evolutionary process that continuously strengthens their ability to maintain service during disruptions.

Similarly, Toyota's experience during the Japan earthquake and tsunami led to significant improvements in their business continuity approach.

The company conducted extensive analyses of their response, identified vulnerabilities in their supply chain visibility, and implemented new systems to address these gaps. These improvements were then tested and further refined through subsequent disruptions, creating a continuous cycle of enhancement.

Organizations seeking to implement continuous improvement in business continuity should consider adopting maturity models that provide structured frameworks for assessing and developing capabilities over time. These models typically define progressive levels of capability across multiple dimensions of business continuity, allowing organizations to benchmark their current state and plan systematic advancement.

The Capability Maturity Model for Business Continuity provides one such framework, defining five maturity levels:

1. Initial: Business continuity processes are ad hoc and largely reactive
2. Managed: Basic processes are established but may be inconsistently applied
3. Defined: Standardized processes are documented and implemented across the organization
4. Quantitatively Managed: Processes are measured and controlled using quantitative techniques
5. Optimizing: Continuous improvement is embedded in the organization's approach

By assessing their capabilities against such models, organizations can identify specific improvement opportunities and track their progress over time. This structured approach to continuous improvement ensures that business continuity capabilities evolve in alignment with changing organizational needs and emerging best practices.

6.7.3 Developing capabilities to manage continuity planning across different geographies

In today's globalized business environment, many organizations operate across multiple countries and regions, each with distinct risk profiles, regulatory requirements, and cultural contexts. Developing effective business continuity capabilities across different geographies requires balancing global consistency with local adaptation.

The Qatar diplomatic crisis demonstrates the importance of geographical considerations in business continuity. Qatar's heavy reliance on imports through neighboring countries created a specific geographical vulnerability that became critical during the blockade. Their recovery involved reconfiguring supply chains to create new geographical patterns of trade and developing domestic capabilities to reduce dependence on imports. This case illustrates how geographical factors can fundamentally shape both vulnerabilities and response options.

Organizations operating across multiple geographies face several specific challenges in business continuity management:

Regulatory Variation: Business continuity regulations and standards vary significantly across jurisdictions. Some countries have mandatory requirements for specific sectors, while others rely on voluntary standards. Organizations must navigate this complex regulatory landscape while maintaining consistent internal practices.

Risk Diversity: Different locations face different risk profiles based on factors such as natural hazard exposure, political stability, infrastructure reliability, and security conditions. Business continuity planning must account for this diversity while ensuring comparable resilience across all locations.

Cultural Differences: Approaches to risk, authority, communication, and decision-making vary across cultures. These differences can significantly impact how business continuity plans are developed, communicated, and implemented in different regions.

Resource Disparities: Organizations often have varying levels of resources and capabilities across different locations. Business continuity programs must account for these disparities while ensuring that all critical operations maintain appropriate resilience.

To address these challenges, organizations should consider implementing a globally coordinated, locally adapted approach to business continuity management across different geographies. This approach includes several key elements:

Global Governance Framework: Establish a central governance structure that defines common principles, minimum standards, and key performance indicators for business continuity across all locations. This provides consistency while allowing for necessary local adaptation.

Tiered Planning Approach: Implement a tiered planning structure with global plans addressing enterprise-wide risks and dependencies, regional plans addressing shared regional issues, and local plans addressing location-specific risks and requirements.

Standardized Methodology with Local Application: Use consistent methodologies for business impact analysis, risk assessment, and plan development across all locations, but apply these methodologies to address local conditions and requirements.

Cross-Regional Coordination Mechanisms: Develop formal mechanisms for coordination across regions during disruptions that span multiple geographies. This includes clear escalation paths, communication protocols, and resource-sharing agreements.

Cultural Adaptation: Adapt business continuity communication, training, and exercises to align with local cultural contexts while maintaining consistent underlying principles and objectives.

The benefits of this approach can be seen in multinational organizations that have successfully managed cross-border disruptions. For example, during the 2011 Thailand floods that disrupted global supply chains, companies with strong cross-geographical business continuity capabilities were able to coordinate responses across multiple regions, reallocating production, sharing resources, and maintaining customer service despite significant operational disruptions.

Organizations can assess their geographical business continuity capabilities by examining several key indicators:

Plan Integration: How well integrated are business continuity plans across different locations? Do they account for cross-border dependencies and potential cascading impacts?

Resource Mobility: Can resources (people, equipment, information) be effectively deployed across geographical boundaries during disruptions?

Communication Effectiveness: Do communication systems and protocols function effectively across different languages, time zones, and cultural contexts?

Regulatory Compliance: Do business continuity arrangements meet regulatory requirements in all relevant jurisdictions while maintaining operational coherence?

By developing robust capabilities to manage business continuity across different geographies, organizations can transform what might otherwise be vulnerabilities into strategic advantages, leveraging their global presence to enhance overall resilience.

6.7.3.1 Understanding disruptive incidents

A disruptive incident interrupts business activities by making necessary resources unavailable. Common causes include natural disasters (e.g., Hurricane Sandy, New Orleans tornado, Nepal earthquake), man-made threats (e.g., fire, cyberattacks, data breaches, workplace violence), pandemics, and the loss of key suppliers or partners. These incidents can cause significant resource loss, highlighting the importance of pre-planned strategies for business continuity.

In most organizations, business continuity encompasses more than just a program designed to react to a threatening event. It also involves proactively implementing controls to mitigate the impact of threats affecting the organization or reducing the severity associated with resource downtime during disruptions. To achieve an appropriate level of preparedness, Business Continuity comprises four related processes:

Risk Management: Focuses on analyzing the business to identify key business continuity risks and then treating those risks to decrease the likelihood of disruptive incidents occurring.

Crisis Management: Involves designing strategies and actions to respond to disruptive incidents, assessing the situation to protect people, property, and business activities, while preparing for business recovery.

Business Recovery: Resumes critical activities and resources within an acceptable timeframe, often involving alternate resources or processes.

IT Disaster Recovery: Encompasses the resumption of information technology assets, including infrastructure, applications, data, communications, as well as PCs and servers, based on business requirements. IT is a critical dependency of the business, and business recovery cannot occur without IT recovery. Given its criticality and complexity, IT unavailability can lead to disaster.

6.8 THE BCM LIFECYCLE

The BCM lifecycle concept is derived from the Good Practice Guidance of the BCI. In biology, a biological life cycle refers to a series of changes in form that an organism undergoes, ultimately returning to its initial state. Similarly, the BCM lifecycle delineates the stages of activity that an organization progresses through and repeats with the overall objective of enhancing its continuity.

Here are the six steps of the Business Continuity Management (BCM) lifecycle:

6.8.1 BCM policy and program management

The lifecycle diagram is circular to signify that the individual activities should be repeated periodically and are directed by a defined program framework or management system. This includes clear goals, assigned responsibilities, guidance, standards, and performance monitoring.

6.8.2 Understanding the organization

This step involves conducting a Business Impact Analysis (BIA) and Risk Assessment (RA). The BIA determines how quickly the impacts of business interruptions become unacceptable, identifies process interdependencies, and specifies the assets needed to sustain operations. It provides the basis for deciding which parts of the organization require Business Continuity Plans.

The RA leverages the BIA to determine the impact of critical asset loss and (where possible) the likelihood of undesirable incidents leading to such losses. It forms the basis for implementing controls to reduce the likelihood of asset loss and reactive controls to respond to it. An all-hazard Risk Assessment informs the organization's Incident Response Plans.

6.8.3 Developing the BCM strategy

This strategy utilizes the BIA and RA to enable Executive Management to make informed decisions regarding which risks are acceptable and which must be mitigated. It determines where resources will be allocated to create and maintain the plans and arrangements necessary to ensure business continuity.

6.8.4 BCM response

This phase details the Plans and Arrangements required to ensure business continuity. It encompasses both proactive controls to reduce the likelihood of an interruption and reactive controls to respond to incidents.

6.8.5 Exercises and maintenance

Checking that plans and arrangements are fit for purpose and updating them as necessary is vital to maintaining business continuity capability. Technology and other recovery arrangements must be tested, and people must understand their plans and practice their responses. Anything untested is almost certain to fail when most needed.

6.8.6 Awareness and training

Awareness and training should occur at every stage, ensuring that staff are well-informed and prepared to implement the BCM effectively (Figure 6.1).

6.8.6.1 Types of business continuity plans

There are four main types of business continuity plans:

- Crisis Management Plan supports senior management in quickly assessing the situation, initiating the initial response to the disruptive incident, and leading to the recovery of essential products and services.
- Crisis Communication Plans identify who to contact both internally and externally within the organization and how to contact them. These plans also include pre-drafted approved messages that can be updated when necessary and identified spokespersons.
- IT Disaster Recovery Plan ensures the timely and complete recovery of core technology assets within the management-approved time frame.

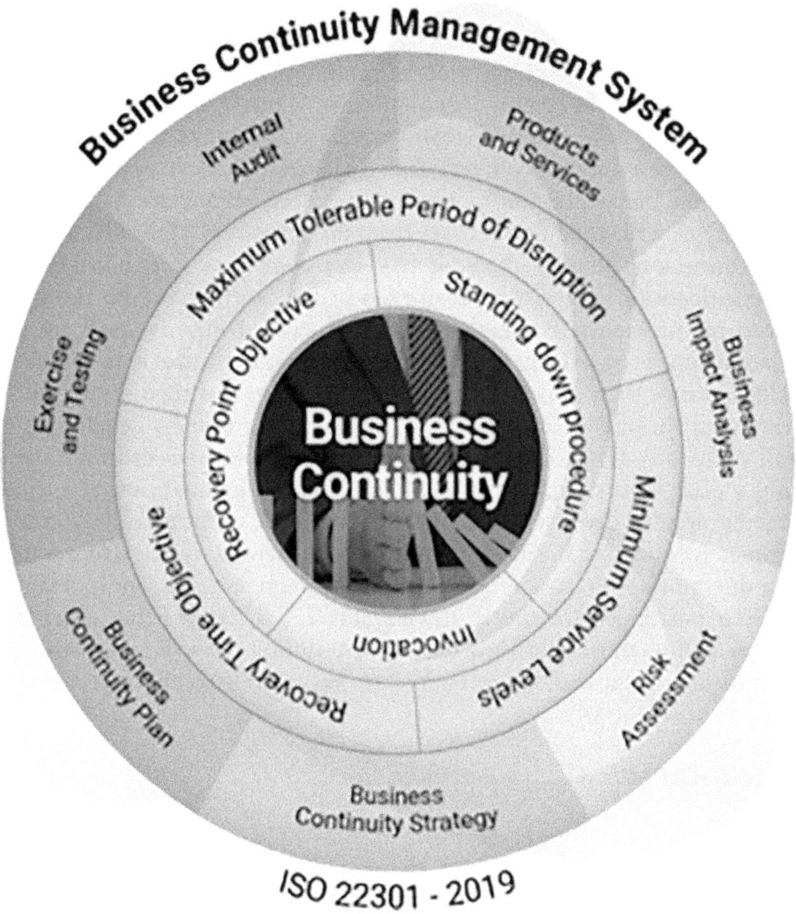

Figure 6.1 Business continuity management lifecycle.

These plans also include predetermined data loss tolerances, known as recovery point objectives (RPO).

- Business Recovery Plan ensures the timely and complete recovery of key business activities within the management-approved timeframe, ensuring core products and services are available to meet stakeholder expectations.

6.9 CONCLUSION

Business continuity planning is a critical component of organizational resilience in today's complex and interconnected business environment. Through the case studies of Netflix's Chaos Engineering, Toyota's response to the Japan earthquake and tsunami, Ochsner Health System's response to Hurricane Katrina, and Qatar's management of the diplomatic blockade, we have explored different approaches to building and maintaining business continuity.

These approaches—graceful degradation, agile restoration, critical thinking, and strategic response and recovery—provide frameworks that organizations can adapt to their specific contexts and challenges. By developing capabilities in anticipation, preparation, response, and recovery, organizations can enhance their ability to withstand and recover from disruptions of all kinds.

The continuous improvement of business continuity capabilities ensures that organizations evolve their resilience in line with changing threats and business requirements. By implementing structured improvement processes and measuring progress against maturity models, organizations can systematically enhance their ability to maintain operations during disruptions.

For organizations operating across multiple geographies, developing integrated yet locally adapted business continuity capabilities is essential. By balancing global consistency with local relevance, organizations can leverage their geographical diversity as a source of resilience rather than vulnerability.

Ultimately, effective business continuity management is not just about surviving disruptions—it's about emerging from them stronger, more adaptable, and better positioned for future success. The organizations that excel in this discipline will be those that view business continuity not as a compliance exercise but as a strategic capability that creates sustainable competitive advantage.

BIBLIOGRAPHY

Andrus, K., Gopalani, N., & Schmaus, B. (2014). FIT: Failure injection testing. Netflix Technology Blog.

Business Continuity Institute (2018). Good practice guidelines 2018 edition. BCI.

International Organization for Standardization. (2019). ISO 22301:2019 Security and resilience—Business continuity management systems—Requirements. ISO.

Quinlan, K. P., & Sacks, J. J. (2002). Preparedness for terrorism: Managing nuclear, biological and chemical threats. The Annals of the American Academy of Political and Social Science, 584(1), 184–200.

Sheffi, Y. (2015). The power of resilience: How the best companies manage the unexpected. MIT Press.

Ulrichsen, K. C. (2017). The Qatar crisis. International Affairs Institute.

Chapter 7

Learning and innovation

Learning Objectives

- How to enable organizations to continuously learn, adapt, innovate, and improve in order to navigate uncertainties, capitalize on opportunities, and sustain long-term resilience and competitiveness.
- Learn to create an environment that encourages continuous learning and adaptation.
- Understand the balance between maintaining operational stability and fostering innovation.

7.1 FOSTERING INNOVATION AND CREATIVITY

Building a culture that promotes innovation and agility in product development, process improvement and re-engineering, or groundbreaking service is fundamental to the success of a business in building competitive advantage and deriving a first-mover advantage in its respective industry. An organizational system where innovation and creativity are always encouraged and rewarded and where generation of new ideas is recognized as a key to its performance.

Innovation is essential for any organization's success, whether it takes the form of incremental improvements or transformational shifts. A structured approach to innovation is critical for ensuring long-term prosperity and sustainability, as it enables organizations to systematically harness creativity, manage risk, and align innovation efforts with strategic objectives.

7.1.1 Why innovation matters

Competitive Advantage: Innovation allows organizations to differentiate themselves in crowded markets, develop unique products or services, and respond proactively to evolving customer needs.

Growth and Adaptability: Both incremental (evolutionary) and transformational (revolutionary) changes are necessary for growth. Incremental

DOI: 10.1201/9781003597520-7

innovation drives continuous improvement and efficiency, while transformational innovation can open new markets or redefine industries.

Resilience and Sustainability: Organizations that innovate are better equipped to anticipate and respond to disruptions, making them more resilient in the face of market or technological changes.

7.1.2 The importance of a structured approach

A structured approach to innovation ensures that creativity is not left to chance but is embedded in the organization's strategy, processes, and culture. This involves:

- Portfolio Management: Balancing incremental, breakthrough, and transformational innovations to optimize both short-term gains and long-term impact.
- Clear Processes: Establishing frameworks for idea generation, evaluation, development, and scaling, so that promising innovations are systematically identified and nurtured.
- Supportive Culture: Encouraging risk-taking, learning from failure, and rewarding innovative thinking at all levels of the organization.
- Alignment with Strategy: Ensuring that innovation initiatives support the organization's broader goals and are resourced appropriately.

7.1.3 Case study: IBM innovation journey

International Business Machines (IBM) stands as one of the most enduring examples of how innovation management and organizational learning can drive multiple successful business transformations over more than a century. From its origins as a collection of disparate companies to becoming a global technology leader, IBM's journey illustrates key principles of fostering innovation, managing organizational change, and building resilience through continuous learning and adaptation.

IBM's commitment to innovation began with the establishment of the Watson Scientific Computing Laboratory at Columbia University in 1945—the first corporate pure-science research facility in the United States. This laboratory, which would eventually evolve into IBM Research, was founded with an unusual mandate: "explore science, forget profits." This philosophy established a foundation for innovation that prioritized scientific discovery and collaboration over immediate commercial returns.

Thomas J. Watson Sr., IBM's early leader, made a strategic decision to place the laboratory on a university campus rather than in corporate buildings, emphasizing the importance of proximity to academic researchers and fostering an open environment for scientific freedom. The laboratory's first director, Wallace Eckert, articulated this ethos clearly: "Problems will be accepted because of scientific interest and not for any other considerations."

This early commitment to pure research established a culture where innovation could flourish independently from short-term business pressures—a radical approach that would become central to IBM's long-term success and resilience.

IBM's history of innovation is inseparable from its capacity for strategic transformation. The company's origins as Computing-Tabulating-Recording Company (CTR) in 1911 represented an amalgamation of businesses with little synergy, heavy debt, and overvalued stock. The hiring of Thomas J. Watson Sr. as general manager in 1914 marked the beginning of IBM's first major transformation.

Watson implemented several strategic initiatives that laid the foundation for innovation:

1. Building a culture of execution by aligning daily actions with measurable targets that were part of the company's strategy
2. Creating cross-functional collaboration by bringing product developers and manufacturing staff into the same building
3. Developing a shared system of beliefs and practices that empowered employees to make consistent decisions
4. Establishing customer training programs that generated valuable feedback and ideas

These initiatives transformed a struggling conglomerate into a cohesive organization with a clear purpose, eventually renamed as International Business Machines (IBM). This early transformation demonstrates how leadership that fosters collaboration, clear communication, and customer engagement can create an environment where innovation thrives.

In 1956, IBM formalized its commitment to innovation by creating an independent research division, bringing together the Watson Lab and three other small labs. This decision institutionalized innovation within IBM's organizational structure and business model.

Today, IBM Research stands as the largest corporate research organization in the world, with 3,000 scientists across 12 labs on six continents. This global research network has been responsible for numerous breakthrough innovations, including:

- The development of the first magnetic hard disk drive (RAMAC)
- The invention of the relational database
- Pioneering work in artificial intelligence, including Deep Blue and Watson
- Fundamental advances in quantum computing

IBM's research model demonstrates how sustained investment in innovation—even during economic downturns—can build organizational resilience and create long-term competitive advantage. The company has led

U.S. companies in patents received annually for 29 consecutive years, with more than 8,500 patents in recent years.

Perhaps IBM's most valuable innovation capability has been its willingness to reinvent itself in response to changing market conditions. IBM scientists and engineers have been at the heart of this "relentless reinvention," guided by the core principle of delivering innovation that matters for both the company and the world.

Major transformations in IBM's history include:

1. From hardware to services: In the 1990s, under CEO Lou Gerstner, IBM pivoted from primarily selling hardware to becoming a services-led company, recognizing the changing needs of enterprise customers.
2. From services to solutions: In the early 2000s, IBM further evolved to focus on integrated business solutions, acquiring PwC Consulting and emphasizing high-value offerings.
3. Embracing cloud and AI: Most recently, IBM has transformed again to focus on hybrid cloud computing and artificial intelligence, including the acquisition of Red Hat for $34 billion in 2019.

Each transformation required not only technological innovation but also organizational learning and adaptation. IBM's ability to recognize change early and decisively transform its business has been crucial to its longevity.

IBM's approach to innovation management combines structured processes with cultural elements that encourage creativity and risk-taking:

IBM maintains a portfolio approach to innovation, investing simultaneously in:

- Incremental innovations that improve existing products and services
- Adjacent innovations that extend current capabilities into new markets
- Transformational innovations that create entirely new markets or business models

This balanced approach ensures both short-term results and long-term growth opportunities.

IBM has embraced open innovation models, including:

- Contributing to open-source projects (e.g., Linux, Apache)
- Establishing collaborative research partnerships with universities
- Creating innovation hubs that bring together clients, partners, and researchers

These collaborative approaches expand IBM's innovation capacity beyond its organizational boundaries.

IBM employs formal processes to manage innovation, including:

- Innovation Jams: Large-scale collaborative events that generate and develop ideas
- First-of-a-Kind (FOAK) projects: Partnerships with clients to develop novel solutions
- Emerging Business Opportunities (EBO): Internal incubators for promising new business areas

These structured approaches ensure that creative ideas are systematically identified, developed, and scaled.

A critical aspect of IBM's innovation culture has been its approach to failure. The company has demonstrated that learning from setbacks is essential for long-term innovation success.

Notable examples include:

- The failure of OS/2 operating system, which led to valuable lessons about platform ecosystems
- Early struggles with PC manufacturing, which informed later strategic shifts
- Challenges in the early days of cloud computing, which shaped IBM's hybrid cloud strategy

By treating failures as learning opportunities rather than career-ending events, IBM has created an environment where calculated risks are encouraged and the knowledge gained from unsuccessful ventures contributes to future success.

Today, IBM's innovation efforts are focused on addressing major global challenges through accelerated discovery—the combination of high-performance computing, AI, and quantum computing integrated through the hybrid cloud.

As stated by IBM leadership: "Our priority has always been leading the frontiers of computing and its relationship to business, science, professions, and society." This focus on applying technological innovation to meaningful problems continues to drive IBM's research and development activities.

IBM's century-plus journey offers several key lessons for organizations seeking to build innovation capabilities:

1. Institutionalize innovation through dedicated research functions with appropriate autonomy
2. Balance short-term results with long-term exploration
3. Create a culture that values scientific inquiry and learning from failure
4. Develop the strategic instinct to recognize when transformation is needed
5. Maintain close connections between innovation activities and customer needs
6. Foster open collaboration across organizational boundaries

By embodying these principles, IBM has demonstrated remarkable resilience and adaptability, transforming itself multiple times while maintaining a consistent commitment to innovation that creates value for business and society.

This case illustrates how effective innovation management—combining structured processes, cultural elements, and strategic leadership—can enable an organization to continuously learn, adapt, and thrive through changing market conditions and technological disruptions.

7.1.3.1 Conclusion

Innovation—whether incremental or transformational—is not a one-off event but a continuous, structured process. Organizations that adopt a disciplined approach to innovation are better positioned to thrive, adapt, and sustain success in a rapidly changing world.

7.2 INNOVATION MANAGEMENT

Innovation management plays a critical role in building resilient organizations by enabling them to anticipate, adapt to, and thrive amid disruptions. Resilient organizations are characterized by agility, robustness, and the ability to integrate new ideas quickly, which are all fostered by effective innovation management practices.

Key Aspects of Innovation Management for Organizational Resilience

1. Decentralized and Inclusive Innovation

   Encouraging innovation at all levels—rather than restricting it to a central team—empowers employees throughout the organization to contribute ideas. This decentralized approach increases the diversity and volume of ideas, enhancing the organization's capacity to respond quickly and effectively to unexpected challenges.

   Collaboration with customers and external partners further broadens the pool of potential solutions, increasing adaptability and preparedness for future crises.
2. Pre-Shock Strategic Emphasis on Innovation

   Organizations that prioritize innovation before a crisis are better positioned to maintain stability and flexibility when disruptions occur. Empirical research shows that firms with a track record of product introductions and a top management focus on innovation weather systemic shocks (like the Global Financial Crisis or the COVID-19 pandemic) more successfully than those that do not.

   This proactive stance ensures that innovation is embedded in the company's DNA, making it easier to pivot and adapt when needed.

3. Agile and Flexible Processes
   Innovation management encourages experimentation, rapid prototyping, and iterative development. These agile methodologies allow organizations to test assumptions, learn quickly, and make necessary adjustments in real time, which is essential for resilience in volatile environments.
   Flexibility is a core asset, enabling companies to shift strategies and operations swiftly in response to changing circumstances.
4. Organizational Learning and a Growth Mindset
   Resilient organizations foster a culture of continuous learning, where failures are viewed as opportunities for growth and improvement. This mindset supports both innovation and resilience, as teams are more willing to experiment and adapt to new realities.
   Organizational learning acts as a mediator between innovation management and resilience, enhancing the ability to absorb shocks and maintain high performance.
5. Leadership Commitment and Supportive Culture
   Leadership buy-in is essential for embedding innovation into the organization's strategy and culture. Leaders must communicate the importance of innovation, provide resources, and incentivize creative behaviors across all levels.
   A supportive culture, where risk-taking is encouraged and recognized, helps sustain innovation efforts and ensures resilience is a shared organizational value.
6. Human-Centered and Strategic Alignment
   Aligning innovation activities with the organization's broader goals ensures that efforts are purposeful and contribute to long-term resilience.
   Human-centered approaches, such as design thinking and scenario planning, keep innovation relevant to customer needs and market realities, further strengthening organizational adaptability.

7.2.1 Real-World example

Resource Group, a technology leader in the Middle East and Africa, exemplifies how innovation drives resilience. By embracing change and prioritizing innovation-even in unstable environments-the company has emerged stronger from challenging periods. Leadership's focus on sustainable change and a culture that encourages new ideas have been key to their ongoing success.

7.2.2 Case study: Google's acquisition of DeepMind

Google's acquisition of DeepMind in 2014 stands as a landmark example of innovation management driving organizational resilience, technological leadership, and transformative impact.

7.2.3 Background

DeepMind was founded in 2010 in London by Demis Hassabis, Shane Legg, and Mustafa Suleyman, with a mission to push the boundaries of artificial intelligence by combining machine learning and neuroscience to build general-purpose learning algorithms.

In 2014, Google acquired DeepMind for a reported $400 million, integrating its expertise and research-driven culture into Google's broader innovation ecosystem.

7.2.4 Innovation management insights from the acquisition

1. Strategic Alignment and Vision

   Google recognized AI as a critical driver for its future products and services, from search and speech recognition to autonomous vehicles and healthcare.

   DeepMind's mission to develop general-purpose AI was directly aligned with Google's ambition to lead in AI-driven innovation, making the acquisition a strategic fit.
2. Empowering Breakthrough Research

   DeepMind operated with a research-focused business model, prioritizing scientific discovery and long-term impact over immediate commercial returns.

   Google provided DeepMind with resources, computational power, and global reach, amplifying its ability to pursue ambitious projects like AlphaGo and AlphaFold.

   Notably, AlphaGo's 2016 victory over a world champion Go player marked a milestone in AI, demonstrating the power of reinforcement learning and deep neural networks.
3. Fostering a Culture of Innovation

   Google allowed DeepMind to maintain a degree of independence, preserving its startup culture and commitment to scientific rigor.

   This autonomy enabled DeepMind to attract top-tier AI talent and pursue high-risk, high-reward research, fueling ongoing innovation.
4. Application to Real-World Problems

   The collaboration has led to advancements in healthcare (e.g., AlphaFold's protein structure prediction, AI-powered medical imaging), energy efficiency, and climate change solutions.

   DeepMind's research has been applied to optimize Google's own operations, such as reducing energy usage in data centers.
5. Ethical and Responsible Innovation

   DeepMind and Google have emphasized the importance of ethical AI development, including the establishment of review boards and guidelines for responsible research.

   This approach reflects innovation management principles that balance breakthrough progress with societal impact and risk mitigation.

Outcomes and Impact

- Technological Leadership: Google DeepMind has cemented Google's position at the forefront of AI research and application, outpacing many competitors.
- Organizational Resilience: The acquisition enabled Google to adapt rapidly to the AI revolution, integrating transformative technologies into its core products and services.
- Cross-Industry Influence: DeepMind's breakthroughs have influenced not only technology but also healthcare, life sciences (spawning Isomorphic Labs), and other sectors.
- Sustained Innovation: The partnership exemplifies how structured innovation management-through strategic vision, resource allocation, talent empowerment, and ethical oversight-can deliver continuous, industry-defining advancements.

7.2.5 Conclusion

Google's acquisition and management of DeepMind illustrate how innovation management can be leveraged to build a resilient, future-ready organization. By aligning strategic goals, empowering research, fostering a culture of autonomy and ethics, and applying AI to real-world challenges, Google has turned DeepMind into a powerhouse of innovation with global impact.

7.3 INNOVATION PROGRAM

To build an innovation program in a resilient organization, you need to integrate innovation management practices with resilience-building strategies. This ensures the organization can adapt, thrive, and maintain a competitive edge even during disruptions. Here's a detailed approach, supported by real-world insights:

Key Steps to Building an Innovation Program in a Resilient Organization

1. Foster a Culture of Innovation and Psychological Safety
   Encourage employees at all levels to share ideas, experiment, and take calculated risks without fear of failure or stigma. Celebrate both successes and lessons learned from failures to normalize experimentation and continuous improvement.
2. Align Innovation with Organizational Strategy
   Ensure innovation initiatives directly support the organization's core mission and long-term goals. Regularly communicate how innovation efforts contribute to resilience and strategic objectives, keeping everyone aligned and motivated.

3. Invest in People and Well-Being
   Provide training, mentoring, and resources that empower employees to innovate and adapt. Support mental and emotional health, creating an environment where employees feel safe to challenge the status quo and propose new solutions.
4. Promote Continuous Learning and a Growth Mindset
   Offer regular opportunities for upskilling, cross-functional collaboration, and exposure to new ideas. Encourage curiosity, adaptability, and learning from both internal and external sources to stay ahead of industry trends.
5. Establish Agile and Flexible Processes
   Implement agile methodologies, such as iterative development, rapid prototyping, and cross-functional teams, to accelerate innovation and responsiveness to change. Streamline decision-making and resource allocation to quickly pivot and scale promising ideas.
6. Create Structures for Idea Generation and Experimentation
   Set up regular brainstorming sessions, innovation labs, or digital platforms where employees can submit and develop ideas. Provide resources and time for experimentation, and establish clear pathways for scaling successful innovations.
7. Leverage Technology and Data
   Use digital tools, analytics, and automation to support innovation, enhance agility, and inform decision-making. Embrace digital transformation to unlock new business models and operational efficiencies.
8. Build Strong Internal and External Relationships
   Encourage collaboration across departments and with external partners, such as startups, research institutions, and strategic allies. Tap into diverse perspectives and expertise to fuel innovation and resilience.
9. Recognize and Reward Innovation
   Publicly acknowledge and reward innovative contributions, reinforcing the value placed on creativity and risk-taking.
10. Monitor, Measure, and Adapt
   Continuously assess the impact of innovation initiatives and adjust strategies based on feedback and changing circumstances. Use data-driven insights to refine the innovation program and maintain alignment with resilience goals.

7.3.1 Practical example

A resilient organization like Microsoft under Satya Nadella transformed its culture by prioritizing psychological safety, cross-functional collaboration, and continuous learning. The company aligned innovation with strategic goals, invested in employee growth, and adopted agile processes-enabling it to pivot quickly, embrace cloud computing, and regain industry leadership.

Summary Table: Building an Innovation Program for Resilience

7.3.2 In summary

A resilient organization's innovation program is built on a foundation of culture, strategy alignment, employee empowerment, agile processes, and continuous learning. By embedding these practices, organizations can anticipate change, adapt rapidly, and turn uncertainty into opportunity.

7.3.3 Qualify ideas for innovation projects

To effectively collect and qualify ideas for innovation projects, organizations use structured templates and key qualifying questions. These tools ensure ideas are captured consistently, evaluated objectively, and developed into actionable projects.

Key Questions to Collect and Qualify Ideas

- When gathering and screening ideas, use the following questions:
- What is the problem or opportunity?
- Clearly describe the issue or opportunity the idea addresses.
- What is your proposed solution?
- Summarize the idea or concept in simple terms.
- Who is the target user or customer?
- Identify who will benefit from this idea.
- What is the expected value or impact?
- Explain the potential benefits (e.g., revenue, cost savings, customer satisfaction, efficiency).
- What resources are required?
- List the people, technology, budget, or partnerships needed to implement the idea35.
- What are the potential risks or unknowns?
- Highlight uncertainties, challenges, or barriers to success.
- How does this align with organizational strategy?
- Explain how the idea supports company goals or strategic priorities.
- What is the estimated timeline?
- Provide a rough timeline for development and implementation.
- How will success be measured?
- Define key metrics or indicators for success.
- Sample Idea Collection and Qualification Template

Below is a structured template, inspired by best practices and widely used innovation frameworks:

Tip: Many digital platforms (e.g., Airtable, Stackby, Miro, Ideanote) offer customizable templates for idea management and innovation funnels, making it easy to collect, review, and advance ideas through your innovation pipeline.

By using these questions and templates, organizations create a transparent, repeatable process for turning creative ideas into high-impact innovation project (Tables 7.1 and 7.2).

Table 7.1 Template for Idea Management

Section	*Guiding questions/fields*
Idea title	What is the name of your idea?
Problem/opportunity	What problem or opportunity does this address?
Proposed solution	Briefly describe your idea or solution.
Target user/customer	Who will benefit from this idea?
Value/impact	What benefits or value does this idea offer?
Resources needed	What people, technology, or budget are required?
Risks/unknowns	What are the main risks or uncertainties?
Strategic alignment	How does this support organizational goals?
Estimated timeline	What is the expected timeline for development?
Success metrics	How will you measure success?
Submitted by	Who is submitting this idea?
Date submitted	When was the idea submitted?

Table 7.2 Sample innovation idea template (filled example)

Section	*Guiding questions/fields*
Idea title	Smart Inventory Management System Submitted By: Priya Sharma Date Submitted: April 29, 2025
Problem/opportunity	Our retail stores frequently experience stockouts and overstock situations, leading to lost sales and increased holding costs. Current manual inventory tracking is inefficient and error-prone.
Proposed solution	Develop and implement an AI-powered Smart Inventory Management System that uses real-time sales data, predictive analytics, and automated alerts to optimize stock levels and reorder points.
Target user/customer	Store managers, inventory staff, and supply chain teams across all retail outlets.
Value/impact	Reduces lost sales due to stockouts by 25% Lowers inventory holding costs by 15% Improves staff productivity by automating manual tasks Enhances customer satisfaction through better product availability
Resources needed	AI software development team Integration with existing POS and ERP systems Training sessions for staff Budget estimate: $150,000

(Continued)

Table 7.2 Sample innovation idea template (filled example) *(Continued)*

Section	*Guiding questions/fields*
Risks/unknowns	Integration challenges with legacy systems Change management and staff adoption Data privacy and security concerns
Strategic alignment	Supports our digital transformation initiative and the company's goal to enhance operational efficiency and customer experience.
Estimated timeline	Prototype: 3 months Pilot in 2 stores: 2 months Full rollout: 6 months
Success metrics	Stockout incidents per month Inventory turnover rate Staff hours spent on inventory tasks
Submitted by	Who is submitting this idea?
Date submitted	When was the idea submitted?

7.3.4 Customer satisfaction scores

This template ensures all key aspects—problem, solution, impact, resources, risks, alignment, timeline, and metrics—are covered, making it easier to evaluate and advance the idea into a full project.

7.3.5 Evaluate the effectiveness of the innovative idea

To evaluate the effectiveness of your innovation template, you should track a mix of metrics that assess idea generation, process efficiency, project progress, and ultimate outcomes. These metrics ensure your template not only captures quality ideas but also helps move them efficiently through the innovation pipeline toward impactful results.

Key Metrics to Track

1. Idea Generation and Engagement
   - Idea Generation Rate: Number of new ideas submitted over a specific period.
   - Employee Participation Rate: Percentage of employees actively submitting or collaborating on ideas.
   - Diversity of Ideas: Variety of departments, roles, or backgrounds represented among idea submitters.
2. Screening and Qualification
   - Idea-to-Project Conversion Rate: Percentage of submitted ideas that pass screening and are qualified as projects.
   - Idea Kill Rate: Percentage of ideas rejected or not advanced beyond initial screening.
   - Time to Qualify an Idea: Average duration from idea submission to decision on qualification.

3. Process and Pipeline Efficiency
   - Cycle Time per Stage: How long ideas/projects spend in each stage of the innovation process (e.g., screening, validation, development).
   - Average Duration in Pipeline: Total time from idea submission to project launch or termination.
   - Milestone Completion Rate: Percentage of projects meeting defined milestones on schedule.
4. Output and Impact
   - Number of Projects Launched: Count of qualified ideas that become active innovation projects or products.
   - New Product/Service Launches: Number of new offerings brought to market as a result of the innovation process.
   - Customer Adoption Rate: Percentage of target users adopting new products or services.
5. Value and ROI
   - Revenue from New Products/Services: Income generated from innovations launched through the template.
   - Return on Investment (ROI): Financial return versus cost of innovation initiatives.
   - Market Share Gained: Growth attributable to new products or services.
6. Learning and Improvement
   - Assumptions Validated/Falsified: Number of key hypotheses tested and validated or disproven during the process.
   - Experimentation Rate: Number of experiments or prototypes developed per idea/project.
   - Lessons Learned Documented: Frequency and quality of post-project reviews and learnings captured.

7.3.6 Portfolio-level metrics

- Percentage of Projects in Each Stage: Helps visualize flow and identify bottlenecks in your innovation funnel.
- Weighted Portfolio Risk Score: Assesses the overall risk profile of your innovation pipeline.

7.3.7 Qualitative metrics

- Employee Satisfaction with Innovation Process: Survey responses on ease of use and perceived value of the template.
- Quality of Ideas Submitted: Subjective assessment of idea relevance, feasibility, and alignment with strategy.

Table 7.3

Resilience metrics	*Description*
Supporting organizational resilience	Innovation significantly enhances organizational resilience by enabling companies to anticipate, adapt to, and recover from disruptions, ensuring sustained competitiveness and long-term success. Multiple studies and real-world cases highlight how innovative practices and cultures directly contribute to resilience.
How innovation supports organizational resilience	Anticipating and Adapting to Change: Innovative organizations are better equipped to foresee market shifts, technological advancements, and emerging risks. By continuously developing new products, services, or business models, they can pivot quickly in response to external shocks
Problem-solving and agility	Innovation fosters a culture of experimentation and learning, allowing organizations to solve problems faster and implement change more effectively than competitors.
Leveraging digital tools and networks	The adoption of digital technologies and collaborative networks accelerates innovation and strengthens resilience, as seen during the COVID-19 pandemic when firms used digital platforms to maintain operations and customer engagement

7.3.8 Summary table

Tracking these metrics will help you continuously improve your innovation template, ensuring it drives both creative engagement and tangible business results (Table 7.3).

7.3.9 Organizational learning

Resilient organizations often have strong learning mechanisms, using feedback from failures and successes to drive continuous improvement and innovation.

Real-World Examples and Case Studies

1. Amazon: Reinvention and Service Innovation

   Amazon began as a bookseller and evolved into a global leader in e-commerce and cloud computing by continuously innovating its business model and services. This relentless reinvention allowed Amazon to anticipate market changes, address new customer needs, and maintain a competitive edge-even in volatile environments. The company's agility and willingness to innovate have been central to its organizational resilience, enabling it to thrive through economic downturns and industry disruptions.

2. Microsoft: Strategic Transformation
   Microsoft demonstrated resilience by shifting from a software licensing model to cloud-based services under Satya Nadella's leadership. This transformation, driven by innovation in both technology and business strategy, allowed Microsoft to recover from stagnation and regain industry leadership. The company's ability to innovate in response to changing market demands has been key to its sustained performance and adaptability.
3. Service Firms During the Pandemic
   A study of Spanish service companies during the COVID-19 pandemic showed that those with strong innovation management practices—such as digital service delivery and collaborative networks—were more resilient. These firms adapted quickly to disruptions, maintained customer relationships through digital channels, and outperformed less innovative competitors.
4. Hospitality Sector in Ghana
   Research in Ghana's hospitality industry found that resilient firms were more likely to engage in exploratory innovation, developing new products and services unrelated to their existing offerings. This adaptability helped them survive in a highly uncertain and volatile environment, highlighting the link between resilience capabilities and innovation performance.

7.3.10 Empirical evidence

Firms with high innovation capabilities show greater resilience during crises, outperforming less innovative peers in terms of financial performance and competitive advantage. Organizational resilience and innovation are mutually reinforcing: resilient organizations foster innovation, and innovative practices strengthen resilience (Table 7.4).

Table 7.4 Innovation and organizational resilience

Example	*Innovation practice*	*Resilience outcome*
Amazon	Continuous reinvention, new services	Maintained market leadership, adapted to change
Microsoft	Digital/cloud transformation	Recovered from stagnation, sustained growth
Service firms	Digital tools, collaboration	Quick adaptation during pandemic
Hospitality	Exploratory innovation	Survival in uncertain markets

7.3.11 In summary

Innovation is a cornerstone of organizational resilience. It enables companies to anticipate and respond to disruptions, solve problems creatively, and maintain a competitive advantage in uncertain environments. Leading organizations like Amazon and Microsoft, as well as firms studied across industries, demonstrate that a strong innovation culture is essential for resilience and long-term success.

7.3.12 Successful innovations

Here are five successful innovations from the recent past that have helped organizations build resilience:

- Digital Transformation and Cloud Computing Companies like Amazon and Netflix leveraged digital transformation-migrating operations to the cloud, automating processes, and using data analytics-to quickly adapt to market disruptions, scale operations, and maintain business continuity during crises like the COVID-19 pandemic. Cloud-based platforms also enabled seamless remote work and collaboration, ensuring operational agility and resilience.
- AI and Automation for Crisis Decision-Making: The adoption of artificial intelligence and automation has empowered organizations to make faster, data-driven decisions during uncertainty. For example, AI-driven supply chain management and automated customer service have helped businesses respond to sudden market changes and resource constraints, reducing human error and enabling teams to focus on higher-level crisis response.
- Agile Work Processes and Collaboration Tools: The implementation of agile methodologies (such as Scrum and Kanban) and digital collaboration tools (like Slack, Jira, and Trello) has given organizations the flexibility to rapidly adjust projects, priorities, and workflows. This adaptability was crucial for businesses to pivot during disruptions and maintain productivity in distributed or remote work environments.
- Cybersecurity and Data Resilience: As cyber threats increased, organizations invested in robust cybersecurity measures and data resilience strategies to protect digital infrastructure. This included advanced threat detection, regular backups, and incident response plans, which safeguarded business operations and enabled quick recovery from cyber incidents.
- Unified Customer Service Platforms: Companies such as R Cable y Telecommunications Galicia created unified customer service workbenches by integrating APIs into legacy systems. This innovation enabled them to deliver customer service improvements 50–70% faster than before, maintaining high service levels and customer satisfaction even during periods of rapid change or crisis.

These innovations collectively demonstrate how technology, process improvement, and a focus on adaptability have become central to building organizational resilience in a rapidly changing world.

BIBLIOGRAPHY

Ackerman, E. (2014). The evolution of IBM research. Europhysics News, 45(2), 16–19.

Argyris, C., & Schön, D. (1978). Organizational learning: A theory of action perspective. Addison-Wesley.

Chesbrough, H. W. (2003). Open innovation: The new imperative for creating and profiting from technology. Harvard Business School Press.

Christensen, C. M. (1997). The innovator's dilemma: When new technologies cause great firms to fail. Harvard Business School Press.

Crossan, M. M., Lane, H. W., & White, R. E. (1999). An organizational learning framework: From intuition to institution. Academy of Management Review, 24(3), 522–537.

Nadella, S., Shaw, G., & Nichols, J. T. (2017). Hit refresh: The quest to rediscover Microsoft's soul and imagine a better future for everyone. HarperBusiness.

Schmidt, E., & Rosenberg, J. (2014). How Google works. Grand Central Publishing.

Chapter 8

Adaptability and flexibility

In today's rapidly changing business environment, adaptability and flexibility have become essential characteristics of successful organizations. This chapter explores how companies can anticipate and respond to change effectively, develop diversified strategies, and maintain resource flexibility to ensure resilience and sustainable growth in the face of uncertainty.

A highly resilient organization distinguishes itself by proactively identifying and adapting to change and uncertainty-often before external pressures make change urgent. This anticipatory approach enables the introduction of new methods, ideas, and products that exploit emerging opportunities and control vulnerabilities. It also fosters a culture where everyone is encouraged to learn and innovate, continually addressing the shifting needs of the organization as its environment evolves.

8.1 ANTICIPATING AND RESPONDING TO CHANGE

Organizations that thrive in volatile environments share a common trait: they don't just react to change—they anticipate it. Anticipatory adaptation involves developing systems to detect early warning signals, creating scenario plans for multiple futures, and building organizational capabilities that enable quick pivots when necessary.

Effective Change Response Requires

- *Environmental Scanning*: Successful organizations continuously monitor their external environment for signals of impending shifts in technology, consumer behaviour, regulations, or competitive landscapes. This involves not just collecting data but interpreting it through multiple lenses to identify potential impacts.
- *Scenario Planning*: Rather than betting on a single future, adaptive organizations develop multiple scenarios and prepare contingency plans for each. This approach ensures they're never caught completely off-guard, regardless of which future materializes.

DOI: 10.1201/9781003597520-8

- *Organizational Learning*: Organizations that respond effectively to change have robust systems for capturing lessons from both successes and failures. They create feedback loops that allow rapid incorporation of new knowledge into operational processes.
- *Agile Decision-Making*: Traditional hierarchical decision processes often prove too slow in rapidly changing environments. Adaptive organizations push decision authority to appropriate levels, enabling faster responses to local conditions while maintaining strategic alignment.

8.1.1 Case study: McDonald's response to the COVID-19 pandemic

McDonald's response to the COVID-19 pandemic exemplifies how a global organization can rapidly adapt to unprecedented disruption through anticipatory planning, operational agility, and strategic pivoting.

1. *Rapid Operational Transformation*
   When the pandemic hit in early 2020, McDonald's quickly implemented comprehensive safety protocols across its global network of restaurants. Within weeks, the company:
   - Redesigned restaurant layouts to accommodate social distancing
   - Installed protective barriers at service counters and drive-thrus
   - Implemented enhanced cleaning and sanitization procedures
   - Mandated masks and temperature checks for employees
   - Introduced contactless payment and delivery options

   These operational changes required significant investment and coordination across thousands of locations, yet McDonald's executed them with remarkable speed, demonstrating the value of standardized processes that can be rapidly modified during crises.
2. *Digital Acceleration*
   While McDonald's had been gradually investing in digital capabilities before the pandemic, COVID-19 prompted a dramatic acceleration of these initiatives:
   - Mobile ordering capabilities were expanded and enhanced
   - The McDonald's app was redesigned to improve user experience
   - Drive-thru operations were optimized with AI-powered menu boards
   - Partnerships with third-party delivery services were strengthened

   This digital pivot wasn't merely reactive—it represented an acceleration of McDonald's existing "Velocity Growth Plan," which had identified digital engagement as a strategic priority. By the end of 2020, digital sales (including delivery, mobile app, and kiosk orders) represented over 20% of system-wide sales in McDonald's top six markets.

3. *Menu Simplification and Supply Chain Resilience*
   Facing supply chain disruptions and staffing challenges, McDonald's temporarily simplified its menu, focusing on core items that:
   - Required fewer ingredients and preparation steps
   - Maintained high customer satisfaction
   - Optimized kitchen operations with reduced staff

   This strategic simplification improved operational efficiency while reducing complexity during a period of extreme uncertainty. Simultaneously, McDonald's leveraged its global scale and supplier relationships to mitigate supply chain disruptions, demonstrating the value of supply chain resilience.
4. *Franchisee Support and Stakeholder Management*
   Recognizing that its franchisees faced unprecedented financial pressure, McDonald's provided substantial support:
   - Deferring rent and royalty payments
   - Providing financial assistance for restaurant modifications
   - Sharing best practices across the franchise network
   - Accelerating the disbursement of marketing funds

   This approach acknowledged the interdependence of corporate success and franchisee health, illustrating how adaptive organizations consider their entire ecosystem when responding to crises.

8.1.2 Impact and lessons

McDonald's pandemic response yielded several key insights about organizational adaptability:

- *Preparation Enables Agility*: McDonald's pre-pandemic investments in digital infrastructure and delivery capabilities provided a foundation for rapid adaptation.
- *Centralized Strategy, Localized Execution*: The company balanced global coordination with local flexibility, allowing individual markets to adapt based on their specific pandemic conditions.
- *Crisis as Catalyst*: Rather than merely surviving the pandemic, McDonald's used it to accelerate strategic initiatives that positioned the company for long-term success in a changed marketplace.
- *Stakeholder-Centric Approach*: By considering the needs of employees, franchisees, suppliers, and communities, McDonald's maintained the trust and cooperation essential for effective crisis response.

By the end of 2021, McDonald's had not only recovered but was outperforming pre-pandemic levels in many markets, demonstrating how effective crisis adaptation can create competitive advantage. The company's experience shows that organizational resilience isn't just about weathering storms—it's about emerging stronger from them.

8.2 DIVERSIFIED STRATEGIES AND RESOURCE FLEXIBILITY

Resilient organizations develop two complementary capabilities: diversified strategies that spread risk and create multiple paths to success, and resource flexibility that enables rapid reallocation in response to changing conditions.

8.2.1 Diversified strategies

Strategic diversification involves developing multiple approaches to creating and capturing value, ensuring that the organization isn't overly dependent on any single business model, market, or growth path.

Multiple Business Models: Organizations that operate several complementary business models simultaneously can better withstand disruptions to any single revenue stream. For example, Microsoft's diversification across cloud services, software licensing, hardware, and gaming creates multiple paths to growth and reduces vulnerability to sector-specific downturns.

Geographic Diversification: Companies with operations across multiple regions can offset localized disruptions, whether from natural disasters, political instability, or economic downturns. This approach requires balancing standardization with localization to achieve both efficiency and market relevance.

Innovation Portfolios: Rather than betting on a single "next big thing," resilient organizations maintain a balanced portfolio of innovations spanning incremental improvements, adjacent opportunities, and transformative possibilities. This approach increases the odds of capturing emerging opportunities while managing risk.

Risk Distribution: Strategic partnerships, joint ventures, and ecosystem participation allow organizations to pursue opportunities that would be too risky or resource intensive to tackle alone. These collaborative approaches distribute both risk and reward across multiple entities.

8.2.2 Resource flexibility

While diversified strategies create options, resource flexibility enables organizations to pursue those options effectively by reallocating capabilities, assets, and investments in response to changing conditions.

Flexible Resource Allocation: Organizations with agile resource allocation processes can quickly shift investments toward emerging opportunities and away from declining areas. This requires not just financial agility but also governance structures that enable rapid, evidence-based decisions.

Modular Systems and Processes: Modular approaches to both technology and operations enable components to be reconfigured, replaced, or scaled independently. This architectural flexibility allows organizations to adapt specific elements without disrupting entire systems.

Redundancy and Slack: While efficiency often drives organizations to eliminate redundancy, strategic redundancy in critical areas provides insurance against disruption. Similarly, maintaining some organizational "slack" creates capacity for experimentation and rapid response.

Data-Driven Adaptation: Organizations that continuously gather and analyze performance data can detect changing conditions early and make evidence-based adjustments before problems escalate or opportunities disappear.

Examples of Strategy Diversification and Resource Flexibility

- *Supply Chain Diversification:* During the COVID-19 pandemic, organizations that had multiple suppliers across regions (instead of relying on a single source) were able to maintain operations and adapt faster to disruptions.
- *Operational Flexibility:* Alcohol distilleries pivoting to produce hand sanitizer, or apparel manufacturers making medical masks, show how flexible resources and modular processes enable rapid adaptation in crisis.
- *Cross-Training*: Companies that cross-train staff can reassign employees to critical roles during surges or shortages, maintaining productivity and service levels (Table 8.1).

8.2.3 In summary

A resilient organization requires diversified strategies to spread risk and seize new opportunities, and resource flexibility to reallocate, adapt, and maintain operations under changing conditions. This dual approach ensures the organization is not only protected from shocks but also positioned to thrive in an unpredictable world.

8.2.4 Case study: Netflix's transition from DVD rentals to streaming services

Netflix's transition from DVD rentals to streaming services is a textbook case of how diversified strategies and resource flexibility underpin organizational resilience and long-term success.

Table 8.1 Resilience Strategies: Netflix's transition from DVD rentals to streaming services

Requirement	*Key actions/elements*
Diversified Strategies	Multiple business models, supply chain diversity, innovation, risk management
Resource Flexibility	Flexible allocation, cross-training, modular systems, redundancy, data-driven decisions

8.2.5 Diversified strategies

8.2.5.1 Business model evolution

Netflix started as a DVD-by-mail rental service, disrupting traditional video rental stores with a subscription model that eliminated late fees and offered convenience. Recognizing technological trends and shifting consumer preferences, Netflix didn't remain static. In 2007, it launched a streaming platform, allowing instant access to a vast library of content online. This shift fundamentally changed how people consumed entertainment and set a new industry standard.

8.2.5.2 Expanding revenue streams

Netflix didn't stop at streaming. It diversified further by investing in original content production (e.g., "House of Cards," "Stranger Things"), which reduced dependence on third-party studios and increased brand value. More recently, Netflix has expanded into live content (such as sports events), retail (pop-up stores and merchandise), and even video games, targeting new audience segments and creating multiple paths for growth.

8.2.6 Global and local diversification

Netflix adopted a strategy of "glocalization," producing and licensing content tailored to diverse markets around the world. By investing in local-language originals and supporting cultural diversity, Netflix appeals to micro-targeted audience groups while also creating globally popular shows.

8.2.7 Resource flexibility

8.2.7.1 Technological adaptation

The move from physical DVDs to streaming required massive investment in cloud infrastructure, content delivery networks, and user interface design. Netflix's ability to quickly scale its technology stack and leverage advances in internet speed and compression algorithms made streaming viable and seamless for users worldwide.

8.2.7.2 Agile operations and talent deployment

Netflix's workforce adapted from managing logistics and physical inventory to developing software, data analytics, and content production expertise. The company invested heavily in acquiring new skills, retraining staff, and hiring talent aligned with its evolving needs.

8.2.7.3 Financial and strategic resource allocation

Netflix demonstrated flexibility in reallocating capital—from logistics and postage for DVDs to technology, content acquisition, and original production. This financial agility allowed Netflix to weather the high content acquisition costs of streaming and to invest in new areas as opportunities emerged.

Table 8.2 Diverse Strategies of Netflix

Diversified strategies	*Key actions/elements*
DVD rentals → Streaming → Originals → Games	Tech stack evolution (cloud, AI, UI)
Global/local content production	Workforce retraining and agile talent deployment
Live events, retail, merchandise	Financial agility and strategic capital allocation

8.2.7.4 Impact and lessons

Customer-Centric Innovation: Netflix's diversified strategies ensured it could serve changing customer needs—offering instant, personalized, on-demand entertainment.

Market Leadership: By not relying on a single business model or content source, Netflix outpaced competitors and set new industry benchmarks.

Resilience and Growth: Resource flexibility enabled Netflix to pivot quickly, scale globally, and experiment with new business lines, making it resilient to industry disruptions and changing consumer habits (Table 8.2).

8.2.8 In summary

Netflix's journey from DVD rentals to a global streaming powerhouse demonstrates how diversified strategies and resource flexibility enable an organization to anticipate change, adapt rapidly, and maintain resilience in a volatile market.

8.2.9 Cultivating adaptability and flexibility: practical approaches

Developing organizational adaptability and flexibility isn't just about responding to immediate challenges—it requires systematic cultivation of specific capabilities and mindsets throughout the organization.

8.2.9.1 Building an adaptive organizational mindset

Creating a culture that embraces change rather than resists it begins with leadership but must permeate all levels of the organization:

- *Leadership Modeling*: Leaders must demonstrate comfort with ambiguity, willingness to experiment, and openness to changing direction based on new information. When leaders visibly adapt their own thinking and approaches, it signals that flexibility is valued rather than punished.
- *Psychological Safety*: Organizations where people feel safe to voice concerns, suggest alternatives, and acknowledge mistakes are better positioned to detect early warning signals and course-correct before problems escalate. This requires deliberate efforts to reward candor and treat setbacks as learning opportunities.

- *Learning Orientation*: Adaptive organizations frame challenges as opportunities to learn rather than threats to avoid. This perspective shift encourages experimentation, reduces defensive routines, and accelerates the acquisition of new capabilities.
- *Distributed Intelligence:* Organizations that tap into the collective intelligence of their entire workforce—not just senior leadership—can sense and respond to changes more effectively. This requires communication systems that enable information to flow in all directions, not just top-down.

8.2.10 Strategies for rapid transformation during crises

When faced with sudden, disruptive change, organizations need specific approaches to accelerate adaptation:

- *Crisis Response Teams*: Cross-functional teams with clear authority and minimal bureaucracy can make and implement decisions quickly during crises. These teams should include diverse perspectives to ensure comprehensive problem-solving.
- *Scenario-Based Planning*: Rather than attempting to predict a single future, organizations should develop multiple scenarios and identify trigger points that signal which scenario is unfolding. This approach enables faster recognition and response when conditions change.
- *Rapid Prototyping*: During crises, perfect solutions are less valuable than timely ones. Organizations that can quickly develop, test, and refine prototypes—whether of products, services, or processes—can adapt faster than those seeking comprehensive solutions from the outset.
- *Stakeholder Communication*: Transparent, frequent communication with all stakeholders—employees, customers, suppliers, investors—builds trust and cooperation during periods of change. This communication should acknowledge uncertainty while providing clear direction on immediate priorities.

Developing Skills for Flexible Business Models: Organizations can systematically build their capacity to implement flexible business models through:

- *Dynamic Capability Development:* Beyond operational capabilities that enable efficiency in stable environments, organizations need dynamic capabilities that enable reconfiguration in changing environments. These include sensing (detecting opportunities and threats), seizing (mobilizing resources to address them), and transforming (continuously renewing processes and business models).
- *Ecosystem Thinking*: Viewing the organization as part of a broader ecosystem rather than a self-contained entity enables more flexible responses to change. This perspective highlights interdependencies and potential partnerships that can enhance adaptability.

- *Technology Architecture*: Systems designed with flexibility in mind—using microservices, APIs, and modular components—enable faster reconfiguration than monolithic architectures. Similarly, data architectures that facilitate information sharing across organizational boundaries support more responsive decision-making.
- *Talent Strategies:* Organizations with flexible talent strategies—including cross-training, skill development pathways, and appropriate use of contingent workers—can more quickly reallocate human resources as needs change.

Here are *50 Key Questions* to assess the attributes of adaptive capacity to achieve organizational resilience level (Table 8.3).

Table 8.3 Key Questions for assessing Adaptability and Flexibility

Attribute 1: Room for autonomous change	Autonomous change culture involves balancing pre-planned responses with adaptive actions. It modifies structures and behaviors to adjust to new conditions while maintaining core values. Actors must improvise during crises and adapt to everyday challenges and opportunities. Institutions support this by continuously monitoring vulnerabilities, valuing improvisation, and promoting self-organization.
1.	Is the organization adaptable to remain relevant?
2.	Is there a framework for change management within the organization?
3.	Does the organization possess a comprehensive understanding of its internal and external environment, monitor key drivers, and anticipate and respond to necessary changes effectively?
4.	Does the organization show their capability to make well-informed, adaptable, and prompt decisions, based on available information, past experience, and considering the potential impact of their decisions?
5.	Does the organization develop strategies to engage with external stakeholders to understand and respond to their needs and expectations, establish shared values, and gain their support and involvement for long-term mutual benefit?
6.	Does the organization manage changes through structured project management and focused process improvements as appropriate, monitor and review the effectiveness of changes, and share the knowledge gained?
7.	Are the inputs for change identified, and is a sense of urgency created?
8.	Is the process considered contemporary and agile in accordance with current business environments?
9.	How do the leader and board demonstrate change management, including its purpose, vision, values, and strategy?
10.	How does the organization deploy resources, including financial, technology, infrastructure, and people, at all levels of the change?

(Continued)

Table 8.3 (Continued)

Attribute 1: Room for autonomous change	Autonomous change culture involves balancing pre-planned responses with adaptive actions. It modifies structures and behaviors to adjust to new conditions while maintaining core values. Actors must improvise during crises and adapt to everyday challenges and opportunities. Institutions support this by continuously monitoring vulnerabilities, valuing improvisation, and promoting self-organization.
11.	Are people empowered and aware of their roles and responsibilities in the change process?
12.	How does the organization communicate with all stakeholders to build an adaptive organization?
13.	Have transformational changes been approved by all stakeholders, including the board?
14.	Is there a process for fast-tracking emergency changes?
15.	When the organization has a close call, does it use the opportunity for self-evaluation instead of confirming its success?
16.	Has the organization actively participated in industry and sector groups during times of change or crisis?
17.	In a crisis situation does the organization seek opportunities for their organization?
18.	Does the organization tend to be optimistic and find positives from most of the situations?
19.	Do engineering and change management reviews take into account the entire lifecycle of new projects, modifications, and operational changes, including their impact on inventories of aspects and impacts?
Attribute 2: Learning Capacity	The degree to which institutions integrate knowledge is reflected by the inclusion of diverse policy frameworks, problem definitions, and solutions; engagement with multiple actors, levels, and sectors throughout policy development and implementation processes; and the capacity to foster differentiated policy options and develop customized solutions and redundancy. These aspects must be accurately documented in the knowledge database.
20.	How does the organization ensure that the knowledge obtained from knowledge management is accessible to all its stakeholders (both internal and external) for input into change management?
21.	How is the organization equipped with tools and techniques to support knowledge management, enabling the application of learnings for building adaptive capacity? This includes the availability of domain and sector experts, trade associations, and special interest groups.
22.	How are the best practices, both within and outside the organization, being archived and utilized for future reference—covering reactive usage, adaptive usage, and routine business operations?
23.	Does knowledge management receive inputs from horizon scanning, risk management, and incident reporting?

(Continued)

Table 8.3 (Continued)

24.	Does single-loop learning (learning from past experiences) and double-loop learning (learning from underlying changes in assumptions) occur?
25.	Who has been given the accountability, responsibility, operationalizing, and review of Knowledge Management in the organization to identify opportunities for transformational change?
Attribute 3: Leadership Role	Establishing and fostering a culture of adaptive capacity in leadership involves providing external sense giving to enhance teams' cognitive ability to promote team psychological collectivism. Three types of leadership can be identified: visionary leadership (the ability to link short-term and long-term goals), entrepreneurial leadership (the ability to facilitate action), and collaborative leadership (the ability to connect levels and create networks and alliances).
26.	How does the leader use psychological collectivism to ensure teams share information and adapt strategies effectively?
27.	How does a leader develop the ability to process different perspectives in various contexts?
28.	How does the leader enable and reward adaptive capacity?
29.	Can the leadership collaborate with industry peers to handle unexpected challenges?
Attribute 4: Resources	A critical external factor that affects and enhances the adaptive capacity of organizations is the availability of resources. Without adequate resources, including financial support, technical knowledge and expertise, and human capital, projects may not be successfully initiated or executed.
30.	Is authority provided at the right level to approve resources for incremental and transformational changes as well as dealing with disruptions?
31.	How many changes were rejected due to budget constraints despite a cost-benefit analysis indicating higher benefits?
32.	What is the time required to acquire individuals with core competencies?
Attribute 5: Workforce Resilience	A resilient workforce can handle minor issues without becoming stressed. They perform well under pressure, adapt flexibly to changing circumstances, and recover from challenges and setbacks effectively.
33.	Does the individual adapt to different situations effectively and possess the resources to rebound successfully?
34.	Does the individual become attuned to the surrounding environment and develop the ability to regulate impulses, thereby becoming less fearful and more manageable?
35.	Does the individual have the capability of aligning their internal needs and motivations with their external surroundings?
36.	Can the individual adapt to environmental stress, uncertainty, conflict, or imbalance?

(Continued)

Table 8.3 (Continued)

Attribute 5: Workforce Resilience	A resilient workforce can handle minor issues without becoming stressed. They perform well under pressure, adapt flexibly to changing circumstances, and recover from challenges and setbacks effectively.
37.	Do changes in the workplace environment affect individual productivity?
38.	Is the individual resourceful and adaptive to changing circumstances, analytical for finding the best fit between situational demands and behavioral possibilities, and flexible with problem-solving strategies?
39.	Does the individual have the ability to elicit positive responses and establish positive relationships with others?
40.	Does the individual possess problem-solving skills, including the ability to plan, control, and demonstrate resourcefulness in seeking assistance from others?
41.	Does the individual have a sense of their own identity and an ability to act independently and exert some control over their environment?
42.	Does the individual possess a sense of purpose, future goals, aspirations, persistence, hopefulness, and an optimistic outlook on the future?
43.	Does the individual have the ability to recover or bounce back in the face of adversity and possess sufficient internal and external resources, strong thinking skills, demonstrate effective leadership, and have high expectations placed on them?
44.	Does the organization prioritize positive organizational behaviour (POB)?
Attribute 6: Culture of promoting adaptive capacity	Adaptive culture fosters employee confidence, encourages risk-taking, promotes leadership that drives change, and prioritizes evolving customer needs.
45.	Does the culture encourage risk-taking and employee confidence?
46.	Does the organization's culture exhibit political and bureaucratic tendencies?
47.	Does the organization have a shared mission with a commitment to reliable safety and production operations?
48.	Are employees encouraged to switch departments or roles to gain experience?
49.	Is there teamwork and camaraderie in the organization?
50.	Are there minimal barriers preventing employees from collaborating effectively internally and externally?

8.2.11 Change ready

To become *change ready*—a core characteristic of organizational resilience as described in the chapter on Anticipating and Responding to Change—organizations must move beyond simply reacting to disruptions. Instead, they proactively anticipate, prepare for, and embrace change as a continuous opportunity for growth and improvement.

What Does It Mean to be Change Ready?
Being change ready means your organization is:

- *Prepared, willing, and able* to implement change at all levels.
- Able to *anticipate, predict, and prepare* for future challenges and opportunities, not just respond to them as they arise.
- Culturally and structurally equipped to *adapt, innovate, and learn* continuously.

Key Steps to Becoming Change Ready

1. *Foster a Change-Ready Mindset and Culture*
   - *Embrace Change as Normal:* View change as a natural part of business, not a threat.
   - *Promote Openness and Experimentation:* Encourage new ideas, risk-taking, and learning from mistakes
   - *Build Psychological Safety:* Create an environment where employees feel safe to express concerns and try new approaches without fear of blame
2. *Leadership Commitment and Role Modeling*
   - *Visible Sponsorship:* Leaders must actively champion change, communicate its purpose, and model adaptability
   - *Empowerment:* Leaders should empower teams to make decisions and act on opportunities, building confidence and buy-in.
3. *Continuous Foresight and Environmental Scanning*
   - *Monitor Internal and External Signals:* Regularly scan for weak signals, trends, and emerging risks or opportunities.
   - *Scenario Planning:* Prepare for multiple plausible futures, not just the most likely one.
   - *Encourage Vigilance:* Train employees to notice and report early warning signs or potential issues.
4. *Structured Change Management Processes*
   - *Assess Change Readiness:* Use surveys, interviews, and workshops to gauge attitudes and readiness for change across the organization.
   - *Apply Proven Frameworks:* Models like Prosci's ADKAR (Awareness, Desire, Knowledge, Ability, Reinforcement) help guide and sustain change.
   - *Continuous Improvement:* Review and learn from past change initiatives to refine your approach.
5. *Agility and Adaptability*
   - *Rapid Decision-Making:* Streamline processes to enable fast responses to new information or conditions.
   - *Cross-Functional Collaboration:* Break down silos to encourage knowledge sharing and collective problem-solving.
   - *Resourcefulness:* Build redundancy and flexibility into systems, processes, and talent so the organization can pivot as needed.

Table 8.4 Steps for becoming change ready

Step	*Description*
Change-ready culture	Embrace change, promote safety, and encourage innovation
Leadership commitment	Leaders champion and model adaptability
Foresight and scanning	Monitor environment and plan for multiple futures
Structured change management	Assess readiness, apply frameworks, and review lessons
Agility and collaboration	Enable rapid decision-making and cross-functional teamwork
Learning and knowledge sharing	Capture and disseminate insights and best practices

6. *Learning and Knowledge Management*
    - *Capture and Share Lessons:* Systematically document and share what works and what doesn't.
    - *Invest in Training:* Equip employees with the skills and tools needed to thrive in changing environments.

8.2.12 Practical example

At *Bose*, leadership embedded change readiness by being visible sponsors of change, engaging directly with projects, and fostering open communication. They learned from past mistakes, celebrated successes, and made adaptability a core part of their operations—demonstrating that when leaders lead by example, the whole organization becomes more change ready (Table 8.4).

8.2.13 In summary

To anticipate and respond to change—and truly become change ready—organizations must embed foresight, adaptability, and a proactive mindset into their culture, leadership, and systems. This not only prepares them to withstand disruptions but also positions them to seize new opportunities for growth and innovation.

Chapter 9

Supply chain resilience

9.1 INVENTORY MANAGEMENT

Case Study: Toyota During the 2011 Earthquake

9.2 DIVERSIFICATION AND REDUNDANCY

Case Study: Apple's Supply Chain Resilience

9.2.1 Supply chain resilience

An organization's resilience is no longer defined solely by its internal strengths; it is deeply influenced by its position within a complex web of suppliers, partners, outsourcers, and other stakeholders. Building resilience across these networks is essential for withstanding disruptions, adapting to change, and sustaining long-term performance.

Organizational Characteristics for Networked Resilience

1. *Deep Network Understanding*
   - *Mapping Interdependencies:*
     Resilient organizations invest in understanding the full extent of their supply chains and value networks, including upstream (suppliers and their suppliers) and downstream (customers and end-users) relationships. This mapping helps identify critical nodes and potential vulnerabilities that could impact operations during disruptions.
   - *Situation Awareness:*
     Staff are encouraged to maintain vigilance not only about internal performance but also about external signals from partners and the broader network. Early warning signs-such as delays, shortages, or shifts in demand-are quickly reported and acted upon.
2. *Collaboration and Effective Partnerships*
   - *Strong Relationships:*
     Building and maintaining robust partnerships with suppliers, logistics providers, and other stakeholders ensures access to resources,

DOI: 10.1201/9781003597520-9

expertise, and support during crises. These relationships are nurtured through trust, transparency, and regular communication.

- *Breaking Silos:*
  Collaboration within and between organizations is encouraged to foster innovation, shared understanding, and coordinated responses to challenges.

3. *Resourcefulness and Redundancy*
   - *Alternative Suppliers and Redundant Systems:*
     Organizations develop flexibility and redundancy by diversifying suppliers, maintaining backup systems, and cross-training employees. This ensures continuity even if a key partner or process is disrupted.
   - *Stress Testing and Scenario Planning:*
     Regular simulations and scenario planning exercises help organizations and their networks prepare for a range of disruptions, validating contingency plans and building collective readiness.
4. *Agility and Adaptability*
   - *Flexible Strategies:*
     Organizations with resilient networks can quickly adapt strategies, processes, and structures in response to changing circumstances. This agility is supported by continuous learning, innovation, and the ability to seize emerging opportunities.
   - *Proactive Posture:*
     Rather than waiting for problems to escalate, resilient organizations take a proactive approach to monitoring and responding to early warning signals in their networks.
5. *Leadership and Governance*
   - *Adaptive Leadership:*
     Leaders play a critical role in promoting a culture of resilience across the network. They provide clear direction, empower teams, and foster open communication with external partners.
   - *Unity of Purpose:*
     There is a shared understanding across the network of the organization's core priorities and minimum operating requirements, especially during disruptions.
6. *Learning and Knowledge Sharing*
   - *Leveraging Knowledge:*
     Critical information, best practices, and lessons learned are captured and shared not just internally, but also with key partners. This collective knowledge base strengthens the entire network's ability to respond and recover.
   - *Continuous Improvement:*
     Organizations and their networks regularly review and refine their resilience strategies based on feedback and evolving risks.

Why Networked Resilience Matters

- *Supply Chain Disruptions:*
  Events such as natural disasters, pandemics, or geopolitical shocks can affect suppliers or partners far upstream, with cascading impacts on the organization. A resilient network can absorb shocks and recover faster.
- *Customer Expectations:*
  Downstream resilience ensures that products and services reach customers even during disruptions, preserving reputation and trust.
- *Competitive Advantage:*
  Organizations that build resilience across their networks are better positioned to seize opportunities, innovate, and outperform less connected competitors.

9.2.2 In summary

Resilient organizations

- Map and understand their full network of relationships and dependencies.
- Build strong, collaborative partnerships with key stakeholders.
- Develop redundancy and flexibility in resources and processes.
- Foster agility, proactive monitoring, and adaptive leadership.
- Share knowledge and continuously improve resilience strategies across the network.

By embedding these characteristics, organizations ensure that resilience is not just an internal capability but a shared strength across the entire ecosystem—enabling them to anticipate, withstand, and recover from disruptions more effectively than those who operate in isolation.

A strong case study illustrating the importance of building resilience not just within an organization, but across its networks and interactions with suppliers, partners, and stakeholders, comes from the *food and beverage sector's response to global supply chain disruption* during the COVID-19 pandemic.

Case Study: Building Networked Supply Chain Resilience in a Global Food & Beverage Company

9.2.3 Background

One of the world's largest food and beverage companies, managing hundreds of brands, faced severe challenges as the pandemic disrupted global supply chains, created labor shortages, and shifted consumer demand patterns. The company's ability to keep grocery shelves stocked was compromised, with service levels (Case Fill Rate, CFR) dropping to 84%-well below pre-pandemic performance.

Organizational Characteristics for Networked Resilience

1. *Deep Network Understanding*
   The company recognized that resilience could not be achieved in isolation. It needed a clear understanding of its entire supply network, including upstream suppliers and downstream retailers. By mapping these relationships and flows, the company could identify bottlenecks, vulnerabilities, and opportunities for collaboration.
2. *Collaboration and Partnerships*
   To address complex challenges, the company broke down internal silos and fostered collaboration both within the organization and with external partners. It established a new Sales and Operations Execution (S&OE) team dedicated to handling short-term supply issues, freeing up the supply chain planning team to focus on long-term strategy. This cross-functional approach encouraged transparency, accountability, and agility across the network.
3. *Resourcefulness and Redundancy*
   The company improved its use of existing tools and data by integrating analytics dashboards with ERP systems and other data sources. This allowed for predictive reporting and proactive alerts, addressing potential issues up to six weeks in advance. By creating redundancy in processes and information flows, the company could better absorb shocks and maintain service levels.
4. *Agility and Adaptability*
   With end-to-end visibility and efficient organization, the company was able to make rapid, informed decisions. New routines and best practices were implemented to connect disparate teams and ensure that supply chain issues were managed proactively, not reactively.
5. *Leadership and Governance*
   Leadership played a key role in orchestrating the change, supporting a culture of networked resilience, and ensuring that all stakeholders-from suppliers to retailers-were aligned with the company's goals and minimum operating requirements during the disruption.
6. *Learning and Knowledge Sharing*
   Continuous improvement was embedded by capturing lessons learned during the crisis and sharing best practices across the network. This collective knowledge strengthened the entire ecosystem's ability to respond to future disruptions.

Results

- *Improved Service Levels:* The company's case fill rate surpassed 90%, reaching record volumes not seen in over two years.
- *Proactive Disruption Management:* The new system enabled the company to anticipate and adapt to supply chain disruptions, market changes, and evolving customer demands.

- *Stronger Network Resilience:* By building resilience across its network, the company ensured that retailers received the products they needed, when they needed them, keeping shelves stocked and consumers satisfied.

9.2.3.1 Key takeaway

This case demonstrates that organizational resilience is deeply connected to the resilience of the broader network. By understanding, collaborating, and sharing knowledge across all stakeholders-suppliers, partners, and customers-organizations can anticipate disruptions, respond effectively, and sustain performance in complex, interconnected environments.

9.2.4 Supply chain governance

Supply chain governance refers to the structures and processes that coordinate and integrate the various dimensions of supply management, directly influencing the resilience and performance of the entire supply chain. It is not just about managing the day-to-day flow of goods and services, but about establishing a framework that guides decision-making, sets standards, and aligns the interests and actions of all supply chain participants.

Key Elements of Supply Chain Governance

1. *Structures for Coordination and Power Sharing*
    - *Governing Bodies or Councils:*
      These are cross-functional teams or committees (including logistics, procurement, operations, and sometimes external partners) that make strategic decisions and oversee the implementation of supply chain initiatives.
    - *Defined Roles and Responsibilities:*
      Clear delineation of authority ensures that every stakeholder knows their part in the chain, from suppliers to end customers. This clarity is crucial for rapid response and coordinated action during disruptions.
2. *Processes for Integration and Oversight*
    - *Policies, Procedures, and Standards:*
      Governance frameworks set out how procurement, production, logistics, and distribution should operate, including quality, safety, and sustainability standards.
    - *Risk Management:*
      Robust risk assessment and mitigation processes are embedded, enabling the supply chain to anticipate, absorb, and recover from disruptions.
    - *Transparency and Reporting:*
      Mechanisms such as contracts, reporting systems, and digital dashboards provide visibility into operations, enabling stakeholders to monitor performance and compliance.

3. *Stakeholder Engagement and Collaboration*
   - *Multi-Stakeholder Involvement:*
     Governance frameworks involve suppliers, manufacturers, logistics providers, and customers in decision-making and continuous improvement, promoting alignment and shared objectives.
   - *Open Communication:*
     Regular information sharing and feedback loops foster trust and facilitate rapid, coordinated responses to emerging challenges.
4. *Strategic Alignment and Continuous Improvement*
   - *Alignment with Business Strategy:*
     Supply chain governance ensures that operational activities support the organization's broader goals, such as growth, profitability, and sustainability.
   - *Adaptability:*
     Governance structures are reviewed and updated regularly to remain effective amid changing market conditions, customer needs, and technological advancements.

How Governance Shapes Resilience

- *Empowers Collective Action:*
  By sharing power and decision-making, governance enables the supply chain to respond as a unified system rather than as disconnected parts.
- *Enhances Flexibility:*
  Clear processes and open communication allow for quick adaptation and reallocation of resources when disruptions occur.
- *Drives Compliance and Risk Mitigation:*
  Oversight mechanisms ensure adherence to regulations and standards, reducing legal, financial, and reputational risks.
- *Promotes Innovation:*
  Collaborative governance encourages stakeholders to contribute ideas, leading to innovative solutions and continuous improvement.

9.2.4.1 Example of supply chain governance in action

A global food and beverage company, when facing pandemic-related disruptions, established a cross-functional governance council including procurement, logistics, and key suppliers. This body set new protocols for risk management, streamlined communication, and empowered rapid decision-making. As a result, the company maintained supply continuity and quickly adapted to changing market demands—demonstrating how effective governance structures and processes underpin resilience (Table 9.1).

Table 9.1 Supply Chain Governance

Governance element	*Role in resilience*
Governing bodies	Strategic oversight, rapid decision-making
Policies and standards	Consistency, compliance, risk mitigation
Stakeholder engagement	Alignment, collaboration, innovation
Transparency	Visibility, accountability, early problem detection
Continuous improvement	Adaptability, sustained performance

9.2.5 In summary

Supply chain governance-the structures and processes for coordination, integration, and power sharing-determines how well a supply chain can anticipate, withstand, and recover from disruptions. Effective governance fosters alignment, transparency, and collective action, making the entire supply chain more resilient and responsive to change.

Supply chain governance-the structures and processes that coordinate and integrate supply management-plays a decisive role in determining the resilience of a supply chain. Effective governance not only clarifies roles, responsibilities, and accountability but also shapes how power is shared among supply chain partners, influencing both individual and collective actions. Here's an elaboration with a case study and example:

Case Study: Private Label Cheese Supply Chains in Greece

A multi-case study of four large Greek retail chains managing private label cheese (specifically feta) illustrates how supply chain governance shapes resilience and performance.

Governance Structures and Processes

- *Integration and Coordination:*

  Retailers managing private label cheese exercised significant control over upstream supply chain activities—such as food quality standardization, packaging, and logistics. They synchronized warehouse and logistics processes by moving processing and packaging units closer to their main warehouses, which would be unfeasible with branded suppliers.
- *Long-Term Partnerships and Power Sharing:*

  Retailers committed to medium- and long-term partnerships with small suppliers, providing them with training and development. This approach fostered trust and mutual investment, shifting away from purely transactional relationships toward collaborative governance.
- *Standardization and Compliance:*

  Both government and retailers enforced strict standards for product quality and safety. Contracts detailed not only product specifications but also information management protocols, ensuring transparency and traceability throughout the supply chain.

- *Innovation Through Collaboration:*
  Governance frameworks allowed for joint innovation, such as improvements in packaging, which required shared investment and risk-taking. These collaborative processes were enabled by the trust and stability established through long-term contracts.

Resilience Outcomes

- *Agility in Disruption:*
  By integrating logistics and standardizing processes, retailers could quickly adapt to supply or demand shocks, reroute products, or adjust production schedules as needed.
- *Sustainable Competitive Advantage:*
  The governance model supported small suppliers, helping them scale and meet quality requirements, which diversified the retailer's supplier base and reduced dependency on any single source.
- *Collective Action:*
  Power was shared through contracts and ongoing dialogue, enabling both retailers and suppliers to act collectively in response to market changes, regulatory updates, or disruptions.

Key *Takeaways*

- *Supply chain governance* determines how well a supply chain can coordinate, integrate, and adapt across multiple organizations and interests.
- *Structures* (such as councils, contracts, and standards) and *processes* (like joint planning, shared innovation, and compliance monitoring) enable both resilience and efficiency.
- *Power sharing* and long-term relationships foster trust, innovation, and the ability to respond collectively to disruptions.

9.2.6 Additional example: Enterprise software company

A large enterprise software company implemented supply chain management best practices by establishing governance frameworks for open-source software use. This included:

- *Supplier management automation*
- *Mandatory documentation and compliance reporting*
- *Continuous improvement via workshops and feedback loops*

This governance structure improved transparency, compliance, and the company's ability to respond to supply chain risks or changes in regulatory requirements.

9.2.7 In summary

Supply chain governance—through its structures and processes for coordination, integration, and power sharing—directly shapes the resilience and adaptability of the entire chain. Effective governance enables collective action, fosters innovation, and ensures that the supply chain can withstand and recover from disruptions.

9.2.8 Visibility

Supply chain visibility is the capability to track and monitor products, materials, and information as they move from the very start of the supply chain (raw materials) to the end customer. It provides a clear, real-time view of upstream and downstream inventories, demand and supply conditions, and production and purchasing schedules, as well as internal alignment on key operational data-often referred to as "one set of numbers."

Key Elements of Supply Chain Visibility

- *End-to-End Transparency:*
  Visibility means being able to see every stage of the supply chain—from suppliers' suppliers to customers' customers. This includes inventory levels, order statuses, shipment locations, and production schedules, both upstream (suppliers, manufacturers) and downstream (distributors, retailers, customers).
- *Real-Time Data and Tracking:*
  Technologies such as IoT sensors, RFID, GPS, and cloud-based platforms enable companies to monitor goods, inventory, and shipments in real time. This allows for immediate detection of delays, shortages, or disruptions.
- *Data Integration and Centralization:*
  Supply chain visibility relies on integrating data from various sources-ERP, warehouse management, transportation systems, and external partners-into a unified platform. This centralization ensures all stakeholders have access to accurate, up-to-date information and agree on a single version of the truth.
- *Internal Alignment:*
  Visibility is not just external. Internally, it requires clear lines of communication and consensus on key metrics, forecasts, and inventory levels so that all departments operate with "one set of numbers."
- *Analytics and Predictive Insights:*
  Advanced analytics and AI tools help companies forecast demand, identify bottlenecks, and proactively manage risks by analyzing real-time and historical data.

Why Supply Chain Visibility Matters

- *Operational Efficiency:*
  Real-time tracking helps identify bottlenecks, optimize processes, and minimize delays in production and delivery.
- *Risk Mitigation:*
  Early detection of potential disruptions (e.g., supplier delays, inventory shortages) enables proactive responses before they impact operations.
- *Improved Decision-Making:*
  Unified, accurate data supports better forecasting, resource allocation, and inventory management, reducing costs and improving service levels.
- *Customer Satisfaction:*
  Visibility allows companies to provide customers with accurate order updates and delivery estimates, increasing trust and loyalty.
- *Regulatory Compliance:*
  Transparent, traceable supply chains facilitate compliance with industry regulations and audit requirements.

How to Achieve Supply Chain Visibility

- *Invest in Technology:*
  Implement ERP, SCM software, IoT sensors, and cloud-based platforms for real-time data capture and integration.
- *Standardize and Integrate Data:*
  Ensure data from all partners and systems is standardized and consolidated for a unified view.
- *Foster Collaboration:*
  Encourage open communication and data sharing among all supply chain stakeholders-suppliers, logistics providers, and customers.
- *Leverage Analytics:*
  Use analytics and visualization tools to monitor performance, forecast trends, and make data-driven decisions.

9.2.9 Example

A company with strong supply chain visibility can track an order from the moment raw materials are sourced through manufacturing, shipping, warehousing, and final delivery to the customer. If a delay is detected at a supplier, the company can immediately reroute shipments, adjust production schedules, or inform customers of new delivery timelines—minimizing disruption and maintaining trust.

9.2.10 In summary

Supply chain visibility is the ability to see and understand every aspect of the supply chain in real time, both externally and internally. It enables better decision-making, risk management, efficiency, and customer service by ensuring all stakeholders operate with accurate, unified information from end to end.

A compelling real-world case study of *supply chain visibility* is Walmart's implementation of real-time shipment visibility platforms to manage its vast, global supply chain. This example illustrates how having a clear view from one end of the pipeline to the other—including upstream and downstream inventories, demand and supply conditions, and production and purchasing schedules—can transform operations, efficiency, and resilience.

Case Study: Walmart's Supply Chain Visibility

9.2.11 Background

Walmart operates one of the world's largest and most complex supply chains, with over 10,500 stores, more than 150 distribution centers in the U.S. alone, and a network of over 100,000 suppliers globally. Managing this scale requires precise coordination and real-time insight across all supply chain activities.

Challenges Before Enhanced Visibility

- Limited visibility into the status and location of shipments.
- Difficulty predicting accurate delivery times.
- Inefficient inventory management leading to stockouts or overstocking.
- Challenges in coordinating with thousands of suppliers and carriers.
- Increased costs due to inefficiencies and lack of transparency.

9.2.12 Solution: real-time shipment visibility platforms

Walmart invested in advanced digital platforms that provide end-to-end supply chain visibility. Key features include:

- *End-to-End Tracking:*
  Every order is tracked from placement with the supplier to final delivery at the store or customer's door. This allows Walmart to monitor every step, from upstream procurement to downstream distribution.
- *Data Integration:*
  The system integrates data from suppliers, carriers, and Walmart's internal systems, providing a holistic, unified view of the supply chain. This ensures all stakeholders operate with "one set of numbers," eliminating discrepancies and confusion.
- *Predictive Analytics:*
  Using historical data and machine learning, the platform predicts potential delays or disruptions, enabling proactive intervention before issues escalate.

- *Real-Time Alerts:*
  Automated alerts notify relevant teams of deviations from planned schedules or emerging issues, supporting rapid response and problem-solving.
- *Mobile Accessibility:*
  Supply chain managers can access real-time information from anywhere, ensuring continuous oversight and decision-making capability.

Results and Benefits

- *Improved Inventory Management:*
  Real-time visibility into incoming shipments allows Walmart to better manage inventory, reducing both stockouts and excess stock.
- *Enhanced Customer Service:*
  Accurate delivery predictions improve Walmart's ability to inform customers about product availability and delivery times.
- *Cost Reduction:*
  Optimized routing, reduced delays, and improved efficiency have significantly lowered logistics costs.
- *Stronger Supplier Relationships:*
  Enhanced visibility and data sharing have improved communication and coordination with suppliers, strengthening partnerships.
- *Greater Agility and Resilience:*
  The ability to quickly identify and respond to disruptions has made Walmart's supply chain more agile and robust in the face of global challenges.

9.2.13 Overcoming implementation challenges

Walmart addressed several hurdles to achieve this level of visibility:

- *Technology Integration:*
  A phased approach was used to integrate new visibility platforms with legacy systems.
- *Data Standardization:*
  Walmart collaborated with partners to standardize data formats and protocols across the network.
- *Change Management:*
  Comprehensive training and clear communication drove adoption among employees and partners.
- *Data Security:*
  Robust cybersecurity measures were implemented to protect sensitive supply chain data.

9.3 CONCLUSION

Walmart's case demonstrates that true supply chain visibility means more than just tracking shipments-it requires integrated data, real-time analytics, clear internal communication, and agreement on "one set of numbers" across the entire network. This visibility enables better decision-making, risk management, and customer service, setting a benchmark for global supply chain excellence

9.3.1 Supply chain risks

Outsourcing a business function—such as manufacturing, IT services, or logistics—does not eliminate or transfer the underlying business risks associated with that function to the supplier or service provider. Instead, the original organization retains significant exposure to supply chain risk, which can manifest in various ways and have substantial impacts on business continuity, reputation, and financial performance.

Why Outsourcing Does Not Transfer Business Risk

- *Responsibility Remains with the Outsourcer:*
  Even when a process is outsourced, the original company is still responsible for the final product or service delivered to its customers. If a supplier fails to deliver, delivers late, or provides substandard quality, it is the outsourcing company's operations and reputation that suffer.
- *Shared and Residual Risks:*
  Outsourcing introduces shared risks, where both the buyer and supplier are exposed to disruptions, and residual risks, which remain with the buyer regardless of contractual arrangements. For example, a supplier's financial instability, labor disputes, or compliance failures can directly affect the outsourcing company's ability to meet its obligations.
- *Complexity and Interconnectedness:*
  Global supply chains are highly interconnected. Disruptions at a supplier—such as shortages, natural disasters, cyberattacks, or geopolitical events—can quickly cascade through the chain, impacting the outsourcer's ability to operate. The COVID-19 pandemic highlighted how reliance on external suppliers for critical components (e.g., semiconductors) led to production halts across entire industries.
- *Legal and Regulatory Accountability:*
  Outsourcing does not absolve a company from regulatory compliance or legal responsibility. If a supplier fails to meet standards (e.g., safety, environmental, data privacy), the outsourcing company may still be held liable by authorities or customers.

9.3.2 Real-World example

Automotive Industry and Semiconductor Shortage:

During the COVID-19 pandemic, many automotive manufacturers outsourced the production of critical electronic components to third-party suppliers. When semiconductor suppliers faced disruptions, automakers could not meet production targets, leading to plant shutdowns and lost revenue. The risk of supply disruption was not transferred; automakers bore the consequences, demonstrating that outsourcing critical components does not eliminate associated risks.

9.3.3 Risk management implications

Because outsourcing does not transfer risk, organizations must:

- *Conduct Thorough Supplier Risk Assessments:*
  Evaluate the financial stability, operational resilience, and compliance of suppliers before and during the relationship.
- *Diversify Suppliers and Build Redundancy:*
  Avoid dependency on single suppliers or regions by engaging multiple sources and maintaining backup options.
- *Implement Robust Contracts:*
  Clearly define performance metrics, contingency plans, and risk-sharing mechanisms in supplier agreements.
- *Maintain Supply Chain Visibility:*
  Use digital tools to monitor supplier performance, inventory, and risks in real time.
- *Collaborate and Share Information:*
  Work closely with suppliers to identify vulnerabilities and improve collective risk management.

9.3.4 In summary

Outsourcing a business function does not transfer the associated business risk to the supplier. The outsourcing company remains ultimately responsible for disruptions, quality issues, and compliance failures. Effective supply chain risk management—including supplier assessment, diversification, robust contracting, and real-time monitoring—is essential to mitigate these persistent risks.

9.3.5 Supplier engagement

Supplier engagement is a strategic process where organizations identify, segment, and develop suppliers and partners across the value chain-including within group businesses and functions-to align with policy, strategy, and the organization's vision. The goal is to generate stakeholder value by leveraging supplier competencies, resources, and knowledge. This approach transforms suppliers from mere vendors into collaborative partners who contribute to innovation, resilience, and sustainability.

Key Elements of Effective Supplier Engagement

1. *Clear Goal Setting and Alignment*
   - Organizations must define what they aim to achieve with supplier engagement (e.g., cost efficiency, sustainability, innovation, risk reduction) and communicate these objectives internally and externally.
   - Cross-departmental unity is critical-procurement, sustainability, product development, finance, and other teams should be aligned on supplier engagement goals.
2. *Supplier Segmentation*
   - Suppliers are strategically categorized based on criteria such as value, risk, business impact, and criticality to operations (using models like the Kraljic Matrix).
   - Segmentation allows organizations to allocate resources and tailor management approaches, focusing more on strategic suppliers while streamlining for non-critical ones.
   - This ensures that attention and development efforts are directed where they can generate the greatest value and mitigate the most significant risks.
3. *Collaboration and Partnership Building*
   - Engagement goes beyond transactions; it involves collaborative planning, joint problem-solving, and co-development of products or solutions.
   - Early involvement of suppliers in product development taps into their expertise and fosters innovation.
   - Long-term partnerships, rather than short-term contracts, build trust and mutual investment in success.
4. *Supplier Development and Support*
   - Organizations invest in supplier training, provide resources, and share best practices to help suppliers meet performance, compliance, and sustainability standards.
   - This may include workshops, digital tools, or access to traceability platforms that simplify compliance and data capture.
5. *Transparency and Communication*
   - Open, two-way communication is essential for building trust and ensuring alignment on expectations, performance metrics, and improvement areas.
   - Digital platforms and centralized systems (such as PLM or supplier portals) facilitate real-time data sharing and performance tracking.

6. *Performance Measurement and Continuous Improvement*
   - Regularly measure supplier performance using KPIs like on-time delivery, quality scores, and sustainability benchmarks.
   - Use this data to identify opportunities for improvement, recognize high performers, and address underperformance collaboratively.
7. *Governance and Policy Integration*
   - Supplier engagement should be embedded in procurement strategy and supported by clear policies, codes of conduct, and governance structures.
   - Assign roles and responsibilities within the organization to ensure accountability and effective implementation.

Value Creation Through Supplier Engagement

- *Innovation:* Engaged suppliers contribute new ideas and solutions, enhancing product development and market responsiveness.
- *Resilience:* Strong relationships and segmentation help organizations anticipate and mitigate supply chain risks.
- *Sustainability:* Collaborative engagement enables organizations to drive ESG (environmental, social, governance) practices across the value chain.
- *Efficiency:* Tailored management and clear communication reduce errors, delays, and administrative burdens, improving overall supply chain performance.

9.3.6 Example in practice

A global retailer segments its suppliers into strategic, leverage, bottleneck, and non-critical categories using the Kraljic Matrix. Strategic suppliers are engaged through joint innovation projects and regular business reviews, while non-critical suppliers are managed through automated procurement systems. The retailer uses digital platforms for real-time data sharing and performance tracking, and invests in supplier training to align with sustainability goals. This approach has resulted in improved product quality, reduced lead times, and enhanced supply chain resilience.

9.3.7 In summary

Supplier engagement is a holistic, strategic process that involves identifying, segmenting, and developing suppliers in alignment with organizational vision and policy. By fostering collaboration, leveraging technology, segmenting suppliers, and focusing on continuous improvement, organizations can unlock supplier competencies and resources to generate stakeholder value and drive sustainable success across the value chain.

A leading real-world example of supplier engagement—where an organization identifies, segments, and develops suppliers in line with its policy, strategy, and vision to create stakeholder value—is *H&M Group's supplier engagement program* for decarbonization.

Case Study: H&M Group—Supplier Engagement for Decarbonization

9.3.8 Background

H&M Group, a global fashion and design company operating in 79 markets, set an ambitious goal to reach net-zero emissions across its value chain by 2040. Recognizing that a significant portion of its environmental impact lies within its supply chain, H&M Group made supplier engagement a central pillar of its sustainability strategy.

Supplier Identification and Segmentation

- *Supplier Mapping:* H&M Group first identified key suppliers across its value chain, focusing on those with the highest environmental impact and strategic importance.
- *Segmentation:* Suppliers were segmented based on their emissions footprint, criticality to H&M's operations, and ability to influence decarbonization outcomes. This allowed H&M to prioritize engagement with suppliers where the greatest impact could be achieved.

Supplier Development and Partnership

- *Local Engagement:* H&M established local teams to work closely with suppliers, providing hands-on support tailored to each supplier's context and capabilities.
- *Financial Assistance:* The company offered financial support and resources to help suppliers invest in cleaner technologies and energy efficiency improvements.
- *Capacity Building:* H&M provided training, tools, and knowledge-sharing platforms to help suppliers set and achieve emissions reduction targets.

Alignment with Policy and Vision

- *Strategic Integration:* Supplier engagement was directly linked to H&M's overall policy and vision for sustainability, ensuring alignment across the group's business units and functions.
- *Stakeholder Value:* By developing supplier competencies and sharing resources and knowledge, H&M not only reduced its own environmental impact but also helped suppliers become more competitive and resilient—generating value for all stakeholders.

Measurable Outcomes

- *Accelerated Progress:* H&M's supplier engagement model led to faster adoption of emissions reduction targets among suppliers, setting an example for the entire apparel and footwear sector.
- *Systemic Change:* The collaborative approach demonstrated how supplier engagement can drive systemic improvements across the value chain, beyond transactional relationships.

Key *Takeaways*

- *Strategic supplier engagement* involves identifying and segmenting suppliers based on strategic value and impact.
- *Development and partnership* are fostered through local engagement, financial and technical support, and capacity building.
- *Alignment with organizational vision* ensures that supplier engagement supports broader sustainability and business goals.
- *Stakeholder value* is generated by enhancing supplier competencies and resilience, benefiting both the organization and its partners.

9.3.9 In summary

H&M Group's supplier engagement program exemplifies how organizations can strategically identify, segment, and develop suppliers in alignment with policy and vision. Through targeted support and partnership, H&M advanced its sustainability agenda and created lasting value across its supply chain.

9.3.10 Supply chain velocity

To increase the velocity of the supply chain, organizations must reduce the end-to-end pipeline time-the total elapsed time it takes to move products and materials from the initial supplier order to final delivery to the customer. This end-to-end pipeline time is a critical measure of supply chain agility, as it reflects not just the speed of individual processes, but the overall responsiveness and flexibility of the entire supply chain.

9.3.10.1 What is end-to-end pipeline time?

End-to-end pipeline time is the elapsed time from when a company places an order with its first-tier supplier to when it delivers the finished product to its customer. It encompasses all phases:

- Procurement and supplier lead times
- Manufacturing and production
- Warehousing and inventory management
- Order processing and fulfillment
- Shipping, distribution, and last-mile delivery

Why Reducing Pipeline Time Increases Agility

- *Faster Response to Demand Changes:* Shorter pipeline times allow companies to respond more quickly and accurately to shifts in customer demand, market trends, or disruptions.
- *Greater Flexibility:* When pipeline time is minimized, businesses can pivot rapidly, change direction, or introduce new products with less delay, enhancing overall flexibility.
- *Lower Inventory and Costs:* Reducing the time products spend in the pipeline means less capital tied up in inventory, lower storage costs, and reduced risk of obsolescence.
- *Improved Customer Satisfaction:* High supply chain velocity ensures customers receive products faster, improving service levels and loyalty.

How to Reduce End-to-End Pipeline Time

- *Streamline Processes:* Eliminate bottlenecks and redundancies across procurement, production, and distribution.
- *Enhance Visibility:* Use real-time data and integrated systems to monitor inventory, orders, and shipments, enabling proactive adjustments.
- *Automate and Digitize:* Implement automation in order processing, warehouse operations, and logistics to speed up workflows.
- *Collaborate with Partners:* Work closely with suppliers and logistics providers to synchronize schedules and reduce delays.
- *Optimize Inventory:* Use demand forecasting and just-in-time inventory strategies to minimize waiting times and excess stock.

9.3.11 Example

E-commerce companies like Amazon have achieved high supply chain velocity by optimizing every stage of their pipeline—from automated order processing and robotic warehousing to advanced logistics and real-time delivery tracking. This reduces end-to-end pipeline time, allowing them to offer rapid delivery and adapt quickly to demand spikes.

9.3.12 In summary

Reducing end-to-end pipeline time increases supply chain velocity and agility. This enables organizations to respond swiftly to market changes, reduce costs, and deliver superior customer service-key drivers of competitive advantage in today's fast-paced environment

A standout real-world case study of supply chain velocity is *Amazon's supply chain*, which exemplifies how reducing end-to-end pipeline time leads to agility, flexibility, and competitive advantage. However, another instructive example comes from *ShipBob*, a fulfillment provider whose practices have been highlighted for achieving high supply chain velocity.

Case Study: ShipBob's High-Velocity Supply Chain

9.3.13 Background

ShipBob is a tech-enabled third-party logistics (3PL) provider that manages fulfillment for thousands of e-commerce brands. In the post-pandemic era, consumer expectations for fast, reliable delivery have soared, with 67% of shoppers now expecting two-day delivery. Meeting these expectations requires exceptional supply chain velocity.

How ShipBob Achieves Supply Chain Velocity

- *Streamlined Internal Processes:*
  ShipBob documents and optimizes every internal process, from inventory intake to order picking and shipping. This reduces confusion, minimizes delays, and ensures that every team works in sync to move products quickly through the pipeline.
- *Real-Time Supply Chain Visibility:*
  The company leverages technology to provide real-time insights into inventory levels, order volumes, and fulfillment throughput. Their analytics tools alert teams when SKUs are running low, enabling proactive inventory management and rapid reorder decisions.
- *Automation and Digitization:*
  Automated systems handle order routing, inventory updates, and shipping label generation, reducing manual work and speeding up fulfillment. This digitization also facilitates seamless integration with e-commerce platforms, ensuring orders flow instantly from online stores to fulfillment centers.
- *Distributed Fulfillment Network:*
  By strategically placing warehouses close to major customer hubs, ShipBob shortens last-mile delivery times, enabling 2-day or even same-day delivery for many customers.

Results and Impact

- *Customer Satisfaction and Loyalty:*
  Brands using ShipBob can consistently offer fast shipping, which is a key driver of customer satisfaction and repeat business. According to studies, 85% of shoppers are more likely to buy when 2-day delivery is available.
- *Increased Profitability:*
  Faster fulfillment reduces the need for excess inventory and lowers operating costs, allowing brands to reinvest savings and grow their businesses.
- *Resilience and Agility:*
  The ability to quickly adapt to demand spikes or disruptions (such as during the COVID-19 pandemic) demonstrates the agility enabled by high supply chain velocity.

9.3.14 Example in action

"ShipBob's analytics tool is really cool. It helps us a lot with planning inventory reorders, seeing when SKUs are going to run out, and we can even set up email notifications so that we're alerted when a SKU has less than a certain quantity left. There is a lot of value in their technology."

- *Oded Harth, CEO & Co-Founder of MDacne*

Key Takeaways

- *High supply chain velocity* is achieved through process optimization, real-time visibility, automation, and strategic facility placement.
- *Velocity enables flexibility*—companies can respond quickly to market changes, manage inventory efficiently, and deliver on rising customer expectations
- *The result is a more resilient, profitable, and customer-centric supply chain.*

9.3.15 In summary

ShipBob's approach to supply chain velocity demonstrates how reducing end-to-end pipeline time—through technology, process discipline, and network design—enables brands to meet modern delivery expectations, boost profitability, and remain agile in a rapidly changing market.

9.3.16 Communication within supply chain

Effective communication and information sharing within the supply chain-and even with competitors-are essential for identifying, managing, and mitigating risks, as well as for capitalizing on opportunities. This collaborative approach enhances overall supply chain resilience and can create mutual benefits for all parties involved.

Why Communication and Information Sharing Matter

- *Enhanced Risk Management:*
  Openly sharing information about risks, incidents, near misses, and vulnerabilities allows all parties to respond more quickly and effectively to disruptions. For example, if a supplier notifies partners about a cyber-attack or a production delay, downstream companies can activate contingency plans or adjust schedules, minimizing the impact on customers.
- *Improved Incident Response:*
  Timely communication ensures that incidents are not isolated but are addressed collectively. This can include sharing lessons learned from past disruptions, which helps prevent recurrence and improves preparedness across the network.

- *Opportunity Identification:*
  Sharing market insights, demand trends, or technological advancements can help supply chain partners-and even competitors-identify new opportunities for collaboration, innovation, or efficiency gains.
- *Building Trust and Collaboration:*
  Transparent communication fosters trust among partners, which is crucial for collaborative problem-solving and long-term relationships. Regular meetings, feedback loops, and clear protocols ensure that all stakeholders are aligned and can act cohesively in the face of uncertainty.

Practical Strategies for Effective Communication

- *Establish Clear Protocols:*
  Define what information needs to be shared, who the recipients are, and the channels to be used (e.g., email, phone, supply chain management platforms). This clarity prevents misunderstandings and ensures critical information reaches the right people quickly.
- *Leverage Technology:*
  Use digital tools and platforms to enable real-time information sharing, status updates, and collaborative decision-making. This is especially important for managing risks that evolve rapidly.
- *Segment and Prioritize Stakeholders:*
  Not all partners require the same level of information. Segment stakeholders based on their criticality and tailor communication accordingly, focusing more attention on those whose actions have the greatest impact on supply chain continuity.
- *Promote Transparency and Proactivity:*
  Encourage proactive reporting of potential issues, near misses, or vulnerabilities, rather than waiting for problems to escalate. This culture of openness supports early intervention and collective action.
- *Risk-Sharing Contracts:*
  Formalize collaboration through risk-sharing contracts, where partners agree to share the burden of disruptions or uncertainties. This approach aligns incentives and strengthens the collective ability to manage supply chain risks.

9.3.17 Example: cross-industry collaboration

During the COVID-19 pandemic, pharmaceutical companies and logistics providers, including competitors, shared information about supply chain bottlenecks, transportation delays, and regulatory changes. This collective effort ensured the efficient distribution of vaccines and medical supplies, demonstrating how transparent communication and collaboration-even among rivals—can deliver mutual benefits and protect public health.

9.3.18 In summary

Sharing information and collaborating about risks, incidents, near misses, vulnerabilities, and opportunities within the supply chain-and even with competitors-enables all parties to respond more effectively, build trust, and realize mutual benefits. Clear communication protocols, technology, transparency, and risk-sharing agreements are key enablers of this collaborative, resilient approach.

A strong real-world case study illustrating the value of communication, information sharing, and collaboration about risks and opportunities across the supply chain comes from the *oil and energy sector's response to weather-related disruptions in Alaska*, as documented in academic research on supply chain communication systems.

Case Study: Oil Supply Chain Communication During Gulf of Alaska Storms

9.3.19 Background

Oil companies operating in Alaska rely on a complex supply chain involving crude oil extraction on the North Slope, transportation via tankers, and delivery to customers. Severe storms in the Gulf of Alaska can delay crude oil tankers, threatening production shutdowns and delayed customer deliveries.

Communication and Collaboration in Action

- *Rapid Information Sharing:*
  When storms threatened tanker schedules, companies quickly relayed information about the delays to all relevant supply chain partners—including suppliers, transporters, and customers.
- *Collaborative Problem Solving:*
  This timely communication allowed suppliers to prioritize available oil volumes, minimizing the overall impact of the disruption. Customers, upon receiving early notice, could seek alternative sources or adjust their own production schedules, reducing the risk of operational shutdowns.
- *Mutual Benefit:*
  By sharing information about near misses, vulnerabilities (such as weather risks), and incidents, all parties in the supply chain—including competitors—were able to coordinate their responses and mitigate the negative effects of the disruption. This collective approach ensured business continuity, preserved customer trust, and reduced financial losses for everyone involved.

Lessons Learned

- *"Information Friction" Management:*
  The case highlights the concept of "information friction"—delays or distortions in communication that can worsen supply chain problems. By addressing and minimizing information friction, the oil companies improved their ability to manage risks and respond to incidents collaboratively.

- *System Redundancy and Open Channels:*
  The companies used multiple communication systems (from phone calls to electronic data interchange) to ensure that critical information reached all stakeholders, even in emergencies.

9.3.20 Broader implications

This case demonstrates that:

- *Open communication and information sharing about risks, incidents, and vulnerabilities across the supply chain—including with competitors—can deliver mutual benefit by enabling faster, more coordinated responses.*
- *Proactive collaboration helps all parties anticipate and mitigate disruptions, enhancing overall supply chain resilience and performance.*

9.3.21 In summary

The oil industry's approach to managing storm-related disruptions in Alaska exemplifies how transparent, timely communication and collaboration about risks and incidents across the supply chain can protect all stakeholders, reduce losses, and realize mutual benefit-even among competitors.

9.3.22 Product stewardship

Product stewardship is a comprehensive, product-centered approach to minimizing the health, safety, environmental, and social impacts of a product and its packaging throughout all stages of its lifecycle, while maximizing economic benefits. This philosophy places primary responsibility on manufacturers or producers, who have the greatest ability to influence a product's impacts, but it also recognizes the important roles played by suppliers, retailers, consumers, and other stakeholders.

Key Principles of Product Stewardship

1. *Lifecycle Management*
   Product stewardship covers every stage of a product's existence—from the sourcing of raw materials, design, and manufacturing, through packaging, transportation, use, and ultimately to end-of-life disposal, recycling, or reuse. At each stage, actions are taken to minimize negative impacts and maximize resource efficiency.
2. *Shared Responsibility*
   While manufacturers are central, stewardship is a shared responsibility. Suppliers must provide safe and sustainable inputs, retailers should educate consumers and ensure safe handling, and consumers are encouraged to use and dispose of products responsibly. Governments

may enforce stewardship through regulations, but many programs are voluntary or industry-led.

3. *Design for Environment (DfE)*
   Stewardship starts at the design phase, where products are engineered to use fewer hazardous substances, be more durable, easier to repair, reusable, and recyclable. This reduces environmental and health risks throughout the lifecycle.
4. *Extended Producer Responsibility (EPR)*
   Manufacturers may be required to take responsibility for their products at end-of-life, including organizing take-back, recycling, or safe disposal programs. This shifts the focus from just selling products to managing their entire lifecycle.
5. *Supply Chain Transparency*
   Effective stewardship requires transparency and collaboration throughout the supply chain. Companies must work with suppliers who share their commitment to ethical and sustainable practices, ensuring traceability and compliance with global regulations.
6. *End-of-Life Management*
   Proper disposal, recycling, or reuse of products and packaging is crucial. Companies may implement recycling initiatives or design products for easier disassembly and material recovery, reducing landfill waste and environmental pollution.

Business Benefits

- *Regulatory Compliance:* Staying ahead of evolving global regulations (such as REACH, GHS, TSCA) and avoiding penalties.
- *Brand Enhancement:* Demonstrating a commitment to sustainability builds trust and loyalty among customers and stakeholders.
- *Cost Savings:* Efficient use of resources, reduced waste, and streamlined processes lead to lower operational costs.
- *Market Access:* Many markets require proof of stewardship for product entry, especially in sectors like electronics, chemicals, and packaging.

Real-World Examples

- *Apple:* Developed the "Daisy" robot to disassemble iPhones for material recovery, illustrating end-of-life stewardship and circular economy principles.
- *Patagonia:* Runs the "Worn Wear" program, encouraging customers to repair, reuse, and recycle clothing, extending product life and reducing waste.
- *Fertilizers Europe:* Requires member companies to follow stewardship requirements at every lifecycle stage, from raw material sourcing to safe use and disposal, to minimize environmental and safety risks.

A highly effective real-world case study of *product stewardship* is Maine's "Bottle Bill" beverage container deposit program, which demonstrates how shared responsibility among manufacturers, retailers, consumers, and recycling companies can minimize environmental and social impacts throughout a product's lifecycle while creating economic value.

Case Study: Maine's Bottle Bill—Beverage Container Product Stewardship

9.3.23 Background

Maine's Bottle Bill is a product stewardship law that requires manufacturers to take responsibility for the collection and recycling of beverage containers. Under this system, producers, retailers, consumers, and recyclers all share responsibility for reducing waste and environmental impact.

How the Program Works

- *Deposit System:*
  Manufacturers charge a 5¢ deposit on each beverage container delivered to retailers. Retailers, in turn, charge this deposit to consumers at the point of sale.
- *Consumer Participation:*
  Consumers return empty containers to collection sites, where they receive their 5¢ deposit back. This incentivizes recycling and reduces litter.
- *Producer Responsibility:*
  Producers collect the empty containers from the redemption centers, pay a handling fee (3.5¢–4¢ per container) to cover sorting and recycling costs, and ensure the containers are properly recycled.
- *Innovative Partnerships:*
  Companies like CLYNK partner with grocery chains (e.g., Hannaford) to provide convenient drop-off locations for consumers. CLYNK's system allows customers to track returns and even donate redemption value to charities.

Outcomes and Benefits

- *High Recycling Rates:*
  Maine boasts a 90% recycling rate for beverage containers, significantly reducing litter and landfill waste.
- *Shared Responsibility:*
  The system distributes responsibility across the value chain: producers fund recycling, retailers facilitate returns, consumers participate in recycling, and processors like CLYNK manage collection and sorting.
- *Economic and Social Value:*
  The program has created jobs (e.g., CLYNK employs 30 full-time staff), spurred innovation in recycling logistics, and provided a profitable business model for redemption centers.

- *Environmental Impact:*
  Studies show Maine's beverage container litter was reduced by 69–77% after the law's implementation, demonstrating substantial environmental benefit.
- *Voluntary and Regulatory Elements:*
  While the program is mandated by law, it also encourages voluntary innovation and partnerships, such as CLYNK's customer-focused services.

9.3.24 Product stewardship in action

"Producers, consumers, and beverage-related businesses all share responsibility in our system, and it works-we have a 90% recycling rate for beverage containers here in Maine because of the bottle bill."
– Paul Coburn, Owner, Old Mill Redemption Center

Key *Takeaways*

- *Lifecycle Impact:* The program minimizes environmental and social impacts from production through end-of-life.
- *Stakeholder Involvement:* Manufacturers, retailers, consumers, and recyclers all play active roles.
- *Economic and Environmental Value:* The system creates jobs, reduces waste, and keeps resources in the economy.
- *Scalability:* Maine's model is a benchmark for other regions seeking to implement effective product stewardship.

9.3.25 In summary

Maine's Bottle Bill is a leading example of product stewardship in action, showing how shared responsibility, innovative partnerships, and regulatory frameworks can deliver health, safety, environmental, social, and economic benefits throughout a product's lifecycle.

9.3.26 Improving the resilience of your supply chain

Supply chains face increasing risks of disruption, with the greatest threats often originating from the wider supply network rather than within the company itself. Most organizations still focus on continuity planning for their own operations, despite the growing complexity and vulnerability of supply chains due to outsourcing, globalization, and market volatility.

External risks like war, epidemics, and natural disasters can now cause widespread disruptions affecting entire businesses or industries. These risks are intensified by long global supply chains, short product cycles, and unpredictable markets.

Effective resilience management requires a systems view, acknowledging interdependencies between organizations. This means considering the resilience of key partners. The emerging field of supply chain event management is valuable in handling operational disruptions.

This section explores recent research on enhancing organizational resilience through stronger supply chains.

The term "supply chain" emerged in the early 1980s to describe a new management discipline. This approach sought greater efficiency by integrating logistics (transport, warehousing, distribution) and operations management (purchasing, order and inventory management, production planning, and customer service) to deliver better value to customers and shareholders.

In the 1990s, supply chain management aimed to enhance product flow efficiency by integrating logistics, operations, and marketing into inter-organizational processes. This was driven by rapid IT advancements, which improved efficiency and awareness of market changes and customer needs.

A real-world case study that highlights how managers perceive supply chain risks differently from insurers or crisis managers—focusing instead on performance issues rooted in managerial decisions and industry dynamics—can be found in the supply side risk assessment of Huawei's supply chain. This example reveals the nuanced tensions between process performance measures, strategic decisions, safety-critical constraints, and industry structures.

Case Study: Huawei's Supply Side Risk Assessment

9.3.27 Managerial risk perceptions

During interviews, Huawei managers did not primarily focus on catastrophic risks like fire or terrorism (the typical concerns of insurers or crisis managers). Instead, they highlighted operational and strategic risks that directly impact supply chain performance:

- Poor Coordination and Communication:
  Managers identified that poor coordination between suppliers and Huawei led to delays in receiving components, which in turn caused issues with delivery lead times and information sharing. This directly affected customer satisfaction and operational efficiency.
- Quality and Skills Risks:
  Production managers pointed out risks related to the quality of supplied components and the skill levels within the company, both of which could disrupt production and sourcing, ultimately increasing costs and reducing profit margins.
- Hidden and Strategic Costs:
  Managers were concerned about hidden costs arising from changes in tariffs, duties, and taxes, which could unpredictably erode profitability.

- Industry and Structural Dynamics:
  The interviews revealed that rapid evolution in supply chain structures (to gain competitive advantage), technical changes, and exposure to global competitive pressures were creating new and more severe risks than in the past (Table 9.2).

9.3.28 Risks identified

Table 9.2 The case study illustrates several risks

Risks	*Example from Huawei case*
Individual process performance measures	Delays in component delivery and poor information sharing affecting lead times.
Strategic business decisions	Shifting supply chain structures and sourcing strategies to remain competitive.
Safety-critical product constraints	Quality and skills risks impacting the reliability and safety of end products.
Industry/supply chain structures	Managing risks in a rapidly evolving, globally competitive supply chain network.

9.3.29 Distinct managerial focus

Unlike insurers, who focus on rare but catastrophic events (fire, terrorism), Huawei's managers prioritized risks that stem from everyday decisions and industry trends:

- They saw the cumulative impact of quality, coordination, and cost risks as more significant to business performance.
- Their concerns centered on operational continuity, customer satisfaction, and margin protection, rather than on insurable, low-probability events.

Lessons and Implications

- Risk management must address both strategic and operational dimensions, not just external shocks.
- Managerial decisions about supplier relationships, process integration, and industry adaptation are central to supply chain resilience.
- Tensions between efficiency (process performance), flexibility (strategic decisions), safety (product constraints), and adaptability (industry structure) must be continuously balanced to sustain performance and competitiveness.

9.3.30 In summary

The Huawei case study demonstrates that managers often perceive—and prioritize—supply chain risks differently than crisis managers or insurers. Their focus is on the performance risks arising from managerial decisions, process integration, and evolving industry dynamics, highlighting the need for a holistic and adaptive approach to supply chain risk management.

9.3.31 Supply chain risk as seen by supply chain managers

Reduced supply chain performance due to managerial decisions and industry trends

- Individual process performance measures
- Impact of strategic business decisions
- Constraints imposed by complex safety-critical nature of the products
- Industry or supply chain structures

9.3.31.1 Complexity

Counteracting complexity was a recurrent theme. The demands of the marketplace, constant changes in product specifications, together with other continuous improvement initiatives within the organizations and the wider industry as a whole, meant that the supply chains never actually reached a stable "steady state."

Furthermore, product and supply chain complexity meant that although interviewees were implicitly or explicitly adopting a process-based view of risk in their supply chains, this was certainly not an "end-to-end" supply chain perspective. Though it was clear that extant managerial practices reinforced a much truncated view of the supply chain.

None of the organizations concerned routinely monitored beyond their immediate customers or suppliers.

9.3.32 Leaner supply chains and the move towards JIT delivery

All of the manufacturing or processing organizations consulted have streamlined operations in recent years and are actively pursuing further opportunities to reduce overheads and inventory holdings.

Nevertheless, several managers expressed concerns that while leaner operations are recognized as a commercial necessity, an overzealous application of lean principles could restrict growth opportunities. For example, the oil company noted that, in some markets it serves, there is insufficient capacity to meet short-term increases in demand.

Managers from the grocery retail business also believed that excessive leanness might limit future expansion opportunities, not only in terms of organic growth but also considering industry dynamics and strategic changes. Similarly, the packaging manufacturer and a public sector healthcare organization aimed to significantly reduce costs by lowering inventory holdings. In uncertain and dynamic environments, they faced the dilemma of determining the appropriate depth of these cuts.

The issue of managing obsolescence was raised by aerospace managers and highlighted by the packaging company and automotive spare suppliers. They identified the conflicting requirements of lean supply chains and the necessity to manage obsolescence. For the packaging company, managing inventory holdings of capital equipment spares posed the most significant challenges. The automotive spare supplier acknowledged the need to buffer with "all-time buys" to address obsolescence issues and protect future service commitments.

One interviewee, a purchasing specialist, suggested that many problems with managing obsolescence stemmed from purchasing managers who originally sourced parts based on price at the time of order, without dealing with subsequent issues. He indicated that the "part not current" problem was particularly common with U.S. suppliers.

Reduced supply chain resilience as a result of the smaller supplier base and longer supply chains

- Results in bigger order quantities, higher inventory, and higher storage costs
- Risk associated with the migration of a parts supplier from one location to another
- Changes the risk profile at an operational and strategic business level
- Lower level of managerial skills, political instability, and lawlessness

The interviews conducted for this research corroborate previous assertions that the globalization of business has intensified the tension between price-focused purchasing and the management of supply chain risk.

A manager from an automotive spares company observed that materials sourced from the Far East at a lower unit cost led to increased order quantities, higher inventory levels, and elevated storage costs; however, these additional costs were not borne by the purchaser. This manager also emphasized another theme identified in aerospace findings—the risk associated with relocating a parts supplier from one location to another. Such relocations seldom proceeded smoothly, primarily due to the loss of experienced staff during the transition. Consequently, companies had to maintain buffer stock to mitigate these disruptions.

For transport and logistics providers serving these companies, globalization has altered the risk profile at both operational and strategic business levels. The managing director of a third-party logistics provider (3PL) explained that while developing markets presented numerous opportunities, the risks related to operational control had increased significantly. He attributed this to a lower level and breadth of managerial skills within the local populations, as well as risks stemming from political instability, lawlessness, and other factors.

9.3.33 Consolidation of production and distribution

Many manufacturing organizations aim to consolidate sites for better asset returns. For example, a pharmaceutical company faced constraints from government contracts and FDA rules when optimizing their operations. Meanwhile, an oil company planned fewer larger terminals, aware of increased disruption risks due to cost pressures and low hydrocarbon margins.

Similarly, food manufacturers and 3PLs worried about supply chain resilience with a smaller supplier base and longer chains, especially against natural disasters. A UK retailer planned to consolidate its domestic distribution network into fewer larger centers, recognizing the vulnerability of leaner supply chains and higher reliance on technology, including IT and automation risks.

9.3.34 Reduction of the supplier base

Several organizations have been rationalizing their supplier base. The pharmaceutical company, as part of its post-merger optimization, opted for single sourcing. While this increases supply-side risks, it minimizes inventory and demand risks through improved quality control and consensus forecasting.

Similarly, the packaging manufacturer reduced its suppliers from over 7,000 to a more manageable number, enabling a supplier development program with first-tier suppliers. Like the pharmaceutical company, they see benefits in fewer production issues due to consistent inputs despite potential challenges in switching suppliers.

9.3.35 The trend to outsourcing

Opinions on outsourcing varied among managers. Some saw it as irrelevant, while others viewed it as necessary. It was least relevant to managers in oil and petrochemicals, who had a vertically integrated process with no secondary distribution responsibilities. Supermarket managers recognized benefits in outsourcing transport to mitigate risks, maintaining control through a mixed strategy.

A pharmaceutical manager highlighted evaluating outsourcing's internal impact both functionally and process-wise. However, outsourcing sometimes backfired, as seen when they lost key staff and knowledge after outsourcing certain processes. Similar issues arose with IT outsourcing.

The electronics manufacturer reported over 85% of their internal processes were outsourced, prompting a focus on supply chain redesign for brand protection. As a result, contract management skills became crucial for supply chain managers.

9.3.36 The four levels of risk

Improving supply chain resilience requires understanding that vulnerabilities in the supply chain can arise in various forms, and risk factors operate at multiple levels. These interconnected levels are described here for clarity within four interrelated levels of analysis:

- Level 1—Process/Value Stream
- Level 2—Assets and Infrastructure Dependencies
- Level 3—Organizations and Inter-organizational Networks
- Level 4—The Environment

Level 1 examines the supply chain from an integrated end-to-end supply chain management perspective. Levels 2–4 introduce sources of risk that can cause disruptions, affecting the efficiency and effectiveness of supply chain management and potentially threatening business continuity.

Level 1 views supply chain vulnerability through a process engineering lens, treating the supply chain as a linear pipeline between organizations. The focus is on efficient management of individual workflows and their associated information by product or product class. Supply chains carry one or more "Value Streams." Reliable information is crucial and depends on parties' willingness to share it, requiring high trust and cooperation between neighboring organizations.

In summary, this approach aims to achieve a seamless flow of information and materials by encouraging all supply chain partners to think and act cohesively. These process management principles support the foundations of both "lean" manufacturing and agile supply chain management methods.

From a process-based perspective, supply chain risks primarily involve financial or commercial risks resulting from poor quality, sub-optimal performance, demand fluctuations, and changing market requirements.

The popular analogy of a supply chain as a seamless "pipeline" serves as a useful metaphor but can be misleading when considering supply chain vulnerability. This analogy promotes a vision of stability and control by depicting a linear, self-transporting flow that is shielded from external disruptions. In reality, supply chains are seldom fixed, discrete, self-propelling, or self-protecting entities.

Furthermore, the adoption of lean and agile practices, particularly Just-In-Time (JIT) delivery, has increased the dependency on a reliable, secure, and efficient communication, transportation, and distribution infrastructure.

Level 2 of the framework focuses on supply chains' asset and infrastructure dependencies. Here, nodes become fixed commercial sites like factories and retail outlets, as well as IT assets. These sites are connected through national and international communications infrastructure and transportation networks, including roads, rail, waterways, and air routes. Assets such as trucks, trains, boats, and planes operate along these links, all maintained by skilled personnel.

At Level 2, the resilience of the network should be evaluated based on the impact of the temporary or permanent loss of links, nodes, and other essential operating assets. Maintaining their operation typically falls under the responsibility of business continuity managers, logistics, operations, IT, human resource professionals, and emergency planners.

Level 3 views supply chains as interorganizational networks, elevating vulnerability to business strategy and microeconomics. In this framework, nodes represent organizations that manage assets and infrastructure, and links are trading relationships with power dependencies. Integrated supply chain management relies on strong organizations not exploiting weaker ones and sharing information and risk for mutual benefit. However, commercial interests, competition, and strategic differences often oppose these goals. Network instability can result from reconfigurations like outsourcing, business failures, or mergers. Dominant organizations managing collaborative supply chains lead to "extended enterprises," but maintaining partnerships is resource-intensive. To lower costs, many large customers have reduced suppliers, favoring single sourcing, which increases the risk of disruptions from supplier failure.

Level 4 – This final level involves the macroeconomic and natural environment affecting organizations, assets, infrastructure, supply chains, and value streams. Key factors include political, economic, social, and technological elements, alongside natural phenomena like geological, meteorological, and pathological events.

Risks at this level are often beyond direct control but can be anticipated for informed risk management decisions. Technological advances impact product demand, business models, and supply chain cooperation. Socio-political disruptions and geopolitical changes also influence international trade and supply chain structures. Macroeconomic fluctuations due to terrorism, war, or currency shifts affect demand, pricing, and purchasing.

Natural events like earthquakes and hurricanes disrupt supply chains, while pathological threats such as diseases and computer viruses highlight vulnerabilities in distribution and information systems.

9.3.37 A new risk

Companies today often outsource goods and services to focus on core competencies, improve financial performance, and mitigate cost-related competitive risks. However, this practice may introduce unforeseen risks not apparent at the decision-making stage. For example, manufacturers like Nokia, Ericsson, and Land Rover use common components across product lines to reduce costs and boost efficiency, which benefits supply chain management when assessing risk from a functional or internal perspective.

Using common components helps planners reduce forecasting and inventory risks, as aggregate forecasts are typically more reliable. These components also ensure quality consistency and lower unit costs due to larger order quantities. However, a supply disruption can impact multiple product lines instead of just one. As third parties often produce goods or services, competitors and users in other sectors may also use them. During shortages, the largest customer typically gets priority.

Manuj, I. and Mentzer, J.T. (2008) Global Supply Chain Risk Management. *Journal of Business Logistics*, Vol. 29, No. 1, pp. 133–155.

9.3.38 The five steps

Global supply chain risk management follows a classic circular risk analysis paradigm: Identify > Assess and Evaluate > Mitigate > Monitor and Re-assess. The steps are:

- Risk Identification
- Risk Assessment and Evaluation
- Selection of Risk Management Strategies
- Implementation of Risk Management Strategies
- Mitigation of Supply Chain Risks

9.3.39 Types of risks

Classify risks into qualitative/quantitative and atomistic/holistic. They identify the following types:

- *Supply Risks*: Disruption of supply, inventory, and schedules
- *Operational Risks*: Operations breakdown, technology changes
- *Demand Risks*: Demand variations
- *Security Risks*: Theft, sabotage, terrorism, counterfeiting, infrastructure breakdown
- *Macro Risks*: Economic shifts, recession, wage hikes, exchange rate variations
- *Policy Risks*: Government actions, legislative changes
- *Competitive Risks*: Competitor uncertainty
- *Resource Risks*: Resource availability uncertainty

The first four are supply chain risks; the latter four are environmental risks. It is important to:

- Inventory the extended enterprise and integration points with overseas entities:
  - Identify origins of critical services and products.
  - Pinpoint single points of failure in the supply chain.
  - Locate single- and sole-source suppliers.
  - Check if contingency plans cover supply chain disruptions.
  - Determine sourcing and shipping methods for crucial products from overseas.

In a global economy, materials come from around the world. Assessing your mission-critical supply chain is essential, though challenging. You may receive critical inventory from countries affected by avian flu. The following checklist offers guidance on assessing your supply chain.

When assessing products:

- Identify minimum inventories needed for critical supplies, considering peak periods.
- Collaborate with suppliers on plans for addressing supply chain disruption during a pandemic.
- Determine whether critical vendors pose exposure risks.
  - Evaluate your vendors' pandemic plans.
  - If some vendors lack adequate plans, consider partnering with competing firms.

Roundtable participants discussed helping vendors ensure pandemic readiness and considered incentives for service/product availability, though current plans did not include such incentives. Some companies are adding pandemic planning requirements in new contracts.

9.3.40 Risk management strategies

Manuj and Mentzer, following the approach outlined by Jütner, Peck, and Christopher (2003), classify risk management strategies into seven categories:

- Avoidance: exiting or delaying entry into a market or product.
- Postponement: delaying resource commitment to maintain flexibility.
- Speculation: assuming risk to gain competitive advantage.
- Hedging: globally dispersing portfolios of suppliers, customers, and facilities.
- Control: integrating vertically and laterally with suppliers and business partners.
- Transferring/sharing risk: outsourcing, offshoring, contracting.
- Security: identifying unusual movements and protecting against unwanted penetration.

In selecting an appropriate strategy, managers should consider both market risk and business risk, seeking to balance these factors.

9.3.41 Scanning the landscape – a managerial framework

Given the inter-organization, international, and inter-industry nature of contemporary supply chain networks, a managerial toolkit for identifying and managing supply chain risk and vulnerability represents a practical approach to addressing the issue. At the beginning of this report, it was suggested that supply chain risk can originate from sources within the supply chain and/or external sources.

However, the application of a managerial toolkit advances from the perspective of a manager in an organization or business unit—a single node in one or more of the inter-organizational networks described in the earlier framework. It has also been established that organizations rarely have comprehensive knowledge of the workings of their customers or suppliers beyond those immediately adjacent to them.

Consequently, a structured analytical framework has been provided, using this limited supply chain perspective as a starting point. The framework guides management in considering how, where, when, and why supply chains may be vulnerable at each of the four levels of the landscape (i.e., value-stream, asset/infrastructure, organizations, environment).

9.3.42 The managerial framework

The managerial framework categorizes the sources of risk based on the location of a potential risk or event manifestation into three stages:

- Internal to the focal firm:
  - Process
  - Control
- External to the focal firm but internal to the supply chain network:
  - Demand
  - Supply
- External to the network:
  - Environment

The first two "internal" categories of the framework pertain to elements within the control of the focal firm, typically within the firm's legal boundaries.

Processes are sequences of value-adding and managerial activities conducted by the firm. The execution of these processes depends on internally owned or managed assets and functioning infrastructure. Hence, the reliability of these assets and supporting infrastructure should be carefully evaluated. Process risk involves disruptions to these processes.

Controls are the assumptions, rules, systems, and procedures that govern how an organization manages its processes. In terms of the supply chain, they include order quantities, batch sizes, safety stock policies, and regulations governing asset and transportation management. Control risk arises from the application or misapplication of these rules.

9.3.43 Process risk

Processes and control mechanisms should align to support corporate and supply chain strategies. The following two categories are external to the focal firm but remain internal to the inter-organizational networks through which materials, products, and information flow. Ideally, the focal firm should be aware of potential or actual disturbances to the expected flow of product and information within and between every node or link in the supply chain networks through which its value streams flow. While this may not always be possible in practical terms, the focal firm should at least aim to familiarize itself with known or likely issues affecting adjacent organizations.

The focal firm is unlikely to have detailed knowledge of all potential risks; however, appropriate monitoring should increase awareness and provide early warning of actual events. Demand risk pertains to potential or actual disruptions to the flow of product, information, and cash within the network, between the focal firm and the market. This includes processes, controls, assets, and infrastructure dependencies of downstream and adjacent organizations.

Supply risk is the upstream equivalent, relating to potential or actual disturbances to the flow of product or information within the network, upstream of the focal firm.

The final category involves disruptions external to the network of organizations through which value streams/product supply chains flow. Environmental events may directly impact the focal firm, upstream or downstream organizations, or the marketplace itself. They may affect a particular value stream (e.g., product contamination) or any node or link in the supply chain (e.g., accidents, direct actions, extreme weather, or natural disasters). These events can result from socio-political, economic, or technological factors far removed from the focal firm's supply chains but may have knock-on effects through connections to other industry networks. While some of these events may be predictable (e.g., regulatory changes), many will not be, although their impacts can be assessed.

Controls are the assumptions, rules, systems, and procedures that govern an organization's processes. In the supply chain, they include order quantities, batch sizes, safety stock policies, and asset and transportation policies. Control risk arises from the proper or improper application of these rules.

Environment—Events can impact the focal firm, those upstream or downstream, or the marketplace. These events may affect a specific value stream (e.g., product contamination) or any part of the supply chain (e.g., accidents, direct actions, extreme weather, natural disasters). They may stem from socio-political, economic, or technological events far from the firm's supply chains but still cause knock-on effects through industry networks. Some events may be predictable (e.g., regulatory changes), but many are not, though their impacts may be assessed.

Principles of resilience: Supply chain resilience means agility. Managing supply chain vulnerability depends on context and the need for operational excellence. Four principles are identified:

- Risk should influence supply chain design and structure.
- Risk management requires high visibility, process alignment, and cooperation among all partners.
- Supply chain resilience implies agility, meaning the ability to react quickly to unpredictable events.

Establishing a risk management culture within the organization, based on well-defined performance requirements and communication channels among all supply chain entities, will enhance and enable supply chain resilience. At a tactical level, specific activities should be undertaken to prepare for and address disruptions.

These activities include the following processes:

- Risk identification process, such as identifying product, supplier, and supply chain-related risks.
- Risk assessment process, including evaluating likelihood, impact, and cost.
- Supply chain continuity management and coordination processes.
- Processes to ensure learning from experiences.

9.3.44 Supply chain reengineering

Traditionally, supply chains were designed to optimize cost and customer service, with resilience rarely being a focus. Given current risks, this must change. Recommendations for designing resilient supply chains include:

Understanding the Supply Chain

- *Mapping Tools*: Identify "pinch points" (capacity bottlenecks) and "critical paths".
  - Pinch Points: Bottlenecks where alternative options are limited.
  - Critical Paths: May have long lead-times, single-source supplies, poor visibility, or high risk.

Risk Assessment

- Create a risk register noting vulnerabilities of critical nodes and links.
- Define procedures for monitoring, mitigation, and management of these risks.

9.3.45 Supplier base strategy

While there has been a trend toward reducing the supplier base in many companies, it is important to recognize the potential limits of this approach. Single sourcing, where one supplier is responsible for providing a specific item or service, may offer benefits in terms of cost and quality management but poses significant risks regarding resilience.

Although having a lead supplier may be desirable, it is crucial to have alternative sources available whenever possible. For companies with multiple sites, employing a single source for an item or service at each site can capture some advantages of single sourcing while mitigating associated risks. Similarly, manufacturing firms producing a range of products might achieve single sourcing by product line, thereby maintaining an alternate supply source.

A key criterion for selecting suppliers should be their awareness of supply chain risk. For instance, have they audited their own supply chain risk profile? Do they have established procedures for monitoring and mitigating risks?

It may be beneficial for the company to adopt a proactive strategy of supplier development, working closely with key suppliers to enhance their supply chain risk management practices.

9.3.46 Design principles for supply chain resilience

A number of principles have emerged which should be considered when (re) engineering supply chains to improve resilience:

- Choose supply chain strategies that keep several options open.
  This may not be the lowest cost course of action but may be the lowest risk. There is an analogy here with "Real Options Theory" in investment planning. Thus a strategy that is based around centralization of distribution facilities may be the lowest cost option but it could also shut down other options and hence increase vulnerability.
- Re-examine the "efficiency vs. redundancy" trade-off.
  Conventionally surplus capacity and inventory have been seen as undesirable. However, the strategic disposition of additional capacity and/or inventory can be extremely beneficial in the creation of resilience within the supply chain. Capacity is a form of inventory but is often more flexible in that inventory may already be committed to its final form or destination. Both capacity and inventory can provide "slack" in a supply chain to enable surge effects to be coped with.

Inventory, carried in a generic or semi-configured form, can enable the creation of a "de-coupling point" that, together with additional capacity (e.g. production, transport, people), can enable demand uncertainty to be more effectively managed.

9.3.47 Supply chain collaboration

A high level of collaborative working across supply chains can help significantly to mitigate risk. The challenge is to create the conditions in which collaborative working becomes possible. Traditionally, supply chains have been characterized by arm's-length, even adversarial, relationships between different participants. There has not been a history of sharing information either with suppliers or customers. More recently, however, there have been signs that a greater willingness to work in partnership is emerging in many supply chains.

In the fast-moving consumer goods (FMCG) industry, there is now significant collaboration between manufacturers and retailers through Collaborative Planning, Forecasting, and Replenishment (CPFR) initiatives. The underlying principle of collaboration in the supply chain is that the exchange of information and application of shared knowledge can reduce uncertainty.

Thus, a key priority for supply chain risk reduction should be the creation of a supply chain community to enable the exchange of information between members. The aim is to create a high level of "supply chain intelligence," ensuring

Figure 9.1 Supply chain knowledge can be divided into strategic, tactical, and operational categories as given in the figure.

greater visibility of upstream and downstream risk profiles (and changes in those profiles) at each node and link in the supply chain, and at each level of analysis, i.e., environment, network, asset/infrastructure, and process (Figure 9.1).

Strategic knowledge involves understanding trends and emerging issues that may affect future supply chain continuity. This can be generated through formal "P.E.S.T." analyses (Political, Economic, Social, Technological) to appraise the operating context.

Tactical knowledge focuses on assessing risks to current operations in areas such as market volatility, product life cycle, lead-times, supplier consolidation, bottlenecks, variability, visibility issues, and data integrity.

Operational knowledge pertains to daily business management. Supply chain event management is valuable for handling operational disruptions.

9.3.48 Agility – responding to change

Supply chain agility refers to the capability to quickly adapt to unpredictable changes in demand or supply. Many organizations face risks due to their lengthy response times to such changes or disruptions. Agility encompasses various dimensions and is relevant to networks as well as individual companies. A critical factor for an agile response is the presence of agile partners both upstream and downstream of the focal firm. Two crucial components of agility are:

- Visibility
- Velocity

9.3.49 Supply chain visibility

Supply chain visibility is the capability of all members of the supply chain to monitor the entire pipeline from one end to the other. It involves having a clear view of upstream and downstream inventories, demand and supply conditions, and production and purchasing schedules, facilitated by transparent communication and agreement on a unified set of data.

A lack of visibility compels supply chain managers to rely on forecasts and build buffer inventories, which may not align with actual demand, thereby exacerbating the issue. These buffers are often created independently by different members of the supply chain, who lack detailed knowledge of activities in the rest of the network, such as information on finished goods inventory, materials inventory, work in progress, demand, capacity, order status, and so forth. Visibility can be further distorted by the bullwhip effect, which amplifies minor fluctuations in market demand as they move back up the supply chain.

9.3.50 Supply chain risk management: processes and tools

The research indicated that companies across all sectors were involved in general corporate risk management and supply chain management, although inter-organizational supply chain resilience was not the primary motivation. When asked to evaluate the risk management tools and techniques available for managing supply chain resilience, managers sometimes found it challenging to respond. There was uncertainty regarding the concepts of supply chain vulnerability and resilience. Consequently, there was some ambiguity about the relevance of managerial tools currently used for other purposes.

With further clarification, most interviewees could identify with at least some of the tools highlighted in the aerospace case study. Occasionally, they suggested additional tools that they had found useful in their specific contexts.

Challenges

- There is a gap between business strategy decisions and their impact on supply chain vulnerability.
- Globalization and cost-cutting pressures create supply chain risks.
- Supply chain managers generally focus on internal operational risks, not on supply chain vulnerability or resilience.
- Business continuity planning often overlooks that the greatest risk may come from the wider supply chain rather than within the business.
- There is a disconnect in organizations between the determination of business strategy and the recognition of the impact of these strategic decisions upon supply chain vulnerability.
- The globalization of business and the pressure for cost reduction have in turn created supply chain risks.
- Managers with supply chain responsibilities generally focus on internal operational risks. They are not explicitly required to address supply chain vulnerability or resilience.
- Business continuity planning tends to focus on the internal network; however, it should be understood and acted upon that the greatest risk to business continuity may stem from the wider supply chain rather than from within the business.

9.3.51 Recommendations

9.3.51.1 Why businesses should act

Supply chains are networks linking businesses, industries, and economies. A modest incident can expose weaknesses if viewed in isolation without recognizing the interconnected system. Current supply chain risk understanding is underdeveloped, missing the bigger picture.

While IT-related business continuity and risk management are well understood and applied, the same can't be said for supply chain risk management. Major barriers include a lack of:

- An integrated action program incorporating the supply chain function
- Access to an appropriate toolkit (Figure 9.3)

Addressing supply chain vulnerability requires a change management approach that considers industry culture, structure, and business drivers. We identified four key success factors for supply chain continuity management:

- Risk awareness among top managers
- Integrating risk awareness into supply chain management
- Awareness by employees of their role in risk management
- Recognizing that changes in business strategy alter supply chain risk profiles (Figure 9.2).

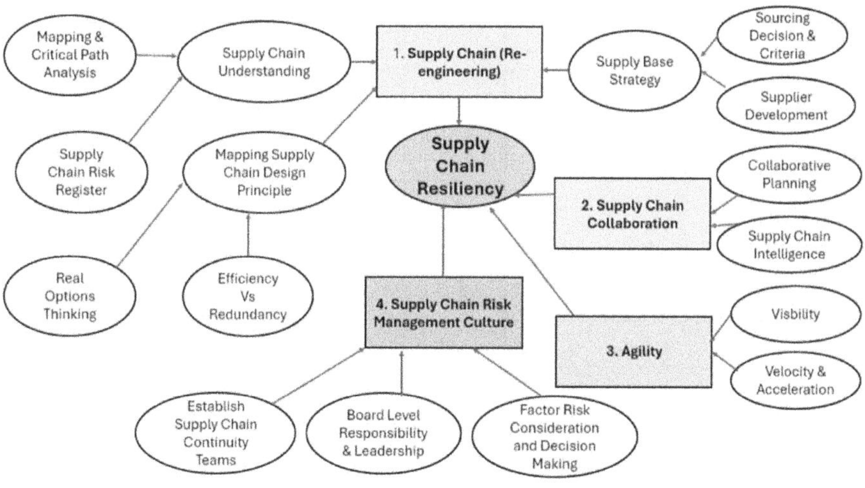

Figure 9.2 Supply Chain Resiliency

Six Sigma Methodology (DMAIC)	Define & Measure	Analyse	Improve	Control
Supply Chain Process Risk Management IMPARC	**Identify, Measure & Prioritise**	**Analyse**	**Reduce**	**Control**
Tools and Techniques				
Scenario Planning	x			
Delphi Forecasting	x			
Brainstorming	x		x	
Failure Modes and Effect Analysis (FMEA)	x			
Flowcharting	x			
Supply Chain Mapping	x			
Critical Path Analysis	x			
Bottleneck Identification	x			
Statistical Process Control	x	x		x
Process Capability Analysis	x	x		x
Simulation Modelling	x	x	x	
Root Cause Analysis	x	x		
Fishbone Diagram	x	x		
Pareto Analysis	x		x	
Process Decision Program Chart			x	
Benchmarking		x	x	
Business Process Re-engineering			x	
Time-based Process Mapping		x	x	

Figure 9.3 Six Sigma Methodology - Toolkit

Many companies have outsourced parts of their operations, which could be disrupted during regional or national disasters.

- Contact key suppliers or contractors to determine the types of contingency plans they have in place.
- Since most supply chains operate on a just-in-time model, many core items and critical inputs may become unavailable.

To mitigate this risk:

- Identify core items and critical inputs.
- Categorize critical inputs as follows:
  - "Vulnerable"—Potentially not available.
  - "Non-vulnerable"—Likely to be available.

Develop contingency plans for unavailability of supplies and inputs
Identify alternative supply chains

- Moving from international to local

Create emergency purchase orders ahead of time that can be executed when needed
Negotiate with vendors ahead of time
Provide a prioritized list of key customers who will receive products by type and channel – and develop plans for scaling back production to these customers (Figure 9.3)

BIBLIOGRAPHY

(2003), "Creating Resilient Supply Chains: A Practical Guide," Cranfield School of Management, ISBN 1 861941 02.

(2003), "Understanding Supply Chain Risk: A Self-Assessment Workbook," Cranfield School of Management, ISBN 1 861941 03 X

Sheffi, Y., (October 2005). Building a resilient supply chain. Harvard Business Review, 1(8) 1–4.

Chapter 10

The interconnectedness of organizations

LEARNING OBJECTIVES

By the end of this chapter, you will be able to:

- Establish Robust Communication Practices: Develop comprehensive communication strategies that build trust, manage reputation, and promote collaboration across all stakeholder groups.
- Manage Crisis Communications Effectively: Learn to coordinate internal and external communications during crises, maintaining message consistency and stakeholder confidence.
- Build and Maintain Stakeholder Trust: Understand the critical importance of transparency, accountability, and consistent messaging in preserving long-term stakeholder relationships.

10.1 INTRODUCTION

In an increasingly interconnected and volatile world, an organization's ability to withstand and recover from disruptions hinges not only on its operational robustness but also on its communication and stakeholder engagement strategies. Effective communication builds trust, manages reputation, fosters collaboration, and ensures that all stakeholders are informed and engaged, especially during times of crisis. This chapter explores the fundamental principles and practices of communication and stakeholder engagement that are vital for organizational resilience.

10.2 INTERCONNECTEDNESS

In an increasingly interconnected and volatile world, an organization's ability to withstand and recover from disruptions hinges not only on its operational robustness but also on its communication and stakeholder engagement strategies. Effective communication builds trust, manages reputation, fosters

 DOI: 10.1201/9781003597520-10

collaboration, and ensures that all stakeholders are informed and engaged, especially during times of crisis. This chapter explores the fundamental principles and practices of communication and stakeholder engagement that are vital for organizational resilience.

Key Dimensions of Interconnectedness in Organizational Resilience

1. *Internal and External Networks*

   Organizations exist within complex webs of relationships that extend far beyond their organizational boundaries. These networks encompass suppliers, partners, regulators, customers, and even competitors, creating an ecosystem where resilience is determined not just by internal capabilities but by the strength and agility of these interconnected relationships.

   Supply chain networks represent a critical dimension of this interconnectedness. Effective supply chain management, characterized by strong collaboration and information sharing among suppliers and partners, is crucial for resilience. Disruptions in one part of the network can quickly cascade across the entire system, making the quality of these relationships paramount to organizational survival and success.

   Stakeholder engagement forms another vital component of organizational interconnectedness. Building trust-based, stable relationships with key actors—including buyers, suppliers, and external agencies—enables coordinated responses to crises and opportunities. These relationships serve as both early warning systems and resource pools during times of disruption.

   - *Supply Chain Networks:* Effective supply chain management, with strong collaboration and information sharing among suppliers and partners, is crucial for resilience, as disruptions in one part can quickly cascade across the network.
   - *Stakeholder Engagement:* Building trust-based, stable relationships with key actors—including buyers, suppliers, and external agencies—enables coordinated responses to crises and opportunities.

2. *Boundaryless Capability*

   Modern resilience thinking emphasizes the importance of boundaryless capability—the ability to connect and reconfigure resources, knowledge, and processes across traditional organizational boundaries. This capability involves two key elements that fundamentally reshape how organizations operate and respond to challenges.

   Openness to external influences requires organizations to be receptive to signals and changes from the broader environment. This means actively integrating external knowledge and adapting to global or societal shifts rather than operating in isolation. Organizations that excel in this area maintain extensive sensing mechanisms that allow them to detect weak signals and emerging trends before they become major disruptions.

Flexible structures represent the internal counterpart to external openness. Traditional organizational silos are broken down, and cross-functional teams or networks are empowered to respond to disruptions and innovate quickly. This structural flexibility enables rapid reconfiguration of resources and capabilities in response to changing circumstances.

This involves:

- *Openness to External Influences:* Organizations must be receptive to signals and changes from the broader environment, integrating external knowledge and adapting to global or societal shifts.
- *Flexible Structures:* Internal silos are broken down, and cross-functional teams or networks are empowered to respond to disruptions and innovate quickly.

3. *Learning and Adaptation*

Interconnectedness enhances resilience through organizational learning—surfacing lessons from near-misses, failures, and successes, and embedding these learnings into systems and culture.

This learning occurs not just within individual organizations but across networks of connected entities. Mindful organizing represents a key aspect of this learning orientation. Organizations remain vigilant, continually scanning for weak signals and proactively addressing vulnerabilities before they escalate. This requires maintaining awareness of both internal conditions and external environmental changes.

Continuous improvement processes ensure that insights gained from one part of the organization or network are shared and applied elsewhere, strengthening the whole system. This creates a multiplier effect where learning in one area benefits the entire interconnected network.

- *Mindful Organizing:* Organizations remain vigilant, continually scanning for weak signals and proactively addressing vulnerabilities before they escalate.
- *Continuous Improvement:* Insights gained from one part of the organization or network are shared and applied elsewhere, strengthening the whole system.

4. *Systemic Perspective and Nonlinear Dynamics*

Interconnectedness means that organizations operate as complex adaptive systems, where traditional linear cause-and-effect relationships give way to more complex dynamics. Understanding these dynamics is crucial for building resilience in interconnected environments.

Emergent properties characterize these complex systems, where small changes or disruptions in one area can have unpredictable, amplified effects elsewhere in the system. This means that resilience strategies must account for the possibility of unexpected consequences and cascading effects.

Co-evolution represents another key characteristic of interconnected systems. Organizations and their networks adapt together, with changes in one part stimulating broader evolution and innovation across the entire network. This co-evolutionary process can create new opportunities even as it presents new challenges. means that organizations operate as complex adaptive systems:

- *Emergent Properties:* Small changes or disruptions in one area can have unpredictable, amplified effects elsewhere in the system.
- *Co-evolution:* Organizations and their networks adapt together, with changes in one part stimulating broader evolution and innovation.

5. *Strategic Adaptability and Robust Governance*

   Interconnectedness supports strategic adaptability—enabling organizations to take measured risks, respond quickly to threats and opportunities, and maintain robust governance across all functions and relationships.

   Practical Benefits of Interconnectedness

   - *Agility:* Organizations can rapidly reconfigure resources and processes to respond to changing conditions.
   - *Robustness:* Diverse and redundant connections reduce vulnerability to single points of failure.
   - *Visibility:* Information sharing and business intelligence across the network allow for early identification of risks and formulation of contingency plans.
   - *Collective Resilience:* Collaborative networks can pool resources, share knowledge, and mount coordinated responses to large-scale disruptions.

Example: Supply Chain Resilience During COVID-19

The pandemic revealed how interconnected supply chains are-disruptions in one region quickly affected production and delivery worldwide. Organizations that had invested in collaborative relationships, flexible sourcing, and real-time information sharing across their networks were better able to adapt, recover, and even seize new opportunities.

10.2.1 Conclusion

Interconnectedness is foundational to organizational resilience. It is about building, managing, and leveraging a web of relationships, knowledge flows, and adaptive capabilities—internally and externally—so that organizations can not only withstand shocks but also thrive in a volatile, uncertain world.

A compelling real-world case study that demonstrates *interconnectedness as a driver of organizational resilience* is the *Puget Sound supply chain collaboration during the onset of the COVID-19 pandemic* in the United States. This case highlights how pre-existing networks, cross-sector partnerships, and shared information enabled organizations to adapt and thrive amid unprecedented disruption.

Case Study: Puget Sound Supply Chain Resilience During COVID-19

10.2.2 Background

In 2019, the Cybersecurity Infrastructure and Security Agency (CISA) initiated a proof-of-concept project in the Puget Sound region (Washington State, USA) to explore strategies for supply chain resilience in the face of a catastrophic earthquake. The project fostered *private-private and private-public relationships* among grocery retailers, logistics providers, government agencies, and critical infrastructure operators, focusing on how to maximize grocery flows following a disaster.

10.2.3 Interconnectedness in action

When the COVID-19 pandemic struck in early 2020, the relationships and principles established during the earthquake preparedness project were rapidly repurposed to address pandemic-induced supply chain shocks:

- *Cross-Sector Collaboration:*
  Private companies and public agencies shared data, resources, and logistical capabilities to manage surges in consumer demand and supply disruptions. This interconnectedness allowed for coordinated responses, such as prioritizing essential goods, rerouting shipments, and sharing warehouse space.
- *Information Sharing:*
  Real-time communication channels established during the 2019 exercise enabled stakeholders to quickly identify bottlenecks, anticipate shortages, and adapt distribution strategies. This transparency reduced duplication of effort and allowed for more efficient allocation of scarce resources.
- *Networked Problem-Solving:*
  The collaborative network included not just direct supply chain partners, but also regional and national actors. For several weeks, the Puget Sound group's approach influenced broader policy and operational decisions, demonstrating how local interconnectedness can scale to wider systems resilience.

Outcomes

- *Rapid Adaptation:*
  The region was able to maintain grocery flows and critical supplies despite unprecedented spikes in demand and logistical challenges.
- *Resilience Beyond the Individual Organization:*
  The success was not due to any single entity, but to the interconnected web of organizations acting in concert, leveraging their collective strengths and resources.
- *Model for Future Crises:*
  Participants recognized that the groundwork of interconnectedness—built before the crisis—was essential for their agile and effective response.

Key Lessons

- *Preparedness through Interconnectedness:*
  Building networks and collaborative frameworks before a crisis enables rapid, coordinated action when disruptions occur.
- *Shared Information and Resources:*
  Open communication and resource sharing across organizational and sector boundaries multiply resilience far beyond what any one organization could achieve alone.
- *Scalability:*
  Local interconnectedness can influence and strengthen resilience at regional and national levels when leveraged effectively.

10.2.4 In summary

The Puget Sound case shows that organizational resilience is fundamentally rooted in interconnectedness—across private and public sectors, supply chain tiers, and even geographic boundaries. By nurturing relationships, sharing information, and collaborating proactively, organizations can collectively withstand and adapt to even the most severe disruption.

Here are several real-world examples of organizations achieving resilience through interconnectedness, as demonstrated by collaborative networks, cross-sector partnerships, and integrated systems:

1. *Coca-Cola's Resilient Supply Chain*
   Coca-Cola is widely recognized for its resilient and interconnected supply chain. The company achieves this through:
   - *Consistent collaboration with suppliers:* Coca-Cola works closely with a vast network of suppliers, sharing data and best practices to anticipate and mitigate disruptions.
   - *Deeper partnerships:* It invests in long-term relationships with logistics providers and bottlers, enabling rapid adaptation to changing market conditions.
   - *Sustainability integration:* Coca-Cola incorporates environmental and social goals into its supply chain strategy, aligning all partners toward common objectives.
   - *Scenario-based resilience planning:* The company regularly runs simulations and develops contingency plans with its partners, ensuring a coordinated response to crises. This interconnected approach has enabled Coca-Cola to remain agile and operational even during global disruptions such as the COVID-19 pandemic.
2. *Singapore's Smart Nation Initiative*
   Singapore launched the Smart Nation Initiative to build a resilient and sustainable city-state by leveraging interconnected digital infrastructure:
   - *National sensor networks:* Real-time data on air quality, traffic, and water levels is shared across government agencies and the public, enabling proactive responses to issues like flooding or congestion.

- *Smart home technologies:* IoT devices empower residents to monitor and optimize energy and water use, while authorities use aggregated data for resource planning and emergency management.
- *Cross-sector collaboration:* The initiative brings together government, businesses, and citizens to co-create solutions, enhancing the city's capacity to withstand and recover from shocks.

  This interconnected digital ecosystem has made Singapore more adaptable and resilient to urban challenges and resource constraints.

3. *New York City's "Big U" Project (Rebuild by Design Competition)*

   After Hurricane Sandy, New York City launched the "Big U" project to protect Lower Manhattan from future storm surges:

   - *Integrated physical and social resilience:* The project combines flood walls and deployable barriers with public spaces, serving both protective and community-building functions.
   - *Community engagement:* Residents and stakeholders were actively involved in planning and design, fostering a sense of ownership and shared responsibility for resilience.
   - *Multi-stakeholder collaboration:* The initiative united city agencies, nonprofits, and local communities, demonstrating the power of interconnectedness in disaster preparedness and recovery.

4. *Healthcare Networks During Epidemics*

   During localized epidemics such as MERS and SARS, interconnected health systems demonstrated resilience by:

   - *Early warning systems:* Sharing data across hospitals and public health agencies enabled rapid identification and containment of outbreaks.
   - *Resource pooling:* Hospitals coordinated the distribution of medical products and staff, ensuring continuity of care even as individual facilities faced surges in demand.

5. *Regenerative Agriculture Movement in Australia*

   In response to climate-induced challenges, Australian farmers adopted interconnected regenerative agriculture practices:

   - *Knowledge sharing:* Farmers, researchers, and industry groups collaborate to develop and disseminate sustainable farming techniques.
   - *Collective adaptation:* By working together, the agricultural community has increased its resilience to droughts, heatwaves, and extreme weather events.

10.2.5 In summary

Organizations achieve resilience through interconnectedness by building collaborative networks, sharing information and resources, and engaging diverse stakeholders in joint problem-solving. These examples-from global corporations to city governments and community initiatives-demonstrate that resilience is strongest when organizations are deeply connected internally and externally, enabling them to anticipate, adapt, and thrive amid disruption.

10.3 COMMUNITY RESILIENCE

Societal and community resilience are deeply strengthened by organizational resilience, especially when organizations provide essential products and services to the public. When such organizations are able to anticipate, adapt to, and recover from disruptions, they help ensure that communities can continue to meet their basic needs and maintain social stability even in the face of crises.

How Organizational Resilience Enhances Societal and Community Resilience

- *Continuity of Vital Services:*
  Organizations that deliver critical services-such as utilities, healthcare, food supply, transportation, and social services-are foundational to community well-being. Their ability to withstand and recover from disruptions ensures that communities can access what they need during emergencies, supporting rapid recovery and reducing the broader social and economic impacts.
- *Support for Vulnerable Populations:*
  Social service organizations, in particular, play a vital role in safeguarding vulnerable groups during times of adversity. Organizational resilience in these sectors means that support systems remain operational and adaptable, directly enhancing the community's overall capacity to cope with shocks.
- *Networks and Partnerships:*
  Resilient organizations often maintain strong networks and partnerships with other businesses, government agencies, and community groups. These connections enable coordinated responses, resource sharing, and rapid adaptation when challenges arise, amplifying the resilience of the broader community.
- *Assurance to Stakeholders:*
  Organizational resilience provides confidence and assurance to a wide range of interested parties, including regulators, third parties, government bodies, customers, partners, and shareholders. This assurance comes from the organization's demonstrated ability to manage risks, maintain service delivery, and protect stakeholder interests even during disruptions.
- *Socio-Economic and Environmental Sustainability:*
  Policymakers recognize that organizational resilience contributes to the sustainability of social, economic, and environmental systems. When organizations operate efficiently and can recover quickly, they help stabilize local economies, protect jobs, and support environmental stewardship, all of which are critical to long-term community resilience.

10.3.1 Real-World examples

- *Community Social Services:*
  Studies have shown that resilient social service organizations in Spain were able to adapt and recover from unexpected changes, ensuring positive user experiences and continued support for vulnerable populations during crises.
- *Critical Infrastructure:*
  Owners and operators of critical infrastructure who adopt integrated resilience frameworks can respond more effectively to complex risks, maintaining essential services and providing assurance to stakeholders, including the public and regulators.
- *Collaborative Community Efforts:*
  In East Boston, collaboration between local organizations and residents led to innovative, resilient solutions to flooding, such as citizen science programs and adaptive land use planning, demonstrating how organizational resilience can catalyze broader community resilience.

10.3.2 Conclusion

Organizational resilience is not only about internal survival and adaptation; it has far-reaching impacts on the resilience of society and communities as a whole. By ensuring the continuity of vital services, supporting vulnerable groups, fostering strong networks, and providing assurance to stakeholders, resilient organizations act as pillars of stability and recovery—enabling communities to withstand, adapt to, and thrive after disruptions.

A notable real-world case study that demonstrates how *societal and community resilience are enhanced by organizational resilience*—especially when vital products and services are involved—comes from the experience of a major supermarket chain in China during the COVID-19 pandemic.

Case Study: Chinese Retail Supermarket Chain During COVID-19.

10.3.3 Background

When the COVID-19 pandemic struck, communities across China faced significant uncertainty and disruption, particularly regarding access to essential goods such as food and household supplies. The resilience of retail supermarket chains became critical not only for business continuity but also for the well-being and stability of the broader society.

Organizational Resilience in Action

- *Preparation and Rapid Response:*
  The supermarket chain had invested in robust supply chain management, digital infrastructure, and emergency preparedness. When the

crisis hit, it was able to quickly adapt its logistics, sourcing, and sales channels to ensure shelves remained stocked and customers could access what they needed.

- *Improvisation and System Management:*
  Managers and staff demonstrated improvisational ability-reconfiguring store layouts, implementing new safety protocols, and ramping up online ordering and delivery services. This flexibility ensured that public health measures were met without sacrificing service delivery.
- *Corporate Social Responsibility (CSR):*
  The organization actively engaged in CSR, providing special support for vulnerable groups, stabilizing prices, and sharing information with government and community partners. This not only built trust but also directly supported societal resilience by reducing panic and ensuring equitable access to essentials.

Societal and Stakeholder Assurance

- *Community Impact:*
  By maintaining operations and adapting to new demands, the supermarket chain played a stabilizing role in the community, ensuring food security and supporting social order during a period of widespread disruption.
- *Assurance to Stakeholders:*
  The supermarket's resilience gave confidence to regulators, government agencies, suppliers, customers, and shareholders. Its ability to continue operations and fulfill its public service role reassured all interested parties of its reliability and commitment to the broader good.

Key Lessons

- *Organizational resilience in vital service providers directly supports societal resilience.*
- *Effective leadership, strong networks, and a culture of responsibility are essential for rapid adaptation and stakeholder assurance.*
- *CSR and proactive communication build trust and strengthen the social fabric during crises.*

10.3.4 In summary

This case study shows that when organizations providing essential goods and services are resilient, they not only protect their own operations but also become pillars of support for the entire community. Their preparedness, adaptability, and commitment to stakeholders enhance societal resilience and provide assurance to regulators, partners, and the public (Table 10.1).

Table 10.1 Some key questions you can ask to measure the level of resilience

Sr. no.	*Questions*
1.	In a crisis, does the organization have agreements with others to access their resources?
2.	Has the organization planned how to *support* the community in a crisis?
3.	Has the organization established relationships with other organizations that they may need to collaborate with during a crisis?
4.	Does the organization comprehend its connections with other organizations and actively manage those relationships?
5.	Does the organization understand how government actions would impact their ability to respond in a crisis?

10.4 KNOWLEDGE TRANSFER

The need for knowledge transfer in organizational resilience is critical because it ensures that essential information, expertise, and insights are systematically shared and accessible across and between organizations. This enables decision-makers at all levels to act swiftly and effectively during disruptions, adapt to change, and maintain continuity of operations.

Why Knowledge Transfer Is Essential for Organizational Resilience

1. *Predictor of Resilience and Agility*

   Research consistently shows that knowledge management—including knowledge transfer—is a strong predictor of organizational resilience and agility. Organizations that excel at acquiring, storing, sharing, and utilizing knowledge are better equipped to adapt to environmental shifts, respond to crises, and sustain performance under stress. This is because knowledge transfer:

   - Enhances the ability to sense and respond to changes.
   - Promotes faster adaptation and recovery.
   - Reduces vulnerability to disruptions by spreading critical know-how.
2. *Improved Decision-Making*

   When knowledge is effectively transferred, decision-makers have access to the most relevant and up-to-date information. This leads to better, more informed decisions—especially in high-stakes situations where timely action is crucial. In sectors like healthcare, finance, and emergency management, this can be the difference between success and failure.

   Effective knowledge transfer ensures that decision-makers can draw upon the collective experience and expertise of the entire organization, rather than being limited to their own knowledge and that of their immediate team. This collective intelligence significantly improves the quality and speed of decision-making during crises.

3. *Continuity and Retention of Critical Knowledge*

   Knowledge transfer ensures that critical skills and institutional memory are retained within the organization, even as employees retire, leave, or change roles. This reduces the risk of knowledge loss, which can otherwise compromise resilience and operational continuity during transitions or crises.

   As employee mobility accelerates, organizations face a significant risk of losing valuable organizational memory when individuals depart. This loss includes not just explicit knowledge (like documented procedures), but also tacit knowledge—expertise, skills, and insights gained through experience. Without systematic processes to capture and transfer this knowledge, organizations can suffer from decreased productivity, increased mistakes, lower quality, and diminished competitiveness.
4. *Fosters Innovation and Problem-Solving*

   A culture of knowledge sharing encourages collaboration and the cross-pollination of ideas, which sparks innovation and creative problem-solving. When teams and departments share insights and lessons learned, the organization as a whole becomes more adaptable and resourceful in the face of new challenges.

   Knowledge transfer creates opportunities for unexpected connections and insights that can lead to breakthrough solutions. When knowledge from different domains is combined, it often produces innovative approaches that would not have emerged within isolated silos.
5. *Enhances Organizational Agility*

   Knowledge transfer supports organizational agility by enabling employees to quickly gather and disseminate information about changes in the environment and respond expediently. This agility is vital for resilience, as it allows organizations to pivot and adjust strategies in real time.

   Agile organizations are characterized by their ability to rapidly reconfigure resources and capabilities in response to changing circumstances. Knowledge transfer is essential to this agility because it ensures that information about changes and opportunities reaches the right people at the right time.
6. *Strengthens Collaboration and Reduces Silos*

   By promoting open communication and the sharing of knowledge, organizations break down silos and foster a culture of teamwork and mutual support. This interconnectedness is a cornerstone of resilience, as it ensures that information flows freely and that the organization can act as a cohesive unit during disruptions.

   Silos represent one of the greatest threats to organizational resilience because they prevent the free flow of information and create blind spots that can become vulnerabilities during crises. Knowledge transfer helps break down these barriers and creates a more integrated organizational response capability.

Practical Methods for Knowledge Transfer

- *Mentoring and Coaching:* Pairing experienced employees with newer staff to share tacit knowledge.
- *Job Shadowing and Cross-Training:* Allowing employees to learn from different roles and departments.
- *Knowledge Management Systems:* Using digital platforms to document, store, and share information.
- *Regular Debriefs and After-Action Reviews:* Systematically capturing lessons learned from projects and crises.

10.4.1 Conclusion

Knowledge transfer is not just a support function-it is a strategic necessity for organizational resilience. By ensuring that knowledge and information are actively managed and shared, organizations empower their people to make informed decisions, adapt to change, retain critical expertise, and innovate in the face of adversity. This collective intelligence and agility are what enable organizations to withstand, recover from, and even thrive during disruptions.

A strong real-world case study demonstrating the power of knowledge transfer in achieving organizational resilience comes from research on *Ugandan parastatal organizations* (government-owned enterprises). This case highlights how systematic knowledge management-acquiring, creating, sharing, and utilizing knowledge-enables organizations to adapt, innovate, and remain resilient in the face of disruption.

Case Study: Knowledge Transfer and Resilience in Ugandan Parastatals.

10.4.2 Background

Researchers studied 51 Ugandan parastatal organizations to understand how knowledge management practices influence organizational resilience. These organizations operate in dynamic environments, often facing policy changes, resource constraints, and unexpected disruptions.

10.4.3 Knowledge management practices

The study found that resilient organizations excelled at:

- *Knowledge Acquisition:* Actively seeking new information from both internal and external sources.
- *Knowledge Sharing:* Encouraging open communication and the exchange of insights across departments and teams.
- *Knowledge Storage:* Systematically capturing lessons learned and best practices for future reference.
- *Knowledge Utilization:* Applying accumulated knowledge to solve problems and adapt processes in real time.

10.4.4 The role of knowledge transfer

The research revealed that *knowledge management alone did not directly result in resilience*. Instead, it was the *transfer of knowledge through organizational innovation* that made the difference. When organizations used shared knowledge to drive new ways of working, develop new products, or improve services, they became significantly more resilient to shocks and changes.

For example, when faced with regulatory changes or supply chain disruptions, organizations that had robust knowledge-sharing systems could quickly gather input from across the enterprise, brainstorm solutions, and implement innovative responses. This adaptability allowed them to maintain service delivery and competitive advantage, even in turbulent conditions.

Key Findings

- *Innovation as a Bridge:* Knowledge transfer fostered innovation, which in turn enabled resilience. Organizations that encouraged employees to share experiences and experiment with new ideas were better equipped to adapt and thrive.
- *Organizational Learning:* Continuous learning and feedback loops—where lessons from past disruptions were documented and shared—helped organizations avoid repeating mistakes and improved their response to future crises.
- *Cross-Unit Collaboration:* The most resilient organizations broke down silos, ensuring knowledge flowed freely between departments, levels, and even with external partners.

Practical Implications

Managers in these organizations recognized the need to:

- Invest in knowledge management systems and training.
- Promote a culture of openness and collaboration.
- Encourage innovation as a way to turn knowledge into actionable resilience strategies.

10.4.5 Conclusion

This case from Ugandan parastatals demonstrates that *systematic knowledge transfer—especially when tied to innovation—enables organizations to adapt, respond, and thrive amid disruption*. By managing and sharing knowledge across all levels, organizations build a foundation for resilience that benefits not only their own operations but also the communities and stakeholders they serve.

10.4.6 Knowledge management

As employee mobility accelerates, organizations face a significant risk of losing valuable organizational memory when individuals depart. This loss includes not just explicit knowledge (like documented procedures), but also tacit knowledge-expertise, skills, and insights gained through experience. Without systematic processes to capture and transfer this knowledge, organizations can suffer from decreased productivity, increased mistakes, lower quality, and diminished competitiveness.

The Impact of Lost Organizational Memory

- *Knowledge as a Competitive Asset:* Employees are key holders of an organization's competitive advantage. When they leave, they take with them not only technical know-how but also relationships and contextual understanding that are difficult to replace.
- *Consequences of Knowledge Loss:* The departure of experienced employees can result in knowledge gaps, slower onboarding for new hires, reduced process quality, and even loss of customers or revenue.
- *Organizational Performance:* High turnover rates have been shown to negatively impact organizational performance, especially in complex or emergency situations, as seen in public health departments during vaccination campaigns.

10.4.7 The need for systematic knowledge transfer

To build on lessons from past experiences and ensure continuity, organizations must create structured approaches to identify, capture, and convert individual expertise into organizational resources. This process is often referred to as knowledge continuity management.

Key Strategies Include

- *Knowledge Management Systems:* Develop platforms and databases where critical knowledge, best practices, and lessons learned are documented and easily accessible to all employees.
- *Mentoring and Knowledge Sharing:* Encourage experienced employees to mentor newcomers, participate in after-action reviews, and share insights in team meetings or through internal networks.
- *Formal Documentation:* Systematically document processes, decisions, and project outcomes so that knowledge is not lost when individuals leave.
- *Trust and Culture:* Foster a culture of trust and recognition, as employees are more likely to share knowledge if they feel valued and trust their colleagues to use that knowledge appropriately.
- *Retention Strategies:* While knowledge transfer is essential, retaining key employees also plays a vital role in maintaining organizational memory.

Benefits of Systematic Knowledge Transfer

- *Preserves Critical Knowledge:* Ensures that expertise remains within the organization, even as individuals come and go.
- *Speeds Up Onboarding:* New employees can learn faster and perform better when they have access to accumulated organizational knowledge.
- *Improves Decision-Making:* Leaders and teams can make better decisions with a richer base of organizational memory to draw from.
- *Enhances Resilience:* Organizations are better equipped to adapt, recover, and thrive in the face of change or disruption when they can build on past experiences.

10.4.8 In summary

As workforce mobility increases, organizations must proactively manage knowledge transfer to safeguard their organizational memory. By systematically capturing and sharing individual expertise, skills, and experience, organizations can build on past lessons, maintain continuity, and strengthen their resilience against future challenges.

A real-world case study that vividly demonstrates the importance of knowledge transfer for organizational resilience is found in the Nigerian manufacturing sector, as detailed in a study by Umoh and Amah (2013).

Case Study: Knowledge Management and Organizational Resilience in Nigerian Manufacturing Organizations.

10.4.9 Background

The study examined 34 manufacturing companies in Rivers State, Nigeria, exploring how knowledge management practices influence organizational resilience. The research included both quantitative surveys and qualitative interviews with 128 employees.

Key Knowledge Transfer Practices

- *Knowledge Acquisition:* Organizations actively sought new information and expertise from both internal and external sources to keep up with industry trends and emerging risks.
- *Knowledge Storage:* Companies systematically documented processes, lessons learned, and best practices, ensuring that critical knowledge was retained even as employees left or roles changed.
- *Knowledge Sharing:* There was a strong emphasis on sharing information across departments and teams, breaking down silos and encouraging collaboration.
- *Knowledge Utilization:* The stored and shared knowledge was actively used in decision-making, process improvements, and innovation, enabling organizations to adapt quickly to disruptions.

10.4.10 Outcomes

The study found a *positive and significant relationship between knowledge management and organizational resilience.* Specifically, companies that excelled in acquiring, storing, sharing, and utilizing knowledge were better able to:

- Adapt to unforeseen changes and disruptions.
- Maintain and even increase turnover during crises.
- Respond rapidly and effectively to challenges, demonstrating both resourcefulness and learning capability.

10.4.11 Managerial implications

The research concluded that *systematic knowledge transfer is essential for building and sustaining organizational resilience.* It is recommended that organizations:

- Strengthen knowledge management practices as a core part of their everyday activities.
- Institutionalize processes for capturing individual expertise and converting it into organizational resources.
- Foster a culture of continuous learning and collaboration to ensure that organizational memory is preserved and leveraged for future challenges.

10.4.12 In summary

Nigerian manufacturing companies that prioritized knowledge transfer—through acquisition, storage, sharing, and utilization—were demonstrably more resilient. This case underscores how organizations can safeguard their memory, build on past lessons, and adapt to ongoing change by systematically converting individual skills and experience into shared organizational assets.

10.4.13 Intellectual capital (IC)

IC refers to the collective knowledge, expertise, innovation capacity, and relational networks within an organization. It is a critical driver of competitive advantage, enabling businesses to differentiate themselves, adapt to market changes, and sustain growth. Effective management and sharing of IC across and between organizations empower decision-makers with actionable insights, reduce repeated mistakes, and unlock opportunities. Below is a detailed breakdown:

Components of IC

1. *Human Capital*
   - *Definition:* The skills, creativity, experience, and tacit knowledge of employees.

- *Role in Competitiveness:*
  - Employees' expertise fuels innovation and problem-solving. For example, R&D teams leverage their knowledge to develop new products or optimize processes.
  - Training and development programs enhance human capital, directly improving organizational agility and resilience.
2. *Structural Capital*
   - *Definition:* Institutionalized knowledge embedded in processes, databases, patents, and organizational culture.
   - *Role in Competitiveness:*
     - Systems like CRM platforms or knowledge management tools (e.g., Bloomfire) centralize information, enabling faster decision-making.
     - Codified processes reduce dependency on individual employees, ensuring continuity during turnover.
3. *Relational Capital*
   - *Definition:* Value derived from relationships with customers, suppliers, partners, and stakeholders.
   - *Role in Competitiveness:*
     - Strong supplier networks (e.g., H&M's decarbonization partnerships) enhance supply chain resilience and innovation.
     - Customer loyalty and brand reputation drive market differentiation.

How IC Enhances Competitive Advantage

Exploiting Opportunities

- *Market Responsiveness:* IC enables organizations to identify and act on emerging trends. For example, companies using real-time data from knowledge management systems can pivot strategies to capitalize on new markets.
- *Innovation:* IC fosters R&D breakthroughs. Studies show firms with robust IC are 20–30% more likely to launch innovative products.

Mitigating Risks

- *Reducing Mistakes:* Documenting lessons learned (e.g., after-action reviews) prevents repeat errors. For instance, Ugandan parastatals institutionalized post-crisis reviews to improve future responses.
- *Risk Forecasting:* Shared knowledge across supply chains helps anticipate disruptions. The Puget Sound collaboration during COVID-19 used pre-established networks to manage grocery shortages.

Strategies for Managing and Sharing IC

1. *Knowledge Management Systems (KMS)*
   - Centralize data (e.g., cloud platforms) to ensure easy access to updated information.
   - *Example:* Manufacturing firms in Nigeria improved resilience by systematizing knowledge storage and sharing.

2. *Cross-Organizational Collaboration*
   - *Supplier/Customer Integration:* Share forecasts and insights to align production with demand (e.g., Huawei's supplier risk assessments).
   - *Industry Alliances:* Competing firms sometimes collaborate on sustainability goals, pooling IC for mutual benefit.
3. *Cultural Practices*
   - *Mentorship Programs:* Transfer tacit knowledge from experienced staff to new hires.
   - *Open Innovation:* Encourage idea-sharing across departments and hierarchies to break silos.
4. *Leveraging Technology*
   - AI-driven analytics identify patterns in IC data, revealing untapped opportunities.
   - Digital tools (e.g., Slack, SharePoint) facilitate real-time collaboration across global teams.

Real-World Impact

- *Nigerian Manufacturing Sector:* Companies excelling in IC management saw 20–30% higher turnover during crises by leveraging knowledge-sharing networks.
- *Coca-Cola:* Structural capital in its global supply chain enabled rapid adaptation during COVID-19, maintaining market leadership.
- *Singapore's Smart Nation Initiative:* Integrated IC across public and private sectors to build a resilient urban ecosystem.

10.4.14 Conclusion

IC is the bedrock of modern competitiveness. By systematically managing and sharing knowledge—through technology, culture, and collaboration—organizations transform individual expertise into collective assets. This not only drives innovation and market agility but also builds resilience against disruptions, ensuring sustained growth in a volatile economy.

Here are some key questions which will help you identify the level of resilience pertaining to Knowledge management (Table 10.2).

Table 10.2 Key Questions: Knowledge Transfer

1.	How does the organization manage and access its knowledge?
2.	Do the employees possess the necessary information and knowledge to address unexpected issues?
3.	Do employees know who to contact if an unusual situation arises?
4.	Is the organization's critical information accessible through various means and from different locations?
5.	If key personnel were unavailable, does the organization have trained individuals who could assume their responsibilities?

(Continued)

Table 10.2 (Continued)

6.	Does the organization have access to expert assistance when there is a problem?
7.	Do the staff have the necessary information and knowledge to handle unexpected problems?
8.	If an unusual event occurs, does the staff know who is qualified to respond?
9.	Is the critical information accessible by various means and locations?
10.	If key personnel were unavailable, does the organization have employees capable of taking on their responsibilities?
11.	Does the organization have readily available expert assistance when there is a problem?

10.5 CONCLUSION

IC is the bedrock of modern competitiveness and organizational resilience. By systematically managing and sharing knowledge—through technology, culture, and collaboration—organizations transform individual expertise into collective assets. This transformation not only drives innovation and market agility but also builds resilience against disruptions, ensuring sustained growth in a volatile economy. The Nigerian manufacturing case study demonstrates that organizations excelling in IC management can achieve -% higher performance during crises by leveraging knowledge-sharing networks, proving that IC is not just a competitive advantage but a fundamental requirement for organizational survival and success in an interconnected world.

Chapter 11

AI and organizational resilience

LEARNING OBJECTIVES

By the end of this chapter, readers will be able to:

- Understand how to leverage artificial intelligence technology to enhance decision-making, operational continuity, cybersecurity, supply chain management, customer engagement, regulatory compliance, and cultural transformation within organizational resilience frameworks
- Comprehend the ethical considerations and challenges involved in using AI for organizational resilience, including privacy concerns, security vulnerabilities, and the importance of maintaining human oversight
- Learn practical approaches for integrating AI with human decision-making processes to create robust, adaptive, and sustainable resilience strategies that complement rather than replace human judgment

11.1 INTRODUCTION

In an era of unprecedented global interconnectedness and complexity, organizations face an ever-expanding array of risks and disruptions that can threaten their operational continuity, financial stability, and long-term viability. From natural disasters and cyberattacks to supply chain failures and pandemic-related shutdowns, the modern business environment demands sophisticated approaches to organizational resilience that go beyond traditional risk management frameworks. Artificial intelligence (AI) has emerged as a transformative force in this domain, offering unprecedented capabilities to predict, prevent, respond to, and recover from various forms of organizational disruption. The integration of AI into organizational resilience strategies represents a fundamental shift from reactive to proactive risk management, enabling organizations to anticipate threats before they materialize, optimize resource allocation during crises, and continuously learn from both successful interventions and near-miss events. This technological evolution is not merely about automating existing processes but about fundamentally

 DOI: 10.1201/9781003597520-11

reimagining how organizations can build adaptive capacity, maintain operational continuity, and thrive in the face of uncertainty. The concept of organizational resilience encompasses an organization's ability to anticipate, prepare for, respond to, and adapt to incremental change and sudden disruptions in order to survive and prosper. When enhanced by AI capabilities, this resilience becomes dynamic and intelligent, characterized by systems that can process vast amounts of data in real-time, identify patterns and anomalies that might escape human detection, and provide decision-makers with actionable insights that enable rapid, informed responses to emerging threats. This chapter explores the multifaceted role of AI in enhancing organizational resilience through two primary lenses: first, examining the fundamental ways in which AI technologies strengthen an organization's capacity to withstand and recover from disruptions, and second, investigating successful real-world implementations that demonstrate the practical benefits and challenges of integrating AI into resilience frameworks. Through detailed case studies of industry leaders like Amazon and IBM, we will examine how AI-driven approaches to supply chain management and healthcare resilience have created competitive advantages while also highlighting the ethical considerations and implementation challenges that organizations must navigate.

11.1.1 Role of AI in enhancing organizational resilience

The integration of AI into organizational resilience frameworks represents a paradigm shift that transforms how organizations anticipate, prepare for, and respond to disruptions. AI's role in enhancing organizational resilience extends across multiple dimensions, from proactive risk identification to continuous learning and adaptation, creating a comprehensive ecosystem of intelligent capabilities that strengthen an organization's ability to maintain operations and recover quickly from adverse events.

1. *Proactive Risk Identification and Monitoring*

   One of the most significant contributions of AI to organizational resilience lies in its capacity for proactive risk identification and continuous monitoring. Traditional risk management approaches often rely on historical data and human analysis to identify potential threats, creating inherent delays and blind spots that can leave organizations vulnerable to emerging risks. AI systems, by contrast, can process vast amounts of data from diverse sources simultaneously, including internal operational metrics, supply chain indicators, market trends, weather patterns, geopolitical developments, and social media sentiment. These AI-powered monitoring systems operate continuously, analyzing data streams in real time to detect anomalies, patterns, and early warning signals that might indicate impending disruptions. Machine learning algorithms can identify subtle correlations and dependencies that human analysts might miss, such as the relationship between specific supplier performance metrics and broader supply chain vulnerabilities, or the connection between certain cybersecurity indicators and potential system breaches. The predictive capabilities of AI enable organizations to move from reactive to proactive risk management, identifying potential threats days, weeks, or even months before they materialize into actual disruptions. This early warning capability provides organizations with valuable time to implement preventive measures, adjust operational parameters, or activate contingency plans before crises fully develop. For example, AI systems can analyze satellite imagery, weather data, and historical patterns to predict natural disasters and their potential impact on specific facilities or supply chains, allowing organizations to preposition resources and implement protective measures.

By continuously monitoring these data streams, AI can:

- Detect anomalies or early warning signs of disruption.
- Predict potential risks before they escalate.
- Provide real-time alerts to decision-makers.

2. *Scenario Planning and Simulation*

AI-powered scenario planning and simulation capabilities represent another crucial dimension of enhanced organizational resilience. Traditional scenario planning exercises, while valuable, are often limited by human cognitive constraints and the time required to develop and analyze multiple scenarios. AI systems can rapidly generate and analyze thousands of potential scenarios, considering complex interactions between multiple variables and their potential cascading effects across organizational systems. These AI-driven simulations can model the impact of various disruptions across different organizational functions, geographic locations, and time horizons. By incorporating real-time data and continuously updating their models based on changing conditions, AI systems can provide dynamic scenario analysis that reflects current organizational vulnerabilities and capabilities. This capability enables organizations to test and refine their response strategies under various conditions, identifying potential weaknesses in their resilience plans and optimizing resource allocation strategies. The simulation capabilities extend beyond simple "what-if" analysis to include complex modeling of interdependencies and cascading effects. For instance, an AI system might simulate how a cyberattack on a specific IT system could propagate through interconnected systems, affecting supply chain operations, customer service capabilities, and financial reporting functions. This comprehensive modeling helps organizations understand the full scope of potential impacts and develop more robust response strategies.

AI-powered tools can rapidly generate and analyze multiple "what-if" scenarios:

- Simulate the impact of various disruptions (e.g., cyberattacks, supply chain failures, natural disasters).
- Help organizations test and refine their response strategies.
- Identify vulnerabilities and recommend mitigation measures.

3. *Enhanced Decision Support*

   AI significantly enhances decision-making capabilities during both normal operations and crisis situations by synthesizing complex information from multiple sources and providing actionable insights to decision-makers. During disruptions, when time is critical and information may be incomplete or contradictory, AI systems can rapidly process available data, identify key trends and patterns, and recommend optimal courses of action based on predictive analytics and historical precedents. The decision support capabilities of AI extend beyond simple data analysis to include sophisticated reasoning and recommendation engines that can evaluate multiple response options, assess their potential outcomes, and rank them based on organizational priorities and constraints. These systems can consider factors such as resource availability, regulatory requirements, stakeholder impacts, and long-term strategic implications when generating recommendations. AI-powered decision support systems also excel at managing information overload during crisis situations, filtering and prioritizing information flows to ensure that decision-makers receive relevant, timely, and actionable intelligence. By automating routine analysis and reporting tasks, these systems free human decision-makers to focus on strategic thinking and stakeholder management while ensuring that critical information is not overlooked in the chaos of crisis response.

   AI assists leaders by synthesizing complex information and offering actionable insights:

   - Automates data analysis and reporting, saving time and reducing errors.
   - Recommends optimal courses of action based on predictive analytics.
   - Supports crisis management teams with real-time, data-driven guidance.

4. *Resource Optimization*

   Effective resource optimization during disruptions is critical for maintaining operational continuity and minimizing the impact of adverse events. AI algorithms excel at analyzing complex resource allocation problems, considering multiple constraints and objectives simultaneously to identify optimal deployment strategies for personnel, equipment, inventory, and financial resources. During normal operations, AI systems can continuously monitor resource utilization patterns, identify inefficiencies, and recommend optimization strategies that improve overall organizational resilience. These systems can analyze historical data to identify seasonal patterns, predict future resource needs, and ensure that critical resources are available when and where they are needed most. When disruptions occur, AI-powered resource optimization becomes even more critical. These systems can rapidly reassess resource requirements based on changing conditions, reallocate resources from less critical to more critical functions, and identify alternative resource sources when primary options are unavailable. The speed and accuracy of AI-driven resource optimization can significantly reduce response times and minimize the operational impact of disruptions.

AI algorithms can help organizations allocate resources more efficiently during disruptions:

- Prioritize critical functions and assets.
- Optimize deployment of personnel, inventory, and logistics.
- Minimize downtime and financial losses.

5. *Continuous Learning and Adaptation*

Perhaps one of the most valuable aspects of AI in organizational resilience is its capacity for continuous learning and adaptation. Unlike static systems that require manual updates and modifications, AI systems can learn from every incident, near-miss, and operational experience, continuously improving their predictive models and response recommendations. Machine learning algorithms can analyze the outcomes of past incidents to identify what worked well and what could be improved, automatically updating their models to reflect these lessons learned. This continuous learning capability ensures that organizational resilience capabilities evolve and improve over time, becoming more sophisticated and effective with each experience. The adaptive nature of AI systems also enables them to respond to changing threat landscapes and organizational contexts. As new types of risks emerge or organizational structures evolve, AI systems can adjust their monitoring parameters, update their predictive models, and modify their response recommendations to remain relevant and effective.

AI systems learn from past incidents and ongoing operations:

- Improve their own predictive models over time.
- Help organizations adapt policies and procedures based on lessons learned.
- Foster a culture of continuous improvement and resilience.

6. *Automating Routine Tasks*

AI's ability to automate routine and time-consuming tasks plays a crucial role in enhancing organizational resilience by freeing human resources to focus on strategic and creative aspects of resilience management. During normal operations, AI systems can automate compliance monitoring, regulatory reporting, routine communications with stakeholders, and standard operating procedure updates. This automation capability becomes particularly valuable during crisis situations when human resources are stretched thin and the volume of required tasks may exceed normal capacity. AI systems can automatically generate status reports, send notifications to relevant stakeholders, update emergency contact lists, and maintain documentation of response activities, ensuring that critical administrative tasks are completed even when human attention is focused elsewhere. The automation of routine tasks also reduces the likelihood of human error during high-stress situations, ensuring that standard procedures are followed consistently and that important steps are not overlooked in the urgency of crisis response.

AI can automate repetitive and time-consuming tasks, such as:

- Monitoring compliance and regulatory requirements.
- Generating reports and documentation.
- Managing routine communications with stakeholders.

7. *Supporting Collaboration and Communication*

   Effective collaboration and communication are essential components of organizational resilience, particularly during crisis situations when coordination across multiple teams, departments, and external partners becomes critical. AI-driven platforms can significantly enhance these capabilities by facilitating information sharing, ensuring message consistency, and maintaining communication continuity even when normal communication channels are disrupted. AI-powered communication systems can automatically translate messages between different languages, summarize complex information for different audiences, and ensure that critical information reaches all relevant stakeholders in appropriate formats and through appropriate channels. These systems can also monitor communication flows to identify potential bottlenecks or gaps in information sharing, alerting coordinators to potential issues before they impact response effectiveness. During crisis situations, AI systems can maintain comprehensive logs of all communications and decisions, creating valuable documentation for post-incident analysis and regulatory reporting. This capability ensures that organizations can demonstrate compliance with regulatory requirements and learn from their experiences to improve future response capabilities.

   AI-driven platforms can enhance information sharing and coordination:

   - Facilitate collaboration across teams, departments, and even with external partners.
   - Ensure that accurate, up-to-date information is accessible to all relevant stakeholders during a crisis.

11.1.2 Case study: Amazon's use of AI in supply chain management

Amazon's implementation of AI in supply chain management provides a compelling example of how AI can enhance organizational resilience while creating competitive advantages. As one of the world's largest e-commerce and logistics companies, Amazon faces constant challenges related to demand forecasting, inventory management, supplier reliability, and delivery optimization across a global network of fulfillment centers, transportation hubs, and delivery routes.

11.1.3 Background and challenges

Amazon's supply chain complexity is staggering, involving millions of products, thousands of suppliers, hundreds of fulfillment centers, and billions of customer interactions annually. Traditional supply chain management approaches would be insufficient to handle this scale and complexity while maintaining the high service levels that customers expect. The company faces multiple resilience challenges, including demand volatility, supplier disruptions, transportation delays, seasonal fluctuations, and the need to rapidly scale operations during peak periods like Prime Day and holiday seasons.

The COVID pandemic highlighted both the importance and the effectiveness of Amazon's AI-driven supply chain resilience. While many retailers struggled with inventory shortages, delivery delays, and supply chain disruptions, Amazon was able to maintain relatively stable operations and even expand its capacity to meet increased demand for online shopping and delivery services.

11.1.4 AI implementation strategy

Amazon's approach to AI in supply chain management is comprehensive and multi-layered, incorporating machine learning algorithms, predictive analytics, robotics, and automated decision-making systems across every aspect of its operations. The foundation of Amazon's AI-driven supply chain resilience lies in its demand forecasting capabilities. The company uses machine learning algorithms to analyze historical sales data, seasonal patterns, promotional impacts, external factors like weather and economic conditions, and real-time customer behavior to predict demand for millions of products across different geographic regions and time horizons. These forecasting models are continuously updated with new data and can adjust predictions in real-time as conditions change.

Amazon's inventory management system uses AI to optimize stock levels across its network of fulfillment centers, balancing the costs of holding inventory against the risks of stockouts and customer dissatisfaction. The system considers factors such as demand variability, supplier lead times, transportation costs, and storage capacity constraints when making inventory decisions. Machine learning algorithms continuously analyze the performance of these decisions and adjust parameters to improve accuracy and efficiency.

11.1.5 Supplier risk management

One of the most critical aspects of Amazon's AI-driven supply chain resilience is its approach to supplier risk management. The company uses AI systems to continuously monitor supplier performance, financial health, and external risk factors that might affect supplier reliability. These systems analyze data from multiple sources, including supplier delivery performance, quality metrics, financial reports, news feeds, and social media to identify potential risks before they impact operations.

When the AI system identifies potential supplier risks, it can automatically trigger contingency plans, such as increasing orders from alternative suppliers, adjusting inventory levels, or activating backup sourcing arrangements. This proactive approach has enabled Amazon to maintain supply continuity even when individual suppliers experience disruptions.

The company's AI systems also optimize supplier relationships by analyzing performance data to identify the most reliable and cost-effective suppliers for different products and regions. This analysis considers not only current performance but also predictive indicators of future reliability, helping Amazon build a more resilient supplier network over time.

11.1.6 Transportation and logistics

Optimization Amazon's transportation and logistics operations represent another area where AI significantly enhances resilience. The company uses machine learning algorithms to optimize delivery routes, predict transportation delays, and automatically reroute shipments when disruptions occur. These systems consider real-time traffic conditions, weather forecasts, vehicle capacity, driver availability, and customer delivery preferences when making routing decisions.

During disruptions such as severe weather events or transportation strikes, Amazon's AI systems can rapidly recalculate optimal routing strategies, identify alternative transportation modes, and adjust delivery schedules to minimize customer impact. The system can also predict the likely duration and impact of disruptions, enabling proactive communication with customers and stakeholders.

11.1.7 Warehouse automation and robotics

Amazon's extensive use of robotics and automation in its fulfillment centers is closely integrated with its AI-driven resilience strategy. The company uses AI to optimize robot deployment, predict maintenance needs, and automatically adjust operations when equipment failures occur. Machine learning algorithms analyze equipment performance data to identify patterns that indicate impending failures, enabling predictive maintenance that reduces downtime and improves operational reliability.

When disruptions occur in automated systems, AI algorithms can rapidly reconfigure operations to work around failed equipment, redistribute workloads to functioning systems, and optimize human-robot collaboration to maintain productivity. This flexibility has proven crucial during peak demand periods and unexpected disruptions.

11.1.8 Customer experience and communication

Amazon's AI systems also enhance resilience from a customer experience perspective by providing accurate delivery predictions, proactive communication about potential delays, and automatic resolution of common issues. Machine learning algorithms analyze historical delivery data, current operational conditions, and external factors to provide customers with realistic delivery estimates and proactive notifications when delays are likely.

During disruptions, Amazon's AI systems can automatically adjust customer expectations, offer alternative delivery options, and provide real-time updates on order status. This proactive communication helps maintain customer satisfaction even when operational disruptions occur.

11.1.9 Results and impact

The results of Amazon's AI-driven supply chain resilience strategy have been impressive across multiple dimensions. The company has achieved industry-leading delivery performance, with the majority of Prime orders delivered within one or two days even during peak demand periods. Customer satisfaction scores have remained high even during challenging periods like the COVID pandemic, when many other retailers experienced significant service disruptions.

From a financial perspective, Amazon's AI-driven supply chain optimization has enabled the company to reduce inventory carrying costs while improving service levels, creating a competitive advantage that has contributed to its market leadership position. The company's ability to maintain operations during disruptions has also enhanced its reputation for reliability among both customers and suppliers.

The resilience benefits of Amazon's AI implementation extend beyond operational metrics to include strategic advantages such as the ability to rapidly enter new markets, launch new products, and scale operations in response to changing demand patterns. This agility has been crucial to Amazon's continued growth and market expansion.

11.1.10 Lessons learned and best practices

Amazon's experience with AI in supply chain management offers several important lessons for other organizations seeking to enhance their resilience through AI. First, the importance of comprehensive data integration cannot be overstated. Amazon's success depends on its ability to collect, process, and analyze data from across its entire operation and external environment. Organizations implementing AI for resilience must invest in robust data infrastructure and integration capabilities.

Second, the value of continuous learning and adaptation is evident in Amazon's approach. The company's AI systems are designed to learn from every transaction, disruption, and operational experience, continuously improving their performance over time. This requires a culture of experimentation and learning, as well as technical systems that can rapidly incorporate new insights.

Third, the importance of human-AI collaboration is clear in Amazon's implementation. While AI systems handle many routine decisions and optimizations, human expertise remains crucial for strategic decision-making, exception handling, and system oversight. Successful AI implementation requires careful consideration of how humans and AI can complement each other.

Finally, Amazon's experience demonstrates the importance of viewing AI implementation as a long-term strategic investment rather than a short-term tactical solution. The company has invested consistently in AI capabilities over many years, building sophisticated systems that provide sustainable competitive advantages and resilience benefits.

11.1.11 Conclusion

AI significantly enhances organizational resilience by enabling proactive risk management, smarter decision-making, efficient resource use, and continuous adaptation. Organizations that integrate AI into their resilience strategies are better equipped to anticipate, withstand, and recover from disruptions-ultimately safeguarding their people, assets, and reputation.

Detailed comparison table between *business continuity management (BCM)* and *Generative AI*, highlighting their roles, features, and benefits in the context of organizational resilience and risk mitigation (Table 11.1).

Table 11.1

Aspect	*Business continuity management (BCM)*	*Generative AI*
Primary focus	Risk mitigation and ensuring organizational resilience	Automating and enhancing content creation, decision support, and scenario generation
Role in risk management	Critical aspect of risk mitigation—monitoring, prediction, and analysis	Supports BCM by generating scenarios, reports, and insights to improve decision-making
Functionality	• Real-time monitoring of threats and disruptions • Scenario modeling and analytics • Report generation • Communications, alerts, and resource allocation	• Generates text, reports, and scenarios based on data • Enhances analytics with natural language understanding • Supports rapid information synthesis
Use cases in BCM	• Alerts and decision-making support • Crisis management coordination • Resource and communication management during disruptions	• Automates report writing and documentation • Creates predictive scenarios for planning • Provides intelligent recommendations and insights
Impact on organizational resilience	Ensures resilience against internal and external threats by proactive planning and response	Accelerates response times and improves quality of analysis and communication through AI-driven automation

(Continued)

Table 11.1 (Continued)

Aspect	*Business continuity management (BCM)*	*Generative AI*
Benefits	• Reduces the effects of disruptions • Enhances crisis preparedness • Facilitates coordinated response	• Increases efficiency in data processing and reporting • Enables more comprehensive scenario exploration • Supports continuous learning and adaptation
Limitations	Often manual and process-driven; dependent on human input and timely data	Dependent on quality and scope of training data; requires oversight to ensure accuracy and relevance
Integration potential	Can integrate AI tools to enhance monitoring and analytics	Acts as a powerful augmentation tool within BCM frameworks

11.2 SUMMARY

- *BCM* is the foundational discipline that ensures organizations prepare for, respond to, and recover from disruptions through structured processes and real-time coordination.
- *Generative AI* serves as an advanced enabler within BCM by automating knowledge work, enhancing scenario generation, and providing intelligent decision support, thereby increasing the speed and depth of BCM activities.

11.2.1 AI in business continuity management (BCM) functions

AI is transforming BCM by automating, enhancing, and accelerating critical activities across the BCM lifecycle. Below are key BCM functions where AI plays a pivotal role:

1. *Scenario Planning*
   - AI generates diverse "what-if" scenarios by analyzing historical data, current trends, and external variables.
   - Enables organizations to anticipate potential disruptions and evaluate the impact of different response strategies rapidly.
   - Supports dynamic updating of scenarios as new data emerges.
2. *Automated Notification*
   - AI-powered systems automatically detect anomalies or threats and trigger real-time alerts.
   - Notifications are prioritized and routed to relevant stakeholders based on context and severity.
   - Reduces response time and ensures timely communication during crises.

3. *Risk Assessment and Prediction*
    - AI analyzes large datasets to identify emerging risks and vulnerabilities.
    - Predictive models forecast the likelihood and potential impact of various threats.
    - Helps organizations proactively mitigate risks before they materialize.
4. *Data Analysis and Visualization*
    - AI tools process complex, multi-source data to extract actionable insights.
    - Advanced visualization techniques (dashboards, heat maps) present risk and continuity information clearly.
    - Facilitates better understanding and faster decision-making.
5. *Supply Chain Management*
    - AI monitors supply chain operations in real-time, identifying bottlenecks and disruptions.
    - Predicts supplier risks and recommends alternative sourcing strategies.
    - Enhances supply chain resilience by enabling agile adjustments.
6. *Resource Allocation*
    - AI optimizes the deployment of personnel, equipment, and financial resources during disruptions.
    - Balances competing priorities to maximize operational continuity.
    - Supports scenario-based resource planning.
7. *Training and Simulation*
    - AI-driven simulations create realistic crisis scenarios for training purposes.
    - Enables employees to practice responses in a safe, controlled environment.
    - Improves preparedness and response effectiveness.
8. *Natural Language Generation (NLG)*
    - AI automatically generates reports, summaries, and communications based on data inputs.
    - Reduces manual effort and speeds up information dissemination.
    - Ensures consistency and accuracy in BCM documentation.
9. *Compliance and Reporting*
    - AI monitors regulatory changes and compliance requirements.
    - Automates reporting processes to ensure timely and accurate submissions.
    - Helps avoid penalties and maintain stakeholder trust.
10. *Predictive Maintenance*
    - AI predicts equipment failures and maintenance needs before breakdowns occur.
    - Minimizes downtime and operational disruptions.
    - Extends asset life and reduces maintenance costs.

11. *Continuous Improvement*
    - AI analyzes post-incident data to identify lessons learned.
    - Supports iterative refinement of BCM plans and processes.
    - Promotes a culture of resilience through ongoing learning.

11.3 SUMMARY

AI enhances BCM by providing predictive insights, automating routine tasks, improving communication, and enabling dynamic, data-driven decision-making. Integrating AI into BCM functions allows organizations to anticipate risks, respond swiftly, optimize resources, and continuously improve their resilience posture (Figure 11.1).

11.3.1 AI in risk assessment and prediction for BCM

Key AI-Enabled Functions

1. *Data Integration and Analysis*
    - AI systems gather and synthesize data from diverse sources (internal systems, external feeds, IoT devices, etc.).
    - This integration enables a holistic view of organizational risks and operational status.

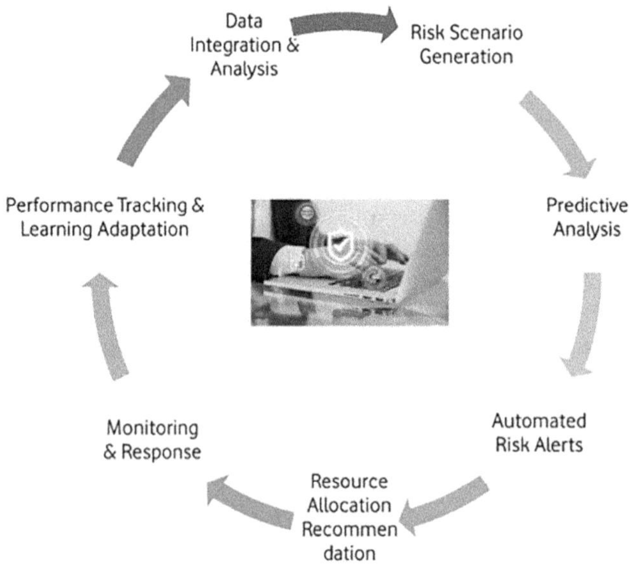

Figure 11.1 AI strengthens BCM Lifecycle

2. *Risk Scenario Generation*
   - AI models simulate a variety of risk scenarios, considering historical data and emerging trends.
   - This helps organizations anticipate potential disruptions and prepare effective response strategies.
3. *Performance Tracking and Learning Adaptation*
   - AI continuously monitors key performance indicators related to risk and continuity.
   - Machine learning algorithms adapt and improve risk models based on new data and outcomes, ensuring ongoing relevance.
4. *Predictive Analysis*
   - AI uses advanced analytics to forecast the likelihood and potential impact of specific risks (e.g., supply chain delays, cyber threats).
   - This predictive capability supports proactive risk mitigation.
5. *Automated Risk Alerts*
   - AI-driven systems provide real-time alerts when anomalies or risk thresholds are detected.
   - These automated notifications enable faster response and escalation.
6. *Monitoring and Response*
   - Continuous AI monitoring ensures that emerging risks are detected early.
   - AI can trigger predefined response actions or recommend next steps to human responders.
7. *Resource Allocation Recommendation*
   - AI analyzes available resources and recommends optimal allocation during a crisis.
   - This ensures that critical functions are prioritized and supported for maximum resilience.

11.3.2 Integration of AI with the BCM lifecycle

AI technologies enhance each stage of the BCM lifecycle by:

- Providing real-time data and predictive insights for risk assessment and scenario planning.
- Automating monitoring, alerting, and reporting functions.
- Supporting resource allocation and decision-making during crises.
- Enabling continuous learning and adaptation by analyzing outcomes and updating models (Table 11.2).

11.3.3 In summary

AI significantly strengthens the BCM lifecycle by enabling proactive risk identification, real-time monitoring, predictive scenario generation, and optimized response strategies. The cyclical nature of BCM, combined with AI's

Table 11.2 AI role in BCM Lifecycle stages

BCM lifecycle step	*AI-driven enhancement*
Policy and Program Management	Automates compliance checks, monitors performance
Understanding the Organization	Integrates data for BIA/RA, generates risk scenarios
Developing BCM Strategy	Predictive analytics for strategy formulation
Response (Plans and Arrangements)	Automated alerts, scenario-based response recommendations
Exercises and Maintenance	Simulates incidents, tracks performance, suggests improvements
Awareness/Training and Improvement	Personalized training, tracks awareness, analyzes audit data

adaptive learning, ensures organizations are continuously improving their resilience and readiness for any disruption.

11.3.4 AI in scenario planning for business continuity management (BCM)

The diagram below highlights how AI enhances scenario planning within BCM by focusing on several key functions:

1. *Data Integration*
   AI systems can aggregate data from multiple sources-internal operations, external events, IoT sensors, industry trends, and more. This comprehensive data integration provides a robust foundation for understanding current risks and predicting future disruptions.
2. *Scenario Generation*
   AI uses integrated data to automatically generate a wide array of possible disruption scenarios. It can model various "what-if" situations, such as supply chain failures, cyberattacks, or natural disasters, helping organizations anticipate and prepare for a range of threats.
3. *Learning and Improvement*
   AI-driven systems continuously learn from new data and past incidents. They refine their models and recommendations over time, ensuring that scenario planning evolves as new threats and business realities emerge.
4. *Resource Optimization*
   AI analyzes scenarios to recommend the most efficient allocation of resources-personnel, equipment, finances-during both crisis planning and response. This ensures critical operations are prioritized and supported for maximum continuity.

5. *Communication and Collaboration*
   AI tools facilitate seamless communication and collaboration among stakeholders. They can automate notifications, share scenario analysis, and ensure everyone has access to the latest information, which is vital during fast-moving incidents.
6. *Simulation and Training*
   AI enables realistic simulations and training exercises. Employees can practice their responses to AI-generated scenarios, improving preparedness and ensuring that plans are actionable and effective.
7. *Scenario Visualizations*
   AI-powered visualizations turn complex scenario data into clear, actionable insights. Dashboards, heat maps, and interactive models help decision-makers quickly grasp risks and responses.

11.3.5 How AI supports the BCM lifecycle

AI's scenario planning capabilities directly enhance each stage of the BCM lifecycle:

- *Policy and Program Management:* AI provides real-time monitoring and performance analytics.
- *Understanding the Organization:* AI integrates data for more accurate BIA and RA.
- *Strategy Development:* AI-generated scenarios inform better risk mitigation strategies.
- *Response:* AI automates alerts and recommends resource deployment.
- *Exercises and Maintenance:* AI simulations offer realistic training and stress-testing of plans.
- *Awareness and Improvement:* AI tracks engagement, analyzes audit findings, and suggests improvements.

11.3.6 Summary

AI in scenario planning empowers organizations to:

- Integrate and analyze complex data,
- Generate and visualize a wide range of risk scenarios,
- Optimize resources,
- Enhance communication and collaboration,
- Support continuous learning and improvement.

When combined with the structured BCM Lifecycle, AI ensures organizations are not only prepared for disruptions but can adapt, recover, and thrive in a rapidly changing risk environment.

AI-Driven Data Visualization in BCM

11.3.7 Importance of data visualization in BCM

Data visualization transforms complex data sets into intuitive, graphical formats such as charts, dashboards, heat maps, and interactive models. This diagram below enables BCM professionals and decision-makers to quickly understand risks, monitor ongoing disruptions, and make informed decisions during crises.

How AI Enhances Data Visualization for BCM

1. *Real-Time Data Integration and Display*
    - AI aggregates data from multiple sources-internal systems, external feeds, IoT devices, social media, weather forecasts, and more-into unified dashboards.
    - Real-time updates ensure that the latest information is always available for situational awareness.
2. *Dynamic Risk Mapping and Heat Maps*
    - AI-powered visualizations highlight areas of high risk or impact, such as geographic regions affected by natural disasters or operational units experiencing supply chain delays.
    - Heat maps use color gradients to represent severity levels, enabling rapid prioritization.
3. *Interactive Dashboards*
    - Users can drill down into specific data points, filter information by criteria (e.g., time, location, department), and customize views to suit their roles.
    - Interactive dashboards support scenario analysis by allowing stakeholders to explore "what-if" conditions visually.
4. *Trend Analysis and Predictive Insights*
    - AI identifies patterns and trends in historical and current data, displaying them visually to forecast potential disruptions.
    - Graphs and charts illustrate trajectories of risk factors, helping organizations anticipate and prepare for future events.
5. *Incident Tracking and Response Monitoring*
    - Visual timelines and status indicators track the progress of incident response efforts.
    - Resource allocation and recovery activities are mapped to provide a clear overview of operational continuity.
6. *Collaborative Visualization Platforms*
    - Cloud-based AI visualization tools enable multiple stakeholders—across departments and locations—to access and contribute to shared dashboards.
    - This fosters coordinated decision-making and communication during crises.

Benefits of AI-Enhanced Data Visualization in BCM

- *Faster Decision-Making:* Visual data reduces cognitive load, enabling leaders to grasp complex situations quickly and act decisively.

- *Improved Situational Awareness:* Real-time, comprehensive views of risks and responses help maintain control during rapidly evolving events.
- *Enhanced Communication:* Visual tools facilitate clearer communication with internal teams, executives, regulators, and external partners.
- *Proactive Risk Management:* Predictive visualizations empower organizations to move from reactive to proactive continuity planning.
- *Continuous Learning:* Visual analytics help identify recurring vulnerabilities and inform continuous improvement efforts.

Real-World Application Examples

- *Supply Chain Monitoring:* AI dashboards displaying supplier performance metrics and disruption alerts enable companies to reroute logistics proactively.
- *Crisis Management Centers:* Integrated visual displays of incident status, resource deployment, and external conditions support coordinated emergency responses.
- *Regulatory Reporting:* Automated visual reports simplify compliance by clearly showing adherence to continuity standards and risk mitigation efforts.

11.3.8 Summary

AI-powered data visualization is a critical enabler of effective BCM. By converting complex, multi-source data into clear, actionable visual formats, AI helps organizations anticipate risks, monitor disruptions, coordinate responses, and continuously improve resilience. This visual clarity supports faster, better-informed decisions that protect people, assets, and reputation during crises.

11.3.9 AI and continuous improvement in BCM

Continuous improvement is essential for organizational resilience. AI technologies significantly enhance this process within BCM by automating, streamlining, and enriching several critical activities:

1. *Incident Analysis*
    - *What it is:* After a disruption or incident, organizations must analyze what happened, why it happened, and how it was managed.
    - *AI's role:* AI can rapidly sift through large volumes of incident data (logs, communications, system alerts) to identify root causes, contributing factors, and patterns that might not be visible to human analysts.
    - *Benefit:* Faster, more accurate insights enable organizations to learn from every incident and prevent recurrence.
2. *Scenario and Predictive Analytics*
    - *What it is:* Exploring potential future disruptions and assessing their impact.

   - *AI's role:* AI can simulate countless "what-if" scenarios, using predictive analytics to estimate the likelihood and consequences of different risks.
   - *Benefit:* Organizations can proactively prepare for a wider range of threats and make data-driven decisions about risk mitigation.
3. *Data Integration*
   - *What it is:* Bringing together data from multiple sources (operations, supply chain, IT, external feeds) for a unified view.
   - *AI's role:* AI platforms can automatically aggregate and harmonize data, making it accessible and actionable for BCM teams.
   - *Benefit:* Enhanced situational awareness and more comprehensive analysis.
4. *Improvement Recommendation*
   - *What it is:* Identifying ways to strengthen plans, processes, and controls.
   - *AI's role:* AI can analyze incident outcomes, performance metrics, and industry benchmarks to recommend specific improvements—such as updating recovery procedures, reallocating resources, or revising training programs.
   - *Benefit:* Continuous, evidence-based enhancement of BCM effectiveness.
5. *Performance Tracking and Feedback*
   - *What it is:* Monitoring the effectiveness of BCM activities and capturing feedback from exercises, audits, and real events.
   - *AI's role:* AI can track key performance indicators, detect trends, and flag areas needing attention. It can also process feedback from staff and stakeholders to identify recurring issues.
   - *Benefit:* Ongoing visibility into BCM performance and early detection of weaknesses.
6. *Report Generation*
   - *What it is:* Communicating findings, lessons learned, and improvement actions to management and stakeholders.
   - *AI's role:* AI automates the creation of clear, comprehensive reports by extracting relevant data and presenting it in accessible formats.
   - *Benefit:* Faster reporting cycles and more actionable insights for leadership.

11.3.10 How AI supports continuous improvement in the BCM lifecycle

AI enhances every stage of the BCM lifecycle, but its impact is especially powerful in continuous improvement:

- *Automates data collection and analysis* for incident reviews and performance tracking.

- *Provides predictive insights* to anticipate future risks and scenario outcomes.
- *Recommends targeted improvements* based on real-time data and industry best practices.
- *Streamlines reporting* so leadership can act quickly on lessons learned.

11.3.11 Summary

- *Continuous improvement* is the heartbeat of effective BCM, ensuring organizations learn, adapt, and grow more resilient over time.
- *AI* supercharges this process by delivering faster, deeper, and more actionable insights—helping organizations move from reactive to proactive continuity management.
- The *BCM Lifecycle* provides a structured path for ongoing improvement, with AI acting as a catalyst at every step.

11.3.12 AI-Enabled predictive maintenance in BCM

Predictive maintenance, powered by AI, is transforming how organizations ensure operational continuity and resilience. Below are the main functions highlighted in the diagram:

1. *Scenario Modeling and Analysis*
   - *What it means:* AI systems use historical and real-time data to model various failure or disruption scenarios (e.g., equipment breakdown, supply chain delays).
   - *Value:* This allows organizations to anticipate potential issues, understand their impact, and plan mitigation strategies before disruptions occur.
2. *Resource Allocation*
   - *What it means:* AI analyzes maintenance needs, risk levels, and operational priorities to recommend optimal allocation of personnel, spare parts, and financial resources.
   - *Value:* Ensures that critical resources are available where and when they are needed most, minimizing downtime and costs.
3. *Data Integration*
   - *What it means:* AI platforms aggregate data from multiple sources-sensors, maintenance logs, operational systems, and external feeds-into a unified view.
   - *Value:* This holistic perspective enables more accurate predictions and better-informed decision-making.
4. *Visual Maintenance Schedule*
   - *What it means:* AI generates visual dashboards and schedules that display upcoming maintenance tasks, asset health, and risk levels.
   - *Value:* Enhances situational awareness for maintenance teams and management, making planning and tracking more intuitive.

5. *Report and Learning*
   - *What it means:* AI automates the generation of maintenance reports, highlighting trends, root causes, and lessons learned from past incidents.
   - *Value:* Facilitates continuous learning and improvement, helping organizations refine their maintenance and continuity strategies.
6. *Real-Time Monitoring*
   - *What it means:* AI continuously monitors equipment and systems for signs of wear, anomalies, or impending failure.
   - *Value:* Enables early detection and intervention, reducing the likelihood of unexpected breakdowns and business interruptions.
7. *Automated Work Orders*
   - *What it means:* When AI detects a maintenance need or predicts a failure, it can automatically generate and assign work orders to the appropriate teams.
   - *Value:* Streamlines response, reduces manual effort, and ensures timely action.

11.3.12.1 The role of AI in the BCM lifecycle

AI, especially in predictive maintenance, enhances every stage of the BCM lifecycle:

- *Policy and Program Management:* AI provides real-time performance metrics and compliance monitoring.
- *Understanding the Organization:* AI-driven analytics improve the accuracy of BIA and RA.
- *Strategy Development:* AI scenario modeling supports data-driven risk mitigation strategies.
- *Response:* Automated alerts and work orders enable rapid, coordinated action.
- *Exercises and Maintenance:* AI simulations and learning from incident data drive ongoing improvement.
- *Awareness and Training:* AI can personalize training and track engagement.

11.3.13 Summary

AI-powered predictive maintenance is a key enabler of business continuity, allowing organizations to move from reactive to proactive risk management. By integrating AI into the BCM lifecycle, organizations can:

- Anticipate and prevent disruptions,
- Optimize resource use,
- Ensure rapid, effective response,
- Continuously improve their resilience.

The BCM lifecycle, supported by AI, becomes a living process that evolves with the organization's needs and the changing risk landscape.

11.4 COMMUNICATION AND STAKEHOLDER ENGAGEMENT

11.4.1 Overview

This section explores how AI can enhance communication and stakeholder engagement within BCM. Effective communication is critical in BCM to ensure all stakeholders are informed, engaged, and able to respond promptly during disruptions.

Key Points

1. *AI-Driven Communication Tools*
    - *Automated Messaging:* AI can automate alerts and notifications across multiple channels (email, SMS, apps), ensuring timely and consistent communication during incidents.
    - *Chatbots and Virtual Assistants:* These tools provide instant responses to stakeholder queries, offer guidance, and disseminate information 24/7, reducing the burden on human teams.
2. *Personalization and Targeting*
    - *Stakeholder Segmentation:* AI can analyze stakeholder data to segment audiences and tailor messages based on roles, locations, or risk profiles.
    - *Adaptive Content:* Communications can be dynamically adapted in real-time to address the specific concerns or needs of different stakeholder groups.
3. *Sentiment Analysis and Feedback*
    - *Monitoring Stakeholder Sentiment:* AI-powered sentiment analysis can gauge stakeholder emotions and reactions from emails, social media, and surveys, helping BCM teams adjust their strategies.
    - *Continuous Feedback Loops:* Automated tools can collect and analyze feedback, enabling rapid improvements in messaging and engagement.
4. *Proactive Engagement*
    - *Predictive Analytics:* AI can anticipate stakeholder concerns or information needs based on historical data and current trends, allowing proactive outreach.
    - *Scenario Simulation:* AI-driven simulations can help stakeholders understand their roles in various scenarios, improving preparedness and confidence.
5. *Crisis Communication*
    - *Rapid Information Dissemination:* AI ensures critical information reaches the right people quickly, minimizing confusion during crises.

- *Consistency and Accuracy:* Automated systems reduce the risk of human error, ensuring messages are accurate and consistent across all platforms.

Benefits of AI in BCM Communication

- *Speed:* Faster dissemination of information and responses.
- *Scalability:* Ability to reach large, diverse audiences simultaneously.
- *Accuracy:* Reduced risk of misinformation through automated, pre-approved messaging.
- *Engagement:* Higher stakeholder engagement through personalized and relevant communications.
- *Insight:* Real-time analytics and feedback to inform decision-making.

Actionable Steps for Implementation

1. *Assess Communication Needs:* Identify key stakeholder groups and their preferred communication channels.
2. *Select Appropriate AI Tools:* Choose AI-driven platforms that integrate with existing BCM systems.
3. *Train Teams:* Ensure BCM and communications staff are trained to use AI tools effectively.
4. *Pilot and Refine:* Start with pilot projects, gather feedback, and refine processes before full-scale rollout.
5. *Monitor and Optimize:* Continuously monitor communication effectiveness and optimize AI algorithms as needed.

11.5 CONCLUSION

Integrating AI into BCM communication and stakeholder engagement strategies significantly enhances an organization's ability to respond to disruptions. By leveraging automation, personalization, and real-time analytics, organizations can ensure stakeholders are informed, engaged, and confident in their roles during any incident.

AI is revolutionizing the way organizations conduct training and simulation by creating highly adaptive, interactive, and data-driven learning experiences. Here's how AI enhances training and simulation:

1. *Avatar and Character Generation*

   AI enables the automatic creation of digital avatars and virtual characters to simulate real people or roles within a BCM training scenario. These avatars can mimic human behavior, expressions, and speech, providing realistic interactions for trainees.

   - *Example:* Simulating stakeholders like emergency responders, media, or executives.
   - *Benefits:* Enhances immersion and human-like decision-making dynamics.

2. *Dynamic Scenario Execution*
   AI-driven systems can execute scenarios that adapt in real-time based on trainee responses and evolving conditions.
   - *Example:* If a trainee delays a decision, the scenario could escalate to simulate real-world consequences.
   - *Benefits:* Provides a non-linear training experience, encouraging critical thinking under pressure.
3. *Decision-Making and Response Training*
   AI supports realistic decision-making exercises by presenting complex problems and evaluating responses.
   - *Example:* Offering multiple evolving choices during a cyberattack simulation.
   - *Benefits:* Builds judgment and reaction skills, highlighting the impact of decisions.
4. *Customized Scenario Creation*
   AI can be used to generate training scenarios tailored to an organization's specific risks, structure, or history.
   - *Example:* Designing a power outage scenario for a data center based on actual risk assessments.
   - *Benefits:* Ensures relevance and practical learning outcomes.
5. *Scenario Replay and Analysis*
   After training, AI can provide playback of sessions with performance metrics and behavioral analysis.
   - *Example:* Highlighting response delays, incorrect decisions, or optimal actions taken.
   - *Benefits:* Enables detailed feedback, continuous improvement, and certification.
6. *Scenario Generation*
   Beyond customization, AI can autonomously create new scenarios by analyzing threat trends, past events, or organizational data.
   - *Example:* Creating a pandemic outbreak scenario with region-specific parameters.
   - *Benefits:* Keeps training current and reflective of emerging risks.
7. *Simulation Environment Creation*
   AI assists in building detailed, interactive environments for training—such as virtual cities, office complexes, or control rooms.
   - *Example:* Simulating a server room fire in a realistic 3D environment.
   - *Benefits:* Immerses users in lifelike situations to test readiness.
8. *Training and Simulation*
   The integration of all the above capabilities forms a comprehensive AI-based training and simulation ecosystem.
   - *Outcome:* Trainees gain hands-on experience in managing crises in a safe, repeatable, and measurable way.
   - *Impact:* Improves organizational resilience, preparedness, and continuity planning.

11.5.1 Challenges and risks of AI in business continuity management (BCM)

While AI brings transformative potential to BCM training and operations, it also introduces several challenges and risks that must be carefully managed. Here's a deeper look at these considerations:

1. *Privacy Concerns*
   AI systems often require access to large datasets, some of which may include sensitive or personal information.
   - *Risk:* Mismanagement could lead to data breaches or violations of privacy regulations (e.g., GDPR).
   - *Mitigation:* Implement strict data governance and anonymization protocols.
2. *Security Vulnerabilities*
   AI systems, if not properly secured, could become targets for cyberattacks or be exploited to manipulate outcomes.
   - *Risk:* An adversary might inject false data or corrupt AI models to produce flawed responses during crises.
   - *Mitigation:* Regular vulnerability assessments and robust cybersecurity practices.
3. *Ethical Implications*
   Using AI in decision-making—especially during emergencies—raises ethical questions about accountability, fairness, and bias.
   - *Risk:* AI might prioritize efficiency over human safety, or replicate biased historical data in its responses.
   - *Mitigation:* Maintain human oversight and ethical review in AI design and usage.
4. *Over-Reliance on AI*
   Excessive dependence on AI could erode human expertise and lead to reduced preparedness if AI fails during a real event.
   - *Risk:* Staff may be unprepared to act if the AI system crashes or gives incorrect outputs.
   - *Mitigation:* Keep humans in the loop and regularly train personnel without AI assistance.
5. *Integration with Existing Systems*
   AI tools must be compatible with current BCM processes and technology stacks.
   - *Risk:* Poor integration could result in fragmented systems and reduced operational effectiveness.
   - *Mitigation:* Plan implementation with cross-functional IT and BCM collaboration.
6. *Model Drift and Obsolescence*
   AI models can become outdated if not regularly updated to reflect new data and threats.

- *Risk:* An AI trained on outdated scenarios might give poor guidance in new crisis types.
- *Mitigation:* Ensure periodic retraining and validation of AI models.

7. *Regulatory and Compliance Challenges*

   The evolving legal landscape around AI may create uncertainty.
   - *Risk:* AI use could unintentionally violate compliance standards or face sudden regulatory changes.
   - *Mitigation:* Monitor legal developments and involve legal teams in AI deployment planning.

8. *Transparency and Explainability*

   AI decisions can often be difficult to interpret, especially with complex models like deep learning.
   - *Risk:* Lack of explainability may hinder trust and accountability in high-stakes decisions.
   - *Mitigation:* Favor interpretable models where possible and provide explanation tools for AI outputs.

11.6 CONCLUSION

Generative and analytical AI can significantly enhance BCM capabilities, but must be deployed with a strong foundation in *ethics, security, oversight, and ongoing validation.* AI should complement—not replace—human judgment, particularly in high-pressure, high-stakes scenarios.

11.7 ETHICAL CONSIDERATIONS AND CHALLENGES IN AI-ENHANCED RESILIENCE

The integration of AI into organizational resilience frameworks, while offering significant benefits, also raises important ethical considerations and challenges that organizations must carefully address. These considerations extend beyond technical implementation issues to encompass fundamental questions about accountability, fairness, transparency, and the appropriate balance between human judgment and automated decision-making in critical situations.

11.7.1 Privacy and data protection concerns

AI systems used for organizational resilience often require access to vast amounts of data, including sensitive information about employees, customers, suppliers, and business operations. The collection, storage, and analysis of this data raise significant privacy concerns that organizations must address through comprehensive data governance frameworks and privacy protection measures.

The challenge is particularly acute in resilience applications because these systems may need access to data that is normally restricted or compartmentalized, such as employee personal information, customer financial data, or sensitive operational details. Organizations must balance the need for comprehensive data access to enable effective AI analysis with requirements to protect individual privacy and maintain data security.

Privacy considerations also extend to the use of AI systems for monitoring and surveillance purposes. While continuous monitoring capabilities are valuable for early threat detection and risk assessment, they may also raise concerns about employee privacy and the potential for misuse of monitoring data. Organizations must establish clear policies and procedures that define appropriate uses of monitoring data and ensure that privacy rights are respected.

11.7.2 Security vulnerabilities and system integrity

The integration of AI systems into critical resilience functions creates new security vulnerabilities that organizations must address. AI systems can become targets for cyberattacks, and compromised AI systems could potentially cause more damage than traditional system failures because of their central role in decision-making and response coordination.

Adversarial attacks on AI systems represent a particular concern, as attackers might attempt to manipulate input data or model parameters to cause AI systems to make incorrect decisions or recommendations. In resilience applications, such attacks could potentially compromise an organization's ability to respond effectively to genuine threats or could cause unnecessary disruptions through false alarms.

Organizations must implement comprehensive security frameworks that protect AI systems from both external attacks and internal misuse. These frameworks should include robust access controls, data encryption, system monitoring, and incident response procedures specifically designed for AI systems.

11.7.3 Algorithmic bias and fairness

AI systems can perpetuate or amplify existing biases present in training data or system design, potentially leading to unfair or discriminatory outcomes in resilience applications. For example, AI systems used for resource allocation during crises might inadvertently favor certain groups or locations over others based on biased historical data or flawed assumptions.

The challenge of algorithmic bias is particularly significant in resilience applications because the consequences of biased decisions can be severe, potentially affecting people's safety, livelihoods, or access to essential services. Organizations must implement bias detection and mitigation strategies that ensure AI systems make fair and equitable decisions across all stakeholder groups.

Addressing algorithmic bias requires ongoing monitoring and evaluation of AI system performance across different populations and contexts. Organizations should establish metrics and procedures for detecting bias and should be prepared to adjust or retrain AI systems when bias is identified.

11.7.4 Transparency and explainability

Many AI systems, particularly those based on deep learning or other complex algorithms, operate as "black boxes" that provide limited insight into how decisions are made. This lack of transparency can be problematic in resilience applications, where stakeholders may need to understand the reasoning behind AI recommendations to make informed decisions or to maintain trust in the system.

The challenge of explainability is particularly acute during crisis situations, when decision-makers may need to quickly understand and validate AI recommendations before taking action. If AI systems cannot provide clear explanations for their recommendations, human decision-makers may be reluctant to rely on them during critical situations.

Organizations should prioritize the development and implementation of explainable AI systems that can provide clear, understandable explanations for their decisions and recommendations. When black-box systems must be used, organizations should implement additional oversight and validation procedures to ensure that decisions are appropriate and defensible.

11.7.5 Human oversight and accountability

The integration of AI into resilience frameworks raises important questions about human oversight and accountability for automated decisions. While AI systems can process information and make recommendations more quickly than humans, ultimate responsibility for organizational decisions and their consequences must remain with human decision-makers.

Organizations must establish clear governance structures that define roles and responsibilities for AI-assisted decision-making, ensuring that appropriate human oversight is maintained while enabling the speed and efficiency benefits of AI systems. These structures should include escalation procedures for situations where AI recommendations are unclear, contradictory, or potentially inappropriate.

The challenge of maintaining human oversight is complicated by the speed at which AI systems can operate and the volume of decisions they may need to make during crisis situations. Organizations must develop procedures that enable effective human oversight without negating the speed and efficiency benefits of AI systems.

11.7.6 Over-reliance and skill degradation

There is a risk that organizations may become overly dependent on AI systems, potentially leading to the degradation of human skills and capabilities that are essential for effective resilience management. If employees become too reliant on AI recommendations, they may lose the ability to make independent judgments or to function effectively when AI systems are unavailable.

This risk is particularly concerning in resilience applications, where human expertise and judgment are often crucial for handling novel or complex situations that may not be well represented in AI training data. Organizations must ensure that AI systems augment rather than replace human capabilities and that employees maintain the skills needed to function independently when necessary.

Addressing the risk of over-reliance requires ongoing training and development programs that maintain human expertise while teaching employees how to work effectively with AI systems. Organizations should also conduct regular exercises and simulations that test human capabilities without AI assistance to ensure that essential skills are maintained.

11.7.7 Regulatory and compliance challenges

The use of AI in organizational resilience is subject to an evolving regulatory landscape that may create uncertainty and compliance challenges. Different jurisdictions may have different requirements regarding AI transparency, accountability, data protection, and algorithmic fairness that organizations must navigate.

The regulatory environment is particularly complex for organizations that operate across multiple jurisdictions, as they may need to comply with different and potentially conflicting requirements in different locations. Organizations must monitor regulatory developments and ensure that their AI implementations remain compliant with applicable laws and regulations.

Compliance challenges are compounded by the rapid pace of AI technology development, which may outpace regulatory frameworks and create uncertainty about appropriate implementation practices. Organizations should engage with regulators and industry groups to stay informed about emerging requirements and best practices.

Chapter 12

A framework for evaluating and enhancing organizational resilience

12.1 EXECUTIVE SUMMARY

The ability of organizations to continue operations during and after crises plays a crucial role in the medium- and long-term recovery and overall well-being of wider society. In today's interconnected world, disruptions within a single organization can trigger widespread global effects, highlighting the increasing need for organizational reliability in the face of adversity.

There is a growing expectation for organizations to operate reliably during unforeseen challenges, not just the predictable ones. Effective resilience requires decision-makers to prepare for both expected and unexpected crises.

Resilience within an organization hinges on three key factors:

- *Situational Awareness:* Understanding internal and external environments to anticipate potential threats.
- *Management of Critical Vulnerabilities:* Identifying and addressing critical weaknesses that could undermine operations.
- *Adaptive Capacity:* The ability to adjust and respond to rapidly changing, complex, and interconnected circumstances.

By strengthening these areas, organizations not only safeguard their operations but also contribute substantially to the stability, health, and recovery of the communities they serve.

The following Resilience Management process can be applied across industries to identify common challenges and improve organizational resilience.

- *Element 1: Raise Awareness.* Use interviews, surveys, feedback, and hazard scenario brainstorming to understand resilience issues.
- *Element 2: Identify Critical Components.* Map essential internal and external organizational functions, including key stakeholders.
- *Element 3: Assess Vulnerability.* Evaluate the criticality and disaster preparedness of essential components on a qualitative scale; assessments may focus on specific events or planning needs.

DOI: 10.1201/9781003597520-12

- *Element 4: Identification and Prioritization of Critical Vulnerabilities.* Vulnerability assessments are visualized in matrices to highlight components posing the greatest threats, using both general and hazard-specific criteria.
- *Element 5: Increasing Adaptive Capacity.* Readiness Exercises and Disaster Simulation (REDS) enable organizations to efficiently practice crisis preparedness and key skills. These exercises are flexible in duration and scope, accommodating groups from a few leaders to the entire organization, and can involve external partners as needed.

From the case study discussed in this book, a set of 15 generic resilience indicators have been identified. These indicators represent the key resilience issues that apply to all of the organizations in this study. They have been subdivided into the specific, but intrinsically related categories of *situation awareness*, *management of critical vulnerabilities*, and *adaptive capacity*. The 15 resilience indicators are outlined in Table 12.1.

Resilience Assessment Approach

- *Quantification of methodology and resilience indicators:* Developing more precise methods to measure and assess organizational resilience. This involves identifying key resilience dimensions and associated objective indicators for quantitative measurement.
- *Resilience Maturity Models (RMM):* Creating frameworks to guide organizations through a structured path of increasing resilience capabilities. These models typically define stages of maturity and the policies to implement to progress.
- *Understanding resilient leadership:* Exploring the qualities, traits, and communication skills necessary for leaders to guide organizations through disruptions and foster resilience.

Table 12.1 Resilience Indicators

Resilience indicators		
Situation awareness	*Management of critical vulnerabilities*	*Adaptive capacity*
Roles and responsibilities	Planning strategies	Silo mentality
Understanding of hazards and impacts	Participation in exercises	Communications and relationships
Connectivity awareness	Capability and capacity of internal resources	Strategic vision and outcome expectancy
Insurance awareness	Capability and capacity of external resources	Information and knowledge
Recovery priorities	Organizational connectivity	Leadership, management and governance structures

- *Communication of resilience concepts:* Developing effective strategies to communicate resilience principles and their importance to stakeholders both internally and externally.
- *International case studies:* Analyzing real-world examples of organizations' experiences with resilience in various global contexts to inform the development of resilience management strategies and determine the range of resilience for organizations.

Key Aspects of Resilience Management

- *Iterative Process:* Resilience management involves continuous cycles of planning, implementation, testing, and refinement, based on feedback and adapting to evolving circumstances.
- *Scalability:* The framework can be tailored to the specific needs and resources of different types and sizes of organizations, allowing for widespread adoption.
- *Holistic Approach:* Resilience considers various aspects including leadership, culture, risk management, business continuity, technology, and partnerships, integrating them into a comprehensive strategy.
- *Focus on learning and adaptability:* Resilience management emphasizes drawing lessons from both successes and failures to adapt and improve an organization's capacity to handle future disruptions.
- *Stakeholder Engagement:* Collaboration with stakeholders, including employees, customers, suppliers, and partners, is crucial for building and maintaining resilience.

In essence, resilience management is a comprehensive and dynamic approach that aims to enhance an organization's ability to navigate unforeseen challenges, recover quickly, and adapt to change for long-term sustainability and success.

Resilience management, especially in the context of major hazard events, is a critical approach for organizations that underpin our infrastructure, economy, and society. Here's a breakdown of the approach to building resilient organizations in the face of such events:

1. *Planning for hazard events*
    - *Proactive Risk Management:* This involves identifying potential hazards, assessing their potential impact on the organization, and developing strategies to mitigate or respond to them.
    - *Comprehensive Crisis-Response Scenarios and Playbooks:* Creating detailed plans for different hazard scenarios, outlining specific actions, roles, and responsibilities for each phase of response and recovery.
    - *Contingency Planning:* Developing plans to ensure business continuity and recovery of critical services in the event of disruptions, including redundancies and alternative solutions.
    - *Continuous Learning*: Drawing insights from past events, whether internal or external, to refine plans and improve preparedness.

- *Understanding Critical Services:* Identifying the most crucial services for customers and the community, assessing their financial and reputational impact, and prioritizing resilience efforts accordingly.

2. *Effective resource direction during crises*
   - *Adaptive Leadership:* Leaders who are visionary, adaptable, and able to make sound decisions under pressure are essential for guiding organizations through crises.
   - *Clear Communication:* Establishing clear and transparent communication channels, ensuring stakeholders are informed and involved in the response and recovery process.
   - *Empowered and Engaged Employees*: A resilient organization fosters a culture where employees feel psychologically safe to contribute solutions and are empowered to act quickly and adapt to changing circumstances.
   - *Resource Mapping*: Understanding the resources needed to deliver critical services and how they are utilized, identifying potential bottlenecks, and developing strategies to optimize resource allocation during disruptions.
   - *Leveraging Technology and Data*: Employing technology and data analytics to optimize operations, increase efficiency, track risks in real-time, and inform decision-making during crises.
   - *Agile Practices:* Adopting agile methodologies allows organizations to adapt and adjust quickly to changes and effectively manage disruptions.
3. *Legal and contractual frameworks and post-disaster reconstruction*
   - *Understanding Legal Requirements*: Ensuring compliance with relevant legal and regulatory frameworks, particularly concerning disaster response, recovery, and reconstruction.
   - *Contractual Resilience:* Developing resilient contractual arrangements that account for potential disruptions and clarify responsibilities, expectations, and compensation in post-disaster scenarios.
   - *Partnerships and Collaboration*: Collaborating with government agencies, NGOs, and community organizations to streamline recovery efforts and ensure essential services are restored efficiently.
   - *Sustainable and Equitable Recovery*: Post-disaster reconstruction should aim not only to rebuild but also to address underlying vulnerabilities and create more resilient and equitable communities.
   - *Community Engagement*: Actively involving community members and local organizations in planning and implementing recovery and reconstruction strategies, as they possess valuable local knowledge and enduring coping strategies.

By focusing on these key aspects, organizations can enhance their ability to respond effectively to major hazard events, minimize service disruption, and support the long-term well-being of the communities they serve.

12.2 USING THIS METHODOLOGY

12.2.1 Situation awareness

Situation awareness is defined as an organization's comprehensive understanding and perception of its entire operational environment. It encompasses several key abilities:

- *Proactive Foresight:* The capacity to anticipate both potential opportunities and impending crises by monitoring trends, signals, and potential shifts in the environment.
- *Accurate Crisis Identification and Impact Assessment:* The ability to precisely identify developing crises and accurately evaluate their potential impacts on the organization.
- *Understanding Crisis Trigger Factors:* A deeper comprehension of the specific events or conditions that can initiate a crisis, allowing for earlier detection and potential intervention.
- *Resource Awareness (Internal and External):* A clear understanding of all available resources, both within the organization (e.g., personnel, assets, capabilities) and externally (e.g., partners, emergency services, government aid).
- *Minimum Operating Requirements (Recovery Focus):* Knowing the absolute essential functions and resources required to maintain operations at a basic level during a crisis and initiate recovery.
- *Stakeholder Expectations and Obligations:* A heightened awareness of the expectations, obligations, and limitations related to all stakeholders, including internal staff and external parties like customers, suppliers, and consultants. This includes understanding their needs, potential reactions, and the organization's responsibilities toward them during a crisis.

12.2.2 Improve situation awareness

12.2.2.1 The 4R's

Diagram showing the use of key performance indicators (KPIs) as a measure of system resilience, where resilience is a function of the area under the curve defined by system vulnerability and system adaptive capacity.

In essence, strong situation awareness allows an organization to see the bigger picture, understand the forces at play, and make informed decisions to navigate complex and uncertain environments.

12.3 MANAGEMENT OF CRITICAL VULNERABILITIES

This aspect focuses on identifying and addressing those organizational elements, both operational and managerial, that could lead to significant negative impacts during a crisis. The text distinguishes between two types of impacts:

- *Instantaneous Impacts*: These occur suddenly and can be triggered by the failure of a single component, leading to immediate significant negative impacts.
- *Insidious Impacts*: These involve a series of small failures of key components that, over time, accumulate and lead to a large-scale cascading failure.

  It's crucial for organizations to understand the interdependencies between components and the vulnerabilities that can arise from these linkages. Critical vulnerabilities can be categorized as:
- *Tangible Organizational Components*: These are physical or easily identifiable assets and roles:
  - Buildings, structures, and critical supplies.
  - Computers, services, and specialized equipment.
  - Individual managers, decision-makers, and subject matter experts (whose absence or failure could cripple operations).
- *Less Tangible Components*: These are often harder to quantify but equally critical:
  - Relationships between key internal and external groups (e.g., strained internal communication, poor supplier relationships).
  - Communications structures (e.g., ineffective channels, lack of clarity).
  - Perception of the organizational strategic vision (e.g., lack of shared purpose or understanding among employees).

Effective management of critical vulnerabilities involves systematically identifying these weak points, assessing their potential impact, and implementing measures to reduce their likelihood of failure or mitigate the impacts if they do fail. This often includes strategies like redundancy, diversification, robust processes, and strong relationship building.

Together, strong situation awareness enables an organization to perceive threats and opportunities, while effective management of critical vulnerabilities helps it build resilience by strengthening its weak points against those perceived threats.

Adaptive capacity, in the context of organizations, refers to the organizational culture and dynamics that enable effective and timely decision-making, not only during routine operations but also in times of crisis. It involves a set of characteristics and processes that empower an organization to anticipate, respond to, and learn from evolving circumstances, ultimately enhancing its resilience and long-term sustainability.

Key aspects of adaptive capacity include:

1. *Leadership and decision-making structures*
   - *Adaptive leadership*: This involves leaders who are flexible, collaborative, empathetic, and embrace uncertainty. They prioritize creating clarity, fostering commitment, and encouraging collaboration and

trust building across all levels of the organization. Adaptive leaders empower their teams, delegate decision-making where appropriate, and focus on mobilizing resources effectively during crises.
- *Decentralized decision-making*: Adaptive organizations often empower teams and individuals at different levels to make decisions within defined boundaries, especially during crises, where swift and localized action is crucial.
- Balancing stability and flexibility: Adaptive leaders strike a balance between maintaining essential structures and procedures while fostering an environment that embraces innovation and responsiveness to change.

2. *Information and knowledge management*
   - *Acquisition, dissemination, and retention of information and knowledge*: This involves the ability to gather, analyze, and share information effectively to gain a clear understanding of the operating environment, including potential threats and opportunities.
   - *Capitalizing on previous experience*: Learning from both successes and failures in past crises or challenging situations helps organizations build a knowledge base of effective adaptive strategies and strengthen their capacity for future adaptations.
   - *Knowledge-sharing culture*: Fostering an environment where knowledge is openly shared and disseminated across the organization is crucial for collaboration and problem-solving, particularly during crises.
3. *Creativity and flexibility*
   - *Embracing creativity and experimentation*: Organizations with strong adaptive capacity encourage employees to think creatively, explore new ideas, and experiment with novel solutions to challenges. They view mistakes as learning opportunities rather than failures.
   - *Flexible processes and structures*: Adaptive organizations are willing to adjust existing procedures, structures, and work practices as needed to respond to changing circumstances, rather than rigidly adhering to established norms.
   - *Cultivating a growth mindset*: A culture that promotes continuous learning and acknowledges the importance of adapting to change is vital for fostering creativity and embracing new approaches.
4. *Other enabling factors*
   - *Strong social capital*: Networks, relationships, and trust within a community facilitate cooperation and collective action, which are essential for building adaptive capacity.
   - *Clarity of objectives and boundaries*: Clearly defined organizational objectives, conditions, and boundaries within which employees operate help guide their actions and ensure they are aligned with the organization's strategic vision, even in rapidly changing situations.
   - *Access to resources*: Having the financial, technological, and human resources required to implement adaptive strategies is also a critical factor.

Essentially, adaptive capacity is about fostering a culture that thrives on change, values learning, empowers its people, and possesses the necessary knowledge and resources to navigate complexity and uncertainty effectively.

A resilient organization distinguishes itself from a non-resilient one through three core qualities:

1. *Greater awareness of itself, its key stakeholders, and its operating environment*

   Resilient organizations possess a deep understanding of their internal strengths and weaknesses, their critical vulnerabilities, and the potential impact these vulnerabilities could have in a crisis. This includes:
   - *Anticipating potential crises and opportunities*: They are proactive in identifying emerging threats and opportunities, rather than reacting only after they materialize.
   - *Understanding crisis impacts and triggers*: They analyze past events and develop a heightened awareness of the factors that can initiate or exacerbate crises, and the potential negative impacts they might unleash.
   - *Knowing available resources*: They have a clear picture of both internal resources (people, assets, etc.) and external support networks (partners, emergency services) that can be leveraged during a crisis.
   - *Identifying minimum operating requirements*: They understand the absolute essential functions and resources necessary to maintain operations at a basic level in a crisis, according to inspenet.com.
   - *Understanding stakeholder expectations and obligations*: They are aware of the needs, expectations, and limitations of all stakeholders, both internal (employees) and external (customers, suppliers, consultants), allowing for effective communication and collaboration during crises.
2. *Increased knowledge of critical vulnerabilities*

   Resilient organizations go beyond simply recognizing vulnerabilities; they actively seek to understand the potential positive and negative impacts these vulnerabilities could have in a crisis situation. This involves recognizing that vulnerabilities can be either:
   - *Instantaneous*: Sudden failures of a single component can have immediate significant negative impacts.
   - *Insidious*: Small failures of multiple components can lead to large-scale cascading failures over time.

   They also recognize that critical vulnerabilities can involve both:
   - *Tangible components*: Buildings, structures, critical supplies, technology, and key individuals.
   - *Less tangible components*: Relationships between groups, communication structures, and perceptions of strategic vision.
3. *Ability to adapt with new solutions or adapt existing tools*

   This quality highlights the organization's dynamic and proactive nature. Resilient organizations are not simply reactive; they possess the capacity to pivot and innovate when faced with unforeseen circumstances. This translates to:

- *Creating new and innovative solutions*: They encourage creativity and foster a culture where employees feel empowered to develop novel approaches to address emerging challenges.
- *Adapting existing tools and processes*: They demonstrate flexibility in modifying current resources, procedures, and systems to effectively cope with new and unforeseen situations.

By embodying these three core qualities, resilient organizations are not only better equipped to survive major hazard events and other disruptions, but also to leverage these challenges as opportunities for growth and innovation. This proactive and adaptable approach minimizes negative impacts and allows the organization to thrive in even the most difficult circumstances.

12.4 SCOPE OF THIS PROJECT

This sample project aims to:

- Identify key features that contribute to organizational resilience across all types and sizes.
- Develop tools to assess and enhance resilience for these organizations.

Ten diverse case-study organizations were chosen for broad representation. A pilot study with the first organization produced an initial Resilience Management framework, which was refined through the remaining nine case studies.

Table 12.2 outlines the key aspects of the research project as described, ensuring clarity on its objectives, methodology, and expected outputs.

Table 12.2 Scope of the Project

Section	*Description*	*Details/examples*
Project title	Building organizational resilience: features and tools	This project focuses on understanding and enhancing organizational resilience to major hazard events
Project purpose	To enhance the ability of organizations to respond effectively following hazard events, minimizing service disruption and promoting community well-being during disasters.	The project aims to improve organizational resilience, which is crucial as organizations manage our infrastructure, economy, and contribute to society.

(Continued)

Table 12.2 (Continued)

Section	*Description*	*Details/examples*
Project objectives	1. Identify features contributing to organizational resilience. 2. Develop tools for assessing and improving organizational resilience.	Features: These are independent of organization size, type, or nature. Tools: Designed for both assessment and improvement of resilience.
Methodology	Case study approach: Ten organizations were selected to represent a diverse range of sizes, types, and industry sectors.	Pilot study with the first case-study organization to develop a preliminary framework for Resilience Management. Subsequent refinement and modification of the framework with the remaining nine organizations.
Key areas of focus (organizational response and recovery)	1. Hazard event planning: How organizations prepare for and mitigate potential impacts. 2. Effective resource direction during crises: How organizations manage resources during crisis situations. 3. Legal and contractual frameworks: The legal and contractual environment in which organizations operate during and after a disaster. 4. Post-disaster reconstruction challenges: Specific issues related to rebuilding and recovery after a disaster.	The project will investigate how organizations plan for, respond to, and recover from hazard events, including the legal and practical aspects of reconstruction.
Target audience	Organizations of all sizes and types, as well as stakeholders involved in disaster preparedness and recovery efforts.	This includes private sector businesses, public institutions, government agencies, non-profits, etc.
Expected deliverables	• A framework for Resilience Management. • Tools for assessing and improving organizational resilience. • Insights and recommendations based on case study findings. • Potential future work under the Resilient Organisations research program.	Deliverables may be presented in the form of reports, guidelines, workshops, and publications.

Table 12.2 provides a concise and clear representation of the project's scope, making it easier to understand its goals, approach, and expected outcomes.

12.5 RESILIENCE MANAGEMENT

In numerous organizations, risk management, business continuity, and emergency management planning are generally recognized as interrelated disciplines; however, effectively integrating these functions is often challenging. The Resilience Management framework unifies all organizational planning activities under a single comprehensive approach known as Resilience Management.

By embedding resilience within daily operations, Resilience Management enables organizations to respond successfully following a crisis, equipping them to manage high-stress situations efficiently. Organizations implementing this approach enhance their situational awareness and gain deeper insights into vulnerabilities that could critically impact performance. Furthermore, adaptive capacity is improved as decision-makers develop a better understanding of the organization's core values and those held by key stakeholders. The process also clarifies expectations for both leadership and stakeholders, facilitating the evaluation of existing plans and the development of new strategies.

The elements within the Resilience Management framework may be utilized individually or in combination, providing a flexible means to incrementally strengthen organizational resilience. For optimal effectiveness, these elements should be applied sequentially and within a condensed timeframe to maximize knowledge retention and application. Depending on the organization's scale and the specific level of resilience targeted—such as leadership versus the entire workforce—the Resilience Management process may require from one week to one month to complete.

This report outlines the tools and techniques devised for conducting Resilience Management using an iterative methodology. The individual components of the process and their corresponding tools are presented in Table 12.3 and discussed in detail in the subsequent sections.

12.5.1 Step 1—Building awareness of resilience issues

For resilience management to be effective, an organization must thoroughly understand the factors influencing its resilience on a routine basis as well as during potential crises. This process, known as building situational awareness, encompasses:

- The current and anticipated operating environment;
- The resources available to the organization;
- The expectations and constraints of all stakeholders; and
- The positive and negative impacts associated with various types of crises.

Table 12.3 The tools used for each element of the Resilience Management process and the relationships between them

<table>
<tr><th>Situation awareness</th><th>Management of critical vulnerabilities</th><th>Adaptive capacity</th></tr>
<tr><td>Element 1
Building an awareness of resilience issues
• Interviews, surveys and reports
Gathering information from key stakeholders and validating that data.
• Impact scenarios building an awareness of crises causes and impacts.</td><td>Element 2
Selection of critical organizational components
Identifying the critical components for continued service, operations and essential functions.
Achieved from an internal and an external perspective.</td><td rowspan="4">Element 5
Readiness Exercises and Disaster Simulation (REDS) improvement of adaptive capacity looking at:
• Environment within which the organization conducts its operations, services and functions.
• Leadership and decision-making for crises
• Communications structures
• Testing and execution of existing or proposed plans including understanding of minimum operating requirements.
• Assessment of organizational strategic vision as a crisis management tool.
• Observation of understanding of key stakeholder limitations, expectations and requirements.</td></tr>
<tr><td>Element 2
Selection of critical organizational components
Building an awareness of essential components for ongoing services, operations and functions from an internal and external perspective.</td><td>Element 3
Self-assessment of vulnerability
A facilitated or independent self-assessment of selected components for criticality, preparedness and susceptibility to determine vulnerability.</td></tr>
<tr><td rowspan="2">Element 5
Readiness Exercises and Disaster Simulation (REDS)
Using the Impact Scenarios to build awareness of the range and impacts of various crisis events.</td><td>Element 4
Prioritization of critical vulnerabilities
Using a vulnerability matrix to map the data from the vulnerability self-assessment, identification and prioritization of critical vulnerabilities is achieved.</td></tr>
<tr><td>Element 5
Readiness Exercises and Disaster Simulation (REDS)
Identification and ongoing testing of identified vulnerabilities in simulated crisis situations.</td></tr>
</table>

Table 12.4 provides examples for each aspect of building situation awareness, a crucial first step in effective resilience management.

By systematically examining these four areas, organizations can develop a more robust and comprehensive understanding of their operational environment, enabling them to anticipate challenges, make informed decisions, and build a stronger foundation for resilience.

Table 12.4 Situation Awareness

Aspect of situation awareness	*Description*	*Examples*
Current and expected future operating environment	Understanding the internal and external factors influencing the organization's operations, including potential opportunities and threats.	Current: Analyzing market trends (e.g., increasing demand for sustainable products), regulatory changes (e.g., stricter data privacy laws), technological advancements (e.g., rise of AI), and geopolitical shifts (e.g., supply chain disruptions). Future: Forecasting demographic shifts (e.g., aging workforce), emerging technologies, potential natural disasters, or shifts in consumer preferences.
Resources at the organization's disposal	Identifying and assessing all available resources, both internal and external, that can be leveraged during day-to-day operations and crises.	Internal: Skills and expertise of employees, financial capital, technological infrastructure, physical assets (buildings, equipment), intellectual property, and existing crisis response plans. External: Partnerships with suppliers, government agencies, NGOs, community support networks, emergency services, and available insurance coverage.
Expectations and limitations of all stakeholders	Understanding the needs, desires, constraints, and potential reactions of all stakeholders, including employees, customers, suppliers, investors, regulators, and local communities.	Examples: Employees: Expectations for workplace safety, clear communication during crises, support for mental health, and fair treatment during layoffs or restructurings. Customers: Expectations for product quality, reliable service, transparent communication during disruptions, and ethical practices. Suppliers: Expectations for timely payments, fair contract terms, collaboration during supply chain disruptions, and adherence to ethical sourcing standards. Regulators: Expectations for compliance with laws, regulations, and reporting requirements related to safety, environment, and financial performance. Community: Expectations for environmental responsibility, ethical behavior, involvement in decision-making, and contribution to local economic development.

(Continued)

Table 12.4 (Continued)

Aspect of situation awareness	*Description*	*Examples*
Positive and negative impacts of various types of crises	Analyzing the potential positive and negative impacts of different crisis scenarios, beyond just the immediate damages.	Crisis Type: Natural Disaster (e.g., Flood) Negative Impacts: Property damage, service disruption, loss of revenue, injury or death, decreased employee morale. Positive Impacts: Opportunities for innovation in infrastructure design, strengthened community ties through recovery efforts, enhanced reputation if response is effective, potential for new business opportunities in reconstruction. Crisis Type: Cyber Attack Negative Impacts: Data breach, financial losses, reputational damage, operational disruption, legal and regulatory penalties. Positive Impacts: Enhanced cybersecurity protocols, improved IT infrastructure, heightened employee awareness of cyber risks, potential for new business opportunities in cybersecurity solutions.

12.5.1.1 Interviews, surveys, and reporting

Interviewing key stakeholders internally (staff, shareholders, etc.) and externally (customers, suppliers, contractors and even the wider community, etc.) is an excellent way to assess situation awareness. Often, during interviewing key decision-makers had a different perspective on the organization and its resilience compared to the views of staff at other levels.

Even when targeting Resilience Management at a senior decision-making level, it is important to gather data from other people in the organization, at a variety of operational and decision-making levels. The validity of viewpoints can be later determined with a targeted survey. Interviewers should have experience, understand resilience management, and offer objective insights. They must recognize that single comments may not reflect the whole organization, but differing views from senior staff may signal key resilience issues. Maintaining objectivity and openness is essential. Use a semi-structured, open-ended interview format to encourage employees to elaborate on leads provided by the interviewer.

12.5.2 Assessing resilience: Stakeholder interview questions for building situation awareness

Interviewing key stakeholders (internal and external) is crucial to gauge an organization's situation awareness and inform its resilience management strategy.

Table 12.5 categorizes sample questions designed to elicit information about the organization's understanding of its environment, resources, stakeholder dynamics, and the impact of potential crises.

Table 12.5 Understanding the Organisation

Category	*Key areas of inquiry*	*Sample interview questions*
Understanding the operating environment	Internal strengths and weaknesses, external opportunities and threats, regulatory landscape, market dynamics.	• What are the key trends affecting the industry in the next 1–5 years? • How are changes in the regulatory environment (e.g., data privacy laws, safety standards) monitored? • What are the organization's greatest strengths and weaknesses? • How does the organization monitor potential threats like cybersecurity risks or supply chain disruptions?
Resource Awareness	Availability and utilization of internal resources (personnel, assets, capabilities) and external support networks (partners, emergency services).	• What internal resources would be most critical in a major disruption? • How well are external partnerships (suppliers, government, community) leveraged for resilience? • Are there any lacking resources that could significantly impact the ability to recover from a crisis?
Stakeholder Expectations and Limitations	Understanding the needs, desires, constraints, and potential reactions of all key stakeholders (employees, customers, suppliers, investors, regulators, community).	• What are the most important customer expectations, especially during a crisis? • How might employee expectations about support and communication differ from senior leadership's? • How are the needs and concerns of suppliers or partners assessed during times of uncertainty? • How transparent is the organization with stakeholders about potential risks or challenges?
Crisis Impact and Learning	Identifying potential positive and negative impacts of various types of crises, and mechanisms for learning from and adapting to crises.	• Can you describe a specific crisis the organization faced and its impact (both negative and potentially positive)? • What specific lessons were learned from that experience, and how were they applied? • How well does the organization learn from mistakes or failures? • Are there any scenarios where a crisis could potentially lead to positive change or opportunity for the organization?

(Continued)

Table 12.5 (Continued)

Category	*Key areas of inquiry*	*Sample interview questions*
Adaptive capacity and decision-making	Leadership's ability to make timely and appropriate decisions, information flow, organizational culture of creativity, and flexibility.	• How effectively can leadership make decisions when facing incomplete or conflicting information during a crisis? • Can you provide an example of a time when the organization had to significantly change course or strategy in response to an unexpected event? • How is it ensured that relevant information reaches the right decision-makers quickly during a crisis? • How much does the organization encourage or tolerate innovative solutions during challenging times?

Note: Varying insights from different organizational levels are important to collect. Interviewers should maintain objectivity and use a semi-structured format to allow for rich, detailed responses.

After interviews are completed and information is gathered, main findings should be shared with the organization. Discussion reports offer an external perspective and reflect internal perceptions or misconceptions the organization may not realize.

Surveys based on these reports can validate interview observations, measure how widespread certain views are within the organization and among stakeholders, and show the effectiveness of strategies or procedures. Staff and stakeholder engagement surveys also provide valuable insight for building resilience management.

12.5.2.1 Impact scenarios

A structured method designed to assist in evaluating an organization's situational awareness is the deployment of Impact Scenarios. These scenarios serve to assess the extent of an organization's understanding regarding potential hazards it may encounter and the corresponding impacts these could have on operations.

Many organizations become preoccupied with daily challenges and consequently neglect to consider unfamiliar events that have not yet occurred. Others tend to focus exclusively on past incidents, preparing primarily for their recurrence. Notably, only a minority of organizations in this study had contemplated the possibility of facing crises simultaneously with maintaining routine business operations, particularly from a human resources standpoint.

Impact Scenarios enable organizations to appreciate that while the range of potential hazards is extensive, there exist universal management strategies suitable for addressing various situations effectively.

A collection of four Impact Scenarios has been developed to enhance organizational awareness of crises and their potential consequences. These scenarios are intended to simulate diverse effects on organizations by shifting the focus from specific hazards to particular event impacts, acknowledging the variability in how threats may manifest.

It is important to recognize that some events will remain unpredictable, and even if anticipated, their impacts may be difficult to accurately forecast. Consequently, the main objectives of the Impact Scenarios are threefold:

- First, Impact Scenarios encourage organizations to identify foreseeable events and consider strategies for managing unforeseen outcomes. They broaden organizational understanding of various hazard types and their potential consequences, moving beyond a focus on only prominent or previously encountered risks. These scenarios serve as effective tools for training decision-makers to respond adaptively to unexpected situations.
- Second, Impact Scenarios support the assessment of an organization's ability to manage the failure—whether temporary or permanent—of interconnected entities. It is essential for organizations to evaluate the implications of the loss of key partners or competitors.
- Third, these scenarios enable organizations to prepare for diverse hazards that may produce similar impacts concurrently, fostering a comprehensive and cost-effective planning approach. Often, mitigation strategies for one hazard can be applied to others, allowing organizations to consolidate critical crisis management elements and optimize resource allocation. Additionally, Impact Scenarios prompt consideration of opportunities that may emerge from a crisis, rather than focusing solely on adverse effects.

The principal characteristics of the Impact Scenarios are presented in Table 12.6.

12.5.3 Impact scenario examples for organizations

These four types of impact scenarios are designed to help organizations develop a more comprehensive understanding of potential threats and build more adaptable resilience strategies.

12.5.4 Element 2—Selection of organizational components

At the outset of the Resilience Management process, it is necessary to define the scope and scale of the assessment. For instance, an organization may focus on developing resilience for its principal decision-maker, senior management team, a specific department such as IT, the entire organization, or in collaboration with related organizations. While enhancing the resilience of the entire organization is typically the broader aim, practical limitations regarding resources, budgets, or organizational support may require constraining the scope. The methodology applies to any scale, provided that the purpose and scope are clearly established to inform the analysis.

Table 12.6 The impact scenarios

Scenario type	*Scenario characteristics*	*Sample scenario*
Regional	Significant physical damage to buildings, contents, and resources, with severe disruptions to essential lifeline services (transportation, electricity, water, telecommunications).	A major earthquake hits the region, collapsing buildings, severing transportation routes, causing widespread power outages, disrupting water supplies, and damaging telecommunications infrastructure.
Societal	Extended staffing absences due to an event, with physical infrastructure remaining largely intact. Staff are either unable or unwilling to be at work.	A widespread pandemic or prolonged severe weather event results in a large percentage of the workforce being unable to come to the physical workplace. Even with remote work options, the overall workforce capacity is significantly reduced due to illness, caregiving responsibilities, or lack of transportation.
Localized	Organization-specific incident causing severe disruption to normal operations, reputation impacts, and potentially loss of life or injury. Intense media and regulatory scrutiny necessitate managing stakeholder perception alongside the physical response and recovery.	A major data breach exposes sensitive customer data, leading to customer distrust, negative media coverage, regulatory investigations, and potential lawsuits. This requires the organization to focus on both technical recovery and a robust communications strategy to rebuild its reputation and maintain stakeholder trust.
Distal	Impacts on business flow through the organizational network (supply chain or customer base) due to an event far removed from the organization's immediate physical location.	A significant geopolitical event or trade dispute in a key manufacturing region leads to government restrictions on the export of critical components, disrupting the organization's supply chain and delaying production. This could also include the collapse of critical infrastructure, like electricity or telecommunications grids, impacting key suppliers or customers, according to inspenet.com.

The role of organizational vision as a crisis response tool was not extensively recognized among the case-study organizations. The organizational vision can offer a framework for determining strategic direction during a crisis. In situations lacking this clarity, some organizations indicated their approach to emergency management was primarily reactive.

Once the scope has been set, the organization can develop a systems map to identify key aspects necessary for ongoing operations. This systems map becomes the foundation for evaluating critical vulnerabilities. To ensure ease of use, the systems map should be created at a level of detail appropriate to the assessment's scope and scale. More detailed maps may facilitate a more accurate evaluation of vulnerabilities but could also increase complexity for managers. Examples of organizational components relevant at the senior management level can be found in Table 12.7.

Table 12.7 An example of the types of internal and external organizational components mapped for organizations in this study

Physical components		*Human components*		*Process components*	
Internal components					
Buildings and equipment	Offices	Communication and Relationships	General staff	Direct planning	Risk management
	IT Hardware		Senior staff		Continuity planning
	Security		Board		Emergency Management
	Vehicles	Management	Leadership		Cash flow
	Software/IP		Succession		Market/brand Knowledge
	Inventory		Staff welfare		Insurance
Services	Generators	Information/knowledge	Backup		
	Fuel supplies		Privacy/protection		
	IT networks		Training/review		
External components					
Services	Electricity	Communication and relationships	Emergency services	Indirect Planning	Inter-connectedness
	Water		Local authorities		Statutory Compliance
	Sewerage		Customers		Contracts
	Telecommunications		Suppliers		Reputation/ image
	Transportation		Media		

A distinction exists between internal and external components within an organization. Internal components are those over which the organization has direct management authority, such as staff employment contracts. External components, by contrast, are those where the organization does not have full control; for example, telecommunications services managed by an external supplier. While the organization may manage its response to service outages, it cannot directly control their underlying causes.

Ongoing situation awareness development is a key element of effective resilience management. Engaging personnel involved in implementing resilience management in the mapping of organizational components supports the development of this awareness.

12.6 ELEMENT 3—SELF-ASSESSMENT OF VULNERABILITY

Conducting a vulnerability assessment plays a crucial role in resilience management by enhancing situational awareness, fostering the development of adaptive capacities, and providing organizations with clear, actionable objectives.

Self-assessment of vulnerability is encouraged to strengthen organizational engagement and buy-in. When assessments are conducted by external facilitators, there is a risk that participants may feel misunderstood or misrepresented, which can result in resistance to the recommendations provided. By employing self-assessment methods, organizations are more likely to take ownership of identified issues and assume responsibility for implementing improvements.

Vulnerability assessments should initially adopt an all-hazards approach, evaluating both the criticality and preparedness of essential organizational elements (Element 2). Where necessary, specific scenarios—such as those outlined in Impact Scenarios—can be utilized to address particular hazards or threats, such as pandemic planning. In these cases, an evaluation of the susceptibility of critical components is conducted. Further details regarding the vulnerability assessment process are outlined below.

Vulnerability assessment is a crucial element of resilience management, contributing to heightened situation awareness, fostering adaptive capacity, and providing organizations with concrete goals for improvement. The self-assessment approach promotes ownership and accountability within the organization. Here are sample tables to illustrate criticality, preparedness, and susceptibility assessments.

12.6.1 Criticality

The critical question when assessing component importance is:

> *How important is this component to the organisation's crisis response and recovery?*

Assessments consider both response and recovery stages. The response phase begins during or just after a crisis and varies by event—lasting hours after an earthquake, but potentially months for a widespread disease. Recovery starts when the organization aims to return to normal operations, though the shift from response is not always clear-cut, and post-crisis conditions may differ significantly from pre-crisis norms (Table 12.8).

12.6.2 Preparedness

Preparedness assessments focus on the following question:

> *What level of planning or redundancy exists to support an effective response and recovery if this component becomes non-functional?*

Table 12.8 Criticality assesses the importance of various organizational components to core operations

Organizational component	*Description*	*Impact of failure (e.g., scale 1–5, where 5 is catastrophic)*	*Recovery Time Objective (RTO) (in hours)*
Mission-critical application	Software essential for core business functions; failure leads to immediate, severe impact on revenue, compliance, and reputation.	5	1
Data center	Houses critical servers and network equipment; failure causes widespread system outages and data loss.	5	4
Key supplier (single source for critical raw material)	Provides essential raw material without which production halts; failure leads to significant delays and potential loss of market share.	4	72
Specialized manufacturing equipment (single point of failure)	Unique equipment required for a critical production process; failure causes production stoppages.	4	24
Customer relationship management (CRM) system	Stores customer data and manages interactions; failure impacts customer service and sales.	3	12
Administrative application (e.g., HR payroll system)	Supports internal functions; failure impacts administrative tasks but not core operations immediately.	2	24
Non-essential office supplies	General office supplies; minimal impact on operations if unavailable temporarily.	1	48

Preparedness is assessed qualitatively as high, moderate, low, or none. For instance, electricity services may be considered highly prepared if a generator has been obtained. In contrast, organizations without generators may assess their planning for power loss as low.

Preparedness measures the organization's readiness to respond to and recover from disruptions impacting critical components (Table 12.9).

Table 12.9 Preparedness Measures

Organizational component	*Current preparedness level (e.g., scale 1–5, where 5 is highly prepared)*	*Existing mitigation strategies*	*Areas for improvement*
Mission-critical application	4	• Redundant servers and network infrastructure. • Automated backup and recovery procedures. • Disaster recovery testing conducted annually.	Improve documentation for manual recovery processes.
Data center	3	• Backup generators and uninterruptible power supplies (UPS). • Off-site data replication. • Limited physical security measures.	Enhance physical security; implement more rigorous access controls.
Key supplier (single source for critical raw material)	2	• Emergency inventory maintained for one week. • Informal discussions about potential alternative suppliers.	Identify and qualify at least one alternative supplier; establish formal contracts.
Specialized manufacturing equipment (single point of failure)	3	• Basic maintenance schedule. • Limited spare parts inventory. • Technicians trained for routine repairs only.	Implement a predictive maintenance program; procure a critical spare parts inventory.
Customer relationship management (CRM) system	4	• Daily backups to cloud storage. • User training for basic troubleshooting. • Help desk support available during business hours.	Extend help desk support to 24/7 during major disruptions.
Administrative application (e.g., HR payroll system)	3	• Weekly backups. • Manual workaround procedures exist.	Automate data entry for backup systems.

12.6.3 Susceptibility

A susceptibility assessment helps organizations identify how specific crises, such as pandemics or earthquakes, could impact different components. For each part of the organization, the question asked is: *"How severely will this component's performance be affected in this scenario?"* For instance, electricity services may be more vulnerable to infrastructure damage from an earthquake than to disruption from a pandemic. Susceptibility is rated as very high, high, moderate, or low.

The assessment context is crucial and can be established through techniques like reflecting on past crises or considering media coverage of potential threats. In this study, Impact Scenarios provide the crisis context, often combining multiple scenarios to simulate the complexity of real crises. This approach reveals organizational vulnerabilities and interconnections, helping clarify strengths and weaknesses.

Susceptibility assesses how vulnerable critical components are to specific threats, potentially using Impact Scenarios (Table 12.10).

By conducting self-assessments using Tables 12.8–12.10, organizations can systematically evaluate their resilience posture, identify key areas for improvement, and develop targeted strategies to mitigate vulnerabilities and build a more resilient organization.

Table 12.10 Impact of threats on Critical Components

Scenario: regional earthquake	*Critical organizational component*	*Susceptibility (e.g., scale 1–5, where 5 is highly susceptible)*	*Impact on component (description)*
Data center	Buildings, structures, equipment	4	Severe structural damage, leading to potential collapse and extensive equipment damage.
Key supplier (single source for critical raw material)	Supply chain, transportation routes	5	Road closures, port damage, and logistical disruptions prevent raw material delivery.
Specialized manufacturing equipment (single point of failure)	Physical integrity of equipment	3	Potential damage from shaking or building collapse; power outages disrupt operation.
Employees	Health and safety, ability to travel to work, housing security	4	Injuries, inability to reach work due to transportation disruption, emotional stress, potential damage to homes.

12.7 ELEMENT 4—PRIORITISATION OF CRITICAL VULNERABILITIES

Identifying vulnerabilities is only the first step in building a resilient organization. The next critical step is prioritizing these vulnerabilities to ensure that limited resources are focused on the areas that pose the greatest risk. This involves combining the vulnerability assessment data (criticality, preparedness, and susceptibility) with a nuanced understanding of how these vulnerabilities can manifest during a crisis.

Critical vulnerabilities are those components or links between components that, if they fail, are likely to have a significant negative impact on the organization. These impacts can be characterized by two key aspects:

1. Speed of Impact:
    i. Rapid: The component failure has an immediate, sudden, and significant negative impact. For instance, a major data breach could result in immediate reputational damage and financial losses.
    ii. Insidious: Small, seemingly insignificant failures of key components accumulate over time, leading to a large-scale cascading failure. For example, a series of minor communication breakdowns could eventually lead to a breakdown in crisis response efforts.
2. Number of Failures Required:
    i. Discrete: The failure of a single component leads to a significant negative impact. For example, the loss of a unique piece of manufacturing equipment could immediately halt production.
    ii. Cascading: A single point of failure within a complex interconnected system propagates failures to other components, creating a domino effect and amplifying the overall impact. This is particularly relevant in areas like critical infrastructure or supply chains.

It is essential to view and treat critical vulnerabilities as interconnected parts of a system rather than in isolation.

12.7.1 Identified critical vulnerabilities in case studies

The study highlighted several components that frequently emerged as critical vulnerabilities across various organizations:

- *Electricity and telecommunications services*: These are foundational for modern operations; disruptions can trigger widespread outages and cascading effects across other systems.
- *Governance structures within the organization*: Inadequate leadership, unclear decision-making processes, or lack of accountability can hinder effective crisis response and recovery.

- *Communications and relationships with key stakeholders*: Poor communication or strained relationships with staff, media, local authorities, and emergency services can impede information flow and coordinated action during a crisis.
- *Flow of information into and throughout the organization*: Blockages or inefficiencies in information flow can lead to delayed responses, misinformed decisions, and a hindered ability to adapt to changing circumstances.

12.7.2 Prioritization framework

A framework for prioritizing critical vulnerabilities could look like this table below:

Table 12.11 provides a framework for organizations to prioritize critical vulnerabilities by considering the nature of the vulnerability (speed and type of impact), its likelihood of occurrence, and its potential impact on the organization's operations, reputation, and stakeholders. According to Brinqa, prioritizing vulnerabilities effectively helps align remediation efforts with business goals and foster trust between security and business teams.

Some components may become more or less vulnerable when viewed within a system rather than alone. For instance, while electricity supply is a vulnerability on its own, its failure can create additional critical vulnerabilities across the system. Conversely, some organizational elements may seem significant in isolation but are less so system-wide. Organizations need effective tools to identify their true critical vulnerabilities and allocate resources accordingly. The vulnerability matrix, developed in this study, visually presents these key vulnerabilities to help organizations identify and prioritize them.

12.7.2.1 The vulnerability matrix

The Vulnerability Matrix (see Figure 12.1) serves as an essential instrument for decision-makers, enabling them to visually pinpoint components that represent the highest potential threats, which can then be addressed appropriately. As such, the matrix is a key tool for prioritizing vulnerabilities within an organization, greatly aiding the effective allocation of attention and resources to areas where they will yield the most value.

Vulnerability matrices are developed using preparedness and criticality data gathered in Element 3, resulting in an assessment of vulnerability across an "all-hazards" spectrum. Additionally, susceptibility information facilitates the creation of context-specific matrices. Both types are illustrated in Figure 12.1.

In these matrices, criticality is mapped on the x-axis and preparedness on the y-axis, with each organizational component depicted as a "hole" within the matrix. In the all-hazards matrix, each hole is uniform in size, and their positions indicate their status as critical vulnerabilities.

Table 12.11 All Hazard Matrix

Critical vulnerability category	*Characteristics (speed and number of failures)*	*Likelihood (qualitative or quantitative scale)*	*Impact (criticality and preparedness ratings)*	*Prioritization ranking (e.g., high, medium, low)*	*Remediation efforts and timelines*
Disruption to electricity and telecommunications services	Rapid and cascading	High (due to aging infrastructure, extreme weather, cyber-attack risks)	Catastrophic (5/5)	High	Implement redundant power systems, develop backup communication channels, establish protocols for remote work during outages, and collaborate with service providers for enhanced resilience.
Weaknesses in governance structures	Insidious and discrete	Medium (depending on culture, leadership and clarity of roles)	Significant (4/5)	Medium-high	Review and refine governance models, establish clear crisis decision-making frameworks, enhance leadership development programs, and foster a culture of accountability.
Poor communication and stakeholder relationships	Insidious and Cascading	Medium (requires ongoing effort to maintain)	Significant (4/5)	Medium-high	Develop comprehensive communication plans, conduct regular stakeholder engagement, train spokespersons for effective crisis communication, and build strong relationships with media, authorities and emergency services.
Ineffective information flow	Insidious and cascading	High (common organizational challenge)	Severe (4/5)	High	Implement clear information sharing protocols, leverage technology for efficient information dissemination, enhance internal communication platforms, and provide training on information flow best practices.

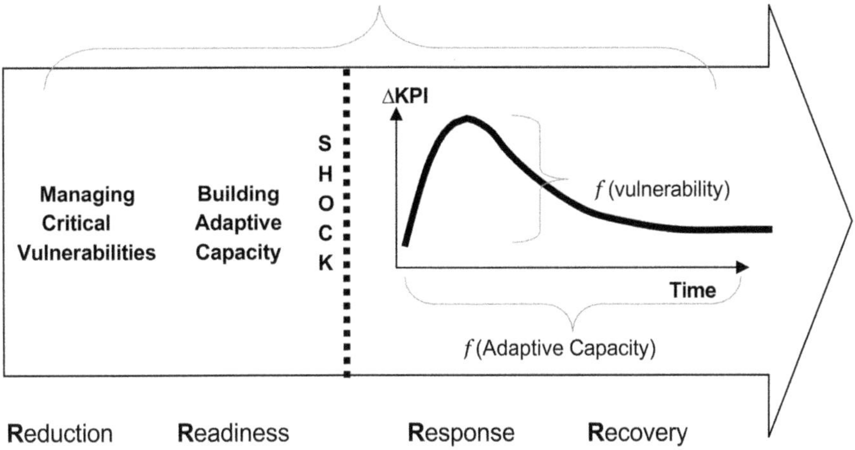

Figure 12.1

For context-specific matrices, susceptibility data is represented by varying the size of the holes; larger holes correspond to greater susceptibility. Here, both the position and size of each hole determine the identification of critical vulnerabilities.

Critical vulnerabilities often include seemingly minor components or links that could significantly disrupt organizational operations. It is imperative to identify these elements promptly, as part of a comprehensive vulnerability assessment. Furthermore, vulnerability matrices can be constructed to analyze various organizational dimensions—such as human resources, external stakeholder relationships, or essential infrastructure—or to evaluate specific business units or departments in comparison to the organization's overall vulnerability profile (Figure 12.2 and 12.3).

Few organizations treat staff as stakeholders, resulting in limited understanding of employee concerns during crises. Large organizations report challenges in involving staff in emergency planning, especially for pandemics, due to reluctance from both staff and decision-makers. Efforts to inform key decision-makers about staff issues are rare.

12.7.2.2 Prioritization of critical vulnerabilities

The Vulnerability Matrix has four categories, with highest vulnerability in the top right quadrant and lowest in the bottom left (see Figure 12.1). In an all-hazards matrix, organizational components in the highest vulnerability categories are critical and should be prioritized in planning. In Figure 12.2, components #10 and #9 are top priorities, followed by #3, #7, and #1, then #5, #2, and #6.

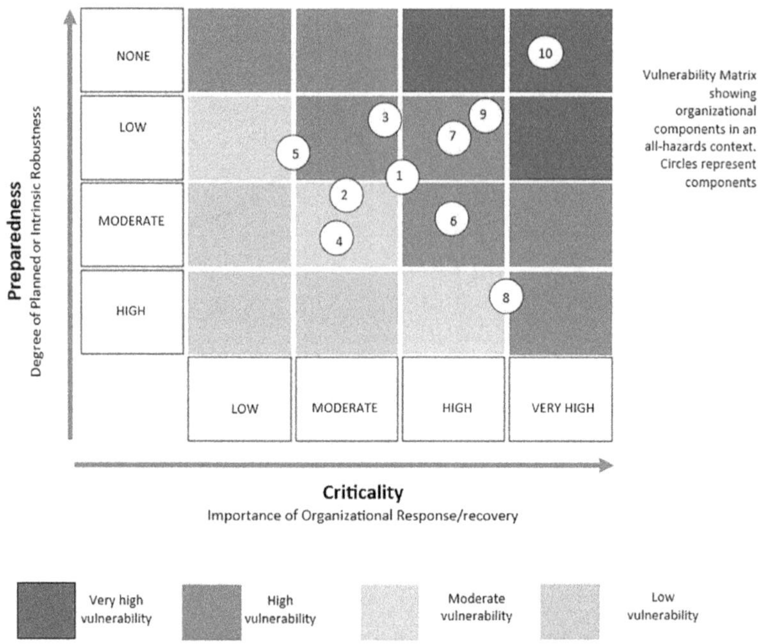

Figure 12.2 Sample vulnerability matrices showing an all-hazards approach and a context specific approach to determine critical vulnerabilities for organizational resilience.

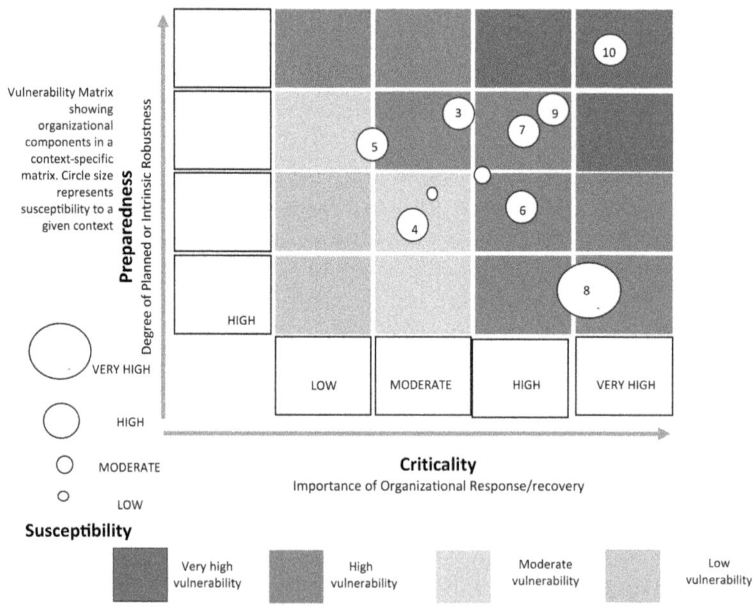

Figure 12.3 Vulnerability Matrix showing Organizational components in an all hazards context. Circles represent components

Organizations use susceptibility data to assess vulnerabilities during specific crises. In a vulnerability matrix, components with larger gaps in the highest vulnerability category are identified as the most critical. For example, in Figure 12.3, component #10 is a greater critical vulnerability than #8 due to its larger gap. Components #8 and #9 also stand out and would typically be addressed before #10 because of their significant impact. This approach enables organizations to prioritize and target the most crucial vulnerabilities relevant to the situation.

12.8 ELEMENT 5—INCREASING ADAPTIVE CAPACITY

Element 5 represents the culminating stage of the Resilience Management process, focusing on practical assessment and improvement of resilience by specifically targeting adaptive capacity, alongside ongoing consideration of situation awareness and critical vulnerabilities. This stage aims to overcome the complexity and resource constraints associated with detailed psychological assessments of organizational culture by providing accessible and actionable tools.

Key Objectives of Element 5

- *Develop Adaptive Capacity:* This is a primary focus, recognizing that the ability to adapt to unforeseen situations is critical for long-term organizational resilience. Instead of delving into complex psychological models, Element 5 provides tools to assess and enhance the cultural and dynamic aspects that foster adaptability, such as leadership styles, information flow, and the organization's openness to creativity.
- *Enhance Situation Awareness:* Building on previous stages, Element 5 continues to refine the organization's understanding of its operating environment, including both day-to-day conditions and potential crisis scenarios. This involves ongoing monitoring of internal and external factors, identifying potential threats and opportunities, and assessing their potential impact.
- *Address Critical Vulnerabilities:* Element 5 leverages the vulnerability assessment data to prioritize and develop targeted strategies for mitigating weaknesses identified through the Vulnerability Matrix. This ensures that efforts are directed toward components or links that pose the greatest risk, considering both the speed and potential for cascading failures.

12.8.1 Tools and approach in Element 5

The tools within Element 5 are designed to be time and resource-efficient, making them readily applicable in real-world organizational settings. They help organizations:

- *Assessing and improving resilience:* By focusing on the practical aspects of adaptive capacity, situation awareness, and critical vulnerabilities, Element 5 provides tangible methods for organizations to gauge their current resilience levels and identify specific areas needing improvement.

- *Developing immediate action plans*: A key output of Element 5 is the creation of actionable plans to address identified resilience gaps. These plans are designed to be specific, measurable, attainable, relevant, and time-bound (SMART), with clear actions, assigned responsibilities, timelines, resources, risks, and goals.
- *Facilitating organizational buy-in*: The self-assessment aspect of vulnerability analysis, as mentioned, encourages ownership of identified issues, fostering accountability and a greater likelihood of implementing recommendations.

12.8.2 Tangible outcomes of Element 5

- *Enhanced adaptive capacity*: Through focused activities and action plans, organizations develop a culture that embraces change, encourages creativity, and empowers employees to respond effectively to unforeseen challenges.
- *Stronger situation awareness*: Continuous monitoring and assessment of the operating environment leads to more informed decision-making and a proactive approach to risk management.
- *Mitigated critical vulnerabilities*: Targeted actions to address weaknesses in systems, processes, or relationships reduce the likelihood and potential impact of disruptions.
- *Immediate action plans*: Organizations leave Element 5 with concrete steps to implement, ensuring that resilience-building efforts translate into tangible improvements.
- *Ongoing improvement*: Element 5 emphasizes the iterative nature of resilience management, recognizing that resilience is not a fixed state but rather a continuous journey of learning, adaptation, and improvement. Organizations are encouraged to regularly revisit assessments and refine their action plans based on new information and experiences.

In summary, Element 5 bridges the gap between theoretical model of resilience and practical implementation. By providing accessible tools and focusing on tangible outcomes, it empowers organizations to actively build and maintain a resilient posture in an increasingly complex and uncertain world.

Table 12.12 provides examples of how organizations can assess and develop adaptive capacity within the framework of Element 5.

Organizations can translate resilience assessments into actions by focusing on these areas and employing practical tools within Element 5. This fosters a more adaptable and resilient culture that is better prepared to navigate future disruptions.

Table 12.12

Adaptive capacity focus area	*Assessment questions/ indicators*	*Practical examples of action plans*	*Desired outcome*
Leadership and decision-making structures	• Are decision-making processes clear and efficient during routine and crisis situations? • Do leaders empower teams to make decisions? • Is there a culture of transparent communication from leadership?	• Implement regular "tabletop exercises" simulating crises to test decision-making under pressure. • Train middle managers in adaptive leadership skills, focusing on autonomy and collaboration. • Establish a clear crisis communication protocol and train designated spokespersons.	Faster, more effective decision-making; increased trust and confidence in leadership.
Acquisition, dissemination, and retention of information and knowledge	• How effectively is information gathered from internal and external sources? • Are knowledge-sharing platforms and practices robust? • How are lessons learned from past incidents documented and integrated into future plans?	• Implement a new internal knowledge management system accessible to all employees. • Conduct post-incident reviews ("lessons learned" sessions) and integrate findings into standard operating procedures. • Establish formal knowledge transfer processes for departing employees.	Improved situational awareness; prevention of repeated mistakes; continuous learning culture.
Creativity and flexibility	• To what extent does the organization encourage experimentation and new ideas? • How easily can processes or structures be modified in response to new challenges? • Is failure viewed as a learning opportunity or something to be avoided at all costs?	• Launch an "innovation challenge" encouraging employees to propose solutions for specific organizational challenges. • Review and streamline change management processes to reduce bureaucracy. • Implement "post-mortems" on failed projects to extract learning without assigning blame.	Development of innovative solutions; rapid adaptation to unexpected situations; enhanced problem-solving capacity.

(Continued)

Table 12.12 (Continued)

Adaptive capacity focus area	*Assessment questions/ indicators*	*Practical examples of action plans*	*Desired outcome*
Actionable outcomes and immediate plans	• What specific actions are identified to address vulnerabilities? • Are responsibilities clearly assigned and timelines defined? • How will progress be tracked and communicated?	• Create a SMART action plan outlining specific steps, responsibilities, resources, timelines, and metrics for addressing a critical vulnerability (e.g., diversifying a single-source supplier, implementing a new cybersecurity measure). • Establish regular meetings to track progress on action plans and make necessary adjustments.	Measurable improvements in resilience; reduced risk exposure; increased accountability for resilience-building efforts.

12.8.2.1 REDS

The Resilience Management process provides decision-makers with practical tools to assess and enhance an organization's resilience during crises. The REDS is one such tool.

REDS allows organizations to identify vulnerabilities and strengths within a simulated crisis environment and serve as a platform for evaluating decision-making and communication processes. Scenario exercises are used to increase awareness of the operating environment during a crisis and examine the potential impacts of various types of events. For organizations that have developed emergency or business continuity plans, simulations provide a method to test these plans before a real incident occurs.

Typically, REDS is conducted with groups of 8–12 individuals who have broad knowledge of the organization and hold key decision-making roles. REDS can be adjusted for smaller organizations, but in larger organizations, group sizes should not exceed 12; additional exercises may be required to involve more participants.

REDS is comprised of six sequential operational stages, which are outlined in Table 12.13 below. Regular use of REDS, incorporating different impact scenarios, can identify cultural characteristics within an organization. These exercises also facilitate assessment and improvement of an organization's ability to fulfil its responsibilities in a range of crisis situations.

12.9 FACILITATING THE REDS EXERCISE

The text outlines the critical role of both participants and impartial observers in the REDS exercise, which aims to enhance an organization's situation awareness and adaptive capacity.

12.9.1 Role of participants

- Active Engagement: Participants are fully responsible for generating outputs throughout the exercise.
- Documentation: They are encouraged to meticulously record everything on wall charts, aiding in the structuring of thoughts and facilitating a shared understanding during the exercise.

12.9.2 Role of impartial observers

Impartial observers play a crucial role in the REDS exercise by providing an objective perspective and insights into various aspects of the organization's resilience. Their observations contribute to a comprehensive evaluation of the organization's capabilities and areas for improvement.

- *Assessing Awareness of Hazards and Impacts*: Observers can gauge the level of understanding participants have regarding potential hazards and their specific impacts on the organization, going beyond the participants' own self-assessment.
- *Observing Decision-Making Processes*: They witness how decisions are made under simulated crisis conditions, including the effectiveness of leadership, communication among decision-makers, and resource allocation.
- *Understanding Minimum Operating Requirements*: Observers assess how well decision-makers comprehend the organization's absolute minimum operating requirements during a crisis and how effectively they communicate these requirements to others.
- *Evaluating Awareness of Roles and Responsibilities*: They assess the clarity and understanding of roles and responsibilities among key stakeholders, both internal and external, during a simulated crisis.
- *Encouraging Internal and External Perspectives*: Observers prompt participants to consider the crisis situation from both an internal organizational perspective (e.g., employee safety, operational continuity) and an external stakeholder perspective (e.g., customer impact, community relations).
- *Assessing Stakeholder Connection Awareness*: They evaluate the organization's understanding of its relationships with various stakeholders (customers, suppliers, partners, regulators) and the potential impacts of disruptions to these links.

- *Evaluating Strategic Vision and Purpose*: Observers assess how well the organization's strategic vision and purpose are understood and integrated throughout the organization, and how this guides decision-making during a crisis.

By actively engaging in the REDS exercise and leveraging the insights provided by impartial observers, organizations can gain a deeper understanding of their resilience strengths and weaknesses. This leads to the development of more effective strategies and action plans to enhance their ability to anticipate, respond to, and recover from disruptions.

REDS offers an effective approach to providing essential context for conducting vulnerability assessments. Through REDS, stakeholders and decision-makers—both internal and external—are able to observe these vulnerabilities within a simulated emergency environment. This process enables organizations to gain a clearer understanding of their own vulnerabilities as well as potential risks associated with interconnected organizations or systems.

Table 12.13 provides a structured approach for impartial observers to assess an organization's resilience during a REDS exercise.

Table 12.13

Observation area	*Questions for observers to consider*	*Sample observations/feedback (positive and negative)*
Awareness of hazards and impacts	• Do participants demonstrate an understanding of the range and scope of potential hazards facing the organization? • Are they able to articulate the potential impacts (positive and negative) of these hazards? • Do they recognize crises beyond those previously experienced or well-known? • Do they consider the possibility of crises occurring concurrently with business-as-usual operations?	Positive: "Participants consistently brought up a wide array of potential threats, including emerging tech risks and geopolitical instability, not just natural disasters." Negative: "The team focused heavily on repeating the response to the last IT outage, seemingly ignoring new cyber threat vectors."
Decision-making process in action	• How are decisions being made under pressure (e.g., collaborative, top-down)? • Are roles and responsibilities clear in the decision-making chain? • How do participants adapt to new information or unexpected turns in the scenario? • Is there a balance between rapid decision-making and considering potential consequences?	Positive: "Decisions were made collaboratively with clear roles. When an unexpected element was introduced, the team quickly reassessed and adjusted their strategy." Negative: "The CEO dominated decision-making, leading to some team members feeling unheard. The team struggled to adapt when the initial plan encountered unforeseen obstacles."

(Continued)

Table 12.13 (Continued)

Observation area	*Questions for observers to consider*	*Sample observations/feedback (positive and negative)*
Understanding and communication of minimum operating requirements (MORs)	• Do decision-makers clearly understand the organization's MORs from a recovery perspective? • How well are these MORs communicated among decision-makers and to other operational levels?	Positive: "The incident commander clearly articulated the MORs to the response teams, ensuring everyone understood what absolutely needed to be maintained." Negative: "There was confusion among different departments about what constitutes 'essential' services, leading to misaligned priorities."
Awareness of roles and responsibilities of key stakeholders	• Do participants clearly understand their own roles and the roles of other internal stakeholders? • Do they recognize the roles and responsibilities of external stakeholders (e.g., emergency services, regulators, community)? • Is there a shared understanding of who needs to be involved at different stages of a crisis?	Positive: "Each team member demonstrated a strong understanding of their specific duties and who to escalate issues to. They also clearly identified key external agencies." Negative: "Several participants seemed uncertain about the responsibilities of the legal department during a crisis, and there was limited interaction planned with local authorities."
Internal and external perspective taking	• Do participants consider both internal (e.g., employee safety, operational continuity) and external (e.g., customer impact, community perception) perspectives during the simulation? • Do they proactively engage in managing stakeholder perception, especially in scenarios with media scrutiny?	Positive: "The team consistently discussed not only the technical fixes but also the potential impact on customer trust and planned media releases carefully." Negative: "The primary focus remained on internal operations, with little consideration for how actions might be perceived by the media or affected customers."
Awareness of stakeholder connections and impacts	• Does the organization recognize its dependence on key stakeholders (suppliers, customers, partners)? • Do they anticipate potential disruptions to these links and their cascading effects?	Positive: "The team quickly identified the vulnerability of a single-source supplier and started exploring contingencies early in the scenario." Negative: "The team overlooked the potential impact on key partners until prompted, revealing a lack of understanding of the interconnectedness of the ecosystem."
Understanding of organizational strategic vision and purpose	• Is the strategic vision or mission guiding decision-making during the crisis? • How well is this vision understood and articulated across the organization (observed through participant comments and actions)?	Positive: "Participants frequently referenced the company's core values and mission when making difficult choices, demonstrating a strong, shared purpose." Negative: "Decisions seemed purely tactical, with little connection to the organization's stated long-term goals or mission."

Key Points for Observers

Objectivity: Remain impartial and avoid influencing participant decisions.
Documentation: Record detailed observations, including specific actions, quotes, and timing, for post-exercise analysis.
Focus: Concentrate on the specific areas outlined above, as well as any others defined in the exercise objectives.
Nuance: Look for subtle indicators and inconsistencies, especially discrepancies between stated policies and actual behavior.
Facilitation (if applicable): While observing, be ready to facilitate discussions or provide guidance if the exercise veers off track, but primarily let the participants grapple with the problem.

This structured approach helps ensure that the REDS exercise yields valuable insights into the organization's resilience, guiding further development and improvement efforts (Table 12.14).

Table 12.14 Description of the six stages of REDS to improve organizational resilience

The REDS process	
Stage 1.	*Group selection and scenario presentation* If a group has more than eight individuals, it is divided into two smaller groups of equal size. Each group receives a detailed event scenario and is assigned to consider the event from a specific time frame during the immediate response phase, which may range from minutes to days depending on the event.
Stage 2.	*The response phase* These four questions are designed to guide the participants' debriefing and analysis after engaging with the REDS (Resilience Evaluation and Decision-Making Simulation) exercise. They aim to translate the simulated experience into actionable insights and concrete plans for enhancing organizational resilience. 1. What are the major issues facing the organization at this time (following the crisis)? • Purpose: To encourage comprehensive brainstorming of all potential problems and consequences stemming from the simulated crisis. This ensures that the full scope of the problem is identified, encompassing both immediate impacts and potential cascading effects. • Discussion points: • Operational disruptions: What services are unavailable? What systems are down? • Financial impacts: Loss of revenue, unexpected costs, market fluctuations. • Human resources challenges: Staff absences, safety concerns, morale issues. • Reputational damage: Public perception, media scrutiny, stakeholder trust. • Legal and regulatory implications: Potential lawsuits, compliance breaches. • Supply chain disruptions: Impacts on suppliers, distributors, or logistics. • Stakeholder relations: Impacts on customers, partners, community. • Desired outcome: A comprehensive list of all identified issues, ensuring no critical aspect is overlooked.

(Continued)

Table 12.14 Description of the six stages of REDS to improve organizational resilience *(Continued)*

The REDS process	
	2. What are the main priorities that the organization must consider? • Purpose: To guide participants in developing a structured response plan, prioritizing actions, assigning responsibilities, and establishing a sequence of steps. This moves beyond simply identifying problems to formulating solutions. • Discussion points: • Immediate actions: What needs to be done right now to stabilize the situation? • Critical functions: Which essential services must be restored first to meet minimum operating requirements? • Resource allocation: How will limited resources (personnel, funds, equipment) be deployed most effectively? • Roles and responsibilities: Who is accountable for specific actions, and who needs to be informed or consulted? • Timeline and sequencing: What steps must be completed before others can begin, and what are the crucial deadlines? • Communication strategy: What key messages need to be delivered to which stakeholders, and through what channels? • Desired outcome: A clear, prioritized action plan outlining the essential steps for immediate crisis response and recovery. 3. What are the lesser priorities, and how long until these become critical? • Purpose: To encourage participants to adopt a longer-term perspective and conduct a horizon scan of emerging issues. This question prompts them to consider the evolution of the crisis and anticipate future challenges that may not be immediately critical. • Discussion points: • Emerging issues: What problems might arise in the coming days, weeks, or months? • Potential cascading effects: What secondary or tertiary impacts might unfold over time? • Thresholds: What conditions or timeframes would cause a lesser priority to escalate into a critical issue? • Long-term recovery: What steps are needed for sustained recovery beyond the immediate crisis phase? • Resource strain: Will current recovery efforts deplete resources needed for later stages? • Desired outcome: An expanded view of the crisis lifecycle, including anticipated future challenges and potential triggers for escalation, allowing for proactive planning. 4. What could the organization do prior to a crisis to better prepare for this situation? • Purpose: To translate lessons learned from the REDS exercise into a practical, implementable action plan for enhancing pre-crisis resilience. This focuses on closing identified gaps and strengthening preparedness. • Discussion points: • Gaps in response: What significant weaknesses were exposed during the simulated response (e.g., lack of resources, poor communication, unclear roles)?

(Continued)

Table 12.14 Description of the six stages of REDS to improve organizational resilience *(Continued)*

<table>
<tr><th colspan="2">The REDS process</th></tr>
<tr><td></td><td>
<ul>
<li><ul>
<li>Proactive measures: What specific actions can be taken now to minimize the impact of a similar future event?</li>
<li>Improvements in situation awareness: How can the organization better monitor threats, understand its environment, and assess potential impacts?</li>
<li>Strengthening adaptive capacity: What changes in leadership, information flow, or culture could improve flexibility and creativity?</li>
<li>Mitigating critical vulnerabilities: How can specific weaknesses identified in the Vulnerability Matrix be addressed (e.g., implementing redundancies, developing alternative strategies)?</li>
<li>Action plan specifics: What are the specific tasks, assigned responsibilities, required resources, and realistic timeframes for implementing these improvements?</li>
</ul></li>
<li>Desired outcome: A concrete, prioritized action plan with assigned responsibilities and timelines, detailing steps the organization can take immediately to enhance its overall resilience posture based on the REDS experience.</li>
</ul>
</td></tr>
<tr><td>Stage 3.</td><td>Break and review

Participants may pause the exercise while facilitators provide feedback on group progress and offer suggestions for improvement. This allows participants to review how they met the given tasks and consider ways to enhance their performance, both individually and collectively.</td></tr>
<tr><td>Stage 4.</td><td>The recovery phase

Following the initial REDS exercise and subsequent organizational recovery, groups reconvene for a crucial debriefing session. This session involves re-evaluating the crisis situation from a different future perspective, often after significant organizational recovery, and integrating feedback from earlier stages. The goal is to deepen learning, refine action plans, and build greater long-term resilience.

Re-answering the stage 2 questions with a new lens

During this recovery phase debrief, participants revisit the four core questions from the previous stage, but with the added context of hindsight, organizational recovery progress, and potentially new information or insights.

<table>
<tr><th>Question</th><th>Original focus (during/ immediately post-crisis)</th><th>Recovery phase focus (after significant organizational recovery)</th></tr>
<tr><td>1. What are the major issues facing the organization at this time?</td><td>Identifying all immediate and potential problems, including cascading effects, arising from the crisis.</td><td>Reassessing the lingering or unforeseen long-term impacts of the crisis, considering secondary effects, and identifying new vulnerabilities that may have emerged during recovery.</td></tr>
</table>
</td></tr>
</table>

(Continued)

Table 12.14 Description of the six stages of REDS to improve organizational resilience *(Continued)*

The REDS process

2. What are the main priorities that the organization must consider?	Establishing immediate response priorities, resource allocation, and responsibilities for stabilization and initial recovery.	Reviewing the effectiveness of the initial priorities and actions, adjusting long-term strategic priorities for sustained recovery and potentially identifying new priorities for post-crisis growth or transformation.
3. What are the lesser priorities, and how long until these become critical?	Scanning the horizon for emerging issues, considering alternative timeframes, and anticipating when secondary problems might escalate.	Evaluating how the previously identified "lesser priorities" evolved, assessing the accuracy of initial estimations, and refining the understanding of timeframes and triggers for future vulnerabilities.
4. What could the organization do prior to a crisis to better prepare for this situation?	Identifying significant gaps in the immediate response, developing initial action plans to minimize impacts, and establishing timeframes for implementation.	Evaluating the effectiveness of the action plan developed in the previous stage, identifying new insights or improvements for the preparedness plan based on the recovery experience, and refining strategies to enhance adaptive capacity for future unforeseen situations.

The value of revisiting these questions

- *Deeper Learning*: Re-engaging with the questions from a recovery perspective allows for a more reflective and nuanced understanding of the crisis, its impacts, and the organization's response.
- *Validation and Refinement*: It helps validate the initial assessments made during the crisis and identify areas where those assessments were accurate or flawed. This refinement improves future decision-making capabilities.
- *Long-Term Resilience*: By considering the long-term consequences and the process of recovery, organizations can develop more sustainable and adaptive strategies, moving beyond mere survival to thriving in a changed environment.
- *Incorporating New Data*: The recovery phase allows for the integration of real-world data and feedback gathered during the actual recovery process, grounding the analysis in empirical evidence.
- *Building a Learning Culture*: This iterative process reinforces a culture of continuous learning and adaptation within the organization, which is a hallmark of resilience.

By systematically revisiting these questions at different stages of the crisis and recovery, the REDS exercise becomes a powerful tool for building not just awareness, but also the adaptive capacity necessary for long-term organizational development and resilience.

(Continued)

Table 12.14 Description of the six stages of REDS to improve organizational resilience *(Continued)*

The REDS process	
Stage 5.	*The External Perspective* Recovery phase: incorporating stakeholder perspectives in REDS debrief In the recovery phase of a REDS (Resilience Evaluation and Decision-Making Simulation) exercise, a crucial activity involves gaining deeper insights into stakeholder considerations. This is achieved by having one individual from each group step into the shoes of key stakeholder groups, providing a more holistic and empathetic view of the crisis and recovery efforts. Process 1. Stakeholder Perspective Assignment: One individual from each participant group is selected and assigned the task of analyzing the scenario from the viewpoint of one or more specific key stakeholder groups. This could include: 1. Customers: Their needs, disruptions to service, communication expectations, and trust levels. 2. Employees: Their safety, well-being, job security concerns, and internal communication needs. 3. Suppliers/Partners: The impact on their operations, contractual obligations, and collaborative recovery efforts. 4. Regulators: Compliance issues, reporting requirements, and potential penalties. 5. Investors/Shareholders: Financial impacts, market confidence, and future viability concerns. 6. Local Community: Environmental impact, safety concerns, and the organization's role in local recovery. 7. Media: Narrative control, transparency, and reputation management. 2. Scenario Analysis from Assigned Perspective: These individuals then analyze the entire scenario, including the organization's initial response and subsequent recovery actions, exclusively from their assigned stakeholder's vantage point. They consider: 1. What were their expectations before, during, and after the crisis? 2. How were they impacted by the crisis and the organization's actions? 3. What were their key concerns, demands, or frustrations? 4. Was communication adequate and timely from their perspective? 5. Did the organization demonstrate empathy and address their needs effectively? 3. Presentation and Debriefing: During the final debriefing session, these individuals present their stakeholder perspectives to the larger group. This presentation highlights: 1. Whether the organization's actions adequately considered the assigned stakeholder's concerns, demands, and expectations. 2. Areas where the organization's response aligned well with stakeholder needs. 3. Significant gaps or missteps in addressing stakeholder concerns. 4. Potential negative consequences arising from inadequate stakeholder engagement.

(Continued)

Table 12.14 Description of the six stages of REDS to improve organizational resilience *(Continued)*

The REDS process	
	Value of this exercise • Enhanced Empathy and Understanding: It forces participants to move beyond an internal-centric view and genuinely understand the diverse impacts of a crisis on different groups. • Improved Stakeholder Engagement Strategies: By identifying gaps in stakeholder consideration, the organization can refine its communication plans, engagement protocols, and overall approach to managing relationships during and after a crisis. • Reputation Management: Understanding how actions are perceived by external stakeholders is crucial for maintaining and rebuilding reputation post-crisis. • Proactive Planning: Insights gained can inform the development of more comprehensive pre-crisis stakeholder analysis and engagement strategies, ensuring these perspectives are considered from the outset. • Stronger Long-Term Relationships: By demonstrating a commitment to understanding and addressing stakeholder needs, the organization can build stronger, more resilient relationships that are vital for sustained success. This activity ensures that the REDS exercise not only focuses on operational resilience but also emphasizes the critical role of stakeholder management in overall organizational resilience.
Stage 6.	*Debriefing and action plans* Post-REDS debriefing: catalyzing immediate action for enhanced resilience The group debriefing session at the conclusion of a REDS (Resilience Evaluation and Decision-Making Simulation) exercise is a pivotal moment. It serves as a crucial platform for consolidating insights, fostering a shared understanding of organizational vulnerabilities, and, most importantly, translating the simulated experience into tangible improvements through the creation of an immediate action plan. Key benefits of the post-REDS action plan 1. Immediate Vulnerability Reduction: The REDS exercise inherently highlights weak points. The debriefing allows for the rapid identification of the most critical vulnerabilities, enabling the organization to formulate and implement quick-win solutions or initiate immediate mitigation efforts. This proactive approach can significantly reduce the organization's exposure to future risks. 2. Enhanced Awareness: Participants leave the REDS with a heightened awareness of potential hazards, their impacts, and the organization's current state of preparedness. The action plan captures this newfound awareness, ensuring that the insights are documented and translated into concrete steps for improving the organization's understanding of its operating environment. 3. Improved Adaptive Capacity: The REDS challenges decision-making and problem-solving under pressure. The debriefing provides an opportunity to reflect on the strengths and weaknesses of the organization's adaptive capabilities. The action plan can then focus on developing specific skills, refining decision-making processes, enhancing information flow, and fostering a culture that embraces creativity and flexibility – all key aspects of adaptive capacity.

(Continued)

Table 12.14 Description of the six stages of REDS to improve organizational resilience *(Continued)*

The REDS process	
	4. Overall Organizational Resilience: By addressing vulnerabilities, improving awareness, and building adaptive capacity, the action plan directly contributes to strengthening the organization's overall resilience. It moves the organization from a reactive posture toward a more proactive and robust approach to managing disruptions. 5. Capitalizing on Momentum and Enthusiasm: The immersive nature of REDS exercises often generates significant energy and enthusiasm among participants. The debriefing provides an immediate outlet for this energy, channeling it into productive planning. This momentum is critical for ensuring that the lessons learned translate into actual change, preventing the insights from fading over time. 6. Fostering Ownership and Accountability: Since participants are directly involved in identifying the problems and co-creating the solutions, they develop a strong sense of ownership over the action plan. This increases the likelihood that the actions will be implemented effectively, as individuals feel accountable for the improvements identified. Creating the action plan The action plan developed during the debriefing should be: • Specific: Clearly define the action to be taken. • Measurable: Include metrics or indicators to track progress. • Achievable: Ensure the actions are realistic given available resources and time. • Relevant: Directly address identified vulnerabilities, awareness gaps, or adaptive capacity needs. • Time-bound: Assign clear deadlines for completion. It should also include: • Identified Gaps: A clear summary of the major vulnerabilities and gaps identified during the REDS. • Proposed Actions: Specific steps to address each gap. • Assigned Responsibilities: Clear ownership for each action. • Required Resources: Identification of necessary resources (e.g., funding, personnel, training). • Timelines: Realistic deadlines for implementation. In essence, the debriefing and the subsequent action plan are the conduits through which the experiential learning of the REDS exercise is transformed into tangible, impactful improvements, solidifying the organization's path toward greater resilience.

12.10 SUMMARIZING THE RESILIENCE MANAGEMENT PROCESS AND ITS APPLICATION

The Resilience Management process highlights its core objectives, methodology, and the value derived from its application, particularly through the use of case studies.

12.10.1 Core objectives of the resilience management process

The overarching goal of the Resilience Management process is to enhance an organization's overall resilience. This is achieved by systematically addressing three interconnected pillars:

1. Improving Situation Awareness: This involves building a comprehensive understanding of the organization's operating environment, including current and future conditions, available resources, stakeholder expectations, and the potential impacts of various crises.
2. Advancing the Identification and Management of Critical Vulnerabilities: The process focuses on pinpointing key organizational components (both tangible and intangible) that, if compromised, could lead to significant negative impacts during a crisis. It also distinguishes between rapid and insidious vulnerabilities, and discrete versus cascading failures.
3. Increasing Adaptive Capacity: This refers to fostering a culture and dynamics within the organization that enable timely and appropriate decision-making, encourage flexibility and creativity, and ensure efficient information flow—all crucial for navigating uncertainty and change.

12.10.2 Methodology: Learning from case studies

The development of this Resilience Management process has been intrinsically linked to the insights gathered from a selection of case studies.

- Diverse Representation: The project utilized ten case-study organizations, deliberately chosen for their diversity in size (large, small), type (private, public), and industry sector. This ensures that the findings and the developed framework are broadly applicable.
- Iterative Refinement: A preliminary framework for Resilience Management was initially developed based on a pilot study with the first case-study organization. This framework was then iteratively refined and modified through engagement with the subsequent nine case studies, indicating a robust, real-world testing approach.

12.10.3 Value of the process and developed tools

The tools and methodologies employed within each step of the Resilience Management process have been instrumental in achieving its objectives:

- Data Collection on Common Resilience Issues: The process, including interviews, surveys, Impact Scenarios, and the Vulnerability Matrix, has been effective in gathering valuable data. This data illuminates common resilience challenges faced by organizations globally, providing generalizable insights beyond the specific case studies.

- Basis for Resilience Profiles: The gathered information serves as the foundation for developing detailed "resilience profiles" for each of the case-study organizations. These profiles likely summarize the organization's situation awareness, critical vulnerabilities, and adaptive capacity, offering a holistic view of their resilience posture.
- Catalyst for Action: The debriefing and action planning components, particularly after REDS exercises, capitalize on participant momentum to translate theoretical learning into immediate, practical steps. This helps organizations quickly reduce vulnerabilities and build a stronger foundation for the future.

In essence, the described Resilience Management process is a structured, evidence-based approach designed to proactively enhance an organization's ability to withstand and adapt to disruptions, ultimately securing its long-term viability and success.

For Product Safety Concerns and Information please contact our EU representative GPSR@taylorandfrancis.com
Taylor & Francis Verlag GmbH, Kaufingerstraße 24, 80331 München, Germany

www.ingramcontent.com/pod-product-compliance
Ingram Content Group UK Ltd.
Pitfield, Milton Keynes, MK11 3LW, UK
UKHW022217190926
475702UK00003B/397
9781032981864